Outdoor Recreation Management:

Theory and Application

Third Edition

Outdoor Recreation Management:

Theory and Application

Third Edition

by

Alan Jubenville

Ben W. Twight

Venture Publishing, Inc.
State College, PA

Copyright © 1993
Venture Publishing, Inc.

No part of the material protected by this copyright notice may be reproduced or utilized in any form by any means, electronic or mechanical, including photocopying, recording, or by any information storage and retrieval system, without written permission from the copyright owner.

Printed in the United States of America

Library of Congress Cataloging in Publication Data

Production: Bonnie Godbey
Printing and Binding: BookCrafters, Inc.
Manuscript Editing: Richard Yocum

Library of Congress Catalogue Card Number 93-85328
ISBN 0-910251-61-4

10 9 8 7 6 5 4 3 2 1

Table of Contents

About the Authors
vii

Preface
ix

PART I	PART II
Management Framework	Recreational Resource Management
1	91

CHAPTER 1
Historical Roots . . . for Framing the Future
3

CHAPTER 2
The Outdoor Recreation Management
Model
13

CHAPTER 3
Theoretical Foundations
31

CHAPTER 4
The Problem-Solving Process
51

CHAPTER 5
Problem Solving and Decision Making in
the Context of Administrative Law
65

CHAPTER 6
Involvement of the Public in Decision
Making
75

CHAPTER 7
Assessing Impacts in the Real World
93

CHAPTER 8
Site Management
105

CHAPTER 9
Turf Management
117

CHAPTER 10
Management of Overstory Vegetation
131

CHAPTER 11
Management of Natural Ecosystems
147

CHAPTER 12
Visual Resource Management
167

PART III
Visitor Management
195

CHAPTER 13
Distribution of Visitor Use
197

CHAPTER 14
Information Services
209

CHAPTER 15
Interpretive Services
223

CHAPTER 16
Public Safety
237

PART IV
Service Management
259

CHAPTER 17
Recreation Area Planning
261

CHAPTER 18
Hazard Management
277

CHAPTER 19
Maintenance Management
289

CHAPTER 20
Concession Management
301

About the Authors

ALAN JUBENVILLE

Dr. Jubenville has had many professional experiences dealing with recreational use of natural resources. Originally from Virginia, he received his early education and experience in the coastal plains of the Southeast. Since that time, he has worked for several state and federal agencies and a private consulting firm. He received a B.S. degree in forest management in 1962 from North Carolina State University, an M.S. degree in silviculture/ecology in 1964 from West Virginia University, and a Ph.D. degree in wildland recreation management in 1970 from the University of Montana. After receiving his doctoral degree, he became the state outdoor recreation extension specialist at The University of Illinois. From there, he moved to the University of Wyoming, where he helped develop the outdoor recreation curriculum and conduct research on river recreation.

In 1979, Dr. Jubenville joined the faculty of the School of Agriculture and Land Resources Management at the University of Alaska-Fairbanks. There, his research interest shifted to recreation management theory. He has authored four books, four contributions to anthologies, twenty journal articles, and many user-oriented publications. His most recent field studies have focused on landscape management, watchable wildlife, and the evaluation of agency recreation management plans. Plus, he has been an expert witness in several cases involving management of parks.

BEN W. TWIGHT

Dr. Twight grew up in the California State Park System, was employed seasonally by the U.S. Forest Service, studied Wildlife Conservation and Forestry at the University of California-Berkeley, and then became a permanent employee of the U.S. Forest Service.

Later transferring to the National Park Service, Twight was a ranger and law enforcement specialist at Yosemite National Park for five years, and manager of the Ohanapecosh District at Mt. Rainier National Park for three years. He returned to graduate school at the University of Washington for his M.S. and Ph.D. degrees in sociology and public administration.

Dr. Twight has authored more than twenty-five journal articles and book chapters. He has taught at West Virginia University and is currently Associate Professor of Forest Resources at The Pennsylvania State University, where he also authored *Organizational Values and Political Power,* a book (now in 2nd printing) on the political battle between the Forest Service and the Park Service over the lands that are now Olympic National Park.

Preface

More people are participating in various outdoor recreation activities than ever before. Because of changing lifestyles, new recreational technology, and improved economic conditions, both the activities themselves and the patterns of participation are more diverse. These have created a need for more new recreational opportunities and changes in many of the existing ones. Management is finding it more difficult to maintain existing opportunities, to try to improve the quality of those, and still respond to the demand for new ones. It is a seemingly thankless job, particularly in the face of shrinking government budgets.

This book offers no instant solutions to the plethora of problems facing the outdoor recreation manager. In fact, we think the worst thing we could do is to offer such solutions (even if they are good ones) because the problem set is constantly changing due to changing social and environmental conditions. The more effective manager, over the long run, is not the one who is solution-oriented, but process-oriented. The process-oriented manager sees the "big picture," understands how the total system works, has knowledge of the causal links within the system, and creates a process by which solutions are carefully developed, analyzed, and implemented.

If one scrutinizes the situational variables in most problems, the major cause is often some current or past management action, or a change in the external social environment. An open-systems approach to management helps to better identify those causal relationships and to isolate the critical variables, including previous management actions.

According to political scientist Florence Heffron, in her book *Organization Theory and Public Organizations: The Political Connection,* an open system organization depends on its social environment for the resources for organizational functioning and for accepting the organization's output. She continues:

> "The overriding goal of the organization in systems theory is survival, which has little connection with the organization's ability to accomplish substantive goals ... If survival is the ultimate measure of organizational effectiveness, the intermediate criteria of effectiveness are the organization's ability to control and manipulate its (social) environment, acquire inputs, process those inputs and maintain stability . . . With a complex and dynamic environment, such as many public organizations have, successful maintenance of organization to social environment relationships can be particularly difficult ... Outputs desired and demanded by one set of environmental actors, the presidency (executive branch) for example, may be received with hostility by another set of environmental actors, the Congress (legislature) for example. The effective organization successfully negotiates with these conflicting actors to avoid negative consequences" (such as budget cuts or loss of administrative discretion; see p. 330).

In this text we attempt to keep the political nature of open-systems theory as Heffron describes it in mind, but we temporize and assume that a currently stable base of political support exists for our outdoor recreation management programs. This assumption allows us to take a transitory positive perspective and emphasize simplified

Preface (continued)

resource management decisions and strategies designed to minimize impact prior to implementation. Despite our tendency to hold the broader political ramifications of recreation management constant, our simplified examples of systems models applied to a given area should help the student be aware of and identify the potentially important social changes (populations, family makeup, satisfaction, participation patterns, etc.) that may affect an area and public support for its management programs. By introducing the student to the idea of anticipating change, we can encourage this future manager to be more active in adjusting the management programs to meet the changes in both the social and natural environments, rather than waiting and then reacting after the impact.

In sum, the one thing this text stresses is the open-systems model. As with any system, when the input is constant, it is said to be in a dynamic equilibrium. Alter any input and you alter the equilibrium. In recreation management, the primary output is the recreational opportunity. If the system is in equilibrium, then we are providing stable opportunities to the using public. Alter the inputs, including those from the external social environment, and you alter outputs. The ultimate measure of success in such an open model is satisfied clientele groups. Stability of the quality of recreation opportunities is critical to keeping clientele satisfied over time. In turn, these groups provide the support for the agency in the political/budgeting process so necessary to maintaining that stability.

All of this points to the significance of Part I, Management Framework, where the recreation management system and the equilibrium theory are fully explained, along with the interaction of the agency with the public in a decision-making mode. The remaining three sections focus on subsystems—the visitor, the resource, and the service—discussing the specific programs under each subsystem. No attempt is made to stereotype management prescriptions for various clusters of similar recreational opportunities. It cannot be done. Ideally the systems approach provides you with 1) a process by which problems and their critical linkages can be identified and 2) assists you in developing legitimate prescriptions for overcoming obstacles—with minimum secondary effects.

PART I

Management Framework

As Florence Heffron points out in her book *Organization Theory and Public Organizations: The Political Connection:*

> "A mission is an organization's function in society—the products it produces and the services it provides . . . the mission and the substantive goals derived from it provide a rationale for organization design and structure . . . . Missions are extremely important to public organizations (such as recreation management agencies). They provide a sense of legitimacy, direction, and purpose, and serve as criteria for performance evaluation for the overall organization and for individual employees . . . . Official goals . . . are the general purposes of the organization as described in the charter (legal mandate) or public statements by key officials . . . and are primarily intended to show the purpose of the organization to key constituencies." (pp. 88-89)

Heffron then suggests that other goals include operative goals, inferred from the actual operating policies of the agency. These indicate what the organization is really trying to do. Then there are operational goals, which are more measurable and are used to guide behavior and evaluate the performance of employees.[16] Goals and their relation to management are discussed further in the problem-solving process described in Chapter 4.

*****

This section of the book is aimed primarily at providing an overview of management as it pertains to recreation areas and clientele—regardless of particular circumstances. It is intended to provide the conceptual framework for succeeding sections, showing readers how the recreation manager, the organization, the resource, and the visitor can be integrated into a systems management approach. Such a holistic systems theory is appropriate for recreation area management in today's complex society. Also, systems models can help us to readily see all the basic elements involved in management and how they relate to one another. In other words, we must first understand the management system on a conceptual level in order to better appreciate what effect our decisions about a single element of a specific subsystem will have on the entire system. In later sections, we will dissect the system into subsystems and then identify specific management programs.

This section does not focus specifically on administrative or organizational management matters such as budgeting and personnel. That is not the intent of the book. Instead it focuses on resource, visitor, and service management in a conceptual framework to provide a better understanding of succeeding sections.

Obviously many management concepts might help in understanding the visitor and thus improve the delivery of public recreation services. Social psychology has contributed much to our understanding of recreationists—their motivations, perceptions, and behavior.

This rich body of literature has provided insights into why people do what they do. However, to be meaningful to management, user response (and that is what we are trying to accomplish when we implement a particular program) must be cast in a managerial context. That is what this section attempts to do—develop the managerial framework. Thus, contrary to social psychological concepts that other authors have emphasized, we have chosen to emphasize managerial concepts—*outdoor recreation* managerial concepts.

CHAPTER 1

Historical Roots... for Framing the Future

Before jumping into a synopsis of the history of outdoor recreation management, we would like to establish a mood or concern for appropriate management of recreational opportunities on public lands. Hopefully this quick digression will firmly establish in your mind a need for both management in general and *appropriate* management specifically.

THE NEED FOR MANAGEMENT

Probably most of us can painfully reflect on some situation which adversely affected our own recreation participation. The situation cried out for appropriate action by the

Figure 1-1. Framing the future? A former U.S. Forest Service officer in his new National Park Service uniform, shortly after North Cascades National Park was established in 1968. (Photo by B. W. Twight)

recreation manager, yet there was no relief in sight. Some of these problems are obvious; others are more subtle. Let's look at some hypothetical situations so that we all have a common understanding of the need for appropriate management strategies.

Developed Sites

A 100-unit forest campground is located in the heavy clay soils of the Piedmont region of North Carolina. The season of use is generally from April 15 to September 15. Your first visit to the site shows almost all the ground vegetation is gone. There has been no effort to harden the heavily used portion of the site, and even the sparsely used portion is showing extreme wear.

Sheet erosion is occurring and almost all of the A_1 soil horizon has been lost. No organic matter can be seen in the upper soil horizons. Siltation is evident in the nearby stream. Some stagheading (dieback) is taking place in the mixed hardwood stand, even though it is only sixty years old.

You show up for a weekend of camping and fishing with the family. It rains. The fishing is nonexistent and the whole site turns to mud. The problems may appear to be obvious, but based on our knowledge of the user/resource interaction, they were highly predictable. Why, then, has this situation been allowed to occur?

A small oval lake is used heavily by water-skiers, fishermen, and swimmers from a local resort. The fishermen usually use the lake early in the morning and late in the afternoon. The water-skiers and swimmers use the lake during the middle of the day. However, conflict often exists between the three groups. Fishermen do not like the water-skiers because they disturb the water

and swamp fishing boats. The water-skiers do not like the other user groups on the lake because they limit the good skiing and create safety problems. The fishermen, with the support of the statewide Izaak Walton League, have even introduced a bill into the legislature that would ban water-skiing.

There has never been a serious accident on the lake, but several incidents have occurred in which minor injuries were reported. One swimmer was bruised by a skier as he swung wide of the boat on a turn. Some minor vandalism of boat trailers has occurred, and exaggerated rumors of other conflicts have circulated. Perhaps you have already formulated some simple solutions while reading about this situation. But, more importantly, you should recognize that it is not going to resolve itself.

Your opening discussion might focus on "appropriate" management actions. Is there such a thing as too much management, overmanagement to the point of detracting from the experience people derive from the particular opportunity? Suppose that to solve the lake problem, you develop a daily schedule of exclusive time periods for each user group. In other words, a certain number of limited-entry permits are established for each group according to time period. To be fair, you establish a random-drawing process twenty-four hours in advance of participation. This action may eliminate the original conflicts between user groups and increase safety, but we might question the wisdom of such a program. Are there other alternatives that would accomplish the same goals, yet allow maximum participation? Would we in effect be creating an undesirable situation for many of the users? Would the involvement of representatives from each user group provide a more acceptable solution? Might the result be underutilization of a valued natural resource? Finally, in terms of management efficiency, have we artificially inflated management costs because we did not seek the least costly solution?

Dispersed-Use Areas

Too often we hear that dispersed-use areas, including wilderness, should not be managed; however, situations do exist that require management action. To procrastinate in implementing this action is really self-defeating—the situation merely gets worse.

For example, much of the traffic in the back-country of the Evergreen Scenic Area, which is a 17,000-acre roadless area, enters through a common point at Sugar Mountain Campground. People travel that trail for a mile or so and then fan out to camp, fish, and relax around the many mountain lakes. As a result, shorelines around the more accessible lakes are showing severe deterioration, litter is strewn everywhere, and horse users and backpackers are even clashing over the better camping and fishing spots. This may be an unusual type of situation, but even to the casual observer this is an unmanaged situation that must be controlled.

Smith Wilderness, a 240,000-acre wilderness in Western Montana, has high concentrations of hiking in one major drainage area. This trail winds its way through several wet meadows, and as trail use creates a rut through the wet meadows, water is funneled onto the trail, causing muddy conditions and then even greater rutting due to compaction and erosion. People fan out to avoid the problem, creating multiple trails. These same problems could have just as easily resulted from motorized, dispersed use. The point is that dispersed recreation, even in designated wilderness areas, is not immune to problems requiring management. However, solutions may be more limited.

In that regard, is there such a thing as overmanagement of dispersed recreation? Assume in the Smith Wilderness problem that the manager responded with some site rehabilitation and limited the number of people using the trail, explaining these actions through an information program. Again, are we underutilizing a resource because we have aimed our management program at maintaining the weakest link in the chain—the trail segments that go through the wet meadows? Have we inflated the cost of management because we did not relocate the trail away from the meadow?

Much has changed in the delivery of public outdoor recreation opportunities, yet change has often come slowly. Perhaps that is the way it should be. Our future, while not a mirror image of the past, certainly reflects our previous managerial experiences. Thus it is important for future management to reflect not only on where we are in state-of-the-art practices, but also how we got there.

Outdoor recreation management has evolved over about a hundred years, but we have only been faced with spiraling recreational use in the face of dwindling resources during the last thirty-five to forty. The following discussion is simply an effort to capsulize this brief history.

Although there are earlier instances of outdoor recreation management to focus on, the one significant event that drastically changed the course of the parks and conservation movement was the establishment of Yellowstone National Park. It was the embryo stage of outdoor recreation management in a public-land context, the ushering in of the "Custodial Era."

Custodial Era

The Yellowstone National Park Act of 1872 opened the door for the establishment of large areas of land for public purposes, including recreation. Several additional national parks were created during the late 1800s.[20] The western national forest lands were established under the Forest Reserve Act of 1891, and other lands were added later.[15,21] The important management strategy that evolved during this early period was that the lands were to be held in reserve— to be protected but not necessarily utilized.[20] Thus, most public lands were held in a custodial state with little access, no recreational facility development, and no sense of urgency for outdoor recreation management.

Even with the establishment of other national parks and the National Park Service in 1916, there was very little change in public use of public lands and in the need for outdoor recreation management, although a strong effort was made by Park Service Director Stephen Mather to build a constituency for parks and wilderness as opposed to forests.[9,22] The Industrial Revolution had brought people to the cities, some of which had expanded to large urban spaces; however, long hours of work in the factories, lack of transportation, and low incomes severely limited participation in outdoor recreation.[19]

Some increased public interest in outdoor recreation and wilderness became apparent in the late 1920s, but even this waned at the onset of the Great Depression.[20] However, the bureaucratic turf battle which began between the U.S. Forest Service and the National Park Service in the late teens, continued throughout the 1920s, climaxing with the Olympic National Park battle in the 1930s and the Grand Teton National Park battle in the next decade.[22,23] In terms of on-the-ground management of user opportunities, once again there was no urgent need for even the most rudimentary technical program. That period did bring transition, and ultimately the end of the Custodial Era, however, in the form of intensive recreation development and the construction of access roads and trails by the Civilian Conservation Corps and the Works Progress Administration.[21,25]

Now all that was needed to usher in the management era was an upgrade in the economy. World War II did just that—propelling the country into a period of economic prosperity. People had more money and time than ever before, and they began to seek pleasurable leisure experiences, particularly in outdoor settings.[14] This new interest in the out-of-doors caused little concern among the land managers (land custodians), since most of them found it difficult to interpret the real significance of increased recreational participation. Nevertheless, the end of World War II marked the end of the Custodial Era and the beginning of the "Extensive Management Era."

Extensive Management Era

Although many people were reluctant to recognize the rise of the new era, its impact did become evident to some concerned observers. During the 1950s and 1960s, public land use expanded greatly, and many agencies attempted to increase facilities and access in order to accommodate more people. Examples of these programs were Mission 66 (National Park Service)[25] and Operation Outdoors (U.S. Forest Service).[21] In addition, increased logging on the national forests accelerated the construction of what has become (for better or for worse) many thousands of miles of coincidental access to formerly isolated areas.[5,6,14,20,23]

The main emphasis of the Extensive Management Era was on increasing the supply of recreational opportunities. Although most of the management programs were extensive in nature, certain fundamental outdoor recreation management programs did evolve:

1. Resource management
   a. Site protection and maintenance
   b. Silvicultural treatment of overstory vegetation
   c. Integration with other resource management programs
   d. Recreation road construction and improvement
2. Visitor management
   a. Informational services
   b. Concession services
   c. Expansion of interpretive programs
   d. Public safety

During the late 1960s, some managers saw a need not only for expanding both resource and visitor management programs, but also for opening up new areas to users.[25] By this time, many new kinds of recreational equipment were becoming available on the market, such as snowmobiles, trail bikes, and ATVs (all-terrain vehicles). Thus there was a need not merely to provide new opportunities and services, but also to integrate these on a systems basis for more efficient management. It was insufficient to provide a few varied opportunities and attempt to reduce possible conflict between visitors. The visitor and his equipment had become technologically sophisticated, which required changes in existing management strategy. There was a need to update the programs—to provide for *resource management* to protect the resource base, and to provide for *visitor management* to maintain opportunities for the various user groups. These two broad programs needed to be integrated to insure congruent decision making that provided sustained-yield public recreation of benefit to all users.[9,13,25]

Intensive Management Era

The beginning of the "Intensive Management Era" is difficult to isolate. Some people feel that we have not yet reached that level; others feel that we may never reach it. Many agencies are trying to coordinate the capability of the resource with the perceived needs of visitors. In this era, the emphasis seems to be the need for developing and updating baseline data on both the effect of visitor use on the resource and styles of visitor participation in a particular area, including the visitor's perceptions of quality recreation experiences.[13]

One prominent strategy that has risen during this era is management by objectives. With this strategy, the recreation manager is forced to evaluate baseline data and develop specific management objectives for each newly planned area. The problem is that we have often couched our objectives in vague generalized terms, sought oversimplified models to achieve those objectives, and measured our output in visitor days.

We need new ideas and recreation managers with increased personal vitality to search for new ways of conducting old business. Research was never designed to solve all problems; its purpose is to improve the existing body of knowledge in order to lessen the uncertainty of managerial decision making. Yet there will always be uncertainty to deal with. To meet those objectives, a framework within which management objectives are developed and a bureaucratic decision maker who is willing to deal with uncertainty in developing programs, are needed.

The Role of the Manager

Historically, the manager has assumed the above role much like the *in loco parentis* of the college set in the 1950s. He or she has simply decided what is in the best interests of visitors, and sets about achieving that outcome. The underlying assumption here is that the manager preserves the outdoor experience for visitors, and that the ends (whatever the manager has decided on as the desired experience) justify the means. Under this paradigm, the manager ignores the role of the individual in producing the recreational experience, and assumes that all desired outcomes can be ultimately achieved through direct manipulation of visitor behavior.

Wilderness epitomizes this situation.[20] Managers have waved the banner, "search for solitude," as the justification for limiting the number of people going into Lake Isolated (a hypothetical area). After all, those poor wretched recreationists could not possibly have a good experience if they had to share

that lake with twenty other people. But the record speaks for itself. How many studies have you read where people were *en masse* dissatisfied with the experiences they had, or were having, in a given environmental setting? We have not located one.

There is good reason for that. People do not choose a particular recreational opportunity, understanding that there is always some uncertainty in any choice, to produce dissatisfaction. *Au contraire,* they make such choices with every intention of being satisfied. That is the role of the user or visitor (see Figure 1-2). The user takes charge of his/her recreational experience by first evaluating an array of potential recreational opportunities within their social, economic, and psychological constraints, then choosing the one that appears to offer the greatest utility, then actually participating. Even after this process, something can go wrong which neither the manager nor the user can control. Maybe the user had a fight with his/her girl/boyfriend before leaving; maybe she and her tentmate

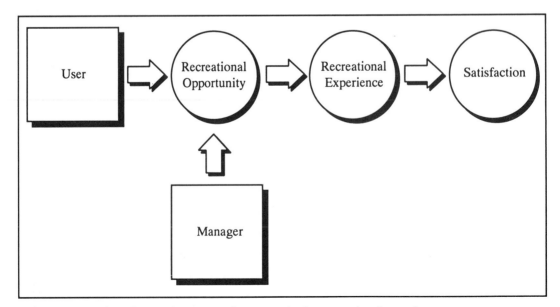

Figure 1-2. Roles of recreation user and manager in the recreational experience.

did not get along; maybe it rained all week, everything got soaked, and they became hypothermic; or maybe . . .

Without getting mired down in details (hopefully these will come later), the point is that the users are in charge of their recreational experiences and that they exercise that authority by choosing their own opportunities and preparing for them prior to actual participation. What does that leave the manager in charge of? The recreational opportunity, of course!

In the Lake Isolated example, the manager has ignored opportunities created by past management such as the realigned trail that reduces the gradient, the widened and surfaced trail, foot bridges across intervening creeks, a paved parking lot at the access point, and, oh yes, the sign—WELCOME TO LAKE ISOLATED. Potentially, each one of these actions creates a new recreational opportunity for some users. Collectively they would spell D-I-S-A-S-T-E-R if the intent was to provide a low-density opportunity at Lake Isolated, an alpine lake setting that was carved out by the last glacial period. Not understanding that past management actions have molded present use patterns, the manager now introduces one more element of change, a limited-entry permit system, which in turn may change users' perception of the opportunity even more.

Again, do not get bogged down in details. This is not an attempt to vilify the manager. What we are trying to say is that he or she is not in charge of the experience of every individual. The job is producing the opportunity—the generic experience associated with the particular environmental setting—by developing and mixing a particular set of management programs. That generic experience places the sideboards or constraints on possible experience outcomes.

All agencies should fit into the concept of the manager being responsible for the recreational opportunities, even though each agency has its own peculiar set of constraints in choosing to develop and promote a given set of recreational opportunities. The general constraints are discussed in Chapter 3.

MANAGEMENT WITHIN AN ORGANIZATIONAL FRAMEWORK

Even if you are comfortable with the idea that the manager provides the recreational opportunity, how efficiently you can perform that role depends much on how you are organized to manage. If decision-making power is held by some central authority, divorced from the resource conditions, management decision making often becomes routinized or stereotyped. Under that type of regime, the benefit of the knowledge of the on-the-ground manager is lost. Unfortunately his or her motivation to implement even the simplest programs is often also lost.

On the other hand, if you were to organize the agency under a completely decentralized authority, each manager might develop his or her own program independently. This may create inconsistencies in program policies, resulting in a total lack of coordination and cooperation—almost organizational anarchy. Obviously there must be some balance to foster decision making at the lowest possible level of the organization and yet maintain some reasonable consistency in those decisions across the organization. While much of this is often determined by the style of management, how you organize to actually accomplish your mission will determine your theoretical efficiency. We say theoretical efficiency because you must also realize that each "pigeonhole" on the organizational chart is filled with a less-than-perfect human being just like most of us.

Rather than lead you through some circuitous discussion about something with which we are not completely familiar, let us make our point with an example about efficiently performing one's role as an outdoor recreation manager. A state's department of natural resources was so hampered by its organizational framework that it had lost much of its effectiveness and efficiency. Each major division had separate regional boundaries, yet the agency was expected to operate as a totally integrated, well-coordinated organization. If a park manager wanted to improve the fishery habitat in a lake, which included removing the existing fishery and draining the lake, he or she may have had to contact the engineer from one district, the fishery biologist for another district, and so on—a complete lack of organizational integrity. The same park manager might have had to go to two different districts to obtain the services of a forest pathologist for a tree disease problem, depending on whether the problem was in the northern or southern portion of the state park. There has since been a reorganization of this agency into an effective operating organization.

The point is that in order to be effective in your management programs, you must first properly organize to be efficient and effective. Otherwise, subsequent management decisions will also be inefficient and ineffective. There is no magic solution; in fact, an effective organization is probably one that continually reevaluates its organizational framework in light of the constantly changing society around it.

SELECTED READINGS

1. Batten, J. D. 1989. *Tough Minded Leadership.* New York, NY: American Management Association.

2. Beck, A. C., and Hillmar, E. D. 1986. *Positive Management Practices.* San Francisco, CA: Jossey-Bass.

3. Cheek, N. H., Jr. 1976. "The Case for the Increased Regulation of Human Access to Parklands: Established Fact or Organizational Myth?" *Proceedings of Recreation Management Institute,* College Station, TX: Texas A & M University.

4. Clark, R. N. 1979. "The Recreation Opportunity Spectrum: A Framework for Planning, Management, and Research," USDA-Forest Service Gen. Tech. Report PNW-98.

5. Clary, D. A. 1986. *Timber and the Forest Service.* Lawrence, KS: University Press of Kansas.

6. Clawson, M. 1983. *The Federal Lands Revisited.* Baltimore, MD: Johns Hopkins University Press.

7. Cox, R. H., and Askham, L. R. 1984. "Implications of Interforest Management Organization." *Journal of Park and Recreation Administration* 2(2):46-53.

8. Downy, K. B., Burke, J. F., and Schreyer, R. 1983. "Recreation Resource Planning and Management and What Defines the Professional." *Journal of Park and Recreation Administration* 1(2):45-60.

9. Everhart, W. C. 1972. *The National Park Service.* Boulder, CO: Westview Press.

10. Gray, D. E. 1983. "American Management Lessons from Japan." *Journal of Park and Recreation Administration* 1(1):1-6.

12. Harris, C. C., Driver, B. L., and Bergerson, E. P. 1984. "Do Choices of Sport Fisheries Reflect Angler Preferences for Site Attributes?" *Proceedings of the Symposium on Recreation Choice Behavior.* USDA Forest Service General Technical Report INT-184.

13. Hartzog, G. B. 1988. *Battling for the National Parks,* Mt. Kisco, NY: Moyer Bell Ltd.

14. Hays, S. P. 1987. *Beauty, Health, and Permanence, Environmental Politics in the United States, 1955-1985.* New York, NY: Cambridge University Press.

15. Hays, S. P. 1959. *Conservation and the Gospel of Efficiency: the Progressive Conservation Movement, 1890-1920.* Cambridge, MA: Harvard University Press.

16. Heffron, F. 1989. *Organization Theory and Public Organizations: The Political Connection.* Englewood Cliffs, NJ: Prentice Hall.

17. Jubenville, A. 1986. "Recreational Use of Public Lands: The Role of the Manager." *Journal of Park and Recreational Administration, 3*(4):53-60.

18. Murphy, J. F., Nupoth, W., Jamison, L., and Williams, J. 1991. *Leisure Systems: Critical Concepts and Applications.* Champaign, IL: Sagamore Publishing, Inc.

19. Myers, P. 1989. *State Parks in a New Era,* 3 Vols., illustrated. Washington, DC: Conservation Foundation.

20. Nash, R. 1982. *Wilderness and the American Mind,* 3rd ed., New Haven, CT: Yale University Press.

21. Steen, H. K. 1976. *The U.S. Forest Service: A History.* Seattle, WA: University of Washington Press.

22. Swain, D. C. 1970. *Wilderness Defender: Horace M. Albright and Conservation,* Chicago, IL: University of Chicago Press.

23. Twight, B. W. 1983. *Organizational Values and Political Power: the Forest Service vs. the Olympic National Park,* University Park, PA: Penn State Press.

24. Walsh, R. G. 1986. *Recreation Economic Decisions: Comparing Benefits and Costs.* State College, PA: Venture Publishing, Inc.

25. Wirth, C. L. 1980. *Parks, Politics, and the People.* Norman, OK: University of Oklahoma Press.

CHAPTER 2

The Outdoor Recreation Management Model

Before we begin a discussion specifically on the outdoor recreation management model, we first need to define what a model is, why a model is needed in outdoor recreation, and why a holistic, or systems, approach is necessary to develop an outdoor recreation management model. *Webster's New World Dictionary* states that a paradigm is a model or pattern, a copy made to represent a real object or situation. This representation can come in many forms. It may be a physical model, such as a statue. It can also be a situational model that depicts events or situations in terms of critical factors and the interrelationships of those factors.

Obviously the static, physical model can be beneficial to the manager in displaying the existing static resource situation, such as a terrain model. However, a situational model, where critical variables are identified and interrelationships established, lends itself more to the dynamic situations with which most managers are faced. The manager can ask the "what if . . ." questions and have a better understanding of the probable outcomes, even if he or she does not know the exact probabilities. For example, if we know that trail use and trail erosion are functions of trail gradient, then we can ask what happens if we increase the gradient and remove the surfacing material on the trail to Lake Isolated (the example in Chapter 1). We can predict that use will probably decrease, and that erosion will increase, even though we cannot predict the exact amount of increase/decrease. The emphasis in the program to maintain low density use in Lake Solitude, however, shifts from a limited-entry permit system to control use to increasing gradient with associated erosion-control measures. Thus, for recreation management, the situational model is the more appropriate of the two models.

The intent of this chapter is to expand our models to show the recreational opportunity as a situation within a managerial context, i.e., as elements, functions, and variables that make up the managerial environment and facilitate the movement of the recreationist from motivation to the recreation experience, and ultimately to a level of personal satisfaction within that experience with the public agency which made the opportunity possible. This level of satisfaction may include active political support of the agency's program or budget either as an individual, or through membership in an interest or constituency group which supports the agency.[10,27] The first step is to describe the elements in this public agency system.

A system is a set of interrelated and interdependent parts, or subsystems, which can react as a total organism under given situations, and this so-called organism resides in an environment which sustains the organism. The "organism" or system exists because of demands for its products or services from elements of its environment, and it produces outputs of products or services which it exchanges with the environment in return for social support. The elements of the environment which consume the system outputs provide positive or negative feedback to the system in regard to the quantity and quality of the system outputs. These feedback signals are often inputs from the public or political leadership and guide the system's production of new outputs so that it survives and grows.[10,22] Feedback also comes from the resources or services which the system manages, signaling problems which may create later negative feedback from the system's interested publics.

Each of the recreation management system's subsystems specialize in different technical aspects of the output production process. Each may have several phases that are also interrelated and interdependent. If one subsystem or phase of a subsystem is altered, then the whole system is affected; therefore the boundary of a system is flexible to meet both external and internal changes. As a model of a system grows and changes, it also develops a history that will have some predictive value. For example, for a given input such as a new law or a budget cut, we may reasonably forecast its effects over the entire system.

A system can be either open or closed. A closed system is theoretically self-contained and does not interact or exchange with its environment. An open system recognizes that certain input from the external environment is vital to its existence and in return it produces certain output (see Figure 2-4, p. 24). By external environment, we mean the social environment (particularly the political environment) which lies outside the system's boundary, but directly affects any subsystem within the boundary.[2,10,22]

The typical outdoor recreation management organization is an open system, directly affected by changes outside its physical, organizational, and legal boundaries such as by degraded water quality due to upstream land use changes or new legal or other policy requirements such as a redesignation of a stream to wild-river status through the political process. Other more regular public policy process changes also routinely impact the recreation management organization, as they do any public agency or public bureaucracy.[10] These include changes resulting from ups and downs in the annual or biennial government budget cycle and the continual inputs of political demands, support, and other exercises of political power by interest groups and legislative committees composing the "iron triangle" of the outdoor recreation agency.[27] Struggle for power and position among interest groups has led to domination of agencies by clientele groups and legislative committees, a factor sometimes unrecognized by professional personnel at lower levels in those agencies.[23]

Because of the obviously complex interrelationships within this open model of the recreation management organization, we must consider the effect of any decision on the total organizational system—not just in solving a particular problem in a given subsystem. For example, while eliminating cattle grazing from a particularly scenic meadow in Grand Mountain National Park may make perfect sense in terms of protection of the recreation resource from severe erosion, it may alienate a rancher who has close ties to the chairman of the Congressional subcommittee on appropriations for the Department of the Interior, creating a threat to the Park's annual budget! Thus, a thorough holistic approach is essential to system management as decisions sometimes can be crucial to the agency's general welfare. A much more politically subtle approach to seemingly "simple" technically logical decisions may occasionally be necessary.

After we get a picture of the total system in our organization, we can dissect it into subsystems and then relate each management program back to the recreational opportunity to be provided. Many detailed, complex subsystems can be reintegrated to form a single highly complex, fully integrated management system. A complex systems model should enable us to understand the interrelationship between subsystems internally and the social environment externally. Theoretically, we could predict the effects of manipulating a given variable in a subsystem on other variables within that subsystem or on the total system. However, we must also keep in mind that this is an open system where external factors are continually affecting the internal operations and changing the program composition of the system. For example, a highly publicized injury in one park or zone can affect how the total system responds to hazard management in the future.

Many of the important problems facing the manager are very complex and affected by various social and political external influences. Thus a model helps us to acquire an understanding of those complexities. Even with the limited information we have about certain environmental and organizational variables, a system model can not only benefit the outdoor recreation manager, but point out the need for baseline information in areas where voids now exist. It may also suggest priorities for future research.

THE PRIMARY INPUTS OF THE SYSTEM

Inputs are the basic descriptors of any system. They place boundaries on what is to be included in the system's management model. In outdoor recreation management there are really three primary inputs after the executive, the legislature, or Congress have provided the legal authority and annual appropriation to work with—the visitor, the natural resource base, and the management organization. We will focus on the nature of the latter three inputs, the general relationships of these inputs, and the overall concept of the system embedded in its external political environment.

The first and probably most important element in the system to be considered is the visitor or recreationist, since he or she—via organized interest groups—creates much of the political demand and support for the recreational experiences that require the other two elements.[10,27] It is for visitors that recreational opportunities are planned and managed in our modern society. Visitors generally have special recreational interests or tastes and expect the system, which is designed to provide recreational opportunities, to meet their needs. However, the political system usually responds to users at the organized interest group level—for example, wilderness hiker groups or auto camper groups—rather than to individual opinions or concerns.

This has worried some managers because they feel that in fairness they should provide for all diverse recreational interests. However, interest groups and leadership elites are the most influential sources of political opinion in our political system.[20,27] As Walker explains: "Political mobilization is seldom spontaneous. Before any large element of the population can become a part of the American political process, organizations must be formed, advocates must be trained, and the material resources needed to gain the attention of national policy makers must be gathered . . . The essential prerequisites for successful political mobilization are mainly organizational . . ." (p. 194).[27]

Further, it seems that when we try to manage for everyone's interest, we end up satisfying no one. As pointed by A. Jubenville, S. C. Matulich, and W. G. Workman:

> Clark and Stankey (1979) recognized that quality is a relevant notion across the entire spectrum but argued, along with much of the profession, that an objective of diversity assures quality. This ill-founded notion is rooted in the belief that recreational quality is so highly personal that management should not be dominated by mass or average tastes. As noted by Davis (1963), it is one of those conceptual weeds that have grown up (and gone to seed) in the outdoor recreation movement.[14]

There are also persons who may not be users but are supporters who are simply glad to know the land and the habitat it provides are there (e.g., bird lovers and wildlife rights groups, watershed protection groups, etc.).

Second, the natural resource base (environmental setting) is the medium in which the activity takes place and which provides the cover for birds, wildlife and watershed protection. This element can be conducive or disruptive in the movement toward satisfying visitors with a single recreational opportunity. It is important to realize that it is absolutely necessary to provide a physical environment that is conducive to pleasant experiences; however, because of the professional value systems of many recreation managers, we have often misjudged what really are the environmental needs of the various types of recreationists.

It is not necessarily the physical characteristics of the recreational site that are important, but rather, how they are perceived by the user. Perhaps we have placed too much emphasis on the resource itself, without regard to how it affects the visitor. We have postulated a need for certain types of environmental settings, such as a pristine environment for the hiker, or maximum privacy for the auto camper, when in fact other environmental settings may be sometimes more satisfying. A pristine environment may be satisfying to an experienced, more highly educated hiker group, but appear hostile to a less experienced one. A modern trailer campground may be very attractive to one camping group, but very unattractive to another.

Indeed, some studies have found that group characteristics such as the educational level of backcountry and wilderness users affects their perception of crowding and thus their desire to restrict numbers in wilderness areas. For example, West found in a study of backcountry campers in the Sylvania Recreation Area in Michigan that it was primarily users with higher education who wished to control the crowding of the area.[28] In a study of two federal recreation areas, Twight et al. found that backpackers had much stronger privacy attitudes than did car campers, particularly backpackers who were both better educated and who wanted to share their experience only with an intimate other.[25] The latter study concluded that restricting backcountry users to designated clusters of campsites was probably detrimental to such shared wilderness experiences.

In other instances, however, it seems probable that the physical characteristics of the resource are a direct indicator of potential recreational pursuits. Given the opportunity, the experienced skier will seek environs that offer challenging skiing conditions over a lengthy season; the experienced sightseer will seek those landscapes that offer maximum aesthetic diversity and unique types of viewing opportunities; and so on.

Finally, management is the third of the three system elements. Again its ultimate goal is to enable various user groups to have satisfying recreational experiences. It coordinates the activities and services on the available resource base with the needs of visitors. Management is the element that protects the integrity of the recreational opportunity and the resource base—the essence of the opportunity.

The interrelationships of all three elements are as follows:

1. The resource affects the visitor.
2. The visitor affects the resource.
3. The resource situation affects management programs.
4. The management programs affect the resource situation.
5. The visitor affects management programs.
6. The management programs affect the disposition of the visitor.

Specific interrelationships are meaningful only in the context of the type of recreational opportunity we are trying to offer in a given situation.

PRIMARY FUNCTIONS

The functions of the system describe the subsystems—visitor management, resource management, and service management. Visitor management is manipulating the visitor (either voluntarily or otherwise) in order to create a pleasing social environment for the activity. Resource management refers to manipulating the resource to enhance the recreational opportunity or protect the site from deterioration. Service management refers to provisioning for certain visitor services within a given recreational opportunity while minimizing the queuing associated with that opportunity. The three subsystems, or primary functions, must be integrated to produce a given recreational opportunity.

Resource Management

The resource management subsystem consists of two phases—resource input and the resource management programs aimed at managing those input (see Figure 2-1, p. 18). Maintaining resource values is important and is accomplished through monitoring the effects of current custodial programs on the resource base at some prescribed level. It is not a matter of eliminating the impact of use on the resource. Instead it is aimed at keeping impact within some acceptable level or improving the resource's ability to sustain a higher level of use within acceptable limits. Monitoring, then, is carried out at the interface of the resource with human use. It tells us how well we are doing and indicates what direction we should shift the program to move it within acceptable limits.

Resource management programs vary from the very site-specific, such as the introduction of a hardy ground cover to stabilize a site under intensive use, to the environmentally protective, as in maintaining secondary vegetation through the introduction of fire. In all programs, the emphasis is not on maintaining the resource as an end in itself, but on achieving some desired outcome—a specified recreational opportunity.

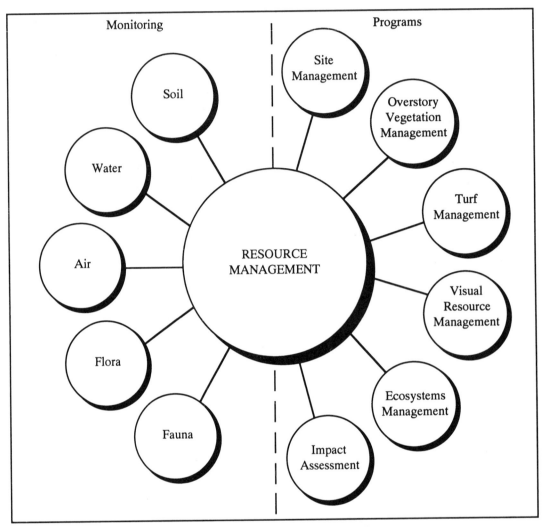

Figure 2-1. Resource management subsystem.

Resource management programs include:

1. Site Management. This is the manipulation of the developed site to maintain the quality of the resource setting and to rehabilitate it where necessary. Site management is an intensive program whose functions are to protect the site from overuse by recreationists and to maintain a desirable, aesthetic environment in which the activity is to take place.

2. Overstory Vegetation Management. This primarily includes silvicultural practices related to the management of intensive use areas, such as developed sites along roads and trails and around bodies of waters. Many of these practices are initiated prior to any recreational development in order to prepare the site, and they may continue throughout the life of the development.

3.   *Ecosystems Management.* Here we focus on specific controversial areas of management concern as they relate to the fragments of ecosystems that remain. The most controversial management strategy concerning ecosystems has been the suppression of fire in the large public areas dedicated to dynamic natural ecosystems. Thus our specific discussion will deal primarily with fire-management programs.

4.   *Visual Resource Management.* This is a program designed to assess the visual impact of any man-made activity or development, and, where appropriate, to enhance the appeal of the landscape. It is a process in which the characteristics of the landscapes are inventoried, analyzed, and classified based on their ability to absorb development with minimum visual impact. This process incorporates the perceptions of visitors.

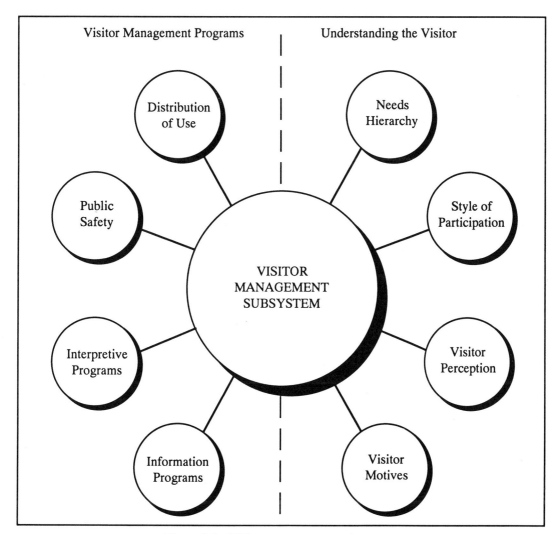

Figure 2-2. Visitor management subsystem.

We often do not give enough consideration to the visual effects of a development, even a recreational development. The public that uses these resources demands that we retain the aesthetic appeal that attracted them there in the first place.

Visitor Management

The functions of visitor management are depicted in Figure 2-2, p. 19. The manager has a visitor information and education program at his or her disposal in order to help visitors choose various opportunities or to manipulate visitor use. Information systems are marvelous management tools; they can help inform users so that they can choose rationally between environmental settings and management-influenced sites that best suit their interests. Such information has been successful in influencing the choices of "new" visitors to an area, but the "old hands" typically ignore it.

Public safety is of concern to management regardless of the type of recreational opportunity being provided. However, the specific public safety program, as will be shown later, must be consistent with the requirements of the opportunity. In some instances, a simple sign or brochure may be sufficient; others may require strict regulatory enforcement. Educational efforts are also important, and should be used to improve both the users' understanding of the landscape and their use of that landscape. Many of the negative effects for which users are blamed are often due to ignorance rather than willful intent. Good educational techniques can help to alleviate some of these problems.

You can also direct your visitor management program toward specific user groups, creating a dialogue in which the user and manager attempt to understand each other. In addition, the manager should consider visitor input in developing management programs. These include the visitors' needs hierarchy, style of participation, and perception.

1. Needs Hierarchy. The needs of the individual in terms of what he wants from the recreational experience are important. These needs have been summarized by Maslow in a hierarchical structure.[16] Maslow theorized that needs are the primary influences on an individual's behavior and each lower need on the hierarchy must be satisfied to some minimal level before the next higher need becomes a motivator of consequence. When a particular need emerges, it shapes the individual's behavior in terms of motivation, priorities, and action taken. Motivated behavior is the result of the tension—either pleasant or unpleasant—experienced when a need presents itself. The goal of this behavior is the reduction of the tension or discomfort, and enables the individual to satisfy his or her need. Only unsatisfied needs are prime sources of motivation, though A. S. Mills suggests this theory may not hold for leisure time.[17]

2. Style of Participation. Style of participation is important to the proper management of the recreational opportunity. There can be great differences in the way people participate in a given activity. For example, one study found differences in styles of elk hunting (trophy hunter, meat hunter, and equipment hunter). These are called the macrocharacteristics, or macrobehavioral patterns or participation. J. A. Wagar[26] separates camping into seven styles: transient, central, long-term, forest, peak-load, backcountry, and wilderness. All activities can be divided into distinct styles of participation that should help the manager to better structure management strategies for enhancing macrobehavioral patterns.

The microbehavior is also important, but unfortunately we do not have many studies that focus on participant microbehavior. Such conduct in hikers would include, for example, how they travel a wilderness trail, interact with one another, and respond to various environmental stimuli. This information could help managers maintain or enhance normal visitor reactions. If it becomes necessary to alter use patterns, a knowledge of the microbehavior can also help managers understand the potential effects of specific management strategies.

3. Visitor Perception. Ultimately, how people participate is based on their perception of the recreational opportunity provided by management. That perception includes not only the resource such as a lake and surrounding shoreline, but also man-made provisions such as roads, boating facilities, services, etc. Even in the absence of empirical data, we should be able to predict general user response to obvious program changes. Others may be more subtle and less predictable. The point is that managers must be able to link management action to visitor perception.

Service Management

Service management refers to the provisioning of facilities, services, and related ancillary programs to accommodate the user (see Figure 2-3, p. 22). This provisioning must fit within some appropriate criteria. The basic framework for judging appropriateness is the Recreational Opportunity Spectrum, which will be discussed in more detail in Chapter 3. Its logic dictates that toward the more primitive portion of the outdoor recreation spectrum there should be fewer facilities and that these should be more rustic in character, requiring less service and more self-reliance.

The service management subsystem can be separated into several programs:

1. Area planning is a resource allocation process where natural and fiscal resources are allocated to provide specified recreational opportunities. As part of that process, managers provide access and facilities for visitors. These are the man-made attributes that visitors initially respond to in choosing a particular site to recreate. Thus the area planning process is very important to service management, but it also creates the need for ancillary programs such as concessions, maintenance and hazard management.

2. Concession management is directed toward providing specialized facilities/services in order for the visitor to enjoy a particular environmental setting. What kind of accommodations are needed? What services should be provided? Who will provide them? How will they be regulated? The using public is generally charged directly for the specialized facilities/services. The question becomes: What is the better vehicle for doing this? Typically this has been a concession lease where a private entrepreneur pays a fee to the public agency for the right to provide the facility/service. In some cases however, it has been necessary for the agency itself to provide either the facility used for the service or both the facility and the service.

3. The maintenance subprogram is aimed at protecting public investment in the facilities and maintaining acceptable accommodations for the using public. It is the first level of management, whether it is done on trails or modern buildings. Other services may enhance the use of the site, but maintenance is absolutely essential.

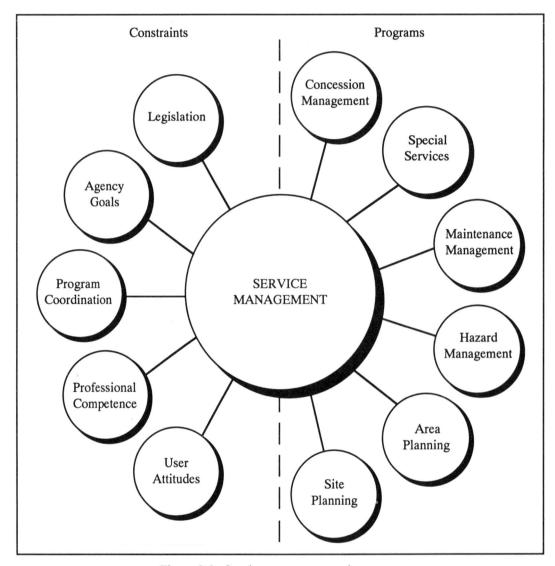

Figure 2-3. Service management subsystem.

4. *Hazard management* is a subprogram directed at reducing the risk of natural or man-made hazards to visitors. It is not risk management, a business-management term which means to minimize the risk of losses to the firm. Here, in a broader sense, it means that the recreation user acts as the firm to minimize his/her personal risk involved in a given recreational opportunity. The recreation manager carries out specific activities to "accommodate" or assist the user in minimizing risk, but the user is still the actual decision maker—still in charge of his/her own behavior.

INTEGRATION OF THE FUNCTIONS

The integration of functions is a difficult process because of the number of possible interactions among all the programs in each subsystem. A diagram of this would create such a maze of lines that we would have difficulty in tracing interrelationships. We must realize, however, that there is an interdependence within the system; that is, a decision made in one program area can have a drastic effect on other programs (see Figure 2-4, p. 24). Thus the manager must consider all the ramifications of a particular decision since one can, with an understanding of these interactions, manipulate one program to produce a desired outcome in another.

For example, suppose you need to improve site conditions in a wilderness area where outfitters (a service management function) have tended to camp near a lake, causing the resource to deteriorate—a resource management problem. Since in a wilderness area we are not allowed to manipulate the resource directly (in terms of culturally treating or hardening the site—see Chapter 8), we can either redistribute use by voluntary cooperation, or, through an outfitter permit, limit his/her use to allow the site to recover naturally.

In a more complex interaction example, let's look at a segment of a major river system that is by federal law designated as a wild river under the jurisdiction of a particular federal land management agency. The designated management agency receives additional inputs of annual appropriations and regulatory authority from the political environment of its agency system. The supervisor or superintendent of the wild river is regularly informed by his agency superiors of the institutional constraints upon the agency, such as

agency goals, new legislation, and the political demands of interest groups such as the rafting outfitters national association, the American Rivers Council (which represents individual floaters and floater groups), and the Izaak Walton League (representing fishermen). By law, this river is managed for two primary activities: scenic floating and fishing. There are only three access points along the federally designated "wild" portion of the river.

Now let's suppose that the visitor (visitor subsystem) is a novice floater who has depended primarily on the commercial outfitters with concession leases for floating the river. He is attracted to the area by the outstanding scenery, and regards floating only as a secondary activity. He enjoys the experience and does not perceive any problems (such as crowding, noise, and so on) that would affect the quality of his experience.

Information on floating is available through the agency and through advertisements by the commercial outfitters. A recent study showed that most people found out about floating trips through contact with friends. Education is primarily through natural history interpretation during the float trips, but other subtle kinds of education can take place because of the surroundings. Each outfitter, as a condition of his permit, is required to present a minimal interpretive talk. A self-guiding brochure of the area is being developed by the agency for the private floater.

Use has increased rapidly, especially on the commercial float trips. At certain times of the day, several boating parties must wait their turns to launch. According to agency regulations (in Title 36 CFR), the policy on launching is that the previous boat must be out of sight before the next one can be launched; this is done to reduce congestion on the water.

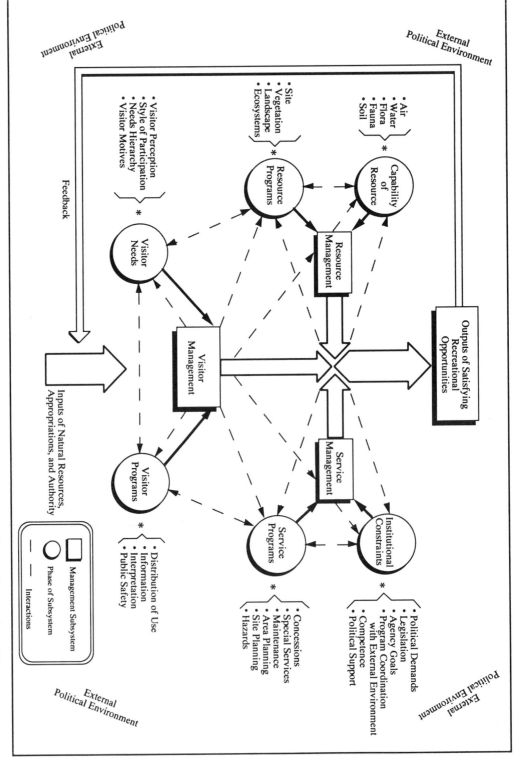

Figure 2-4. The Outdoor Recreation Systems Model. This model shows the integration and interaction of the subsystems. An asterisk (*) indicates areas where the external environment may affect the operation of the system.

Public safety has not been a problem since most people go out on a commercial raft under the guidance of a skilled boatman. All craft must meet minimum safety standards (according to both state law, agency and Coast Guard regulations), and agency rangers permit no one to launch his/her craft, except at the designated access points. The few safety problems have been caused by several unskilled private floaters who did not appreciate their own limitations in craft maneuvering. No serious accidents have occurred.

Resource management problems are minimal except those related to fishing, since floaters are not allowed to stop and get out of their craft. This eliminates environmental impact except at or near the access points, where some site deterioration from boaters and from fishing use is taking place. No overnight use is allowed, although budgetary limits on ranger personnel makes enforcement difficult.

Service management has probably the greatest effect on the entire system. Several concessionaires have special use permits to operate on the river and these outfitters encourage participation by advertising float trips. Most permittees offer a good service that is well-received by the commercial floater. Few complaints of any substance have been received from the clientele using the commercial services, but the outfitters' association has pressured the agency to relax its insurance requirements and raft inspections.

Others are also not entirely happy with the management of the Wild River. The local chapter of the Izaak Walton League has complained about disturbance of fishing conditions and line entanglements involving the increase in numbers of floaters and outfitters permitted. The American Rivers Council has asked that the balance between commercial

and individual floating craft numbers be discussed at the next meeting of the agency advisory board. And finally, the Gold Dredgers' Association has begun a petition-signing campaign among nearby residents of the area to open up the river to their use, on the basis that Wild River status precludes many jobs which would otherwise be available in the local economy. Some members of that association have recently attempted to open up the river on their own through minor trespasses. The river management agency wanted to overlook these trespasses in order to avoid creating local political antagonisms, but was sued by the Sierra Club, which obtained a court order forcing the agency to take law enforcement action against the dredgers.

Access to the river area is currently limited to gravel roads leading to the three access points. These roads, in effect, restrict the total amount of use that the river can receive. Total commercial use is also limited in a more formal manner through a quota system of 75,000 visitor-days per year, which is made a part of each special use permit issued to a concessionaire. Psychological barriers to river use have been overcome by the permits' requirement of qualified boat operators handling each trip. The agency also uses a river patrol to enforce regulations, permit requirements, and to otherwise enhance visitors' safety on the water.

Obviously, additional factors could be mentioned. The purpose here is to delineate a management system and indicate how it operates without passing judgment on any phase of it. Now, with our knowledge of the system and how it works, we can better understand the effects that a given decision may have on the various subsystems and on the system's environment. Each phase may have an effect on every other phase.

SUMMARY

The visitor is the main beneficiary of an outdoor recreation systems management model. There is a need for service and resource management in recreation only if there are inputs of political environmental demands and support for the agency's programs. Agencies develop specific visitor management programs in response to user demands for satisfying experiences. By so doing, they gain the user support.

The service management subsystem offers basic features, including access, facilities, and other accommodations, which are commensurate with institutional constraints, resource limitations, and visitor needs. Resource management programs attempt to maintain the existing resource base within accepted limits of change (based on either legislation, agency goals, visitor perceptions, or all of these). When use exceeds these limits, feedback through the system may indicate a need to reduce the impact by means of a visitor redistribution program (visitor management), which in turn should signal a need to adjust area or site planning, number of accommodations, and services. Another possibility is to manipulate the overused site by using cultural site treatments to increase its durability—as long as this manipulation is acceptable under law, as well as to the user and the agency, and does not disrupt the activity or the services provided. Even temporary disruption is permissible if the majority of the people support the temporary inconvenience in order to have a better-managed site in the long run.

A systems model is the only logical approach to managing the natural resource base for recreational use because it simply depicts the highly complex interaction of visitor, resource, and the manager in the context of the public policy system. While all possible interactions may not be fully appreciated, we understand enough to know that the three subsystems are linked together and that any change in one can affect the others. Without that knowledge, we could continually solve problems in one area and possibly cause catastrophes in others.

However, it is important that you use an open model in your system's management. As pointed out in Figure 2-4 (p. 24), external political factors and institutional constraints influence and/or govern individual recreational subsystems, thus affecting the entire system. Since a closed, static model cannot realistically describe the dynamic changes that occur in a recreation system or its embedded setting in the larger political environment of society, the open model is invaluable for its great emphasis on monitoring external factors. When management does not adapt quickly to changes in external forces, public support wanes for *all* agency programs.

A closing observation: In regard to public support for better management of outdoor recreation lands at the state level, we have noticed several situations where—for efficiency purposes—park and recreation agencies have been combined with environmental regulatory agencies and/or public land commodity production agencies to form the mega-resource agency. Such action may reduce administrative costs and be politically advantageous, but there is a little-recognized but deleterious effect on the quality and quantity of service provided by park and recreation agencies. We think the political reasons for creating the mega-agencies (under the cloak of efficiency) are:

1. The regulatory agencies are required to perform certain functions by law, yet their budgets and other efforts are

opposed by the regulated—generally certain private sector organizations and trade groups.

2. The mega-agency administrators, particularly at the state level, need a public-minded constituency (such as park and recreation agency constituents) to broaden the issues and to balance or play off against the political pressures of the regulated commodity interests.

3. These state administrators, often political appointees, are rewarded for their actions in so neutralizing political pressures by receiving more federal environmental aid (e.g., EPA) for their rapidly growing regulatory agencies.

4. However, in the process, the now less visible park agency gets short shrift, and is often prevented by the mega-umbrella agency from presenting its programs on their own merits to the legislature. The park agency can quietly have constituency groups work with legislative committees to reinstate some of its priorities, but it is an uphill battle through the back door.

Thus, it is in the interest of quality parks and recreation not to be combined with environmental regulatory agencies in a mega-agency. If the pollution regulatory agencies require a balanced political setting for effectiveness, then placement in a health department might be best, where the independence and stature of the medical profession can fend off the political pressures from the reluctant regulated polluters of water, land and air.

Further, when park and recreation agencies are combined in a mega-agency with commodity-oriented agencies, such a mega-agency often treats commodities (e.g., forests) as singularly important and ignores priorities for recreational use that it cannot quantify in a benefit-cost analysis. Chapter 17 indicates that this problem can be overcome if the agency is willing. In such a superagency, recreation philosophically seems to play second fiddle.

Finally, in a commodity-oriented mega-agency, the interaction of its subsystems is often not understood and appreciated. Consequently, impacts of other resource uses on recreation or caused by recreation are often treated simplistically—frequently as simple cause-effect relationships within a single subsystem and not the system as a whole. As much as this is a concern, we think that in the future the role of parks and recreation will be elevated—to the point of recreation becoming one of the dominant themes in multiple-use management agencies. Management must listen to constituency groups, because if they do not, those groups will be heard at the legislative level. People are demanding more recreational and aesthetic opportunities on their public lands, and they will get them.

SELECTED READINGS

1. Alden, H. R. 1973. "Systems for Analyzing Impacts of Outdoor Recreation Programs on Environmental Quality," *Outdoor Recreation and Environmental Quality.* Foss, P.O. (ed.). Ft. Collins, CO: Colorado State University.

2. Boulding, K. E. 1956. "General Systems Theory: The Skeleton of Science" *Management Science* 2(3):198.

3. Buckley, W. 1967. *Sociology and Modern Systems Theory.* Englewood Cliffs, NJ: Prentice Hall.

4. Chase, G., and Reveal, E. 1983. *How to Manage in the Public Sector,* New York, NY: McGraw-Hill, Inc.

5. Cordell, H. K. 1990. "Outdoor Recreation and Wilderness (Chapter 10)." *Natural Resources for the 21st Century.* R. N. Sampson and D. Hair (eds.). Washington, DC: Island Press.

6. Cox, R. H., and Askham, L. R. 1984. "Implications of Interforest Management Organizations." *Journal of Park and Recreation Administration* 2(2):46-53.

7. Crompton, J. L., Mackay, K. J., and Fesenmaier, D. R. 1991. "Identifying Dimensions of Service Quality." *Journal of Park and Recreation Administration* 9(3):15-28.

8. Davis, R. K. 1963. "Recreation Planning as an Economic Problem." *Natural Resources Journal* 3(10):329-349.

9. Goodsell, C. T. 1985. *The Case for Bureaucracy: A Public Administration Polemic.* 2nd ed. Chatham, NJ: Chatham House Publishers, Inc.

10. Heffron, F. 1989. *Organization Theory and Public Organizations: The Political Connection.* Englewood Cliffs, NJ: Prentice Hall.

11. Hellriegel, D., and Slocum, J. W., Jr. 1982. *Management: A Contingency Approach.* Reading, MA: Addison-Wesley Publishing, Co.

12. Hendee, J. C., Stankey G. H., and Lucas, R. C. 1990. *Wilderness Management,* 2nd ed. Golden, CO: North American Press. Chapters 9, 14-17.

13. Johnson, R. A., Kast, F., and Rosenzweig, J. E. 1967. *The Theory and Management of Systems.* New York, NY: McGraw-Hill Book Co.

14. Jubenville, A., Matulich, S. C., and Workman, W. G. 1986. *Toward the Integration of Economics and Outdoor Recreation Management.* Bulletin 68, Agricultural and Forestry Experiment Station, Fairbanks, AK.

15. Lange, O. 1965. *Wholes and Parts: A General Theory of System Behavior.* New York, NY: Pergamon Press.

16. Maslow, A. H. 1970. *Motivation and Personality,* Second Edition. New York, NY: Harper & Row.

17. Mills, A. S. 1985. "Participation Motivations for Outdoor Recreation: A Test of Maslow's Theory." *Journal of Leisure Research* 17(3):184-199.

18. Morgan, G. 1986. *Images of Organizations.* Beverly Hills, CA: Sage Publications.

19. Murphy, J. F., Niepoth, E. W., Jamison, L. M., and Williams, J. G. 1991. *Leisure Systems: Critical Concepts and Applications.* Champaign, IL: Sagamore Publishing, Inc.

20. Neuman, W. R. 1986. *The Paradox of Mass Politics,* Cambridge, MA: Harvard University Press.

21. Pezoldt, C. 1985. "Park Management in the Year 2001." *Journal of Park and Recreation Administration* 3(4):viii-x.

22. Scott, W. R. 1992. *Organizations: Rational, Natural and Open Systems,* 3rd ed., Englewood Cliffs, NJ: Prentice-Hall.

23. Seidman, H. 1986. "The Politics of Government Organization," Chapter 27 in Rourke, F. E., ed., *Bureaucratic Power in National Policy Making,* 4th ed., Boston, MA: Little, Brown & Co.

24. Stankey, G. H. 1972. "A Strategy for the Definition and Management of Wilderness Quality," in *Natural Environments: Studies in Theoretical and Applied Analysis.* Baltimore, MD: The Johns Hopkins Press.

25. Twight, B. W., Smith, K. L., and Wissinger, G. H. 1981. "Privacy and Camping: Closeness to the Self vs. Closeness to Others." *Leisure Sciences, 4*(4):427-441.

26. Wagar, J. A. 1966. *Campgrounds for Many Tastes.* USDA-Forest Service Research Paper INT-6.

27. Walker, J. L. 1991. *Mobilizing Interest Groups in America.* Ann Arbor, MI: University of Michigan Press.

28. West, P. 1981. "Perceived Crowding and Attitudes Toward Limiting Use in Backcountry Recreation Areas," *Leisure Sciences, 4*(4): 419-425.

CHAPTER 3

Theoretical Foundations

Recreation management is a relatively new professional field with roots in both ecology and social psychology. Many theories have been advanced to explain user behavior, most of which have been drawn from motivational literature. Thus, much of the theory reflects the demand, or user side, of the recreation equation. On the other hand, there appears to be a renewed interest in the study of what the manager provides—the "supply side." We have to remember that the manager and much of the "supply" would not be there unless *someone* wanted it in the first place and had enough political support to have the "supply" established and maintained up to the present time. Under the systems approach, the *real* test of demand is whether it can positively or negatively influence the legal authority and appropriations which reward the recreation supplier agency and its managers.

In any new profession, there is always an internal struggle in searching for the truth. Of course we all understand that this struggle never ceases, but at least searching for the truth usually adds other pieces to the total puzzle. We all gain a little bit professionally and personally because of the effort. Rather than try to cover the waterfront of all possible theories and concepts dealing with recreation management, we confess to being mere mortals and will simply limit discussion to the interface of demand and supply. While this interface has many paradigms, two primary patterns filter out of the literature recreational carrying capacity (RCC) and recreational opportunity spectrum (ROS). Many of us have at times felt that we had arrived at the truth, that the struggle was over. We felt comfortable with one of the paradigms. If you feel this way, don't proceed, clinging tightly to your own biases, looking for a slip, a mistake, or a fault in logic. You will certainly find them. Instead, relax and enjoy the discussion. View it with an open but critical eye.

Actually we find both paradigms, RCC and ROS, to be conceptually sound in the abstract. The problem has been that, in the rush to solve management problems, we operationalized the paradigm without first fully exploring the concept and then seeing if it applies to how the world (the interface between user and manager) really works. Fittingly, then, this chapter steers away from operational aspects and looks at both RCC and ROS in the abstract. Not only are they sound concepts, they are not competing models and actually compliment one another. Together they form the theoretical foundation of outdoor recreation management. Keep in mind, however, that this management theory must operate within the context of the larger system model and its social political environment described earlier in Chapter 2.

RECREATIONAL OPPORTUNITY SPECTRUM

While many authors have suggested a recreation-management continuum, J. A. Wagar was probably the first to advance the idea from a purely managerial perspective.[48] However, the first definitive publications were probably the ones published by P. Brown, et al.,[5] and B. L. Driver and P. Brown.[10] The later publications concerned themselves with the theoretical production of distinctive recreational experiences or psychological outcomes.[11] R. N. Clark and G. H. Stankey described the continuum as a spectrum of recreational opportunities and the role of the manager as a provider of those opportunities.[9]

One of the significant mistakes that was made was confusing the recreational opportunity with the recreational experience. As shown in Figure 1-2 (see p. 8), the manager provides the recreational opportunities (RO) by mixing specific inputs (Figure 3-3, p. 37) and the user creates his/her own recreational experience. People may bring different sets of motives, participate in various activity aggregates, but utilize the common RO to produce their own individual experiences. In the process, how we as managers mix those inputs will put sideboards on the options people have to create their own outputs. This gives the manager a certain control over recreational use patterns, and leaves the recreationists free to participate in whatever manner they choose, but the options are limited by previously-determined managerial actions. See Chapter 17 on Recreational Area Planning for more detail.

The Operationalized ROS

Clark and Stankey define the setting for a recreational opportunity as *the combination of physical, biological, social, and managerial conditions that give value to a place.*[9] An opportunity involves qualities provided by nature (vegetation, landscape, topography, scenery), qualities associated with recreational use (levels and types of use), and conditions provided by management (development, roads, regulations). By combining variations of these qualities and conditions, management can provide a variety of opportunities for recreationists.

This variety can be expressed in a continuum called the Recreational Opportunity Spectrum (see Figure 3-1). This framework recognizes the link between the environmental setting and the psychological outcome, the recreational experience itself. It is based on the assumption that recreationists choose to participate in those activities that are consistent with a particular environmental setting

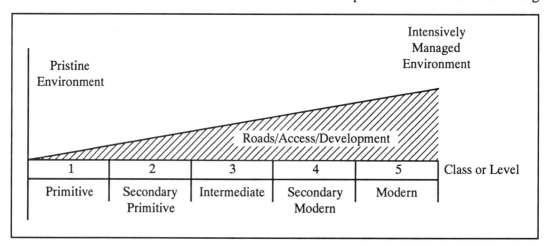

Figure 3-1. The Recreational Opportunity Spectrum.

and that the setting may be managerially influenced to provide different types of recreation opportunities. Thus ROS was intended as a "fundamental [aid] to multiple-use natural resource planning and management decisions."[5]

Clark and Stankey go on to suggest that it is not necessary to understand the exact linkage between recreational opportunities and psychological outcomes in order to be an effective manager.[9] In fact, although some studies have shown such a linkage, most indicate that the motives that direct recreational experiences vary considerably even within a given activity, environmental setting, or individuals.[13] The literature is in agreement that people are driven by their motives but that those at specific sites do not necessarily share common motives. In other words, we may do the same thing at the same site, but for different reasons that produce different outcomes; or we may do different things.

Unfortunately, the remaining factors offered by Clark and Stankey—social, managerial, biological, and physical—are not evaluated in terms of their own interrelationships and their effects on the user's perception of the opportunity.[9] They are simply dropped into the management blender, mixed, and then poured out, as suggested in Figure 3-1, in neatly packaged, equal-interval classes of opportunities.

There is actually a strong cause-effect relationship between the three ROS factors of social, biophysical, and managerial. People's perceptions of the particular RO are defined primarily by the biophysical attributes (natural attractors and the generalized landscape in which they occur), and the managerially determined attributes of physical development (access and facilities), services, etc. The generalized social setting on the ground (activities, patterns of participation, etc.) is the product of the biophysical and managerially determined attributes—not homogenized to produce the RO. The homogenization process does not follow logic.

We suggest that the cause-effect relationship can be described as follows:

For a given environmental setting (holding the biophysical inputs constant):

Managerially Determined Attributes → Drive Social Norm's

A restatement of this, since the primary managerially determined attribute to which people respond is physical development (access and facilities, see also Chapter 17) is:

Jubenville's Law

Development Norms Drive → Social Norms

(Jubenville and Becker, 1984)[25]

As restated from Chapter 17, since facilities almost always correspond to the character and scope of the access transportation system:

For a given environmental setting—

Character and Scope of the Access Transportation System Drive → Generalized Social Norms

While the present treatment in the literature may not follow simple logic, it has been operationalized by the U.S. Forest Service and the Bureau of Land Management into similar cookbook versions of ROS. Because the concept was never fully developed, there are four major problems with the operationalized version:

1. It fails to recognize the importance of the specific biophysical attributes of the site. Based on the present process, we could inventory our lands into various ROS classes. If sufficient acreage were placed into a particular class, we could assume that we are providing a sufficient supply for that opportunity. For that to be true we would also have to assume that specific biophysical attributes are *not* central to the recreationist's choices. Yet we know that use is not evenly distributed; it tends to be concentrated at the various natural attractors in the landscape and absent in areas having little attraction. Obviously, managerial actions may determine the general types and levels of use at these concentration points, but as suggested in the preface by Clark and Stankey, biophysical attractors are generally the focal points of recreational use in the landscape, regardless of managerial action.

Furthermore, we would argue that the physical component in the operationalized version (remoteness, size, and evidence of humans; see USDA-Forest Service ROS User Guide)[44] is not the physical or biophysical inputs but rather managerially determined inputs. The real biophysical inputs are first the natural attractors—whitewater rivers, scenic waterfalls, mountain peaks, prime deer habitat, good fishing streams, good bird-watching habitat, etc.—and then the quality of the generalized landscape in which they occur. If that were not true, why aren't people willing to use the 10 million-acre bog called the Tanana River Valley I gaze upon through my window while writing this chapter? According to the operationalized ROS, the area would classify as large, remote, and little evidence of humans—a superior primitive RO in which few recreationists, if any, are really interested.

Ironically the same ROS User Guide [p. 29] tells you to adjust whatever ROS classification you may have for a given piece of land based on observed social (recreational use) patterns. We think that if you use the concepts developed in this chapter and applied through area planning (Chapter 17), the only observations needed will be to determine how well you created the desired recreational use patterns. Then all you need to do is to make the micrometer adjustments to obtain the desired equilibrium.

The attractiveness rating of the RO in the Guide is covered in one sentence on [p. 31] almost as a casual afterthought. Forget about PAOT's (People At One Time) unless it is a specific site with a physical capacity such as a 10-unit campground or 25-unit picnic site. And forget about expressing PAOT/acre because use is not spread evenly over all acreages; that is not a desirable management goal. People are concentrated on the acreage around the attractors, and along the ribbon called the access transportation system.

If you properly design and locate the access transportation system and associated sites and facilities, and strive to maintain the desired equilibrium, you will accomplish exactly what the public expected. The actual number then will vary based on variables that affect people's actual participation over which you or the participant have little control—weather, timing of three-day weekends, etc.

2. It fails to recognize cause-effect relationships. ROS literature indicates that physical setting, managerial setting, and social setting combine to produce the recreational opportunity. Social setting is described as density, or use per amount of area per unit of time, and ignores causal relationships in producing that density. However, as stated earlier in the chapter, the social parameters of a site are not something that can simply be manipulated by the direct intervention of management. Rather, the generalized density of a site is a direct function of management provisions such as increased access, increased visitor facilities associated with access, change in services, etc. Densities are always going to be higher at specific local natural attractors—a mountain lake, a unique geological feature, prime elk habitat, and so on—even where you have low density zones.

Thus, there appear to be important linkages that have been overlooked. The core of the opportunity are the specific biological and physical attributes of the site. These are what attract people. The social factor (primarily density in the literature) is considered a function of management actions in a particular environmental setting. Who is actually attracted is determined by these actions.

As you increase access, recreational use increases. Hold access constant and increase services, and the clientele will probably increase. In both cases, the aggregate makeup of the user group will likely shift to those preferring more access and/or services. The only situation in which this would not be true is where you would have a reasonably strong attractor and no physiographic constraints, as the case of the Southern California desert, where use has to be artificially constrained through regulation.

Without the understanding of cause-effect relationships, managers have often attempted to directly intervene to "create" the desired opportunity with limited-entry permit systems. The problem is that it becomes economically inefficient to provide increased access, facilities, and/or services that encourage a particular general density level and then spend additional operating dollars to limit use to some lower level.

3. It fails to recognize that indirect managerial input such as permit systems have an effect on the opportunity produced. Yet for many users, indirect input may have a dramatic effect on the user's perception of the site, even if all else is satisfactory. For some users, the imposition of direct behavioral restrictions may not only discourage use of a RO, it may in fact cause them to move to another site where there are no restrictions. Knopf suggests that the aggregate attributes of the site, including management programs, influence the user choice.[28] This is further discussed in Chapter 17.

4. It assumes that a maximum variety of opportunities are offered through direct management action. The operationalized model does not guarantee that a variety of opportunities will be offered on a large area or regional basis, even though it is often touted as ensuring such variety. Even if you were to institute a regional oversight committee or superagency to direct subordinate agencies in such a manner that a variety of management actions were assured, there would still be no guarantee of variety because such a method ignores the specific biophysical inputs which attract people in the first place.

As suggested in Item 1, biophysical inputs are central to the individual's choice of recreational opportunities; thus it would seem that a variety of opportunities should be linked to a variety of biophysical attributes. Assuming that maximizing recreational opportunities is a goal of the planner, the first step in achieving that goal would be proper resource management to ensure natural variation in the biophysical makeup of the landscape protection, enhancement or rehabilitation.

With all its suggestions that help managers allocate and plan recreational resources, inventory recreational opportunities, conduct impact analyses, and match desired experiences with available opportunities, ROS appears to be nothing more than an inventory classification scheme in which the most important single ingredient is left out—the specific biophysical attractors.

The Conceptual ROS

The Conceptual version developed by Driver and Brown,[10] and Clark and Stankey,[9] recognized separate and distinct roles for the manager and user. The manager provided the opportunity and the user created his/her own unique experience within that opportunity.

1. The Role of the User. As shown in Figure 3-2, the user is driven by motives to participate; however, because of personal constraints such as lack of time or money or personal commitment to others, the actual choice is typically more constrained than the set of opportunities that is theoretically available. Within that constrained choice, a user then chooses a site and pursues a recreational experience that leads to personal satisfaction. This is very similar to models by R. Schreyer, R. C. Knopf, and D. R. Williams,[35] and C. C. Harris, B. L. Driver, and E. P. Bergerson.[18]

Satisfaction means how well the experience meets the expectations of the user.[35] Most studies that have measured satisfaction have found the users satisfied. After all, the site is deliberately chosen within the constraints of the user, to produce satisfaction. People make such choices to maximize their satisfaction, according to a recent article by R. Schreyer, D. W. Lime and D. R. Williams.[36] These authors discovered that participants on eleven wild rivers rated the rivers between 2.9 and 3.2 on a five-point scale; yet their levels of satisfaction, using the same scale, varied between 4.6 and 4.8. While the rivers were not rated very high, people were well-satisfied with their choices.

R. A. Holmes[22] measured a similar choice/response pattern for anglers on the upper Chena River, where enjoyment was rated

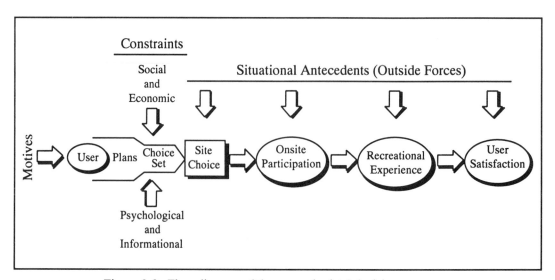

Figure 3-2. Flow diagram of the recreationists' decision process.

good to excellent (1.92 on a 4-point scale where 1 equals excellent, 2 good, 3 fair and 4 poor). Yet they rated their perception of the fishing only fair to good (2.81 on the same scale). He found the two most important constraints on choice to be lack of leisure time (41.8%) and costs (15.3%).

Choice of site, on-site participation, and the experience derived may also be influenced by external factors beyond the control of the manager or the user such as weather, spontaneous actions of others, etc.[23] These external factors, or exogenous input into the recreational experience, are beyond the control of the user or the manager, yet can exert tremendous influence over the quantity and quality of the recreational experience. A week of rain on your wilderness vacation in the Bridger Mountains would most likely produce a dissatisfying experience, yet may not negatively affect your perception of the recreational opportunity at all, particularly if you are convinced that the rainstorm was an atypical occurrence.

2. The Role of the Manager. Figure 3-3 shows all the input into a recreational opportunity. The environmental setting and managerial actions reflect the supply-related function of the manager. While he or she does not create the environmental setting, it is the manager's responsibility to evaluate, dedicate, and manage sites for specific uses. Where he/she chooses to operate on the ROS is known as the "anchor point" for the specific recreational opportunity. All programmatic decisions must conform to the requirements of this anchor point.

From a recreational perspective, every acre is not of equal value; specific environmental attractors tend to be of greater value than the generalized landscape within which

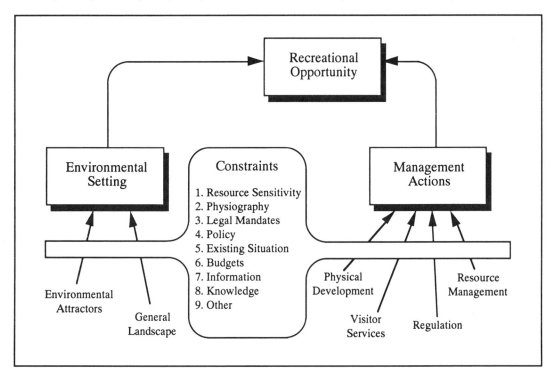

Figure 3-3. Input and constraints in the production of the recreational opportunity.

they occur. For example, bodies of water, prime wildlife habitat, and natural movement in the landscape such as waterfalls are more attractive to the user than the surrounding generalized landscape. The generalized landscape is important for visual continuity.[29] A waterfall would lose its attractiveness if the surrounding landscape were denuded; a rustic visitor center may be perceived as aesthetically pleasing and appropriate to a setting accessed by road, but inappropriate in a roadless area with primitive trail access.

Managerial actions are specific and may be applied to a site to attract certain user types, to protect or enhance resource attributes, or to maintain opportunities for specific experiences. These are the management devices that can be used to alter the value of the site to the user.[27]

If you are to manage for particular opportunities, it is important to understand what people are responding to and how you can managerially influence choice. Yet little is known about how people respond to the various attributes of a site. For discussion purposes, we have divided the attributes of a recreational opportunity into direct and indirect. Direct attributes are the obvious, tangible ones—environmental setting and physical developments (shown under Management Actions in Figure 3-3, p. 37).

According to Jubenville and Becker, recreationists respond initially to the direct attributes that connote the essence of the site. More specifically, use tends to concentrate at the natural attractors, the more valued portions of the site. The type of user and level of use at these locations also generally reflect the type and level of access and associated facilities.[25] Thus, from a perceptual perspective, physical developments become as much an inherent quality of the site as the environmental attributes.

Indirect attributes such as visitor services, resource management programs, and regulations tend to be perceived as less tangible, unless the environmental setting is enhanced or there is a direct link between a physical development and a given service. Managers often ignore the effects of indirect attributes, or treat them as insignificant. Yet recent studies have shown them to have a significant impact on the users' perception of the site. For instance, users were displaced due to increased information services,[2] and wilderness hikers showed strong behavioral modification in response to the impact of a permit system on their recreational experiences.[44] Thus, while direct attributes represent the essence of the opportunity, indirect ones may ultimately affect choice.

Furthermore, that choice appears to be a multiplicative model rather than an additive one.[27] In the additive model, several factors contribute or add to overall user satisfaction. The environmental setting contributes so much, physical developments add so much, and so on. Management has typically dealt with each input on an individual basis, with the assumption that each adds or detracts from overall visitor satisfaction. In multiplicative models users' perception of the site is based on an interaction of inputs. You could test for multiplicity if there was an interaction of input which was valued by some clientele group at zero. This follows the basic mathematical theorem that anything multiplied by zero is zero. It would be very rare in an additive model to have all attributes go to zero value. R. Gum, S. Garifo, and J. Loomis[15] found demand for steelhead fishing dropped to zero when water quality was perceived as poor, regardless of the level of access to the fishing streams. A. Jubenville and J. K. Feyhl[26] found a similar choice pattern for recreational development of a proposed hydroelectric project reservoir once people were made aware of the cold, silt-laden glacial water feeding the system. Birch Creek, a designated national wild river in Alaska, is no longer attractive to the canoeist because of the heavy siltation of the water from upstream placer mining, even though access has been improved greatly.

Rarely would the package of management actions be valued at zero by all potential user groups. However, those who do value an entire package at zero would obviously not choose the opportunity or be displaced. You can also assume that displacement would occur at a much earlier stage, unless the environmental setting was extremely attractive or there were no available substitutes.

What does this mean to the manager? The value to be captured stems directly from the environmental setting. The package of management actions determines who is attracted to the environmental setting and enjoys those values. If an area is naturally unattractive (like the extensive black spruce bogs mentioned earlier) or is allowed to deteriorate beyond some acceptable level, any management program is not likely to capture much public value, unless such action is aimed at rehabilitating the site. You must recognize, of course, that with a changing set of management actions, a new aggregate user population will be attracted. This implies social succession—one social group succeeding another within a particular environmental setting—which will be discussed below as distinct phenomena.

Social Succession

Social succession is simply a user response to a given recreational opportunity based on some change in the total system. People adjust to that change to maintain or enhance their own satisfaction, and the actual impact of change, usually considered negative, can be positive. As pointed out by Jubenville:

> In terms of negative impact, the user can still create a desired experiential outcome through *amelioration* of the impact by changing behavioral patterns (e.g., one now fishes during the week instead of the weekend to avoid the crowds); *adaptation* to the change by lowering expectations for the site (e.g., because of fishing pressure one would expect to catch 10-inch trout instead of 14-inch ones); or *displacement* by voluntarily displacing oneself to a new site in order to be able to produce the desired recreational experience (e.g., switching to a new trout stream). The positive impact will come in the form of *enhancement* of the site in the perception of the existing user (e.g., the access road to the stream has been improved to increase safety and reduce damage to the automobile); and *attraction* where non-users are now attracted to the site by the introduced change.[23]

The change-response pattern is dynamic, and that change is introduced not only by the manager but also the user and the exogenous input. Refer to Figure 3-2 (p. 36) and note that if you change any of the social and economic constraints, the choice set changes, which in turn alters the individuals' decision. As suggested by Jubenville:

> The question, then, from a public land manager perspective, is not one of how to stabilize the change-response pattern, but what will be the effects of particular managerial input on the perception of the user, and thus, the change-response

pattern? The accountability of management must be inextricably confined to the role of the manager, not that of the user.[23]

RECREATIONAL CARRYING CAPACITY

Carrying capacity has been an important theoretical management model since Wagar's monograph in 1964.[48] A lot of rhetoric on carrying capacity has since inked the pages of literature. Our intention here is not to review this literature, but to give a brief overview of the basic theoretical model and offer a critique. More definitive descriptions and critiques of the model can be found in *Leisure Sciences* 6(4)[34] and Hendee, Stankey, and Lucas.[19]

There are at least four described recreational carrying capacities: ecological (the impact of recreational use on the ecology), physical (the number of people an area can handle without queuing), facility (the number of people a facility can accommodate) and social (the number of people an area can sustain and still maintain a quality recreational experience). F. E. Boteler goes on to say that, while each sounds good in theory, they offer little utility to the manager looking for some *rational reason for limiting use.*[4] The manager has sought some magical cutoff limit that is inherent in the area, but there isn't any. A. R. Graefe, et al.[13] after an exhaustive review, conclude there is no inherent limit and that the concept is an elusive one, or perhaps "illusive."[3] W. R. Burch, Jr. suggests that . . . "the universal use of recreation carrying capacity standards may have more to do with coinciding lines of ideology held

by the manager and researcher than by the empirical data."[8] Unfortunately the researcher seems undaunted by it all, and continues to push back frontiers that don't really exist, or don't exist in the form that we envision. Rather than belabor the point that there is no inherent carrying capacity, we are going to offer you an alternative that is real and potentially measurable, but not as exacting as measuring stumpage to the nearest cubic foot.

Carrying Capacity— A Dynamic Equilibrium

We will digress a little in order to lay the groundwork for the equilibrium idea. As reported by G. Bultena, et al. (1981), the backcountry of Denali (Mt. McKinley) National Park is partitioned into thirty-four management zones, ranging from 2,000 to 430,000 acres. Most of the zones radiate from the linear road corridor within the park. Based on some earlier studies of wilderness users in the "Lower Forty-Eight" that indicated most people preferred to see no more than two parties per day, particularly in their evening campsite, use was restricted in the zones to six persons, or three parties of two people each. This represented a hundred percent probability that no parties would see more than two other parties. Four zones were selected as experimental and capacity limits were increased up to thirty persons per day. Daily, the average number of hikers in each of the experimental zones was 14.6 as compared to 2.7 in the thirty control zones (maximum of six people). The average number of daily interparty contacts was 0.9 parties per day in the experimental zones and 0.7 parties per day in the control zones.[7] These numbers do not represent a significant difference, and neither approach the original upper limit of seeing no more than two parties per day.

Furthermore, the data indicate that if the capacity limits are raised dramatically or removed, interparty contacts would not exceed the original standard. The Denali zones are trailless and brushy, and you would not expect much interparty contact. However, wilderness statistics in the Lower Forty-Eight indicate that ninety-nine percent of the use is via trail and that trail systems typically occupy less than one percent of the total physical area. Obviously there is much more interparty contact under these circumstances. Maintain and upgrade the trails and the numbers of users increases. Put in foot bridges across creeks, and the trail system becomes even more attractive.

The point is that general patterns of use, total area used, total number of users, and even activities are primarily a function of the management actions applied to the particular environmental setting. You manipulate some management program such as trail maintenance and you create a new opportunity and attract a new aggregate clientele group. In other words, introduced change creates a new equilibrium. Ironically the data on wilderness users not wanting to see more than two parties per day, particularly when in camp, ignores the fact that use is typically concentrated along the trail. A simpler solution would be to require people to camp away from the trail, out of earshot of other campers, and away from the primary attractors. Shenandoah National Park has effectively implemented such a policy to minimize social and environmental impacts over the past 16 years.

Some people are not bothered by changes. Some ameliorate the impact of more weekend trail users on the improved and maintained trail by visiting during the week or camping well away from the trail. Some adapt by assuming they'll see more people

than they did in the past, but are still attracted by the good fishing in Heart Lake or the beautiful falls on Johnson Creek. Some are actually displaced because of the increased number of people on the trail. Others find the opportunity enhanced because they no longer have to fight the downfall across the trail or wade the streams. Still others are now attracted (another way of saying displaced from somewhere else) because of the improved trail conditions.

Often the new users have different social characteristics (experience, age, education, environmental concern, attitude toward park regulations, etc.) than the displaced users. In fact, managers find (alas!) that changes may sometimes attract a type of person whom they find causes serious management problems. This new clientele may turn out to be destructive to the resource and not politically supportive of the management agency and its programs. In one western state park, for example, management tried to encourage more public use of a traditional low visitation family picnic and camping park. Management provided new large parking areas around a 100-plus acre swimming and boating lake, as well as several unsupervised access and egress routes. They assumed that the additional clientele would be similar to the traditional clientele. However, the unanticipated consequence was the attraction of large crowds of drinking juveniles, displacing the traditional quiet family users, and resulting in many behavior and law enforcement problems, injuries and destruction of property. This problem was solved only by completely fencing off and barricading access to the lake except through a single entrance station. That station was constantly manned by uniformed rangers who charged an entrance fee and took down car license numbers. State highway patrol officers were assigned to weekend duty at the lake also. Numerous arrests for disorderly conduct and alcohol and drug violations were made. The juvenile crowd voluntarily went elsewhere, but only after management had learned a costly lesson.

As suggested in Chapters 2 and 3, if the inputs are relatively constant, there is equilibrium in any system. In the case of recreational use of public resources, there is an equilibrium between the recreational opportunity that the manager provides and the recreational experience that the user has. This might be represented as:

$$RO \xrightleftharpoons{\hspace{2cm}} RUP$$

where RO is the *recreational opportunity* and RUP is the resulting *recreational use pattern*. It is this equilibrium that represents the carrying capacity of an area—the dynamic equilibrium between use and recreational opportunity.[23] Introduce managerial change and you alter the equilibrium. That balance can also be affected by exogenous inputs like weather, wildfire, flood, and changes in potential user population. A new coal mine opens nearby and the aforementioned wilderness area becomes the playground for the local hunter, fisherman, hiker, and horseman; or some local residents take a wilderness orientation course and overcome their fears of visiting such an area. However, even if change is introduced that is beyond the control of the manager, with a little thought, the relative impact and direction of that impact are often predictable and mitigable through management actions. This places great emphasis not only on monitoring patterns of use and associated endogenous variables, but also the exogenous inputs on those patterns.

In sum, managers become prime influencers or determiners of equilibrium by the way they manipulate opportunities. They must have some understanding of the effect on the recreational use pattern when they tweak some particular managerially determined attribute within the system. Without that type of conceptual understanding, even social, managerial or ecological baseline data are not useful for decision making. No research will provide the exacting kinds of answers to specific problems that many managers are seeking from the scientific community. Professional judgments still have to be made, but in a logical framework with predictable results—at least predictable in terms of their general effects on patterns of use.

Carrying Capacity— A Resource Allocation Process

From the manager's perspective, carrying capacity is a resource allocation process where a predetermined recreational opportunity is achieved through the allocation of natural resources (land and water for recreation) and fiscal resources (physical developments, services, resource management programs, and regulations). Economic efficiency is assumed in achieving this equilibrium. Chapter 17 is dedicated to making this happen through the area planning process.

The idea behind resource allocation is the establishment or maintenance of a particular equilibrium. Typically we think of resource allocation as designating the land (resource) for particular uses. But when we do that we are also committing ourselves to certain management programs that are thought to best maintain desired use patterns. Thus, in the original planning stage, all of this should be spelled out. Having to implement a new program later on means that:

1. The original allocation decisions are not achieving the desired equilibrium.
2. The external influences have changed sufficiently to alter the equilibrium needed to maintain the desired RUP.
3. The original equilibrium is no longer desired and new goals have been established that require a reallocation of resources.

Let's look at an example to understand the linkage between the recreational opportunity and user response. The Jones River was recently designated a national wild river. There is very primitive trail access into its headwaters and it is difficult to portage a canoe two miles over a ridge to get to floatable water. To solve this problem, management pushes a road over the ridge to within one quarter mile of Jones River and constructs a new wide trail from the modern parking lot to the river's edge. A canoe rack is also situated halfway so people can rest along the one quarter mile portage.

As a result of these improvements, use doubles the first year and nearly triples the second year. Manager yells, "Too many people on the river. We have to institute a limited-entry system to achieve the 'old' equilibrium." Translated, this means, "We don't like the mess we have created." Fifty thousand dollars have been spent on capital improvements to get more people into Jones Wild River and now management is willing to spend twenty thousand more a year on a limited-entry permit system to keep them from using it.

Worse yet, they will never achieve the previous equilibrium with an artificial rationing system. Assume that one hundred type-A users frequented the upper Jones River when it was a type-A opportunity. Now, with the introduced change and social succession, there

are 950 type-B users and fifty type-A users. If you attempt to achieve the previous equilibrium with a limited-entry system, the response might be something like this: The permit system was the last straw for the type-A users and they were displaced. So you hand out one hundred permits to type-B users. Not necessarily. Now type-C users show up because they can be guaranteed a low density experience with easy access ninety days in advance. The permit system is still another change introduced into the system which causes a new equilibrium with a new aggregate population of one hundred type-B and C users. Through regulation you can achieve former levels of use but you cannot achieve the former equilibrium. To do that on the Jones River would require a rollback of the new access to its former level, while maintaining other input at a status quo.

In the above resource allocation process, it is also important to recognize that what has been produced is a particular recreational opportunity. All subsequent programs must be aligned with that opportunity. For example, while all of us recognize that you cannot have a primitive recreational opportunity in a given environmental setting and put in roads, what about cabins? Footbridges? A map that locates and describes all the hazards? Rustic handrails on steep trails? Beer delivered by mule train? Directional signs on trails? Mandatory two-way radios while hiking? Remember that equilibrium is not something that is achieved with a stroke of the pen. It is based on the perception of users in relation to the total natural and managerially influenced attributes of the site. Also remember that the old users, while not as numerous, are probably not representative of the groups who supported setting the Jones River aside as a Wild River in the first place. What are the political consequences of your management action? Will the new users be more or less supportive of your agency programs? Will displaced users stir up criticism of your agency in the press? Managerial changes have more consequences than just for the resource . . .

Limits of Acceptable Change (LAC)

Frissell and Stankey[12] provided the framework for LAC by focusing on control of human-induced change. The goal was to limit the character and rate of change that would lead to unacceptable conditions, biological or social, within RO's. Probably the most notable application has been in getting a viable wilderness management plan approved for the Bob Marshall Wilderness Complex. While its initial focus of LAC was on wilderness, it is touted as fitting any recreational problem.

As pointed out by Hendee, Stankey and Lucas,[19] LAC is an integral part of the carrying capacity concept where capacity limits are the product of value judgments as well as science. Inherent in this value judgment is the recognition that management of recreation areas is actually a management of users and their impacts. Three factors should be considered in making these judgments: (1) natural resource base, (2) sociopolitical factors, and (3) managerial factors.

It is important to understand change is inevitable. The question is how much is too much. Ecologically, most studies show that most impact from recreational use occurs at low levels of use. Rather than trying to answer "how much is too much," LAC focuses on how much change will be allowed. Ultimately that threshold will have to be translated into number of users. Thus, attention is shifted from initially defining maximum number of users to identifying desired future conditions, then managing use levels or doing resource rehabilitation/enhancement so impacts do not exceed those thresholds.

The LAC system is shown in Figure 3-4. The steps are fairly straightforward. For a detailed description of the process, see Hendee, Stankey, and Lucas, 1990, Chapter 9, pp. 220-228. The process is driven by issues and concerns of both management and visitors. The selection of indicators, or limiting factors, of desired future conditions are at times difficult. The selection is guided by (1) ability to be measured, (2) affectedness by use patterns, (3) social conditions of user concerns, and (4) responsiveness to management control.

The options are supposed to be guided by the concept that minimum regimentation should govern management. At some point, it may become necessary to limit numbers, types of users, or modes of travel. A numerical capacity must be established for the area, and regulated through a limited entry permit system.

In sum, the literature indicates that LAC is not the search for a magic number, but prescribing the desired social and resource conditions and the needed policies and action to maintain or restore the desired conditions. Social or resource indicators can then be used to determine when the capacity has been reached. Management programs then kick in to maintain the desired conditions.

We agree with the basic concepts, except that the process is set up for *ex poste facto* decision making. Our contention is that these types of decisions should be made as part of the original plan and resources allocated with proper design to achieve the desired conditions. You cannot ignore the linkage between access and/or facility development and services, and the resulting user response— the new pattern of use—then hope to contain the unacceptable impacts after the fact.

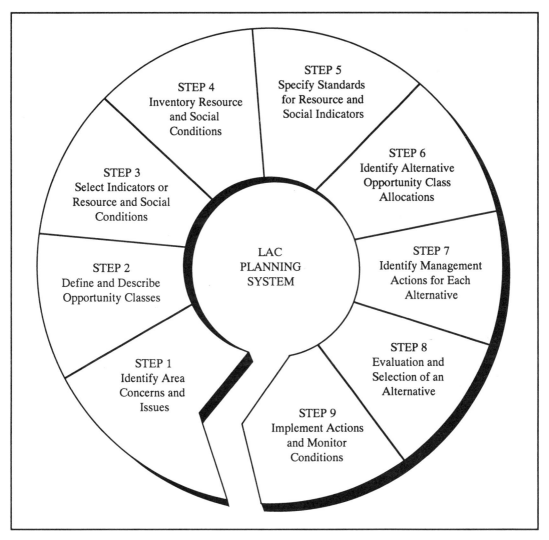

Figure 3-4. Limits of Acceptable Change (LAC) planning system.

LAC is a good tool for identifying all constraints on the system—social, resource, budget, etc. The original resource allocation would be done to keep the pattern of use within the constraints—the equilibrium idea.

SUMMARY

The Recreational Opportunity Spectrum model, as presently operationalized by agencies, ignores input from the environmental setting. This chapter tries to incorporate that input into a holistic view of the recreational opportunity. It is the role of the manager to provide the recreational opportunity through the resource allocation process.

However, it is up to the user to respond to these opportunities, within his/her limitations of time and money, and experience a recreational activity that leads to personal satisfaction. The goal of the user is to maximize, within whatever personal constraints, his/her own utility function. This is the very reason, when we measure satisfaction at a given site, that we find satisfaction to be high with little dispersion around the mean.[4] It is also the very reason that researchers have not been able to establish a relationship between use density and satisfaction.[1,13,14] After all, if you are looking for a low-density opportunity, you don't select a high-density opportunity and expect to be satisfied.

If you try to achieve a given equilibrium on the ground and become frustrated because you always seem to overshoot or undershoot the target, don't give up. Management is not an exacting science. The answers cannot simply be cranked out of a microcomputer with mathematical precision. All decisions must be tempered with professional judgment, not personal value judgments. Even then the "right" answer must be continually refined and nurtured. We believe that what we said was, "All managers are human. They can't be replaced by the computer, so we must continually work hard to achieve any measure of success. And success is judged on how well we achieved the selected anchor point, or equilibrium, on the continuum of recreational opportunities."

In sum, ROS assumes that a population with a particular set of experience tastes, participates in certain activities satisfying those tastes in a conducive environmental setting. That setting has been modified by management—whether apparent or not—through provision of access, development, environmental control, and social control. In the process, the agency develops a loyal clientele of followers, and it works to maintain the support of that clientele, or even to increase it through interpretive programs (see Chapter 15). Without such agency efforts there would be little support for its budgets, policies or general operations.

SELECTED READINGS

1. Absher, J. D. and Lee, R. G. 1981. "Density As An Incomplete Cause of Crowding in Backcountry Settings." *Leisure Sciences* 4(3):231-247.

2. Becker, R., and Niemann, B. J. 1981. "Displacement of Users Between the Lower St. Croix and Upper Mississippi Rivers." *Journal of Environmental Management* 13(3):259-267.

3. Becker, R. H, and Jubenville, A. 1990. "Forest Recreation Management." *Introduction to Forest Science* (2nd ed.), R. Young and R. L. Giese (eds.). New York, NY: John Wiley and Sons.

4. Boteler, F. E. 1984. "Carrying Capacity As a Framework for Managing White Water Use." *Journal of Park and Recreation Administration* 2(2):26-36.

5. Brown, P., Driver, B. L., and McConnell, C. 1978. "The Opportunity Spectrum Concept and Behavioral Information in Outdoor Recreation Resource Supply Inventories: Background and Application." *Integrated Inventories of Renewable Natural Resources: Proceedings of the Workshop.* USDA-Forest Service General Technical Report RM-55.

6. Buist, L. J., and Hoots, T. A. 1982. "The Recreational Opportunity Spectrum Approach to Resource Planning." *Journal of Forestry* 80:84-86.

7. Bultena, G., Field, D., Womble, P., and Albrecht, D. 1981. "Closing the Gates: A Study of Backcountry Use-Limitation at Mount McKinley National Park." *Leisure Sciences* 4(3):249-267.

8. Burch, W. R., Jr. 1981. "The Ecology of Metaphor: Spacing Regularities for Humans and Other Primates in Urban and Wildland Habitats." *Leisure Sciences* 4(3):213-230.

9. Clark, R. N., Stankey, G. H. 1979. *The Recreation Opportunity Spectrum: A Framework for Planning, Management, and Research.* USDA-Forest Service General Technical Report PNW-98.

10. Driver, B. L., and Brown, P. J. 1978. "The Opportunity Spectrum Concept in Outdoor Recreation Supply Inventories: An Overview," *Integrated Inventories of Renewable Resources: Proceedings of the Workshop.* USDA-Forest Service General Technical Report RM-55.

11. Driver, B. L., Brown, P. J., Stankey, G. H., and Gregoire, T. G. 1987. "The ROS Planning System: Evolution, Basic Concepts, and Research Needed." *Leisure Sciences 13*(3):239-246.

12. Frissell, S. S., Jr., and Stankey, G. H. 1972. "Wilderness Environmental Quality: Search for Social and Ecological Harmony." *Proceedings, Society of American Foresters,* Hot Springs, AR.

13. Graefe, A. R., Vaske, J. J., and Kuss, F. R. 1984. "Social Carrying Capacity: An Integration and Synthesis of Twenty Years of Research." *Leisure Sciences 6*(4):395-431.

14. Gramann, J. H. 1982. "Toward a Behavioral Theory of Crowding in Outdoor Recreation: An Evaluation and Synthesis of Research." *Leisure Sciences 5*(2):109-126.

15. Gum, R., Garifo, S., and Loomis, J. 1984. "Methodology and Activity Determinants of Recreational Values." Annual Meeting of the Regional Hatch Project, W-133, USDA, Las Vegas, NV.

16. Hammitt, W. E., and Cole, D. N. 1987. *Wildland Recreation: Ecology and Management.* New York, NY: John Wiley & Sons.

17. Hammitt, W. E., and Patterson, M. E. 1991. "Coping Behavior to Avoid Visitor Encounters." *Journal of Leisure Research 12*(3):225-237.

18. Harris, C. C., Driver, B. L., and Bergersen, E. P. 1984. "Do Choices of Sport Fisheries Reflect Angler Preferences for Site Attributes." *Proceedings Symposium on Recreation Choice Behavior,* p. 46-54.

19. Hendee, J. C., Stankey, G. H., and Lucas, R. C. 1990. *Wilderness Management,* (2nd edition). Golden, CO: North American Press.

20. Heywood, J. L. 1991. "Visitor Inputs to Recreation Opportunity Spectrum Allocation and Monitoring." *Journal of Park & Recreation Administration 9*(4):18-30.

21. Heywood, J. L., Christensen, J. E., and Stankey, G. H. 1991. "The Relationship Between Biophysical and Social Setting Factors in the Recreation Opportunity Spectrum." *Leisure Sciences 13*(3):239-246.

22. Holmes, R. A. 1981. "Angler Effort, Exploitation and Values on the Upper Chena River, Alaska." Unpublished MS Thesis, University of Alaska-Fairbanks, Alaska.

23. Jubenville, A. 1986. "Recreational Use of Public Lands: The Role of the Manager." *Journal of Park and Recreation Administration 3*(4):53-60.

24. Jubenville, A. 1983. "Wilderness Recreation Management: A Conceptual Framework." *Alaska Science Conference Abstracts,* Whitehorse, Yukon Territory.

25. Jubenville, A., and Becker, R. H. 1983. "Outdoor Recreation Management Planning: Contemporary Schools of Thought (Chapter 4, Section 4)," in *Recreation Planning and Management.* Lieber and Fesenmaier (eds.). State College, PA: Venture Publishing, Inc.

26. Jubenville, A., and Feyhl, J. K. 1986. "The Typical Recreation Planning Model Does Not Fit the Large-Scale Alaskan Hydroelectric Projects." Unpublished manuscript, University of Alaska-Fairbanks, AK.

27. Jubenville, A., Matulich, S. C., and Workman, W. G. 1986. *Toward the Integration of Economics and Outdoor Recreation Management.* Bulletin 68, Agricultural and Forestry Experiment Station, University of Alaska-Fairbanks, AK.

28. Knopf, R. C. 1983. "Recreational Needs and Behavior in Natural Settings." *Behavior and the Natural Environment.* I. Altman and J. Wohlwill (eds.). New York, NY: Plenum Publishing.

29. Litton, R. B., Jr., and Twiss, R. H. 1967. "The Forest Landscapes: Some Elements of Visual Analysis." *Proceedings, Society of American Foresters,* pp. 212-214.

30. McCool, S. F. 1989. "Limits of Acceptable Change," Visitor Management Strategies Workshop. Waterloo, Canada: University of Waterloo.

31. Nash, R. 1982. *Wilderness and the American Mind,* (3rd Edition). New Haven, CT: Yale University Press.

32. Patterson, M. E., and Hammitt, W. E. 1990. "Backcountry Encounter Norms, Actual Encounters, and Their Relationship to Wilderness Solitude." *Journal of Leisure Research* 22(3):259-275.

33. Roggenbuck, J. W., Williams, D. R., Bange, S. P., and Dean, D. J. 1991. "River Float Trip Encounter Norms: Questioning the Use of the Social Norms Concept." *Journal of Leisure Research* 23(2):133-153.

34. Schreyer, R. (ed.). 1984. "Theme Issue: Social Carrying Capacity." *Leisure Sciences* 6(4).

35. Schreyer, R., and Knopf, R. C. 1984. "The Dynamics of Change in Outdoor Recreation Environments: Some Equity Issues." *Journal of Park and Recreation Administration* 2:9-19.

36. Schreyer, R., Knopf, R. C., and Williams, D. R. 1984. "Reconceptualizing the Motive/Environment Link in Recreation Choice Behavior." *Proceedings Symposium on Recreation Choice Behavior.* p. 9-18.

37. Schreyer, R., Lime, D. W., and Williams, D. R. 1984. "Characterizing the Influence of Past Experience on Recreation Behavior." *Journal of Leisure Research* 16:34-50.

38. Schreyer, R., and Roggenbuck, J. W. 1978. "The Influence of Experience Expectations on Crowding Perceptions and Social Psychological Carrying Capacities." *Leisure Sciences* (4):373-394.

39. Shelby, B., Bregenzer, N. S., and Johnson, R. 1988. "Displacement and Product Shift: Empirical Evidence From Oregon Rivers." *Journal of Leisure Research* 20(4):274-278.

40. Shelby, B., and Heberlein, T. A. 1985. "A Conceptual Framework for Carrying Capacity Determination." *Leisure Sciences* 6(4):433-451.

41. Shelby, B. and Vaske, J. J. 1991. "Using Normative Data to Develop Evaluative Standards for Resource Management: A Comment On Three Recent Papers." *Journal of Leisure Research* 23(2):173-187.

42. Stankey, G. H., and McCool, S. D. 1984. "Carrying Capacity in Recreational Settings: Evolution, Appraisal, and Application." *Leisure Sciences* 6(4):453-474.

43. Stankey, G. H., McCool, S. D., and Stokes, G. L. 1984. "Limits of Acceptable Change: A New Framework for Managing the Bob Marshall Wilderness Complex." *Western Wildlands* 10(3):33-37.

44. USDA-Forest Service (undated). *ROS User Guide.*

45. Van Wagtendonk, J., and Benedict, J. M. 1980. "Wilderness Permit Compliance and Validity." *Journal of Forestry* 78(7):399-401.

46. Vining, J., and Fishwick, L. 1991. "An Exploratory Study of Outdoor Recreation Choices." *Journal of Leisure Research* 23(2):114-132.

47. Virden, R. J., and Knopf, R. C. 1989. "Activities, Experiences, and Environmental Settings: A Case Study of Recreation Opportunity Spectrum Relationships," *Leisure Sciences* 11(3):159-176.

48. Wagar, J. A. 1964. The Carrying Capacity of Wild Lands for Recreation. *Forest Science Monograph 7,* Society of American Foresters, Washington, D.C.

49. Walsh, R. G. 1986. *Recreation Economic Decisions: Comparing Benefits and Costs.* State College, PA: Venture Publishing, Inc.

CHAPTER 4

The Problem-Solving Process

From our reading prior to this chapter, we know that an agency attempts to provide a given number of recreational opportunities in response to the direction and constraints provided by its legal mandate, policy direction and current demands, and support emanating from the agency's political constituencies. However, we also need to understand the process by which the system responds when something goes awry in creating those opportunities. The term "decision making" suggests a rational process where you choose between conflicting courses of action to accomplish stated objectives based on known inputs from policy makers or constituencies. Uncertainty, both in terms of input and probable outcome, is integral to the process.

In outdoor recreation, we often use limited biophysical and social baseline data in our decision making. The uncertainty caused by the lack of information on a specific situation results in the possibility that a decision may not be the most desirable one. Decisions made with that type of uncertainty and risk— a situation that frequently arises in outdoor recreation—may ultimately lead to failure in accomplishing objectives.

Simon describes the decision-making process in terms of normative decision theory or the logic of deliberate choice under uncertainty.[19] These terms imply a formal and deliberate attempt to evaluate all circumstances, to formulate viable alternatives, and to choose a given alternative that will satisfy both defined goals and constituency demands. For most day-to-day decisions, we do not use either a formal model or a formal process such as the normative decision theory, though we may follow a process subconsciously. In outdoor recreation, however, this process is useful. Problems arise when our orderly process of accomplishing objectives is disrupted.[4] This chapter focuses on the problem-solving process, which can be described as the process that is used to overcome disruptions, retain the support of interested groups and key persons, and continue moving toward long-range goals. By understanding the problem-solving model, managers can better focus their efforts to achieve their goals, thus minimizing the effects of these problems.

THE PROCESS

Problem solving requires four elements: a model, concepts, an analytical process, and data. These need to be understood and then fused together in the problem-solving process.

Model

Before attempting to solve a problem, we must understand the total system—subsystems consisting of program sites, specific programs, and interrelationships—including those with the system's sociopolitical environment, as developed in Chapter 2. Usually a problem is isolated within one subsystem, but understanding the linkage between subsystems or with the political environment can help in identifying potential solutions and also minimize impact on other subsystems. In sum, a management model, if constructed properly, can give the manager a means of systematically and realistically viewing a decision in terms of its effects without using the "trial and error" process. No model is going to eliminate the uncertainty, but a systems approach should reduce it and thus improve decision making.

Concepts

In Chapter 3 we discussed a conceptual understanding of the manager's role in producing recreational opportunity. In summary, that opportunity is the anchor point along the recreational opportunity spectrum (ROS). You remember that the ROS is a continuum of management strategies as applied to a given *environmental setting.* That environmental setting is what attracts the visitor or clientele and gives value to the recreational opportunity. The package of management actions applied to the environmental setting determines the total number of people actually attracted; visitors respond to recreational opportunities in a multiplicative fashion (environmental setting X management action), and equilibrium is achieved between the general pattern of use and the recreational opportunity provided by management. Conceptually, a problem arises when we fail to achieve the desired equilibrium. Problem solving must then be viewed as a new attempt to achieve a given equilibrium, or the predetermined anchor point on the ROS.

Analytical Process

When a manager is confronted with a problem, he or she needs not only a conceptual framework from which to approach the problem and a model to show relationships, but also an analytical process to organize the attack on the problem. The critical aspect is the proper identification of the problem. It can never be solved unless it can be identified, isolated, and articulated in terms that allow a meaningful response by the manager. Another critical necessity is a pool of competing alternative solutions.

Data

Ideally, baseline data collection should be part of the ongoing management program so we can more quickly recognize disruption in the recreation opportunity, or disequilibrium. We also have a better understanding of what conditions existed prior to disequilibrium, and what changes were introduced that may have caused the problem. But data are not always available and may not be worth the cost relative to a particular decision. Understanding the general systems model and the linkages within the system, along with some systematically collected observations over time, should allow you to mentally or graphically simulate the particular situation. Such a simulation may be sufficient for problem solving in the absence of real data.

THE PROBLEM-SOLVING MODEL

The problem-solving model, a synthesis of several potential models, shows the logical flow of events from the initial identification of a problem to the implementation of a course of action (see Figure 4-1). It is commonly called a sequential model because a sequence of events leads to a possible solution—not any single event. After determining that a problem exists, the next step is stating the exact nature of the problem. It needs to be described in a manner that the

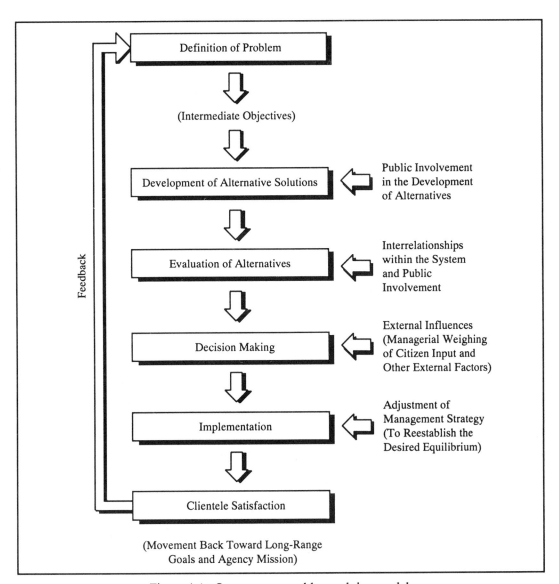

Figure 4-1. Open-system problem-solving model.

manager can respond to; the outcome of the whole process depends upon this. Developing a range or continuum of alternative solutions is the next step. Various alternatives are examined and evaluated in terms of the agency's legal mandate, professional values, constituency relationships and other bases of political support, and the best solution chosen—one that reestablishes the desired equilibrium at the least cost in terms of both the particular course of action and support from the system's social environment.

You should consider three concepts in relation to the problem-solving model:

1. Closed-system Versus Open-system Model. The open model varies in its degree of openness depending on demand and support for the final decision. In a closed model, there is a known set of alternatives, and the manager reaches a decision by a logical process. The closed model assumes the following:

1. Objectives are predetermined.
2. All alternatives are previously defined.
3. Analyses of problems involve identifying and ranking the already defined alternatives.
4. Selected alternatives maximize objectives.

The closed model is typically used for solving routine problems. It helps the manager to handle these kinds of problems with a minimum input of time and effort. Many major management problems are often affected by external influences, but the closed model unfortunately treats them as if they did not exist.

An open model is a dynamic one that is influenced by external factors—including public opinion, as shown in Figure 2-4 (p. 24). This is the typical model for recreation management situations, one where the manager must deal with much uncertainty. By recognizing this, and monitoring external influences as well as internal ones, he or she can make better and more-informed decisions.

2. Rationality of Choice. A decision should be considered rational if it maximizes goal achievement within specified environmental constraints. Decisions have traditionally been viewed on a scale ranging from rational to irrational. The irrational ones are those that don't conform to constraints or maximize goal achievement. D. Hellriegel and J. W. Slocum disagree with the traditional view; they consider a broader perspective of decision making, especially that which

involves value judgments—i.e., the conscious or subconscious choice of values by an individual or organization to be *rational*." Hellriegel and Slocum's model eliminates the problem of having to be either rational or irrational in decision making.[8] We may respond based on our personal value system, which they call being rational and which most of us are already guilty of doing. Irrationality is generally not accepted as a typical characteristic of decision making; however, most people could not function in the role of decision maker if they were not allowed some freedom of choice or personal expression. In other words, complete rationality may not always be achievable. According to H. A. Simon, bounded rationality is what many people perceive as being the rational process. It is based on the following three elements:

1. Instead of seeking a single optimum solution to a problem, an individual might establish a very limited range of outcomes that would be satisfactory. He calls this *satisficing*.
2. An individual, to obtain the specified outcome, undertakes only a very limited search for possible alternatives.
3. Some factors outside the control of the decision maker will ultimately affect the decisions. This further supports the precept that rationality is generally tied to a limited frame of reference from an individual perspective. Sometimes this frame of reference is the result of professional socialization.[19]

Decision making, under bounded rationality, is portrayed as simplistic, pessimistic, and almost wholly rational. Thus, bounded rationality affects the quality of decision making in two ways:

1. The scope of the problem-solving process becomes very limited. All problems are treated as if you are dealing with a closed system. Solutions are often temporary, or worse, they cause problems rather than solving them.
2. Management withholds or omits information from the public so as to minimize the influence of external factors—in essence trying to approximate a closed-system model.

In sum, all decisions are, to a certain degree, rational. In order to reduce irrationality and improve the level of decision making, we must follow a logical, systematic process for arriving at a decision and realize that value judgments may ultimately have to be made. In that vein, it is probably a good idea for all of us to periodically take stock of our professional values and personality characteristics and appraise how they might influence our decisions, in spite of what might be called "the rational choice."

3. Systems Effects. For most problem solving in outdoor recreation management, we must concern ourselves with the effects of our decisions on the total system—i.e., "systems effects." This is not necessarily a simple input/output relationship; a decision that alters a given portion of the system may, in turn, have drastic effects on other portions of the system. For example, a manager may increase the service capacity of a large campground by adding more facilities. The increase in "head count" is based on an increase in demand and user perceptions which indicates that it would still be possible to provide an enjoyable camping opportunity—even with the addition of more people to the camping area.

But suppose the poorly designed new facilities disrupt the visual harmony of the entire site so that previous users rebel at the decision to expand service capacity and are displaced by a less well-behaved class of users. Suppose the increase in service capacity at the campground causes overloading on the adjacent small lake, one of the primary attractors, which then causes increased user conflict and even safety hazards for certain users. Suppose the increased capacity results in an accelerated rate of deterioration for the vegetation on the adjacent sand dunes, which in turn causes the dunes to be closed to all recreationists. This then causes a decrease in attendance, since the dunes are one of the primary attractions for the camper.

This type of vicious circle is a potential consequence of a single decision; however, a knowledge of the systems model can help you to see the potential consequence before you implement the decision.

Definition of the Problem

Before we can solve a problem, we must first define it. According to J. J. Bannon[4] the simplest description is "something is wrong." In recreation, a problem is a deviation from the normal, expected, or desired outcome for a given situation; however, it only becomes meaningful when the manager recognizes it and takes corrective action to remedy it.

After identifying a flaw in the system, you should isolate the specific problem. To do this, you must gather as much information as possible, sort the data, eliminate the insignificant variables, and then try to fit the significant ones together to determine the problem. Isolating the specific problem can sometimes be so complicated that it requires a team of specialists. If it is not isolated, however, managers cannot take any specific actions and their best efforts become a trial-and-error process. The situation is analogous to changing parts on a car, hoping that something will work to make it run better.

To isolate a problem, you must identify all its effects. Individually or in clusters, these effects point to a cause. Sorting and possibly eliminating some of the subproblems should also help to isolate the real problem. Remember that the real problem may continue or even get worse if we only attack the symptoms or subproblems.

In the example of the sand dunes, a problem occurred when the loss of stabilizing vegetation caused management to close them to public use. We are assuming that the dunes are unique; the long-range goal is to maximize the recreational and esthetic potential of the dunes while maintaining their fragile ecosystem. Loss of vegetation is symptomatic of an underlying problem. We can make our decision based only on symptoms and then attempt to reestablish vegetation, but this attempt is doomed to fail simply since the cause of the vegetation deterioration is not eliminated—i.e., overuse.

So we step back one level and look at the overuse problem. Overuse caused the vegetation loss; thus if we control overuse and reestablish vegetation, our problem should be solved. Right? Probably not! Overuse should realistically be viewed as a subproblem. Remember that there was no deterioration of the vegetation until we expanded and changed the campground to meet the increased demand for camping. Perhaps the real problem is the expansion of the campground, which ultimately caused the overuse.

We could even suggest that the real problem is in the area plan, which allocates the resource for specific recreational opportunities. If there is a growing demand for both "duning" and camping, the manager may want to separate the two activities yet keep each of them reasonably available. In the long run, we may be causing or greatly contributing to the site deterioration of the magnificent dunes by allowing camping immediately adjacent to them.

We encourage much use by the casual camper merely through location, access, and attractiveness. This may reduce the availability of the dunes for those who are actually seeking that specific opportunity. If we do not recognize the link between management programs and user response, we may further complicate the malady by increasing the automobile camping opportunities adjacent to the dunes while trying to reestablish dune vegetation.

A third step in problem definition is articulating the symptoms, subproblems, and finally the real problem. We must be able not only to isolate the real problem but also to describe it in terms of present form, causes, and significant historical data. Without this articulation, managers and their staffs may not be able to reduce or eliminate the causes and will simply revert to the trial-and-error solution method.

We must establish some intermediate goals to resolve the problem once it has been isolated and articulated. We can then put the entire system back on course, moving toward our long-range goals. This could be compared to a sailor who sets off for a distant island. He is right on course when the rudder breaks. First he has to isolate the problem—the broken rudder. His intermediate objective is to fix the rudder (eliminate the cause of the malfunction). Once the problem is solved, he regains his original course and continues toward his long-range objective. This example may seem oversimplified, but it does show the proper sequence.

Development of Alternative Solutions

According to Webster's ninth *Collegiate Dictionary* the term *alternative* means a proposition or situation offering a choice between two or more things, only one of which may be chosen. So there must be at least two reasonable solutions proposed in any problem-solving process.

As used here, an alternative solution refers to an overall conceptual direction for all management programs such as that provided by the term "secondary modern" on the ROS continuum. See Figure 3-1, p. 32, Chapter 3. Alternatives may be scaled from one intensity level to the next, representing several intensity levels of management or development modernity on this continuous scale or continuum. Differences between scale levels would thus represent incremental variations in intensity of application of all three recreation management subsystems.

Thus, under a secondary modern alternative, all actions or activities carried out under the manager's Service Management, Visitor Management and Resource Management subsystems would have to be of the intensity suggested by the secondary modern class or level of management environment. For example, under a secondary modern alternative, the quality of comfort station design and maintenance would be that expected under a relatively intensively managed environment with a relatively intensive level of use. Flush toilets and thrice daily cleaning are facilities and care levels that might well be in order under the intensity of service management programs carried out under a secondary modern alternative. Also, law enforcement (Visitor Management Program) intensity would be that expected for a secondary modern area, with a relatively high profile level of enforcement, such as that demonstrated by well-dressed well-trained, class A uniformed enforcement officials, with visible weapons, Sam Browne belts, Mace™ and handcuffs, etc. making regular patrols in well-marked highly visible enforcement vehicles, thus providing a feeling of tight security. All actions under other management programs should be consistent with the management intensity level selected on the ROS for law enforcement.

Resource management activities under a secondary modern alternative thus would also take on an intensity level similar to those suggested for service management and visitor management. Vegetation might well be subject to regular mechanical and chemical manipulation for recreation opportunity purposes, and managers may well take regular day to day actions to mechanically transplant and fertilize new borders of screening trees, or seed, dig in and mulch rehabilitative meadow cover.

Therefore, the term "alternative" *does not refer to any one specific program action or activity* carried out (such as putting in rustic picnic tables), but to the general level of management intensity intended to guide a summation or package of *all* the activities included under each of the management programs: *Service Management, Visitor Management and Resource Management at the selected ROS intensity level or number. Consequently, akin to the secondary modern alternative exemplified above, a "secondary primitive" management environment alternative would suggest a much lower intensity level of law enforcement, vegetation management and restroom design and care.* One-holers with no roof and only a screen of shrubs and trees may do the secondary primitive restroom job quite well, as would law enforcement by a blue-jeaned ranger on horseback, identified only by her uniform shirt and stiff-brimmed Stetson hat. Any police equipment would be concealed in saddlebags or a pack, and a short shovel might be tied across the back of her saddle. At the secondary primitive level, vegetation management would more likely be handled by closure, brush barricades and a small prescribed burn.

According to federal regulations for writing Environmental Impact Statements, a common decision-making process required by law for all major federal land management actions (see Chapter 7), alternatives must be presented in a comparative form, "thus sharply defining the issues and providing a clear basis for choice among options by the decision maker and the public" (see 40 CFR 1502.14). One of the alternatives or potential solutions must be a "no action" proposal. Also, elimination of any other reasonable alternative from consideration in the decision process must be explained in detail.[25] Furthermore, the federal recreation manager must identify his agency's preferred alternative and should remember that *all* alternatives set forth must be feasible (according to judicial rulings made on the subject). No phony alternative may be proposed in order to assure selection of the one preferred by the agency or proposed to please one particular interested group or ideology. The typical problem-solving model worked through by a land manager will generally have three or more alternatives explicitly stated and compared in a detailed analysis.

We suggest that outdoor recreation managers use the above format for alternatives because it is both widely used and it may save some later backtracking. This is because National Environmental Policy Act procedures generally apply not only to federal lands but also to state and local projects carried out with federal funds.

There are many ways of developing a range or continuum of potential alternatives or solutions including:

1. Scoping sessions with staff, based on their previous experiences,
2. Scoping sessions with the interested public, including interested groups,
3. Review of literature, particularly previous management plans, case studies, etc.,
4. Contractual studies, and
5. Expert testimony.

Probably as significant as any of the above are the scoping sessions with your staff. These are the people who are the most knowledgeable and intimately involved with your particular problem. In fact, you should discover the most solutions this way, with the remaining portion coming from the other four alternatives. In most cases, a well-informed public can also contribute greatly to the range of potential solutions.

In Chapter 6 we will discuss the use of *public involvement* as the most important method of developing alternatives for general management plans and similar formal policy decisions. You should refer to that chapter for public involvement processes to be used for any major problem-solving processes requiring use of an open systems model under this section. We also suggest public involvement of some type (key-persons, advisory boards, etc., but not necessarily formal public meetings or workshops) for regular use at the various specified points in the problem-solving process and model (see Figure 4-1, p. 53).

Another process we would like to emphasize here is a way for your staff to expand its ability to discover new, potential solutions to smaller often nagging, chronic problems.

The process is a more closed system approach called *brainstorming,* a term often equated with creative thinking.[4] In this process, the staff is encouraged to offer unrestrained ideas about solving the problem, without regard to the appropriateness of any proposed solution. This is where the problem solver allows him or herself the freedom to conjure up new alternatives for solving a problem without social, legal, or organizational constraints. Brainstorming encourages new ideas without judgments as to quality. Too often, we mentally evaluate an alternative and summarily dismiss it because it is too "far out." Brainstorming encourages new ideas—the "farther out," the better.

It works like this. The problem solver and his staff are seated around a conference table while the specific problem is presented to the team. Everyone is given an opportunity to respond and solutions are initially stated in general terms, though more specific details usually come to the forefront as the group process proceeds. No judgments are passed on the ideas. When a judgment is deferred, there tends to be a maximum output of ideas, both in number and quality. The process continues until a reasonable number of ideas are recorded.

Too often, brainstorming is viewed as an undisciplined, disorganized rap session by a group of organizational misfits. It is not felt to be logical. This type of criticism arises from the bounded mechanism with which most problem solvers surround themselves. Without new ideas, we would stagnate, and brainstorming is one way of reaching out for new, creative approaches to problem solving.

In reality, brainstorming is not something that can be done well without training and practice. It may seem simple on the surface, but it is difficult to actually do. Most people feel strange in their first session; they feel too inhibited to formulate far-out ideas because of their education, professional training, and associations. With time and effort, however, a problem solver can discard bounded rationality and search for new ideas to solve the problems that plague us. If this type of approach to problem solving can be developed through training and practice, there is hope that in the future we will be better able to face and actually solve difficult problems.

Evaluating Alternatives

Judging the alternatives developed during brainstorming has been relegated to a separate step. No alternative should be either dismissed summarily or evaluated superficially and your evaluation should be viewed as reduction or elimination of the worst and reexamination of the best. The process does not simply mean perusing a few alternatives and selecting the best one. It is a concentrated effort in which the problem solver seeks all available information about each alternative, attempts to sort the information based on pertinence to the problem, eliminates undesirable alternatives through a series of reviews, and then ranks the better ones. You should make no attempt, at this point, to reach a decision.

After evaluating, you should also set aside those solutions which do not fit the intermediate objectives. At this point in the problem-solving process, the old-fashioned problem solver often dismisses new ideas or alternatives, claiming that they will not work, that they are too expensive, or that they do not meet objectives. However, this is a cop-out, a reversion to bounded mechanism and a "why bother?" attitude. We have to stay in tune with the whole process if we are really going to solve today's problems today.

Begin by screening and classifying the more viable alternatives. Then sort and classify ideas into groups for analysis. They should be critically evaluated in relation to the established long-range objectives, which of course should not only include legal and ecological requirements, but also constituency support requirements. And this evaluation should be just as judicious and creative as the development phase has been up to this point. In all cases, the effort extended should be equal to the complexity of the problem.

Problems having obvious solutions may not require many steps in the problem-solving process; this is the closed system model of problem solving where you do not need to examine the effects of the decision on the external environment of your agency. In this closed system situation, constituency support is assured, there are no conflicting groups or constituencies, and it is an action that will not require new legislation or new funds. Thus you do not need to spend a great deal of time and effort to arrive at a solution. Staff brainstorming is sufficient in this case. For more complex problems where constituency support is at risk or conflict with other interest groups is possible, you should also employ the open system model and use public involvement (see Chapter 6). In this way, you can search for new ideas among the staff, key legislators and also the public, then spend an appropriate amount of time evaluating each idea. Where a problem is less complex or less volatile, but still possibly of concern to external groups, it may not rate full-scale public involvement. In that case, use key people such as an advisory board, senior agency officials' advice, and key Congressional or legislative committee staff comments.

In the dune problem, interrelated factors would include the following: information about the resource system (the dune ecosystem and the effects of visitor use); the visitor subsystem (including types of behavior patterns, visitors' perceptions of the recreational opportunities, and social impact); and the service subsystem. Questions concerning how the entire area was planned, why that particular campground was expanded, and what effects different decisions have had on existing use patterns must be answered before we can determine, at least hypothetically, what will be the effects of a particular alternative. Remember the immediate objective—to stabilize the dune system—and the long-range objective—to maintain public support by offering a quality hiking experience in that unique dune formation. It is hoped that the final decision reflects a combination of alternatives that best satisfy the problem at hand and consider the interrelated factors of management systems, agency constraints on fiscal resources, public interest, and available information. Perhaps in the future, this approach will provide more and better information for decision making.

Decision Making

The problem solver and the decision maker may be the same person, or the information, analysis, and alternatives (including a priority listing) may be turned over to the manager or decision maker by a staff specialist who has handled the problem. How this is handled is determined by the size and organization of a particular agency and the extent of the problem itself. The decisions made to solve a problem at each step ultimately determine the outcome; thus every step leading to the decision must be given careful attention, particularly those producing public concern during public involvement. The decision maker must be made aware of the potential effects of all alternatives so that when the decision is made, results can be reasonably well-predicted.

The final decision is generally influenced by external factors, including interest-group concerns, legislative concerns, legal mandates, time constraints, budgeting processes, trade-offs in other areas of operation, and so forth. On the dune problem, external factors that affect the decision may include a conservation organization that uses newspapers and television to argue for handling the problem in a particular manner. Perhaps a special envoy is even sent from a conservation organization's national headquarters to persuade the managing agency to permanently close the dunes to recreational use. They may complain to Congress or go to court. To counteract this, a state businessmen's organization may claim that there is no problem and that all that the agency is trying to do is drive them out of business. Then Senator Smith calls on the phone and says that he wants to hold a special hearing. Existing laws do permit this type of hearing, but it is not mandatory.

After reflecting on the existing situation, you may decide that an environmental assessment report or impact statement (see Chapter 7) is necessary before you can proceed with the decision. Has the situation gotten out of control? Has it been blown out of proportion? Probably not! There are other external factors to be considered—environmental effects beyond the immediate area, regional economies, national goals, legal requirements, and reductions in other programs to concentrate on this one. The list may be almost unlimited, but the interest group's criticisms and the Senator's interest might have been avoided if you had systematically involved affected groups in the problem-solving process. Perhaps this is the justification for separating problem analysis from decision making. The problem solver should probably be two people, each with a distinct role. The problem

analyzer (probably a staff person) who would bring the process up to the point of decision making and involve the public, and the decision maker, who would weigh external factors and make a final decision.

As part of the problem-solving procedure, managers may also choose to have alternatives and evaluations reviewed by each major staff person, called jurying. Jurying provides an opportunity for a specialist to weigh the information that is related to his/her own area of expertise and to make certain recommendations which are based on this knowledge. Theoretically, jurying serves two purposes. First, it can create a better, more widely accepted decision because of the quality of the individual input. Second, it can create a more congenial atmosphere for the final decision to be supported and implemented. Also, never forget the potentially interested public. Involve them early in the problem-solving process. They will better support the outcome if they have had part in the decision.

Implementation

A decision can only be as effective as its implementation. Thus you must develop detailed strategies to put a plan into action. These strategies should include how a plan will be accomplished, when it will be accomplished, who will be involved, and what will be needed. The implementation of sensitive decisions may also require additional public involvement because, while they may agree with the proposed course of action, they may not agree with the actual implementation vehicle.

Too often a bad decision is blamed on errors in the problem-solving phase. In fact, most problem-oriented decisions which were well-thought-out, fail in the implementation phase for reasons such as lack of staff support, the unwillingness of a manager to commit the necessary resources, an inadequate time framework, or an uninvolved public.

The success of problem solving depends upon both a decision which is well-conceived and relevant to the specific problem and an implementation plan which is given sufficient staff support, resources, time, and public involvement. Many problems have evolved over years of neglect; it may take many more years to solve them properly. In general, the interested public has to be made aware of the time limitation, and most people are receptive to that limitation. Often, certain phases of a plan must be accomplished before the other phases can be implemented. If we proceed too rapidly, we may skip a step and doom the decision to failure.

In the case of the dune ecosystem, it may take years to fully reestablish vegetation, even though use has been either eliminated or restricted to certain paths. If use is allowed to continue at low levels over the entire area with reasonable controls, it may still take ten to fifteen years to revegetate, or perhaps forever.

For a long implementation period, it is necessary to monitor the results of each phase, possibly changing strategy to better implement the decision. This final phase of problem solving is one of developing strategies, making task-oriented decisions, adjusting strategy, and supervising work needed to fully implement the decision that was reached through problem analysis. We may wish to put the program back on course, guided by our mission (see Part I, Management Framework), proceeding ultimately toward long-range goals while maintaining public support. Remember though, problem solving is not complete until we have fully implemented the decision and returned the errant program to the originally charted course.

SELECTED READINGS

1. Adams, J. L. 1986. *The Care and Feeding of Ideas, a Guide to Encouraging Creativity.* Reading, MA: Addison Wesley.

2. Albrecht, K. 1984. *Brain Building: Easy Games to Develop Your Problem-Solving Skills.* Englewood Cliffs, NJ: Prentice-Hall, Inc.

3. Anderson, B. F. 1980. *The Complete Thinker: A Handbook for Creative and Critical Problem Solving.* Englewood Cliffs, NJ: Prentice-Hall, Inc.

4. Bannon, J. J. 1981. *Problem Solving in Recreation and Parks.* 2nd ed., Englewood Cliffs, NJ: Prentice-Hall, Inc.

5. Carpenter, S. L., and Kennedy, W. J. D. 1988. *Managing Public Disputes, a Practical Guide to Handling Conflict and Reaching Agreement.* San Francisco, CA: Jossey-Bass.

6. Gray, B. 1989. *Collaborating, Finding Common Ground for Multi-party Problems.* San Francisco, CA: Jossey-Bass.

7. Hayes, J. R. 1989. *The Complete Problem Solver.* 2nd Ed., Hillsdale, NJ: L. Earlbaum Associates.

8. Hellriegel, D., and Slocum, J. W., Jr. 1982. *Management: A Contingency Approach.* 3rd edition. Reading, MA: Addison-Wesley Publishing Co.

9. Kaufman, H. 1967. *The Forest Ranger.* Baltimore, MD: The Johns Hopkins Press.

10. Kahney, H. 1986. *Problem Solving, A Cognitive Approach.* Philadelphia, PA: Milton Keynes, Open University Press.

11. Kepner, C. H., and Tregoe, B. B. 1976. *The New Rational Manager.* Princeton, NJ: Princeton Research Press.

12. March, J. G., and Olsen, J. P. 1989. *Rediscovering Institutions, The Organizational Basis of Politics.* New York, NY: Free Press.

13. March, J. G., and Olsen, J. P. 1979. *Ambiguity and Choice in Organizations.* 2nd ed., Bergen, Norway: Universitetsforlaget.

14. Nigro, L. G. 1984. *Decision Making in the Public Sector.* New York, NY: M. Dekker.

15. Pressman, J. L., and Wildavsky, A. 1984. *Implementation.* 2nd edition. Berkeley, CA: University of California Press.

16. Roberts, W. 1990. *Leadership Secrets of Attila the Hun.* London, England: Bantam Books.

17. Sandole, D. J. D., and Sandole-Staroste, I., eds. 1987. *Conflict Management and Problem Solving, Interpersonal to International Applications.* Washington Square, NY: New York University Press.

18. Simon, H. A. 1982. *Models of Bounded Rationality,* 2 vols. Cambridge, MA: MIT Press.

19. Simon, H. A. 1976. *Administrative Behavior,* 3rd edition, New York, NY: The Free Press.

20. Stevens, L. A. 1984. *Thinking Tools.* Stockton, CA: Stevens and Shea Publishers.

21. Twight, B. W., Lyden, F. J., and Tuchmann, E. T. 1990. "Constituency Bias in a Federal Career System, A Study of District Rangers of the U.S. Forest Service," *Administration and Society,* 22(3)November: 358-389.

22. Twight, B. W., and Lyden, F. J. 1989. "Measuring Forest Service Bias," *Journal of Forestry,* 87(5)May: 35-41.

23. Twight, B. W., and Lyden, F. J. 1988. "Multiple Use vs. Organizational Commitment." *Forest Science* 34(2)June: 474-486.

24. Twight, B. W., and Carroll, M. S. 1983. "Workshops in Public Involvement: Do They Help Find Common Ground?" *Journal of Forestry 81*(11)November: 732-734.

25. United States Council on Environmental Quality, 1986, *Regulations for Implementing the Procedural Provisions Of the National Environmental Policy Act,* 40 CFR 1500-1508. Washington, U.S. Government Printing Office.

26. Van Grundy, A. B. 1981. *Techniques of Structured Problem Solving.* New York, NY: Van Nostrand Reinhold Co.

CHAPTER 5

Problem Solving and Decision Making in the Context of Administrative Law

by Harry R. Bader*

INTRODUCTION

Today's outdoor recreation manager may perceive himself as a modern day Jason, sailing uncharted and dangerous waters with little helpful guidance. A paucity of statutory direction for recreational management on public lands in general, and federal lands in particular, makes the already exceedingly onerous task of reconciling conflicting public desires, even more difficult. Congress has clearly articulated its desire to promote recreation on public lands.[a] However, there is much that is left to the manager's discretion through vague and generalized statutes that provide only broad policy pronouncements.

It is, arguably, good public policy for the legislature to use ambiguity in order to allow field professionals the discretion necessary to narrowly tailor individualized solutions to context-specific problems. Unfettered decision making, however, may create an environment where the vicissitudes of favoritism and bias can thrive. Administrative law is designed to ensure that due deference is given to technical decisions made by professionals, while preventing cavalier, capricious, and malevolent choices. Thus, it is essential that effective natural resource professionals have a thorough understanding of the case law which establishes the appropriate processes for reasoned decision making by public officials.

This chapter is designed to introduce the reader to the salient principles found in procedural law as articulated by the federal courts. The vast majority of decisions that an outdoor recreation manager must make fall into the category of "informal" decisions. Informal decision making is well-illustrated by the case of *Overton Park*[b] and its progeny, which exemplify the intended purpose of the U.S. Administrative Procedures Act.[c,d] These cases illuminate the types of decisions in which it is decided whether to grant a permit for a particular use, whether to build a particular trail, locate a campground, restrict access, etc.

Such decisions are called "informal" because they do not require a trial type process incorporating motions, production of evidence from differing parties, cross-examination and other activities of that ilk (Plater, 1992,

---

* Harry R. Bader is with the School of Agriculture and Land Resources Management at the University of Alaska-Fairbanks.

---

[a] For example, see: 16 U.S.C. 460 (1982) and 43 U.S.C. 1781 (1982)

[b] *Citizens to Preserve Overton Park v. Volpe* 401 U.S. 402

[c] 5 U.S.C. 501

[d] 5 U.S.C. 553, 701-706

p. 541). Though judges generally grant recreation managers great deference in exercising professional discretion in such informal decision making (should they be challenged in court),[e] a manager is still required to utilize a process which ensures the integrity of the system. Managers must also provide sufficient information to potential reviewing courts so that they are able to render an incisive review of agency actions (Plater, 1992, 542).

Except for general notice provisions, neither the federal Administrative Procedures Act itself nor promulgated regulations specify exactly what constitutes appropriate process for informal decisions. Therefore, a manager must turn to available case law for guidance. Case law proceeds from a series of judicial decisions addressing a variety of disputes. Based on such cases, an alert judicial observer can divine a common method for resolving questions addressing due process conflicts. The all-important facet of case law is the application of past opinions to new situations to create "a legal concept which is built up as cases are compared" (Levi, 1949, p. 8). Over time, this legal concept becomes relatively fixed, and through reasoning by example, its basic principles continue to classify items as either inside or outside of the concept.

The role then, for judicial review, is to balance the need for oversight of public managers, in order that public confidence is maintained in agency integrity, while at the same time providing sufficient latitude for agency professionals to exercise judgment in highly technical matters. As long as agencies adhere to procedural safeguards in their decision making, courts will not substitute their judgment for that of the agency, unless some specific legal requirement is not being met.[f] Court practice generally holds to the tradition that administrative decisions are set aside only for substantial procedural failure or substantive reasons set out by a specific law, not simply because the court is unhappy with the result of the agency's conduct.[g] Therefore, a judge will overturn a manager's decision only if it appears arbitrary, capricious, an abuse of discretion, or a violation of law.[h]

A manager can create a checklist from a series of cases that guide the manager through a decision-making process which has received judicial sanction.[i] The following elements should be considered essential steps for a legitimate decision building process in regard to natural resources management (Bader, 1990, p. 8). All the elements focus upon the concept of full disclosure and reasoned inquiry as a means to facilitate public understanding of agency logic and considerations.

[e] *Duesing v. Udall* 350 F.2d 748 (D.C. Cir. 1965)

[f] *Kleppe v. Sierra Club* 427 U.S. 390 at 410 (1976) and *Natural Resources Defense Council v. Hodel* 624 F. Supp. 1045 (1986)

[g] *Vermont Yankee Nuclear Power Corporation v. Natural Resources Defense Council* 435 U.S. 519, 558 (1978)

[h] *Citizens to Preserve Overton Park v. Volpe* 28 L.Ed 136 at 153 (1971)

[i] *National Audubon Society v. Hester* 801 F.2d 405 and 627 F.Supp. 1419 (1986), *Sierra v. Clark* 755 F.2d 608 (1985), *Friends of Endangered Species v. Jantzen* 760 F.2d 976 (1985), *Village of False Pass v. Clark* 733 F.2d 605 (1984), *Sierra Club v Clark* 577 F.Supp. 783 (1984), *Baltimore Gas & Electric v. NRDC* 462 U.S. 87 (1983), *Motor Vehicle Mftr. Assoc. v. State Farm* 103 S.Ct. 2856 (1983), *Humane Society v. Watt* 551 F.Supp. 710 (1982), *Cayman Turtle Farm v. Andrus* 478 F.Supp. 125 (1979), *Palila v. Hawaii DLNR* 471 Supp. 985 (1979), *Def. of Wildlife v. Andrus* 428 F.Supp 167 (1977)

Checklist for Rational Legal Decision Making

1. The first step is to identify the purpose of the decision and the goals intended to be achieved.
2. Next, all appropriate policies, management plans, and precedents which establish potential objectives or parameters for problem solving must be explained.
3. The manager must then identify what types of facts are relevant to the issue at hand.
4. The criteria to be used to evaluate the appropriate facts must be explained.
5. Analysis techniques and methodologies used in the collection of facts and their evaluation must be explained.
6. All assumptions, areas of uncertainty, and limitations on accuracy must be disclosed.
7. The effectiveness of the solution selected must be shown to relate directly to the goals and objectives previously identified.
8. The solution selected must be compared to other viable alternatives, and its supremacy must be justified.
9. When competing user groups are involved, the manager must demonstrate that a good faith effort was made to balance the costs and benefits as equitably as possible across all potentially affected groups.
10. If the solution selected constitutes a departure from agency precedent or policy, the manager must indicate what factors brought about the change, and why.

Discussion

All the above steps must be incorporated into some form of record. This record can take the form of a standardized document drafted at the end of the process, or it can be a simple file, indicating what actions were taken at different stages, when they were taken, and why. The record's purpose is to explain to those reviewing the decision just what the manager was thinking at the time of the decision and the reasons for the manager's choices. If at any time the record possesses gaps, or is so ambiguous that a reader is required to guess what the manager was thinking, then the record is incomplete.

No court came down and specified these elements. Instead, courts have only stated that an agency must "examine the relevant data and articulate a satisfactory explanation for its action, including a rational connection between the facts found and the choice made."[j] Thus, all that is called for is a rational decision with sufficient documentation to make it possible for later review.

Because courts are process-oriented, one must decide before solving problems what processes lead to a reasonable decision. Generally, managers already incorporate these elements intuitively into their thinking when making a decision. These elements are already something that each and every one of us does as we think about problem solving. The problem with informal methods of thinking, however, is that we often make "jumps" between steps or omit steps entirely. It is when we "jump" in our thought processes that we make errors in judgment and make irrational decisions.

---

[j] *Baltimore Gas & Electric Co. v. Natural Resources Defense Council* 462 U.S. 87 at 105 (1983)

A preflight aircraft checklist does not teach a pilot how to fly before take off. It just ensures in a formal standardized fashion that the pilot doesn't forget to consider everything he/she already knows needs to be done. Checking for fuel in the wing tanks prior to a flight makes rational sense. The procedures present on the checklist merely guarantee consideration in all circumstances. Likewise, the checklist described here simply ensures, in a formal and systematic way, that everything that ought to be considered in solving a problem is indeed considered. Through procedural safeguards, better, wiser decisions result. From strict adherence to process, substance is begot.

Management agencies are relatively free from judicial interference so long as an agency creates a system of problem solving that is both public in its disclosure and rational in its structure. Failure results in litigation and its attendant consequences of delay, increased costs, and personnel demoralization, as well as lost public confidence in the agency. When public confidence wanes, support for the agency and its agenda will likewise diminish. The public bears an enormous burden in public wildlands recreation management through both lost economic opportunities and fiscal expenditures. These social costs might not be tolerated if the public perceived the decisions, upon which so much cost is the consequence, as casually derived.

Finally, this chapter develops a hypothetical example for the purpose of walking the reader through the ten elements of rational decision making in a public recreation management context. The hypothetical example takes place in Denali National Park. It concerns a decision about whether or not to develop a trail system in the national park.

Step 1 (see checklist on p. 67) requires the manager to identify the purpose of making a decision in the first place. What is the problem and what goals and objectives are to be achieved by its resolution? When looking at the trail question, we find that the problem is one of visitor use concentration. It appears that park visitors are crowding along the existing transportation corridor. This concentration is impairing the quality of the total visitors' experience in the park as well as causing habitat degradation for the park's wildlife. The goal, then, is to disperse recreational use throughout the park in a fashion that will maintain quality visitor experiences while eliminating damage to wildlife habitat.

In **Step 2,** the recreation manager must explain which park policies and prior decisions relate to the matter at hand. It is at this point that the manager must refer to all relevant management plans. The proper role of management and land use plans is to establish the parameters within which a decision must be made. Management plans, whether resource-based or recreational, are designed to preidentify pertinent information and either apply old policies or establish new policies relating to categories of decisions. A plan itself can never dictate a specific outcome for a particular problem. However, a properly developed plan should narrow the field of possible options and alert the manager to potential problems as well as make him/her aware of critical considerations. The decision maker must specifically cite how the plan's information addresses concerns in the issue at hand. It is insufficient to merely review the plan. How the plan specifically applies or does not apply must be stated in a written decision-making record or memorandum.

In the event that a departure from policies contained in the appropriate management plans is necessary, the manager must clearly indicate (1) what new information has subsequently come to light, (2) what inaccurate information has been found in the plan, or (3) what information is lacking within the plan, that justifies a departure from the plan's findings and recommendations for the immediate question being addressed. A manager cannot depart from an established plan without first demonstrating that the plan's provisions are either moot or irrelevant.

Our hypothetical example in Denali requires the manager to make clear that the park's recreation plans have always discouraged the development of a trail system in the park. Instead, the park plan has previously relied upon use zones in order to disperse visitor activities. The intent behind the trailless concept is based upon the objective of minimal impairment of the recreational opportunity. It was believed that users would disperse themselves and concentrate less if not confined by preexisting trails. In effect, each backcountry visitor could tailor his/her own experience to meet their own objectives without being constrained by established campgrounds, picnic sites, water sources, and trails.

To justify a potential departure from the current recreational management plan, if a departure is even warranted, the manager must proceed to step three of the decision-making process.

Step 3 requires the manager to delineate what type of facts are relevant to the problem. This step is important because it prevents a manager from simply relying on what information he/she may already have at his/her disposal. The manager must ask himself what information would a reasonable person want before making such a decision.

Information needed must be identified regardless of its availability or the technical feasibility of retrieving it. This is essential in that it specifically identifies the information horizon, providing evidence of whether the manager has thoughtfully considered all the prominent aspects of the issue. More, however, is required than a simple list. The manager must explain her/his connection to the issue and why the information would be valuable in making a decision. This list should represent the full spectrum of appropriate topics. Following the creation of such a record, the decision maker should be fully informed as to what is pertinent. If he/she chooses to ignore certain facts, our decision maker will do so with his/her eyes open.

Large and cumbersome laundry lists with cavalierly identified topics damage the likelihood of procedural compliance. A reviewing court will not tolerate perfunctory performance of procedural requirements. The intent behind identification of needed facts is to reveal what the manager was thinking while preparing for a decision. Through the formal process of identifying relevant facts needed, it is hoped that the manager will concentrate and focus on the root causes of an issue and not merely treat symptoms. Again, the importance of a high-quality management plan is apparent. Many of the topics and pertinent facts may already be contained within an existing plan.

In the Denali Park scenario, a list of important pieces of information may look like this:

1. What are the needs of the individual backcountry visitors in terms of what they want from the recreational experience?
2. What are the "macrobehavior patterns" of participation?
3. How do people perceive the management scheme and how does this relate to their participation?
4. What is the capability of the resource and how resilient is it to stress or disturbance?

5. What impact is visitor use having upon the resource and how does the impact relate to the park's overall mission statement and management goals?

In addition to this list, the manager would have to explain how the list relates to the issue. For example, visitor needs and perceptions are important because if a new management strategy is developed which fails to meet essential needs or validly held expectations, then the rate of voluntary compliance with the new rules will decline. Management will either become a complete failure, or extremely expensive because of increased enforcement outlays.

In **Step 4,** a manager must prioritize information topics relative to each other, and define means by which to evaluate their importance. This step can be accomplished, in part, by referring to Steps 1 and 2. The goals of the decision, as well as the parameters established by prior policy, partially dictate what is most important.

In our hypothetical example, the Alaska National Interest Lands Conservation Act, which created the enlarged Denali Park, stipulates that the ultimate park objective is to preserve the natural resources of the park in their wild state, ensuring natural and healthy populations of flora and fauna. Given this paramount objective, the most important information will relate to the capability of the resource. Because of visitor activities, potential impacts on air and water quality, and wildlife habitat and behavior, must be more thoroughly examined.

Each topic area must be assigned some ranking relative to the others. This process ensures that the manager will not blindly

overemphasize or undervalue issues in coming to his/her decision. The intent of the process is to force the manager to systematically think about why he/she values one piece of information over another. The purpose is realized because the manager is required to provide an explanation for each relative weight given which relates directly to the goals, objectives, and parameters for the decision. In the course of ranking, no consideration is given to data availability. Lack of availability will be pointed out later in the process.

Step 5, the methodologies, used in the collection of necessary information previously identified, must be explained. This ensures that the agency did not employ irrational methods for calculating the facts upon which it relied in arriving at its decision.[k] This step must be applied on two levels: (a) to the decision-making process as a whole, and (b) to each individual calculus employed in ascertaining information.

Comprehension of how information was derived not only facilitates understanding the meaning of information on the part of a reviewer, but it also forces the decision maker to compare and contrast various techniques that may be equally applicable to a particular problem. It must always be remembered that the methodology chosen establishes the parameters of an inquiry, and therefore predisposes the analysis to certain interpretations. The process of identifying the methodology assists the researcher in refining techniques to ensure that the methods employed are the most appropriate for meeting the task at hand.

Relating this step back to our hypothetical example, we can address the main pieces of information that were most important to the decision maker in solving the issue of

[k] *Perkins v. Bergland* 608 F.2d 803, 807 (1986). *Wilderness Public Rights Fund v. Kleppe* 608 F.2d 1250 (1979).

development of a trail system. For example, in determining the needs of the individual backcountry visitors, the recreation manager must ask him/her self:

1. What method of study will accurately reveal the desires of remote country recreationists?
2. What techniques have been employed in the past in analogous situations that may be helpful to draw upon for this study?
3. What limitations are inherent with the various techniques?
4. What system of analysis best meets the needs for the current study?

In determining the needs of recreationists, the manager may choose to first address the issue of impacts to the park and the park visitor. To do so, the manager must review ways of determining the impact of the recreational use upon the ecology of the park, the number of people an area can handle without queuing, and the number of people an area can sustain and still maintain the desired quality of the recreational opportunity.

The manager must go through this process for each piece of information identified in step three of the decision-making process. It is recognized that this process is time-consuming, but a manager must realize that time spent now in developing the decision-making model will easily save ten times the money, time, morale and energy caused by challenges to a procedurally-flawed decision.

In **Step 6** of our model, all assumptions, uncertainty, and unavailability of information must be disclosed.

Natural systems are dynamic as a result of innumerable influences which sometimes defy identification. The same is true with human behavior. Because resources management is a nexus between natural and social sciences, certain assumptions are essential to permit reasoned decision making. Otherwise, managers might be paralyzed by the inherent lack of available knowledge. It is essential, however, to inform the public and any possible reviewer about the assumptions relied upon and the uncertainty those assumptions create within any model.

As mentioned in prior steps, a recreation manager may find that some of the most pertinent information is impossible to obtain or simply cost-prohibitive. Such information may have been ranked high in step four. It is appropriate to identify all such information at this point. If the most important information cannot be obtained, the relative merit of the manager's solution will have to be correspondingly depreciated.

Identifying study limitations forms the foundation for any full disclosure document. Too often, managers try to hide the fact that much of natural resources management more closely approximates art rather than science. When one claims correctness based upon adherence to "science" without noting the limits of the process, one sets up the opportunity for failed expectations and lost credibility. Always keep in mind to explain what the study does not reveal just as readily as what the study seems to affirmatively conclude.

In addition to identifying the assumptions and uncertainty inherent with a study methodology or model, one must also be prepared to explain the limits in terms of scientific precision and accuracy. The terms are not the same. Precision relates to the ability of the analysis to replicate results in identical situations without variance. Accuracy relates to the degree of error implicit in the process. Thus, any study must explain both the degree of precision and the accuracy within the methodology chosen.

Studying ecosystem stability and sensitivity, as identified in Step 3 and prioritized in step four of the Denali Park hypothetical, is rife with assumptions and uncertainty, all of which must be identified. For example, the inability to isolate interactive variables in natural systems necessarily reduces analytical precision. In assessing the stress induced by recreational use, the manager must carefully explain the problems with environmental science assumptions. The role of such theories as biological magnification, range of tolerance, and niche (Robinson and Boten, 1984, p. 19-24) in environmental assessment and their limitations needs to be developed in this step.

After Steps 1 through 6 have been completed, the manager may begin to assimilate information and carry out the necessary analyses. Once all the appropriate data have been collected and considered, the manager can continue with the decision-making model process. At this point, one should think of Steps 7 and 8 as being performed concurrently in an integrated fashion.

Considering the data, the manager must begin crafting solutions, given the objectives stated in step one and within the parameters established in Step 2. It is important from the very outset that the manager begin developing a set of solutions, each *equally viable.* By being forced to generate a set of solutions, the manager is prevented from developing tunnel vision and fixating upon the first solution conceived. This is important, because more often than not, the first solution proposed is likely the result of personal proclivity and bias rather than reasoned analysis.

The set of solutions developed must represent the full spectrum of possible options within the criteria set in steps one and two. The discussion of each option's benefits and disadvantages must be complete and cannot

contain simple, conclusory statements. At this point in solution finding, it is imperative that the process not become skewed toward a particular end. The importance of the process of comparing and contrasting possible solutions is critical because it serves to confirm the objectivity of the process. In comparing each alternative, the manager must relate the option directly to facts found, objectives specified, criteria established, and the uncertainty and availability of information relied upon.

Through **Steps 7 and 8,** the manager will justify the efficacy of the option selected and, ultimately, the supremacy of the preferred option in relation to all others considered.

For example, the manager in our hypothetical case might develop three potential solutions to the problem identified in Step 1 (p. 67). First, the manager may consider the development of fixed trails. In developing this option, the manager would have to consider the effect of this choice on prior park policies. Also, the manager would have to judge how effectively the option would reduce visitor concentrations and the impact the scheme would have on visitor perceptions and desires. Finally, the impact to the park's flora and fauna, the primary concern identified in Step 3 and prioritized in Step 4 must be addressed.

The same considerations must be made of the other two alternatives, which may include a continuation of current recreation management or a new scheme requiring backcountry visitors to camp at least five miles from the park road, relying on personal, rather than forced, dispersal patterns. An additional, and final consideration, is the attempt to balance the costs and benefits to all parties potentially affected by the manager's decision. The National Park Service was confronted with just such a balancing act when it was forced, because of visitor overuse, to ration permits for floating the Colorado River in the Grand Canyon National Park.

In the Grand Canyon case, the Park Service decided to limit rafting trips to the level experienced in 1972 at approximately 92,000 user days per year. The Park Service then chose to allocate the available permits between commercial operators and private floaters at a ratio of 9:1. Private floaters challenged this decision as an unfair distribution of benefits to the class of commercial operators. The court recognized that if the use of the river has to be limited to protect the resource, then differential allocation is reasonable if done fairly and in a manner that recognizes the interests of each.

The Park's record of decision noted that the trade-off was not between commercial operators and private users, but rather between those who can make the run safely without professional assistance and those who cannot. In general, there are many more who desire that type of recreational experience but lack the ability and equipment necessary. Thus, commercial operators undertake a public function, and the distribution reflects this service. The court upheld the Park Service.

Step 9 concerns balance between competing interests, and the role of personhood values has recently become increasingly important in natural resources management decisions. The conflict between wilderness preservation and logging-dependent communities is a hallmark of when recreational or ecological interests are balanced with the personhood interests maintained through promoting community (human) stability through below-cost timber harvests.

The concept of personhood stems from the recognition that humans are conscious and goal-directed organisms. Attempts at needs satisfaction involve the ordering of one's own personal environment in an effort to maximize creative options and freedom of choice. These options and choices create the opportunities for self-realization (personhood). To achieve this goal, an individual needs some control over personal activities, as well as the assurance that social conditions are stable enough to permit a person to make plans, investments, and commitments.

A chosen lifestyle can provide a unique sense of personal fulfillment. These choices should foster a sense of individual contribution and significance. A social system which trivializes and cancels the choices and expectations people have, trivializes the role that person has within society. When this happens, it is only a small step to perceiving oneself as trivial. Once this occurs, anonymity and alienation set in, emasculating any further participation in social activities, leading to an increasingly degenerative community (Bader, 1986, p. 2-3).

When a decision by a resource manager encroaches upon personhood values, the balance of costs and benefits is automatically tipped strongly in favor of personhood values, and it requires very specific mandates to the contrary to overcome this presumption.

After a comparison is made of the various solutions, the manager must select a preferred alternative. If the selection solution is a material departure from established park policies, as identified in Step 2, then the manager must go into detail about what factors specifically dictated this choice, and why departure is necessary.

Step 10 is implementing the selected alternative: if the manager finds that the choice made will cause a major departure from prior decisions in similar circumstances or change existing policies, a point-by-point analysis, building upon the information identified in Step 3, must be provided. Therefore, in the Denali Park example, a justification for developing a fixed trail system would undergo greater scrutiny than a decision to implement a dispersed system where hikers were required to camp a certain minimum distance from roads and other parties.

SUMMARY

This chapter closes with the understanding that courts recognize that they are not natural resource management experts. However, courts are continually called upon to review agency decisions. In order to carry out their tasks, courts turn to what they are experts at— reasoned decision making. Without intruding upon the professional discretion of resource managers, courts can enforce a process designed to assure that decisions are not the result of arbitrariness, caprice, or avarice, provided it is followed.

SELECTED READINGS

1.   Bader, H. R. 1986. "Re-Inventing Democracy." Harvard Law School paper (unpublished).

2.   Bader, H. 1989. "Wolf Conservation: the Importance of Following Endangered Species Recovery Plans." *Harvard Environmental Law Review, 13*, No. 2.

3.   Bader, H. 1990. *Park Science, 10*(3):13-17 & 20.

4.   Levi, E. H. 1949. *An Introduction to Legal Reasoning.* Chicago, IL: University of Chicago Press.

5.   Plater, Z. 1992. *Environmental Law & Policy: Nature, Law, and Society.* St. Paul, MN: West Publishing Co.

6.   Robinson, W. L., and Boten, E. G. 1984. *Wildlife Ecology and Management,* New York, NY: Macmillan Publishing Co.

CHAPTER 6

be tailored to each p⌐ overriding concern is ⊔⌐ conflicting minority interest gr⌐⌐ satisfaction of a silent majority."[5]

Involvement of the Public in Decision Making

In Chapter 4, we identified several instances where public participation could or should be used in deciding what to do about a problem. In this chapter, we detail the specifics on obtaining participatory input from the social environment of our open system. Twenty-five years ago, public involvement was minimal and public apathy was great. Agencies seemed to prefer this arrangement because it meant little interference with management decisions. It certainly made decision making much easier. Today, we seem to want to go to the other extreme—to maximize user input. Yet we often seem to neither understand the limits of the system feedback we receive, nor have any good notion of how to incorporate it into decision making.

Today's interest in involving the public in decision making is an outgrowth of the environmental movement of the late 1960s and 1970s. People clamored to be heard on environmental issues, and interest groups pushed to institutionalize the process for public involvement, requiring agencies to air issues of resource use before the affected public. We now have laws and regulations in place to guarantee public involvement. However, there is no single guaranteed, foolproof technique for assessing public opinion and incorporating it into decision making. We do know that public involvement strategy must

PUBLIC OPINION

To better understand how public input is related to decision making, we must first understand public opinion in terms of how it is formed, why it is formed, and to what it responds. Public opinion has been summarized by H. Cantril into the following four principles:

1. *Identification Principle.* People ignore an idea, an opinion, or a point of view unless they can see clearly that it effects their personal fears, desires, hopes, or aspirations. Your message must be stated in terms of the interest of your audience.
2. *Action Principle.* People do not buy ideas that lack action. This may be either action taken (or about to be taken) by the sponsor of the idea or action that can be conveniently taken by the people to prove the merit of the idea. Unless a means of action is provided, people tend to shrug off appeals.
3. *Principle of Familiarity and Trust.* We buy ideas only from those we trust; we are influenced by or adopt only those opinions and points of view espoused by individuals, corporations, or institutions in whom we have confidence. A person is not likely to listen to or believe someone unless he or she has confidence in the speaker.
4. *Clarity Principle.* The situation must be clear to us—not confusing. Information we observe, read, see, or

hear must also be clear—not subject to several interpretations. To communicate, you must employ words, symbols, or stereotypes that receivers can understand.[9]

These principles present some interesting characteristics of public opinion. If the public is to respond, information and ideas must affect his or her well-being or self-interest. Self-interest may be based on economic, aesthetic, or other concerns, so an issue, to have meaning and cause the individual to actively respond, must be of personal importance. A person may feel he or she cannot tolerate the situation or contemplated action of the agency, or may feel compelled by the group norms of an organization. Despite involvement in organizational action, that person must still feel a personal commitment in relation to the issue.

None of this may actually take place unless the issue itself is clear. The public will then respond according to self-interest and the sense of urgency that stimulates a personal course of action. For any given issue, only a small portion of the population will become involved. The remainder simply do not feel the need, or are already involved in more important activities. Today as never before, we lead socially complex lifestyles—at work, at home, and during leisure we have overcommitted our time and personal energy. If important social issues are to be faced, we must first reorient our priorities. At best, we can carefully select the issues we become involved with, and there are hundreds to choose from. While it may be easy to narrow down that list, we must still structure our priorities within that list.

Finally, the source of information drastically affects how people respond. If we have confidence in the source and the political system, we may be more willing to respond in a positive, aggressive way. If we are alienated from the source, we may choose to ignore the issue or to respond in a strongly negative fashion.

In sum, influencing public opinion requires: good communication, a clear message, identifying the issue, giving cause for action, and a reliable source. Nevertheless, only a limited number of people become involved at any one time. It is hoped that we can, in some way, dissect this problem to find out not only what sways public opinion, but also how people arrive at their conclusions.

Based on a ten-year study, Cantril summarized public opinion in the following axioms:

1. Opinion is highly sensitive to important events (particularly mistakes).
2. Events of unusual magnitude are likely to swing public opinion temporarily from one extreme to another. Opinion does not become stabilized until the implications of events are seen with some perspective.
3. Opinion is generally determined more by events than by words—unless those words are themselves interpreted as an "event."
4. Verbal statements and outlined courses of actions have maximum importance when opinion is unstructured and people are seeking some interpretation from a trusted source.
5. By and large, public opinion does not anticipate emergencies; it only reacts to them.
6. From the viewpoint of social psychology, opinion is basically determined by perceived self-interest. Events, words, and other stimuli affect opinion only insofar as they relate to

this self-interest, and part of it is stimulated by the leadership in an individual's reference group.

7. Opinion does not remain aroused for any long period of time unless people feel the issue acutely involves their self-interest or unless the opinion aroused by group/community leaders is sustained by events.

8. Once perceived self-interest is involved, opinions are not easily changed.

9. In a democracy, public opinion is likely to be ahead of official policy when it involves self-interest.

10. When an opinion is held by a slight majority or not solidly structured, an acknowledged fact tends to shift opinion in the direction of acceptance.

11. At critical times, people become more sensitive to the adequacy of their leadership. If they have confidence in it, they are willing to delegate greater responsibility; if they lack confidence in it, they become less tolerant.

12. People are less reluctant to have critical decisions made by their leaders if they feel that somehow they, the people, are taking some part in the decisions.

13. People have more opinions and are able to form opinions more easily about goals than about the methods necessary to reach those goals.

14. Public opinion, like individual opinion, is colored by desire, and when opinion is based chiefly on desire rather than information, it is likely to fluctuate sharply with events.

15. By and large, if people in a democracy are provided educational opportunities and ready access to information, public opinion reveals a hardheaded common sense. The more enlightened people

are about the implications of events and proposals for their own self-interest, the more likely they are to agree with the objective opinions of realistic experts.[9]

The above statements summarize public opinion and how it is formed. The public reacts to identified issues, particularly perceived threats. These reactions are caused by events, rumors, prejudices, and stereotypes, and are generally correlated with level of education and perceived personal effects. If the public perceives itself as able to participate in decision making, the intensity of their reaction will be based, to a certain degree, on their level of confidence in the leadership. It is the responsibility of the agency to develop and maintain the public trust. While people are better able to form decisions about goals than about methods of reaching these goals, they often have strong feelings on methods. Maintaining public trust often requires that the public be consulted on methods *as well as* goals, and the manager must be sensitive to public opinion. Finally, people should have access to information and be able to interpret it so that they can formulate a common-sense response to an issue, which is what Phase 1 (p. 79) is all about.

PUBLIC INVOLVEMENT AS A PROCESS

Today's public is better educated, interested in the management of public resources, and often well-versed on local management issues. More people and organizations are demanding the right to participate in the decision making. True feelings, however, are sometimes masked by the game playing that occurs at public meetings. Organized groups may polarize the public in the hope that a compromise decision will be reached in their favor, or they may use the public meeting as an opportunity to deliberately create conflict. In such cases, input often is not very viable, and nothing is really accomplished except for the venting of feelings.

To make public involvement work satisfactorily requires commitment on the part of the manager. The manager's responsibility is to inform the user of the facts about a particular issue and to educate him as to how these facts fit together in the context of decision making. Unfortunately, manager(s) often have only an intuitive feel for the significances of particular variables and how they might affect the outcome of the decision.

For example, a federal agency recently put out a draft resource management plan to which interested members of the public were supposed to respond with useful input that could be incorporated into the final plan. The plan included an inventory, four alternative plans, an environmental impact analysis, and applicable statutes. Detailed review showed that much of the data was not helpful in understanding or evaluating alternatives because of the way the agency had written them; only one of the four alternative plans could actually be implemented (some courts have held that such unfeasible alternatives are illegal). Consequently public input on the document was worthless, except perhaps as a soothing ritual and a guarantee that only what the agency wanted to do in the first place would be selected. To legitimize the final recommended plan (which was alternative B—the only possible choice) pages of names of public participants were incorporated. A summary response stating that an additional 189 written comments had been received,

reviewed and considered was also included. Serious input was obviously not encouraged in this case, nor were the comments apparently given more than a superficial review.

We seemingly solicit public comments because the law requires us to do so. Not much energy or imagination goes into the effort. Yet that is not the impression we get when we talk with managers. They want to improve public participation, but seem to have difficulty in breaking away from proven methods or methods required by law. In that context, this chapter is no revelation either. Hopefully the message that you do receive is that there is nothing wrong with the idea of public involvement but that some adjustments are needed. These include more critical links in the overall process, the applicability of particular ways of involving the public in particular situations, and the realization that the affected public should be involved in goal setting and establishing alternative ways of achieving such goals, as well as selecting the trade-offs.

Before examining this process, we should define "public opinion," the expected input. According to *Webster's New World Dictionary,* it is "the opinion of the people, generally as a force in determining social and political action." By definition, then, an anticipated result is some impact on decision making. Yet many people are alienated because they feel a decision has already been made, and others enter a situation with an even more naive perspective—that they will have an impact on outcome. Tactics may vary from simple shows of power, to the power of logical thinking. Generally the public becomes frustrated because they feel they have little impact. The agency, as suggested in the above example, often spends much time and money for very little useful input while appearing to involve the public in decision making.

The following section attempts to address these concerns, from both the manager's and user's point of view. Rather than immediately assessing the potential of various methods, the discussion will focus on the total process, critical links within it, and the roles/perspectives of the manager and user.

Figure 6-1 presents a flow model of the total involvement process. There are three phases to this process:

1. *Identification and enumeration of the issue.* The public issue is identified, investigated, and reported to the public through various media.
2. *Formulation of public opinion.* The individual, often via community or group leaders whom they respect, filters the information, integrates it with his or her own beliefs, and arrives at a conclusion.
3. *Integration of public input into decision making.* The intent is to obtain feedback that can be used in decision making.

Identification and Enumeration—Phase 1

Identified issues for a particular area may include anticipating problems and needs by an agency, public response, or legal requirements. Some agencies use scoping techniques to identify issues involved with some proposed project, the revamping of a management plan, etc. Issues arise continuously. Some are important and some aren't, so management must determine relative significance in terms of public support of the agency. Usually issues arise because of change, or proposed change, in the agency programs. The question is how much change requires public involvement in decision making. While

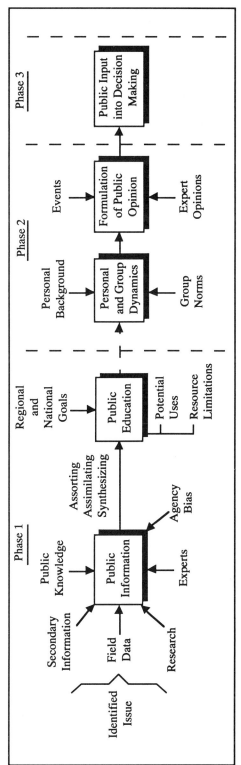

Figure 6-1. Model for formulation and integration of public opinion into management decision making.

there is no absolute answer, the best response is probably that significant issues arise when the recreational opportunity is to be altered or when a well-known environmental feature is to be changed. The assumption is that social succession takes place, significantly altering the benefits to society (see Chapter 3).

While there are legal requirements for involving the public in decision making in certain situations, these do no more than separate the significant from the insignificant issues. Beyond that, it is the responsibility of the manager to identify and prioritize issues where public consultation is important. Failure to do so may ultimately force dissatisfied parties into the political or judicial arena where results are often less than satisfactory. This means that the manager must monitor both the resource and the interested public through various media.

Once the issue has been isolated, the agency must then formally initiate an involvement process so that it can obtain the most useful input from the public. Information and education programs are the responsibility of the manager, and the rest of the process is dependent on the effort extended in the initial phase. In other words, if the manager does not do his job in Phase 1, the collective opinions formed in Phase 2 will probably not be very useful in decision making. All available information should first be collected and then assimilated and verified before any additional field data collection is begun. In this way, field data can be used to verify existing data or to fill in any gaps in the available information. Too often, we duplicate our efforts by initiating field data collection before considering the information that is already available. In our haste, we may either collect too much data or require a greater degree of precision than is really necessary.

Data should be made available to the public in some useful form so that they also have the pertinent information on which to base their opinions. A majority of interested "publics" today are sophisticated enough to understand the information if it is presented in a suitable manner, though they may need some assistance in interpreting data. This openness about the issue and related data can help in obtaining better public input and reducing public suspicion about "closed-shop" decision making.

The manager must also educate the public, through interpretation of data, about the potential and limitations of an area for certain kinds of recreational opportunities. Potential rests with the attractiveness of the resource. It also depends on the ability of the resource to sustain recreational use; institutional constraints such as laws, policies, budget, and past land use; the existing situation; and the

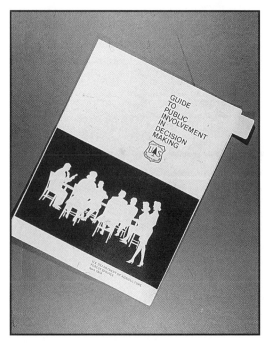

Figure 6-2. An early public involvement manual issued by the U.S. Forest Service. (Photo by B. W. Twight)

vision of management (see Figure 3-3, p. 37). If the manager synthesizes this information and presents it in a straightforward manner to the public so they know that the decision is to be made within a narrow segment of the Recreational Opportunity Spectrum, then feedback is more meaningful to the decision-maker. The example in the introductory section, where among Alternative Plans A, B, C, & D, only B can be implemented, is evidence that the process should have eliminated all but B. Public comments could then be sought on alternative ways of achieving B—B1, B2, . . . B_n. In this way, public input is based on knowledge and rational judgment and useful in the final decision. Furthermore, the public understands the trade-offs if such a course of action is implemented. Trade-offs are the recreational plans that are foregone to develop a particular recreation opportunity.

The need for education, as well as its potential effects, has been misunderstood. Some feel that public opinion should not be "manipulated" by information, that public sentiments should be unconstrained and/or untainted by managers. Yet received input is often unusable because no reason is given for an opinion or it is based on misinformation. Educational sessions can help reduce misinformation, misunderstanding, and misjudgment. As a result, the quality of rational public input improves, and the quantity increases because of greater confidence in the agency. Even so, there are limitations. Each person has a unique personality and, in his or her own way, filters information to arrive at an opinion. Everyone also has biases related to specific situations or objects. We cannot eliminate these, nor should we try, but we can hope that each individual can become better prepared to make a rational, public interest-oriented choice and can better understand his or her reasons for making that choice.

Formulation of Public Opinion—Phase 2

The information and education process completes Phase 1. Phase 2 involves personal decision making in which the individual, having a free choice to make, attempts to formulate his or her own opinions on an issue. There are actually two parts to this phase—personal and group dynamics. The personal involves unique background, beliefs, and biases that affect the information. The group involves responses as a member of a reference group—as a professional, as a conservation club member, as a snowmobiler, or as a businessman. The individual may also incorporate group norms and social expectations into his or her opinion. A decision may be further tempered by trends in events or the opinions of experts in whom the individual has confidence. This is why the television networks were requested to stop issuing election returns until the polls had closed. The networks were, in fact, influencing the final vote.

Phase 2 is the responsibility of the user. As mentioned earlier, on important issues, the user forms an opinion based on available information. This does not mean that what is presented by the manager is received, accepted, and utilized by the individual. However, if done properly, through the proper media, the probability increases that the information affects public opinion. That probability is also influenced by other factors such as individual perception of the issue and individual trust or confidence in the agency.

Integration of Public Input Into the Decision-Making Process— Phase 3

There is a need to effectively and objectively analyze public input on an issue so that managers can evaluate and integrate it into the final decision, modifying the decision as necessary. This has been the greatest shortcoming to proper use of public input. The following four steps can help you integrate public input into a decision.

Analysis. According to R. N. Clark and G. H. Stankey, "the analysis process summarizes and displays the nature, content, and extent of input received."[11] A. Bleiker and H. Bleiker add that its objective should be to relay public messages to the decision maker with minimal distortion and loss of detail.[7] No judgment should be made on its value or its applicability. Clark and Stankey recommend an applied content analysis approach to sort the information relayed in a manner useful to the manager. It is desirable to know not only what was said and who said it but also how it was said. As input, form letters and petitions are generally considered to be less important than personal letters.

Evaluation. Unlike analysis, evaluation is subjective in that the information is filtered and interpreted in relation to the issue; it should follow, however, a logical and objective process that relates information to the maintenance of system support (as shown in Chapter 4), to arrive at some conclusions about the input and incorporate these into the final decision. Noting the principles of public opinion, it is desirable to interpret the input according to specific objectives. Sometimes these objectives can be compatible and accommodated within some overall area goal.

It is important in the analysis process to differentiate among local, regional, and national public input since the nature of the decision may merit weighing input in the evaluation step. Some issues may reflect broad national and regional concerns; others may more directly affect local conditions within minimal regional concerns.

In sum, evaluation is an interpretation of the validity and significance of public comments and an examination of these comments in relation to a particular issue. Knowing both the balance of opinion and the supporting rationale is critical; these elements define public values on any issue, and both are important to maintaining positive support from the social environment of the system.

Integration. Integrating requires consideration of public input, as evaluated by the manager, plus factors such as legal responsibility, fiscal constraints, resource capability, environmental effects, and related social and economic conditions. It should be understood that the public input must be considered by the manager making a decision.

Implementation. Implementation requires program objectives which refine management goals in operational terms. Specific management prescriptions flow from these program objectives. For example, a goal might be to maintain ecological succession under "pre-Columbian conditions" in a particular wilderness. The focus would be on how to best accomplish this—let burn, control burn, or no burn—for each major management unit within the wilderness. Specific prescriptions would show exactly what needs to be done under particular conditions within a management unit, including the fact that public opinion is against the "let burn" policy. This would necessitate a greater interpretive effort, aimed at fire-ecology education.

The question is: How does public involvement really fit into this problem solving and decision process? On the surface, anyone who has ever actively participated as part of the public would give the obvious answer: "It doesn't fit." While this may be a legitimate condemnation of some management planning efforts, it should not arise if public involvement has been conscientiously carried out earlier in the planning process, if *goals, objectives,* and *prescriptions* have been developed. Generally, management puts too much internal behind-the-scenes effort into forming goals and objectives, and thus asks for and judges public input relative to those objectives only. Then the later, inordinate amount of staff time, data collection, and ego involvement is wasted because the agency predetermined the decision anyway.

What should be done, as suggested earlier in Chapter 2, is to use the public involvement workshop to develop the set of objectives. Then groups with differing views can be sure their position is represented, and their workshop representatives can come to grips with costs and trade-offs. In each succeeding level, they can acquire new data as needed and make refinements based on that data. These refinements can include not only strategy but also the goals and particularly the objectives.

If the public is involved at every level, they can help refine goals, objectives, and resulting management prescriptions, which is what T. Gallagher calls *cycle planning.*[19] The problem from a public involvement perspective, which cycle planning helps to overcome, is that with a static set of goals and objectives, the outcome (management prescription) may appear as essentially predetermined. Without being able to influence management objectives, the public understandably feels thwarted—no, frustrated—in its

ability to influence the outcome. With cycle planning they feel they have played a definite part.

APPLICATION

Media for Public Involvement

The following are the various media through which public involvement is encouraged. No one approach is completely satisfactory and each may be applicable for specific situations. Thus an agency may use all these media at any one time, even on a single issue.

Public Hearings. Public hearings are generally formal meetings in which testimony is given about a particular issue. Presentations must be prescheduled and are often recorded. While the potential is to reach large numbers of people at minimal cost, the actual number may be small and the costs very high. If many people *do* turn out for a meeting, feelings are probably very strong and the meeting may degenerate into polarized camps that play more to the audience than to management.[6] Because of this, group leaders often posture and exaggerate their views, hoping to mobilize additional public opinion in their direction. Therefore, issues are rarely discussed in a compromising fashion; that is, the focus is on points about which the various camps do not agree.

Public Workshops. Public workshops are designed to encourage discussion among participants. In order to direct that discussion, managers must establish an agenda. Then participants are presented with information about an issue and segregated into small informal groups for discussion and formulating a course of action. In the final step, the groups interact with one another so that each has the opportunity to hear the others' positions as well as to advocate its own. Ideally this format should allow participants the opportunity to search for those areas of interest that they have in common or can agree on; then negotiations focus on those items about which they do not agree.[6]

If the agency does its part in presenting all available information (defining the arena within which the decision will be made and sticking to the agenda), results should be beneficial to the decision maker. However, members of organized groups often feel disadvantaged without their own information experts, particularly if they do not trust the agency or the opposition.

Solicitation. Solicitation of comments on public issues allows the individual to respond in writing to some prepared statement. Such general solicitation encourages feedback from the public, often in conjunction with a public hearing, public workshop, or prepared statement by the agency. While this may constitute a large percentage of the responses, often the information is not useful because people react to the wrong issue or area, or state their views in terms that are too general. Sometimes responses are even mass-produced, signed, and submitted by people who may have only peripheral interests.

Surveys. Surveys of public opinion on an issue, planning task, or management policy can give insight into visitor perceptions of both the problem and its possible solutions. These can help in making judgments about the effects of particular management strategies on the user or potential user. The potential user is important because often the most significant problems are those created by

change. With change comes a new aggregate user population that may not recognize its self-interest until after the project/program is implemented. Thus surveying potential user populations can give better insight into total public opinion. The problem is that surveys are expensive, time-consuming, and often difficult to properly develop (questionnaire, sampling, and data analysis).

Advisory Committees. These committees may be formal or informal, but they all counsel the manager on general policy or specific issues. They should be aware that their role is only advisory. Each major administrative unit or program should probably have a formal committee that represents major segments of the public and that solicits public opinion. This opens a regular formal channel for public-management interactions but does not eliminate the need for general public input. Such formal interactions allow both committee members and agency people to explore a question more thoroughly, examine information more critically, and arrive at a decision more deliberately. The informal committee can also give the manager a sounding board in lieu of general public input if it is composed of key individuals in dominant social positions. However, management must recognize that while the quality of the input can improve, all committees may not represent the public at large.

Continual Contacts. Continual contact with groups or associations of interested individuals can keep channels of communication open. A manager who is selective in his or her group contacts should also maximize the effectiveness of this technique, e.g., you can't just solicit input from the snowmobile club and ignore the cross-country club, unless the issue is the design and/or improvement of an already allocated snowmobile trail. Nevertheless, if you contact the group on their own turf without an adversary across the table, discussions should be less pretentious and more focused on issues of concern to both the club and management.

Expert Opinion. Expert opinion can be solicited on specific issues in relation to technical aspects—behavioral modeling, resource damage, and so forth—however, it is still up to the manager to make the decision by weighing the evidence and public opinion.

A Plausible Approach—The Workshop

Soliciting and analyzing public opinion are formidable tasks to which there are no easy approaches. A complex approach may cause people not to respond, but a simple one may result in input that is not useful. The public workshop can offer a balanced solution that encourages maximum public input while obtaining useful feedback. It also fits the basic model (see Figure 6-1, p. 79). To produce the workshop model, one additional phase is needed—the interphase, which is between Phase 1 (Identification and Enumeration of the Issues), and Phase 2 (Formulation of Public Opinion).

Small-group communications characterize the workshop model. People and agency members are divided into small groups to discuss the information they have received. Each group, through discussion, should arrive at a compromise solution about the issues. Each member must listen to and assess the discussion of others, express his/her own feelings, and justify opinions to the other group members. The summary of all the groups, including justifications, should reflect the sentiment of those people present.

Under these circumstances, pseudo-polarization diminishes, and real conflict is isolated. The issue is thus reduced in scope, and specific details are refined and re-formed into a more practical, manageable problem. The input received consequently focuses on the real matter rather than a collection of "problems" that are often alluded to in typical public hearings.

Information and education are the two basic management functions that must be required for the workshop approach to work. The information session should focus—without highly technical language—on the visitor, the resource, competing land uses, and both national and regional public input. Experts hired by nonagency interest groups must also be allowed to present alternative technical analyses for consideration.

The education session may be held directly following the information session. For more complex issues involving much information, you may schedule it after some time delay so that people can assimilate the material presented and consult their own experts. The three factors considered in interpreting information are: potential of the resource for certain uses, limitations of the resource for desired activities, and associated trade-offs. Expert views may differ on each of these.

The potential of the resource can be evaluated in two ways: by what it can sustain without suffering permanent physical deterioration, and by what it can be used for. Both factors should be discussed so that people understand the available options, the potential effects of a given option, and the assumptions upon which these views are based.

Trade-offs are difficult to handle even if you know the interrelationships between various resource elements, and difficulty increases when we add the people-use factor. Trade-offs, however, are essential in understanding the potential effects of choosing a given management option to meet a goal or mixture of goals, and in interpreting these efforts for the public. Even if you cannot attach an absolute value to a trade-off, you should still be able to predict, with the assistance of the technical staff, the relative effects on different groups of a given option.

Small-group dynamics is accomplished by dividing the larger body of people into groups that are small enough for people to feel comfortable in informal interactions. You must consider six basic factors in order to ensure the success of small-group dynamics:

1. Size. The size of the group may vary, but a maximum of eight to ten people is generally recommended. In a larger group, most people tend to have fewer interactions, and a few individuals dominate the discussion.

2. Heterogeneity. It is important that people with different views on the issue discuss these openly. If people with the same views make up the discussion group, they do very little critical analysis of the issue. They merely agree with one another without attempting to identify the real issues, formulate a logical response, or even understand their own stance. Heterogeneity does cause some personal tension; however, this is beneficial because it tends to cause each individual to think about the issue, to examine their feelings about it, and to verbalize these feelings.

There are several ways to obtain heterogeneity. One of the more popular is to pass out color- or number-coded agenda sheets on a systematic basis as people enter the meeting room. Individuals can then be assigned to a certain group. You must have a similar technique for doing this; otherwise groups will be homogeneous.

3. Leadership. Leadership is difficult to handle because of the potential effect a leader can have on the group decision. Since the agency is often an interest group itself, agency leaders often tend to create more tension, reducing the effectiveness of the discussion and the final choice of options. Also, their presence sometimes casts suspicion on the whole process.

There are two other possibilities—hire professional leaders or "brokers" who are not agency people but who have the ability to get people involved and negotiating, or allow the leadership to evolve or be selected from each group. The latter method sometimes works well, since in such a small group most participants do not allow the informal leadership to dominate their conclusions. Some theoreticians feel that one way to eliminate the air of dominance is to omit a table where people can establish positions of power, and to arrange chairs in a small circle. The former approach may also work well where there has been conflict and suspicion between interest groups.

4. Deciding on Goals. Participants should understand that they are to focus on those goals which they feel are desirable and obtainable. As was shown earlier in this chapter, people are more able to decide on goals than on methods of obtaining them. Since the agency will be seeking specific kinds of input on the issue, it should develop a set of open-ended questions that people can respond to.

5. Reporting. Each small group should then report their findings and their reasons for these to the whole assembly. They should also report gaps in information or inaccurate data associated with their decisions. This may help the agency in its deliberations and preparations for future workshops. Offer opportunities for minority reports if people disagree with small-group conclusions or if they feel that a single individual dominated the discussion.

6. Information and Education. Desirable small group dynamics are predicated on information and education sessions. These are not designed to eliminate personal bias, but may include professional experts hired by outside groups. It is hoped that more information will give everyone a better background and make them more aware of all the ramifications of the issue.

Transactive Planning Theory

J. Friedmann offers a new approach to involving the public in planning and transactive planning, where the public is the essential decision maker.[17] He describes a process to decentralize, debureaucratize decisions, where the public is involved throughout the entire planning process, even the implementation. The key element, according to Friedmann, is action facilitated by the professional planner but determined by the involved public. This is similar to Gallagher's cycle planning and Bleiker and Bleikers' SEACA, Substantial Effective Agreement on a Course of Action. The difference is that Friedmann tries to develop an underlying theory.

Friedmann identifies three critical components: 1) dialogue, 2) mutual learning, and 3) societal guidance. Dialogue refers to personal communications between the client-public and the planner. Mutual learning occurs where the processed knowledge of the planner and the personal knowledge of the client are shared in a mutual exploration of the problem and possible solutions. Societal guidance occurs when, based on the dialogue and mutual learning, a substantial, effective

agreement on a course of action is reached. Each potentially affected party, though drawn by self-interest, ultimately tempers that motivation with social responsibility as long as there is mutual respect and acceptance. Once the decision is made and implemented, acceptance increases and challenges decrease, at least successful challenges. Ashor and Stokes present two excellent case studies on recreation management problems using the transactive planning approach for the reader who wishes to pursue this further.[4,34]

SELECTED READINGS

1. Alston, R. M. 1972. Goals and Decisionmaking in the Forest Service. U.S. Forest Service Research Paper INT-128.

2. Alston, R. M., and Freeman, D. M. 1975. "The Natural Resource Decision-maker as a Political and Economic Man: Toward a Synthesis." *Journal of Environmental Management* 3:1.

3. Amy, D. J. 1987. *The Politics of Environmental Mediation.* New York, NY: Columbia University Press.

4. Ashor, J. L. 1985. "Recreation Management in the Bob Marshall Wilderness Complex: An Application of the Limits of Acceptable Change Concept and Transactive Planning Theory," Master's Thesis (unpublished). University of Montana, Missoula.

5. Behan, R. W. 1978. "Why the Majority is Silent: Some thoughts to Ponder about Public Involvement While Waiting for the Sierra Club to Arrive." *Proceedings, Society of American Foresters,* pp 168-173.

6. Bleiker, H. 1976. "The Role of Values in Environmental Decision-Making and in Environmental Education," Fifth Annual Conference, National for Environmental Education, Atlanta, GA.

7. Bleiker, A., and Bleiker, H. 1990. *Citizen Participation Handbook.* Carmel, CA: Institute for Participatory Management and Planning.

8. Borton, T. E., and Warner, K. P. 1971. "Involving Citizens in Water Resource Planning: The Communication-Participation Experiment in the Susquehanna River Basin," *Environment and Behavior 3*(9):284.

9. Cantril, H. 1972. *Gauging Public Opinion.* Princeton University Press, pp. 226-230.

10. Carpenter,, S. L., and Kennedy, W. J. D. 1988. *Managing Public Disputes, A Practical Guide to Handling Conflict and Reaching Agreement,* San Francisco, CA: Jossey-Bass.

11. Clark, R. N., and Stankey, G. H. 1976. "Analyzing Public Input to Resource Decisions: Criteria, Principles, and Case Examples of the Codinvolve System." *Natural Resources Journal 16*(1):213.

12. Clark, R. N., Stankey, G. H., and Hendee, J. C. 1974. "An Introduction to CODINVOLVE: A System for Analyzing, Storing, and Retrieving Public Input to Resource Decisions." U.S. Forest Service Research Note PNW-223.

13. Creighton, J. L. 1981. *The Public Involvement Manual.* Cambridge, MA: ABT Books.

14. Daneke, G. A., Farcia, M., and Priscoli, J. D. (eds.). 1983. *Public Involvement and Social Impact Assessment.* Boulder, CO: Westview Press.

15. Deutsch, M. 1977. *The Resolution of Conflict.* New Haven, CT: Yale University Press.

16. Fazio, J. R. and Gilbert, D. L. 1990. *Public Relations and Communications for Natural Resource Managers,* 2nd Ed., Dubuque, IA: Kendall-Hunt Publishing Co.

17. Friedmann, J. 1973. "The Public Interest and Community Participation: Toward a Reconstruction of Public Philosophy." *Journal of the American Institute of Planners 39*(1):1-12.

18. Frome, M. 1992. *Regreening the National Parks.* Tucson, AZ: Univ. of Arizona Press.

19. Gallagher, T. 1987. *Cycle Planning.* University of Alaska-Fairbanks.

20. Gamson, W. A. 1974. *Power and Discontent.* Homewood, IL: The Dorsey Press.

21. Getz, D. 1986. "Management Planning in Public Recreation Agencies." *Journal of Park and Recreation Administration 4*(3):17-31.

22. Gray, B. 1989. *Collaborating, Finding Common Ground for Multiparty Problems.* San Francisco, CA: Jossey-Bass.

23. Hendee, J. C., Clark, R. N., and Stankey, H. 1974. "A Framework for Agency Use of Public Input in Resource Decision-Making." *Journal of Soil and Water Conservation 29*(2):60.

24. Heffron, F. 1989. *Organization Theory and Public Organizations: The Political Connection,* Englewood Cliffs, NJ: Prentice-Hall.

25. Hendee, J. C., Lucas, R. C., Tracy, R. H., Jr., Staed, T., Clark, R. N., Stankey, G. H., and Yarnell, R. A. 1973. *Public Involvement and the Forest Service: Experience, Effectiveness, and Suggested Direction.* Washington, DC: U.S. Forest Service.

26. Hornback, K. E. 1975. "Overcoming Obstacles to Agency and Public Involvement." *Environmental Design Research Association Annual Proceedings.* Lawrence, KS.

27. Hunt, S. L., and Brooks, K. W. 1983. "A Planning Model for Public Recreation Agencies." *Journal of Park and Recreation Administration 1*(2):1-13.

28. Kedder, L. H., and Stewart, V. M. 1975. *The Psychology of Intergroup Relations: Conflict and Consciousness.* New York, NY: McGraw-Hill Book Co.

29. Lipset, S. M., and Schneider, W. 1987. *The Confidence Gap: Business, Labor and Government in the Public Mind,* Baltimore, MD: Johns Hopkins University Press.

30. Lyden, F. J., Twight, B. W., and Tuchmann, E. T. 1990. "Citizen Participation in Long-Range Planning: The RPA Experience," *Natural Resources Journal, 30* (Winter): 123-138.

31. Mager, R. F. 1985. *Goal Analysis* (2nd ed.). Belmont, CA: Davis Lake Publishing.

32. Mills, T. M. 1973. *The Sociology of Small Groups.* Englewood Cliffs, NJ: Prentice-Hall, Inc.

33. Neuman, W. R. 1986. *The Paradox of Mass Politics: Knowledge and Opinion in the American Electorate,* Cambridge, MA: Harvard University Press.

34. Phillips, G. M. 1973. *Communication and the Small Group.* Indianapolis, IN: Bobbs-Merrill Co., Inc.

35. Pressman, J. L. 1970. "Decision-Making and Public Policy: The Perils and Possibilities of Fragmentation." *Elements of Outdoor Recreation Planning.* Driver, B. L. (ed.). Ann Arbor, Ml: University of Michigan Press.

36. Reinke, K. B., and Reinke, B. 1973. "Public Involvement in Resource Decisions: A National Forest Seeks Public Input for Recreation Development." *Journal of Forestry* 71(10):656.

37. Rosenfeld, L. B. 1973. *Human Interaction in the Small Group Setting.* Columbus, Ohio: Charles E. Merrill Publishing Co.

38. Schroeder, T. D. 1987. *Nonparticipants: Barriers to Recreation Participation.* (Public Admin. Series). Monticello, IL: Vance Bibliographies.

39. Shelby, B., and Vaske, J. J. 1991. "Resource and Activity Substitutes for Recreational Salmon Fishing in New Zealand." *Leisure Sciences 13*(1):21-32.

40. Shaw, M. E. 1976. *Group Dynamics: The Psychology of Small Group Behavior.* New York, NY: McGraw-Hill Co.

41. Schweitzer, D. L., Freeman, D. M., and Alston, R. M. 1975. "Ensuring Viable Public Land-Use Decisions: Some Problems and Suggestions," *Journal of Forestry* 73(11):705.

42. Stankey, G. H., Hendee, J. C., and Clark, R. N. 1975. "Applied Social Research Can Improve Public Participation in Resource Decision-Making." *Rural Sociology* 40:65.

43. Stankey, G. H. 1972. "The Use of Content Analysis in Resource Decision Making." *Journal of Forestry* 70(3):148.

44. Stokes, G. L. 1982. "Conservation of the Blackfoot River Corridor: An Application of Transactive Planning Theory." Ph.D. Dissertation (unpublished), Colorado State University, Ft. Collins, CO.

45. Tindall, J. 1984. "Expanding Citizen-Professional Partnerships: 'Grass Roots' Community Development of Leisure Opportunity." *Journal Parks and Recreation Administration* 2(1):64-72.

46. Twight, B. W., Lyden, F. J. and Tuchmann, E. T. 1990. "Constituency Bias in a Federal Career System? A Study of District Rangers of the U.S. Forest Service." *Administration & Society, 22* (3)November: 358-389.

47. Twight, B. W., and Lyden, F. J. 1989. "Measuring Forest Service Bias," *Journal of Forestry, 87* (5)May: 36-41.

48. Twight, B. W., and Carroll, M. 1983. "Workshops in Public Involvement: Do They Help Find Common Ground?" *Journal of Forestry 81*:732-735.

49. Twight, B. W., and Paterson, J. J. 1979. "Conflict and Public Involvement: Measuring Consensus." *Journal of Forestry, 77*(12)December: 771-776.

50. Twight, B. W. 1977. "Confidence or More Controversy: Whither Public Involvement?"*Journal of Forestry, 75*(2)February: 93-95.

51. U.S. Forest Service. 1980. *Public Participation Handbook,* Vol. I & 2. USDA-Forest Service. Washington, DC.

52. Vining, J. (ed.). 1990. *Social Science and Natural Resources: Recreation Management.* Boulder, CO: Westview Press.

53. Wagar, J. A., and Twight, B. W. 1984. "Communication and Public Involvement." Section 23, *Forestry Handbook.* 2nd edition. Wenger, K. F. (ed.). New York, NY: John Wiley & Sons.

54. Wicks, B. E. 1987. "The Allocation of Recreation and Park Resources: The Courts' Intervention." *Journal of Park and Recreation Administration, 5*(3):1-9.

55. Wondolleck, J. M. 1988. *Public Lands Conflict and Resolution: Managing National Forest Disputes,* New York, NY: Plenum Press.

56. Young, R. C. 1970. "Establishment of Goals and Definitions of Objectives," *Elements of Outdoor Recreation Planning.* Driver, B. L. (ed.). Ann Arbor, MI: University of Michigan Press.

PART II

Recreational Resource Management

The management model (Chapter 2) and particularly the underlying theory (Chapter 3) emphasize the importance of the environmental setting—the prime attractors and the generalized landscape in which they occur. This section presents a series of resource management programs directed at maintaining or enhancing the environmental setting. Each chapter has a specific programmatic theme, going from the more intensively used sites, and thus more intensive resource management, to more dispersed-use areas and extensive programs.

Modern man has been caught in a philosophical debate of using versus preserving the ecological setting. The argument is often presented as an all-or-nothing choice. From a programmatic perspective, the argument deals with an illusion. Few if any areas exist that have not been influenced by modern man. Even the wildest have been penetrated, directly manipulated through specific activities, or indirectly influenced by external activities. And no one would suggest that these same areas should be cordoned off to prevent use, or that use, even in an unrestricted form, is going to cause wholesale destruction of the ecological webbing.

The debate from the manager's perspective, then, should not be one of use versus preservation, but *use versus use.* What type of use is appropriate for the area? And how can we best achieve that? How does that translate into specific resource management programs? Intensive versus extensive descriptors are not intended to reflect the relative value of the resource management program. On the contrary, each program is important and its relative worth must be judged in relation to the recreational opportunity to be provided. For a modern to semi-modern opportunity, intensive site management, such as introducing exotic vegetative ground cover and hardening the site, is just as inappropriate for a primitive recreational opportunity as introducing wild fires, and letting insect/diseases go unchecked.

CHAPTER 7

Assessing Impacts in the Real World

by Robert H. Becker*

The relationship between people and their environment is marked by a procession of benefits and costs associated with use of natural resources. These benefits and costs are rarely, if ever, evenly distributed; some claimant groups derive mostly benefits while costs are borne by other claimants, user groups, or society as a whole. While it is impossible in one brief chapter to cover all the impact associated with allocation of resources, we will introduce concepts that may be useful in understanding the consequences of resource allocation and management decisions.

Impact results from disparate views of benefits and differing interpretations of what constitutes a "resource." In 1951, E. W. Zimmerman coined the phrase "Resources Are Not, They Become."[23] This means that objects do not possess inherent value; they become resources when assigned importance or worth by a group of people. These people may claim the object as a resource for a particular value or set of values. Different groups of claimants may seek legitimate but incompatible uses for the object. For example, a tree may be viewed as a source of

fiber for paper or lumber by one group of claimants and valued for aesthetic appreciation and recreation by another group. Both resource definitions of that tree are legitimate and mutually exclusive. Under those circumstances, if one group of claimants wins, the other must lose.

Thus, management of natural areas becomes control of access to, and the balance of legitimate claims for, resources. This balance of claims must involve an examination of trade-offs, which requires enumerating impacts and evaluating the consequences of an action. Therefore, selecting options becomes a statement of values, an expression of the legal and administrative strictures by which resources are offered or withheld.

Because we live in a world of choice and possibility, no one can predict the future. Therefore, projecting probable futures and the consequences of a proposed action is a function of assumptions and random scenarios based upon empirical data rather than prediction. However, the actions taken today form that future. To project some future, then, we should examine our current actions and decisions and see if the foundations upon which those actions are built give us comfort or concern.

As professionals, we typically seek technical solutions to societal problems. This search for ways of assessing the impacts of specific situations is, however, rational. Management based upon science is on the surface more appealing than management based strictly upon judgment. The awe caused by an equation often overrides the conventional wisdom of practical application or understandable explanations. G. M. Weinberg,[22] suggests that "by using words, we shall sacrifice the appearance of elegance, but we shall stay closer to the things we want to think about." So why the drive for explanations of

* Robert H. Becker, Ph.D. is Professor of Parks, Recreation and Tourism Management at Clemson University.

outcomes based upon a quantitative foundation rather than a qualitative approach? Perhaps we believe that "The stature of a science is commonly measured by the degree to which it makes use of mathematics."[19] Or perhaps we were, and possibly still are, obsessed with what F. Egler terms "physics envy."[12] Consequently, we push for the technical solution— the objective answers to the often subjective questions. To discover technical solutions, however, we need a high level of concurrence about social values and scientific facts, a condition rarely met.

Figure 7.1, suggested by Thompson and Tuden, offers a paradigm for selecting decision strategies.[20] To understand this paradigm, let's track the issue of whether a tract of land should be used for dispersed recreation or mineral extraction. The initial decision is political and occurs in an arena of elected officials. These officials consider the arguments of various interest groups who claim the resource and the social benefits of competing claims. Once they have agreed on values—to recreate or to mine—they can begin to assess management options. A technical, computational solution is possible only if agreement is reached about management parameters. Impact assessment is therefore only possible when there is accord about these parameters. Reviewing them results in a solution upon which all parties agree or as an outcome that must be referred to judicial review. Also, while the identification of impacts associated with specific actions or policies is a sound management practice, it is also a requirement of law.

Assessing the consequences of an action involves identifying a variety of impacts. These can be grouped into two general categories: *environmental impacts* which focus on changes to the physical and biological community as the result of some action or management policy; and *social impacts* which focus on the way actions or management policies affect people (including quality of life).

LEGISLATION AND POLICY

Public involvement in issues of natural resource allocation and management crystallized during the 1960's. Concern over development actions such as the Glen Canyon Dam project on the Colorado River, timber

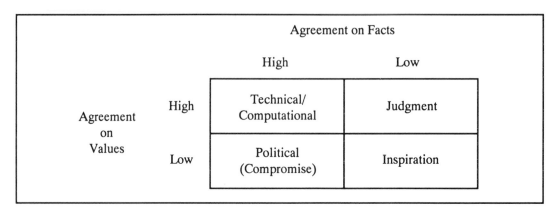

Figure 7-1. Paradigm of decision-making strategies. (from Thompson, J. D., and Tuden, A.)

cutting programs on eastern U.S. Forest Service lands, and large-scale water projects such as the Tennessee-Tombigbee Waterway and the Cross-Florida Barge Canal led to the passage of the National Environmental Policy Act (PL 91-190), commonly referred to as NEPA. The philosophy for NEPA is stated in Title I of the act:

> It is the . . . policy of the Federal Government . . . to use all possible means and measures . . . to create and maintain conditions under which man and nature can exist in productive harmony, and fulfill the social, economic and other requirements of present and future generations of Americans.[11]

NEPA requires a systematic, interdisciplinary approach to integrating the natural and social sciences, along with the environmental design arts, in planning and making decisions which might affect the environment. NEPA also requires that unquantified environmental amenities and values be weighed on balance with technical and economic considerations, and that a detailed statement report the impact of a proposed action along with possible alternatives. This report, known as an environmental impact statement (EIS), has a specific requirement for an environmental impact assessment (EIA) and a social impact assessment (SIA), and must be developed in a manner to assure public involvement.

Further, NEPA requires that all associated impacts be identified and considered as part of the allocation and management decision-making process (see Figure 7-2, p. 96). NEPA tells the agency that it must be comprehensive and consider all factors, but gives no directives as to how this monumental task

is to be accomplished. Additional legislation such as the Clean Air Act, the Clean Water Act, and the Mining Reclamation Act establish similar impact evaluation requirements and established parameters for defining resource quality, but offer little guidance for the affected agencies.

To assure compliance with the wishes of Congress, Title H of NEPA provides for the establishment of a Council on Environmental Quality in the executive branch of government. Regulations developed by the President's Council on Environmental Quality (CEQ) for implementing NEPA offer some procedural direction for conducting impact analysis and producing the necessary documentation. [15] The initial phase of an impact analysis is developing an environmental assessment (EA).

The EA briefly reports evidence based upon existing information about the severity and types of impacts, including areas where effects may be unknown. The EA is used to determine if the impacts are of a sufficient nature to merit a detailed analysis and the preparation of a complete environmental impact statement (EIS). If the EA determines that they are of a significant nature, the agency initiates a complete EIS.

In general, these procedures call for a process known as "scoping" in which interested parties, including affected agencies, are brought together to define the proposed actions and identify possible areas of impact. The scoping phase of impact assessment defines the kind, depth, and intensity of the environmental analysis required to address possible consequences (see Figure 7-3, p. 97).

Few impact analyses proceed beyond the preparation of an EA. For example, in 1980 the U.S. Forest Service prepared almost 13,000 EA's and only 111 EIS's.[8] Critics of the process have argued that EA's have been

Figure 7-2. The absence of impacts is not required for a project to be undertaken. NEPA requires that impacts be identified and considered, and public interests be accounted for. The impact of these elements on this Olympic Pennisula stream (WA) was not considered important. (Photo by B. W. Twight)

prepared without adequately addressing possible social and environmental consequences and further, that initial environmental assessments have been used to undermine the intent of NEPA by providing a thinly veiled rationale for proceeding with projects without adequately considering public interests.

Sometimes, however, agency decisions not to prepare a full EIS have been overturned in court, and the court has required the preparation of the statement. Criticism of this process usually centers on what constitutes major impacts, how well "reasonable" alternatives are developed, and the extent to which the public's interests are considered. But regardless of these criticisms, NEPA remains

the most effective tool for ascertaining the desires of public and special-interest groups which, prior to NEPA, had difficulty voicing concern over public land-management programs.

NEPA continues to be defined through judicial review.* While a great deal of variation exists in case findings, a few general themes have surfaced. First, the courts are

*A summary of the pertinent case is presented in *The Law of Parks, Recreation Resources, and Leisure Services*, by A. N. Frakt and J. S. Rankin.[14] The text includes the Clean Water Act and the roles special-interest groups have played in presenting court actions.

Figure 7-3. Development of recreational facilities in a national recreation area may require an EIS, even though the land is in private ownership. Sawtooth National Recreation Area, Sawtooth National Forest, ID. (Photo by B. W. Twight)

reluctant to give broad interpretations of NEPA requirements. However, they have been willing to specify the roles of various agencies in oversight of granting permits. For example, a recent case involving modification to wetlands established that the U.S. Army Corps of Engineers has permit review authority for modifications to wetlands with areas greater than one acre. In addition, the court clarified the definition of "wetlands" as lands with flora cover typically found on saturated soils. The presence of open water is not required.

The courts have also established the need to thoroughly consider all possible alternatives to proposed projects. This has been referred to as the "hard look" doctrine.[10] Other points of judicial review have centered upon whether public interests are adequately considered. This places considerable pressure upon managers to assure full public participation and increases the importance of the manager as a mediator of competing claimant interest. Thus, it becomes important for managers to involve the public in establishing the guidelines under which an area will be operated. For example, forest managers can involve the public in establishing ROS "anchor points," (see Chapter 3), which are used to govern access and define appropriate activities in specific resource settings. Today public land managers are custodians of access.

A SYSTEMS APPROACH TO IMPACT ASSESSMENT

You should not undertake an environmental impact assessment without first defining a system of variables and associated relationships that are important to understanding the problem. Unfortunately you can usually identify hundreds of variables and thousands of relationships to describe even the most simple system. Reducing any system to a workable model is necessary before you undertake an assessment or environmental impact study. The difficulty in developing a workable model centers on sifting all possible variables to arrive at a parsimonious set that describes the problem and setting. Successful assessment of environmental and social impacts begins with a clear description of the resource setting to be affected and a clear description of the actions likely to cause the change.

Imagine assessing the impact of running a highway through a forest. We may be concerned with alterations to the physical environment and have to assess variables along the route such as soil identification (fragility, productivity, depth to bedrock and type); slope and aspect; presence of water; amount of earth to be removed or relocated; presence of rare or endangered flora and fauna; amount of biomass removal; and habitat classification. (Your own list may be even more inclusive.)

Now consider how the highway may affect the social qualities of the forest. We may speculate that the following variables are important here: noise, traffic levels, proximity to backcountry areas, number of existing trails, location of trails, number of visitors,

type of visitors, attitudes of current visitors (here we could list many specific items), visibility from promontories, and breaks in the natural vista. (Again, your list may be different.)

Proponents of the highway project may also wish to include variables such as driving time between selected destination points, economic return to local communities, local land values, traffic levels on existing proximal highways, and cost of alternative routes. Various claimants will have their own way of describing the situation.

As the list of variables grows, the complexity of assessment grows. The number of potential relationships among variables is the number of variables squared. Thus a system with only fifteen may have as many as two hundred twenty-five relationships to be considered. And a system with twenty may have as many as four hundred! Our task of understanding even simple systems soon becomes enormous; consequently, it is not technically feasible to fully evaluate all of the interactions caused by proposed alterations to natural systems. Instead we must rely on procedures and models which systematically sift out a set of critically important variables and relationships which can be used to assess impacts. To work, this model must have the consensus of those natural resource claimants or users who are, or may be, affected by proposed actions. It must also have the rigor to withstand judicial review.

Intuitively, we may believe that decisions for allocating resources are human judgments. While we may use a technical solution to legitimize a specific conclusion, final decisions are based upon the wisdom of experience. Yet as G. A. Miller points out, the capacity of humans to process information is extremely limited.[16] Their limits in understanding interactions, according to Miller, are about seven relationships, plus or minus two. In other words, a brilliant manager can understand a system that has a maximum of nine possible interactions. Since the number of possible paired interactions in a system is the number of variables in the system squared, the brilliant manager can understand the relationships in a system with only three variables.

Thus, when faced with complex multidimensional choices, people naturally devise "simplifying strategies" and sacrifice a lot of information as they follow some easy road to a decision.[18] Most of these adaptations involve the creation of good/bad evaluation criteria and often result in suboptimal choices in difficult situations. The creation of such valuation scales often tends to characterize situations that are uncertain or that introduce change as "bad." Yet change and uncertainty are among the realities which managers are facing and will continue to face.

By definition, change means moving away from the status quo. Whether induced by socioeconomic forces, shifting cultural mores, or legislative initiatives, change may cause the manager to focus on reactions to its effects and create conflicts. Often these conflicts put managers at odds with their public and support groups. Also, the anxiety created by change and conflict results in decreased agency morale—a loss of a sense of mission. Managers may feel they are perceived as part of an "us versus them" problem. This attitude further crystallizes the conflict, polarizes groups, and heightens anxiety.

The circular relationship of change and conflict is compounded by growing social complexity. Complexity is defined as the number of parts in a system. As systems become more intricate, simple truths and conventional wisdom become difficult to identify and enumerate. A feeling of isolation and a sense of "they don't understand" further separates resource managers from their public.[1]

The number of social groups focusing on special, narrow issues is growing. These groups place demands on resource agencies that are becoming more specific and less negotiable. Thus, as previously mentioned, managers may find themselves becoming mediators between special interests and gatekeepers of resources which are sought for often conflicting uses. Special interests often wax and wane with specific issues, so managers must also deal with groups and interests that seemingly appear without notice.

Resource managers are further stressed by having to anticipate probable conflicts. Similarly, the explosive growth of knowledge and the increasing specificity of laws and regulations heighten complexity. Knowledge is cumulative—the more that is learned, the more elements have to be considered when resolving problems. Laws and regulations are likewise cumulative and further increase complexity. As T. M. Bonnicksen points out, all trends seem to indicate that growth in knowledge, growth in referenda and initiatives, and growth in special-interest groups will accelerate into the foreseeable future.[3] The result is increased complexity and greater uncertainty, so it is reasonable to ask if managers can keep pace with increased complexity and uncertainty.

Coping with complexity requires developing management techniques that are not paralyzed by uncertainty. New resource management arrangements must build on the premise—indeed, the fact—that we live in a world of choice rather than determinism. They must provide frameworks for improving decision making when decisions are ultimately based on judgment.

Assessing impact in resource recreation, park management, or environmental planning requires a systems approach which integrates the characteristics of the setting with the expectations and demands of the claimants. T. M. Bonnicksen and R. G. Lee present biosocial systems analysis as "an approach to organizing and tracking interactions between society and its physical environment."[4] The superiority of biosocial systems analysis is its capacity to require thoroughness from a manager and to explicitly state what a resource decision, policy or study emphasizes or ignores.

CROSS-IMPACTS ASSESSMENT PROCESS

T. M. Bonnicksen and R. H. Becker suggest a technique based on biosocial theory, the cross-impact assessment process (CAP), as an effective approach to integrate the interests of a wide array of groups and enhance the quality of management decisions.[5]

CAP was developed from a number of techniques that are collectively referred to as cross-impact analysis. In general, these techniques estimate future changes in a set of variables based on certain hypothetical relationships among the variables. CAP uses a participatory approach and encourages consensus among claimants as to what variables and relationships are critical in assessing specific site impacts. CAP has proven to be a valuable tool for addressing problems for which no clear, indisputable solutions are apparent. By using a participatory approach in the early stages of impact assessment, the beliefs and claims of different interest groups are expressed and considered during policy creation, thus reducing subsequent conflicts.

CAP relies on the judgment of an interdisciplinary group of well-informed individuals. The assumption is that a concise set of variables which adequately define a complex system is not available. Usually three to four independent and interdisciplinary panels of knowledgeable individuals assemble in face-to-face meetings to define the characteristics and the effects of a specific action. Panelists are selected according to their ability to contribute specific knowledge and the breadth of view necessary to integrate that knowledge with the information provided by other panelists.

The first four panels used in the CAP assessment are called *foundation panels*. Each foundation panel should be limited in size to promote the exchange of ideas (about ten to fourteen people). Multiple foundation panels, as opposed to one, decrease the likelihood of excluding important variables. The final panel in this process is referred to as the *capstone panel* because it uses and refines variables identified by the foundation panels. To insure objectivity, you should select panelists to maintain a balance of expertise and public and private organizational affiliation. Examples of types of panel participants used in previous CAP programs include land developers, investment bankers, engineers, planners, ecologists, recreation specialists, biologists, transportation planners, sociologists, area managers, foresters, water-resource specialists, landscape architects, private citizens, and local and state governmental officials.

The first stage in a foundation panel meeting is a brainstorming session to identify variables relevant to potential impact. Each variable added to the list is given a general name, such as land-use, and then made more specific by the assignment of a unit of measure, such as acres-by-type of use. After the variable identification list is completed, panelists are asked to individually select the twenty variables they believe are the most important. These selections are then tallied to provide a list of the top twenty variables which the collective panel believes are associated with a proposed action or program.

Next, the capstone panel uses the variables identified by the foundation panels to select the final set of twenty to thirty critically important ones which represent a core group. These variables define and assess impact on the park or forest area.

The capstone panel also identifies the relationships which link the final set of twenty to thirty variables together to form a system. This panel systematically decides whether or not a relationship exists between each pair of variables. A relationship is considered to exist when one variable is considered, in the judgment of the capstone panel, to have an impact or cause a change in a corresponding variable. In other words the capstone panel determines whether a change in variable X will cause a change in variable Z. After all possible relationships are identified, panelists rate the relative importance of each.

The cross-impact assessment process distills the conventional wisdom and collective judgments of a broad-based group of interested, knowledgeable individuals. Results allow the agency or area manager to analyze possible impacts and develop site-effect management programs. CAP assessment helps managers move from simply listing perceived impacts to their parks to analyzing why something is a threat or impact. Thus the cross-impact assessment process is a qualitative method which develops a consensus on values and facts needed for effective management.

Today's management environment requires a strong bond between those agencies charged with the stewardship of our public natural resources and those groups which claim resources for a variety of uses. CAP provides a framework for improving decision making and policy formulation when decisions and policies are ultimately based on political or judgmental strategies (see Figure 7-1, p. 94). CAP also recognizes the role of compromise in agreeing on the values and facts needed to implement an impact assessment or management plan.

As we look ahead to a future that is being shaped by decisions made today, we should insist that those decisions are based upon the collective judgments of all interested parties and explore ways to collect those qualitative judgments. As P. W. Bridgeman observes, "In my own case, pursuit of operational analysis has resulted in the conviction . . . that it is better to analyze in terms of doings and happenings than in terms of objects or static abstractions."[7]

Today, too many programs start with a "vaporous wish" phrased in eloquent but elusive language. This penchant for stating policies in vague terms leaves further definition and clarification to the implementation process. Yet as R. T. Nakamura[17] states, conflicts erupt when the implementation process gets underway and policies are more clearly defined. Those charged with implementation disagree over what should be done and how; policymakers intervene to reformulate priorities or to shift direction, and the program bogs down in conflict among various interest groups. The breakdown encountered during implementation is rooted in a lack of consensus and a lack of agreement.

Impact assessment and sound resource management are synonymous. The processes used to allocate resources mirror societal values. For land managers to maintain support and trust they must exercise their stewardship in a manner congruent with the expectations of society. Actions which appear capricious will be challenged. As much as any technical values derived from a systematic approach to resource management, consensus-building and constituent development must be part of strategic management. The techniques suggested in this chapter and throughout this text will help facilitate that goal.

SELECTED READINGS

1. Becker, R. H., Dottavio, F. D., and Bonnicksen, T. M. 1985. "Conventional Wisdom and Qualitative Assessment." In Wood (ed.). *Proceedings 1985 National Outdoor Recreation Trends Symposium 11,* Vol. I pp. 80-88. USDI, National Park Service, Southeast Regional Office, Atlanta, GA.

2. Blomquist, R. F. 1989. "Supplemental Environmental Impact Statements Under NEPA: A Conceptual Synthesis and Critique of Existing Legal Approaches to Environmental and Technological Changes," *Temple Environmental Law & Technology Journal, 8* (Fall): 1.

3. Bonnicksen, T. M. 1985. "Initial Decision Analysis (IDA): A Participatory Approach for Developing Resource Policy." *Environmental Management 9*:379-392.

4. Bonnicksen, T. M., and Lee, R. G. 1982. "Biosocial Systems Analysis: An Approach for Assessing the Consequences of Resource Policies." *Journal of Environmental Management, 15*:47-61.

5. Bonnicksen, T. M., and Becker, R. H. 1983. "Environmental Impact Studies: An Interdisciplinary Approach for Assigning Priorities." *Environmental Management, 7*:109-117.

6. Boulding, K. E. 1961. *The Image.* 175 pp. Ann Arbor, MI: The University of Michigan Press.

7. Bridgeman, P. W. 1959. *The Way Things Are.* Cambridge, MA: Harvard University Press.

8. Bryan, H., and Hendee, J. C. 1981. "Social Impact Assessment in the United States Forest Service and Other Resource Management Agencies." Paper presented at the International Union of Forest Research Organizations (IUFRO) meeting, Kyoto, Japan, Sept.

9. Burch, W. R., Jr., and DeLuca, D. R. 1984. *Measuring the Social Impact of Natural Resource Policies,* Albuquerque, NM: University of New Mexico Press.

10. Coggins, G. C., and Wilkinson, C. F. 1987. "The National Environmental Policy Act," pages 321-356 in Coggins & Wilkinson, *Federal Public Land and Resources Law,* Mineola, NY: Foundation Press.

11. Council on Environmental Quality. 1986. *Regulations for Implementing the Procedural Provisions of the National Environmental Policy Act,* reprint of 40CFR Parts 1500-1508, July 1, 1986. Washington, DC: U.S. Government Printing Office.

12. Egler, F. 1983. Comments made at a wildlife ecology lecture, University of Wisconsin-Madison WI, Oct.

13. Everhardt, G., Becker, R. H., and Dottavio, F. D. 1983. "Assessing Encroachments: A Public Participation Approach." Res. Report, USDI National Park Service, Atlanta, GA., 39 pp.

14. Frakt, A. N. and Rankin, J. S. 1982. *The Law of Parks, Recreation, and Leisure Services.* Salt Lake City, UT: Brighton Publishing Co.

15. Jain, R. K., Urban, L. V., and Stacey, G. S. 1980. 2nd ed., *Environmental Impact Analysis, A New Dimension in Decision Making.* New York, NY: Van Nostrand Reinhold Co.

16. Miller, G. A. 1956. "The Magical Number Seven, Plus or Minus Two: Some Limits on Our Capacity for Processing Information." *The Psychological Review 63*:81-97.

17. Nakamura, R. T. 1981. "Strategies for Defining Policy During Implementation." pp. 113-134. In *Research in Public Policy Analysis and Management.* J. P. Crecine, (ed.). Greenwich, CT: JAI Press, Inc.

18. Shepard, R. N. 1964. "On Subjectively Optimum Selection Among Multi-attribute Alternatives." pp. 257-281. In *Human Judgment and Optimality.* Shelly, & Bryan (eds.). New York, NY: John Wiley & Sons.

19. Stevens, S. S. 1962. "Mathematics, Measurement, and Psychophysics," in *Handbook of Experimental Psychology.* S. S. Stevens, (ed.). New York, NY: John Wiley & Sons. Stevens, Ed. New York, NY: John Wiley & Sons.

20. Thompson, J. D. and Tuden, A. 1959. "Strategies, Structures and Processes of Organizational Decision," in J. D. Thompson et al., (eds.), *Comparative Studies in Administration,* Pittsburgh, PA: The University of Pittsburgh Press.

21. U.S. Bureau of Reclamation. 1990. *National Environmental Policy Act Handbook,* 2nd ed., Denver, CO: U.S. Department of the Interior, the Bureau.

22. Weinberg, G. M. 1975. *An Introduction to General Systems Thinking.* 279 pp. New York, NY: John Wiley & Sons.

23. Zimmerman, E. W. 1951. *World Resources and Industries.* New York, NY: Harper Bros.

CHAPTER 8

Site Management

Protection and renovation are necessary to maintain aesthetic and environmental values associated with developed sites. Trails, backcountry campsites, and other areas can potentially deteriorate if concentrations of recreationists gather there. Site protection means that positive management action reduces the effects of human use, or increases the site's resilience. It is important to correlate future management strategy with the site planning process so that you can protect site values through either proper design, or well-organized management strategies that work within the limits of the design (Figure 8-1).

Site renovation focuses on rehabilitating a deteriorated site. It can be a fallowing process which allows the site to recover naturally, or it can be an active process in which specific treatments speed up recovery (Figure 8-2, p. 106).

The well-managed site is one that is properly selected through the area planning process to provide a particular recreational opportunity and reduce possible environmental degradation. It is designed to fit the natural lay of the land, yet accommodate the normal behavioral patterns of visitors. Management strategies developed in accordance with the variables of site location, resource qualities, and expected use patterns protect the site after its development while complementing the normal use. They are also contingent on uncontrollable environmental conditions, which may cause the manager to periodically adjust his or her strategies according to seasonal conditions.

Program options available to the manager depend on where the particular site (anchor point) lies on the recreation opportunity spectrum. This is determined during the area planning (resource allocation) process. Actual site design also depends on the anchor point and the ability of a particular site to sustain the anticipated type and level of recreational use. The site absorbs recreational use in predictable ways, which you can plan for in initial management programs. However, aberrations can occur which are only detected through continuous monitoring. One significant kind of behavior is vandalism, which occurs out of ignorance or maliciousness (see Chapter 15). Use patterns and impacts may also be different than originally predicted. Strategies to counteract these effects can range from deliberate nonaction to stabilization at present conditions, rejuvenation of degraded sites, and restoration to former conditions.

In sum, site management is first and foremost a function of proper site location. Without this, you can spend inordinate amounts of money to maintain acceptable

Site Management is: f
{
Site Location
Site Design
Recreation Use Patterns
Environmental Conditions
Management Programs

Figure 8-1. Functions in proper site management.

Figure 8-2. The need for site protection and management is more obvious on the intensively used sites. North Cascades National Park. (Photo by B. W. Twight)

conditions. Even then the results may be less than satisfactory to the clientele being served. Whatever programs are needed to maintain ground cover and aesthetics, minimizing aberrations should be a crucial part of your basic commitment to the site. Monitoring indicates the success of these programs and the need to adjust management strategies over time.

CONCEPTS RELATED TO SITE MANAGEMENT

There are three concepts that we should consider before looking at specific management program options:

1. *Durability of the site is important.* Durability refers to the ability of the site to sustain itself under recreational use. The more durable sites are the ones where, if the RO is compatible, use should be encouraged. The durability can be related to ground vegetation, soil conditions, or topography. Given the opportunity, you would focus on the better soils—high organic matter and less erodible. Obviously if you tip the site up to increase topographic relief, you increase the forces of water and the probability of erosion. Within the constraints of the soil and topographic characteristics, the real focus is on the maintenance of ground vegetation. Thus, while the area plan may identify the better locations for a given site, the resource

management prescription within the plan should address the vegetation management within those topographic constraints.

2. Deterioration of vegetation is faster than recovery. Under typical site conditions, the initial, light use causes the greatest impact on ground cover. Additional use causes impact but at a much lower rate.[13] The recovery from this use is typically slow unless reasonably intensive site management programs are implemented immediately. Since the initial light use causes the greatest impact immediately and recovery time is much slower, the manager needs to implement some programs even before use is encouraged on the site. The reason for this is that while mechanical damage may cause direct impact to the vegetation, the more subtle impacts that cause lasting damage often go unnoticed until the ground vegetation is destroyed.

Moderate soil compaction at the surface reduces water infiltration and robs the vegetation of needed moisture. While the percent ground cover may remain essentially unchanged, the species composition may be changing dramatically to favor the drought-hardy plant species. These species are more fragile and thus more easily damaged by recreational use. Ideally we would monitor species composition and use indicator species to tell us that deterioration is underway. However, we typically use general monitoring of percent ground cover, without regard for changing species composition. Two ideas come to mind, if maintenance of ground cover is important: management programs need to be implemented before the use, and where feasible, new, more-hardy ground cover species need to be considered.

3. Resilience of species is important. Some plants are more resilient to recreational use than others.[13] Resilience is the ability to recovery after the use is removed. While some of the lack of resilience can be traced to changing environmental conditions (e.g., a long drought), there are natural differences in resilience among species. We can take advantage of these differences to encourage or discourage certain species, or introduce exotic vegetation. Care must be taken in selecting sites for exotic vegetation as such vegetation can often outcompete native plants to the point of destroying desirable plant associations. Even then, introduction should be limited to the high-density, road-access sites and some sites at the roaded/roadless interface. The extreme primitive end of the spectrum should be avoided to protect the genetic integrity and natural appearance of the site.

BASIC MANAGEMENT STRATEGIES

There are six possible basic strategies for managing recreational sites:

1. Leave Open, Culturally Treat. This is probably the most ideal situation—keeping the site open to public use while implementing some cultural program to maintain ground vegetation and soils. While this may be possible in cases of minimum deterioration, often symptoms of overuse are not evident until major deterioration has occurred. The site sustains heavy use with little external change in other than the species composition of its ground vegetation until it reaches a threshold at which rapid deterioration usually occurs. At that point, it is almost impossible to implement a "leave open and culturally treat" policy except on the most naturally productive, stable sites. It is simply not feasible to reclaim the site under those conditions.

The only effective way to implement this policy is on a regular basis, scheduled well before the threshold of site durability is reached. This means that each site should be thoroughly analyzed to determine the factors that may limit use, such as heavy soil, species composition, soil moisture, and soil nutrients, and that managers solve these problems through specific cultural treatment programs designed for each site. If soil moisture is a limiting factor in maintaining the vigor of vegetation during the heavy use season, it may be necessary to establish an irrigation program, perhaps during low-use periods early in the week. Under these arrangements, light periodic applications are really preventative rather than remedial.

Ideally, we attempt to prevent the problems of overuse and then respond with remedial programs if preventive measures fail. The final decision is based on economics. Often it is more difficult to convince a superior that preventive programs are necessary when there are no external signs of deterioration than it is to justify higher expenditures later to reclaim a worn-out site. In the future, emphasis may fall on preventive measures, which are probably the best choice in the long run for maintaining recreational opportunities, least cost, environmental protection, and efficiency of management.

2. Close, Natural Recovery. If a state shows deterioration from recreational use, we can always consider closing the site and allowing the ground vegetation to rejuvenate itself. The recovery of most recreational sites is slow since recreational use is often relegated to areas that are poorer in terms of natural productivity. Thus, when these sites are in the earlier stages of deterioration, we should predict certain results and close the area at that point, allowing more rapid recovery. This strategy is very appropriate for heavily used sites in wilderness areas, that must be allowed to recover naturally. You should also consider redesigning trail systems to encourage concentrations of use elsewhere. Heavily used developed sites, however, are generally auto-oriented and difficult to close without the loss of a significant recreational opportunity and a tremendous public outcry. Therefore merely closing a site, allowing it to recover naturally, is not an advisable alternative except under specific conditions.

3. Close and Culturally Treat. In this approach, the overused site is closed to public use and certain cultural treatments are introduced to speed recovery. These treatments may include the introduction of exotic species, soil aeration, and fertilization. Closing off the area is necessary if the treatment causes undue inconvenience to visitors, if visitors disrupt the treatment, or if the site does not fully recover while use continues.

Close-and-treat is an especially appropriate strategy for heavily deteriorated sites. It allows maximum recovery while minimizing recovery time and inconvenience to the visitor. Remember, however, to correlate appropriate information programs with any site closing so that people can understand what is being done. If at all possible, make alternate opportunities available to the public.

4. Rest and Rotate. In this program, additional sites are developed so that sufficient facilities are still available when other areas are closed for rejuvenation. This means that certain sites can be "rested" to encourage recovery and rotated on a regular schedule. Some managers are very receptive to this strategy and have tried to implement it in their own administrative units; however, most areas are not planned and developed in such a way as to allow rest and rotation. Often, what is described as a rest-and-rotation program is really a closure program, as described in strategies 2 and 3. This greatly reduces an area's capacity to handle normal visitor loads. Also, rest and rotation, particularly in more primitive portions of the recreational opportunity spectrum, often do not work because deterioration is typically more rapid than recovery and there is little opportunity for intensive programs. The exception would be where alternative sites are more environmentally stable than the original ones, thus one can wait longer for the recovery. All of this assumes that the alternate sites are reasonable substitutes; otherwise an intensive enforcement program is mandated.

5. Hardening the Site. Hardening the site to sustain a higher-than-normal level of use is an option which can take two forms: the introduction of exotic plants (if permitted by policy) that can sustain themselves under particular heavy-use conditions, or surfacing high-use areas. Planting exotic ground vegetation is a viable choice where the site-specific effects of the particular species is known and no impact can be anticipated beyond the site. However, you must consider the economics of introducing and maintaining exotic species, the potential for spreading new diseases and noxious weeds, and the effects on the gene pool.

Surfacing, while it alters the environmental setting, can be made to blend with the requirements of the particular opportunity. On extremely heavy soils where use and precipitation levels are high, paving may be the only reasonable answer, particularly if other soil conditions are neither available nor suitable for development in the general area, or recreational use cannot be diverted to more suitable sites during high-moisture periods.

A more desirable solution may be to surface these high-use areas with other materials, such as gravel or coarse sand. This helps reduce compaction and retard erosion by encouraging water infiltration; it also tends to be more aesthetically pleasing. In moderate-use areas, you can use wood chips with a similar effect. In heavily used portions of a site—like around the picnic table—a reduced amount of erosion and dust is probably the best we can hope for. Plants simply do not survive in those conditions.

The implication here is that the problem should really be eliminated in initial site planning by properly surfacing known or suspected heavy-use areas. Certainly resurfacing on a periodic basis is necessary to check sheet erosion and dusty conditions and to maintain the tread surface; however, it is impossible to eliminate the dust problem that occurs with many medium-to fine-textured soils. Light watering and even some chemicals may help, but too much moisture while recreational use is high can cause severe compaction and surface erosion—the problem that surfacing was supposed to eliminate in the first place.

Remember, too, that some sites are supposed to be hard to accommodate an activity, a mode of travel, etc. Many different materials can be used for surfacing these areas—from wood chips to coarse sand to concrete. Your actual choice depends on use pattern and ROS restrictions. Site developments in the roaded portion of ROS typically feature heavily-used areas that are appropriately hardened to sustain rough treatment. In roadless portions, the decision is not so clear. In zones of easier access with prime attractors, hardening is probably the best answer. But what about the more primitive end of the ROS? While you can argue that surfacing high-use areas in the wilderness is not a viable option, the truth is that in many instances we already have—like the tread of a wilderness trail. Much of the new wilderness in Alaska is suffering from these types of user-impact problems. Do you harden access points along lake shores, gravel-bar landing strips, etc.? Or do you simply live with the consequences of the use patterns?

6. Cut Out, Get Out. In the past we have focused much of our attention in managing public lands on resource uses other than recreation. This has often created a *laissez-faire* approach to recreation management. We have allowed people to do almost anything, anywhere, and the results have often been less than satisfactory—conflict among user groups, resource deterioration, and a general decline in user satisfaction. This is similar to the "cut out, get out" policy of land management a century ago. At that time, the agency or enterprise merely harvested the renewable resource without any consideration for the future. Resources were inexhaustible—or at least we thought so.

In recreation management, some of these philosophies still exist. People seek outdoor recreation experiences on various sites. Yet sometimes, through abuse and overuse, they destroy the very site and opportunity that they so highly value. Their focus is seemingly on the present and not on the future as they destroy one oasis and then move on to another.

Can we afford a *laissez-faire* approach today? The answer has to be no. In view of spiraling demands and diminishing supply, we must protect our existing resources while trying to innovatively increase their use. This does not mean we must rigidly control access to maintain the resource; nevertheless, we must take an active role in managing the site to protect the resource and the opportunity now, ensuring that the site is maintained for future generations.

The "cut out, get out" philosophy will never be formally adopted as modern management policy, but it may become preeminent through benign neglect. The commitment at the time of development is to maintain the site at some acceptable level, yet use patterns and budgets change. Technology can help maintain the site at reduced costs; however, at some point managers may simple have to let the quality of the site slip through benign neglect. Rather than allow a site to die a slow agonizing death so it no longer provides the desired, acceptable recreational opportunity, it should be dispatched. For example, rather than neglecting a series of small family picnic areas because they are so small and scattered, wouldn't it be better to enlarge one or two to handle the load and close the others so you can still provide the opportunity and maintain it within budget limits? Under these circumstances, you must take care in site design so it offers the social intimacy of the smaller sites. Another consideration is the public safety hazards caused by benign neglect. Deferred maintenance on the sites because of budget shortfalls is not a legal defense in the courtroom.

While all the classical strategies are presented and their limitations discussed here, the axiom that deterioration is faster than recovery certainly affects the site management process. The contention is that except on better, more productive sites, recovery is much slower than deterioration, even when combined with specific cultural treatments. This casts doubt on the applicability of management strategies where recovery is extended over a period of time and/or when other sites are going to be affected by the closure of the treated site. While not conclusive, the above suggests that the original site selection process is a preeminent consideration in overall site management. The site should then be designed to handle expected visitor loads and, where necessary, incorporate cultural treatment programs on a regularly scheduled basis from the beginning. All programs must be developed within ROS constraints.

POSSIBLE CULTURAL TREATMENTS

If cultural treatments are to be part of the site-management program, then the manager must choose the proper ones for particular circumstances. There are no universal recommendations because of the tremendous variation that occurs in local situations. Instead, a discussion of possible cultural treatments and their general application follows:

Soil Scarification

Soil scarification is the loosening of the topsoil to reduce compaction, which increases infiltration of water and exposes the maximum amount of mineral soil. This prepares a seedbed, improves soil-moisture conditions, increases soil aeration, and upgrades the physical properties of compacted soil. Scarification seems mandatory for renovating most overused sites in which soils have become compacted, vegetation has been lost, and sheet erosion has taken place. It should be one of the first treatments considered since the effectiveness of some other treatments are dependent upon soil scarification. There are no ROS restrictions on the use of scarification, only on the particular equipment involved.

Degree of scarification depends upon the problems associated with a particular site. To be encouraged, a plant species may not need extensive exposure to mineral soil for germination and survival. Therefore scarification may be light, done with hand tools such as rakes. On the other hand, the soil may be deeply compacted—with an almost total loss of pore space for air and moisture, particularly in the upper six to twelve inches where most root systems are located. This may require mechanical scarification with heavy equipment, such as a tractor disk, to reach the entire compacted area. Even if the deteriorated potion of the site is going to be planted or sodded, it is still advisable to improve the physical properties of the soil by scarifying and leveling.

When you reduce soil clumping caused by compaction, pore space—and consequently, soil aeration—increases. Root respiration depends on the amount of oxygen (O_2) available in the soil. At low oxygen levels, root respiration is reduced. In turn, mineral absorption by roots is directly associated with the level of respiration. Fine-textured soils such as clays may become compacted under heavy recreational use, particularly during periods of extremely high moisture.

Irrigation

Water seems to be a major limiting factor in site renovation.[1] Regardless of other treatments used, irrigation seems mandatory for heavily deteriorated sites. Better results seem to come from watering, fertilization, and seeding, or from watering and seeding. No other treatment or combination of treatments bring significant results in reestablishing ground vegetation without adequate water.

Two types of irrigation are possible— flood and aerial. In flood irrigation, portions of the site are surface-flooded by a ditch system that transports the water. However, the site must be closed during the irrigation period, and flood irrigation is difficult to design where there is much topographic variation. It is seldom used on recreation sites.

Aerial irrigation is used fairly extensively on medium- to high-density sites because of the ease of control, flexibility of application, and efficiency of water use. Aerial irrigation systems can be portable or permanently installed, as with an underground sprinkler system. It is easier to direct and control the volume of waterflow using the aerial system, and a portable system allows flexibility in handling local, isolated problems. For permanent sites in which irrigation is done on a continuous basis, an underground system is more efficient and can be regulated so that any portion of it works independently of the rest of the network. It can also be shut down and drained during cold-weather periods.

Some problems associated with irrigation are beyond the immediate concern of improving site conditions. W. G. Beardsley and R. B. Herrington[1] list these as site design, cost, engineering, and public relations. Site design is important so that irrigation can be done with minimum inconvenience to visitors. Unfortunately, long-term management programs are typically not addressed when most sites are planned.

If you decide to use irrigation as a means of site maintenance or site renovation, you must also face the problem of public relations. You should make people aware of any inconveniences and offer an explanation so that people understand the need for the irrigation program. If a site is closed, there should ideally be information available on an alternate site. Good public relations through a strong, positive, information program make people aware of the situation and of the action being taken (see Chapter 12).

Fertilization

Fertilization implies adding commercial fertilizers to the soil to improve plant growth. Too often, managers use some standard fertilizer mix (N-P-K, plus some micronutrients) without understanding the deficiencies of the soil. Proper fertilization requires some knowledge of soil chemistry. Most states have a soil-testing laboratory to examine specific nutrient deficiencies in the local soils and to make recommendations for correcting them. These deficiencies must be related to the plant species that you wish to grow since each species has different nutritional requirements and levels of tolerance for specific mineral elements.

Nitrogen, phosphorus, and potassium are the primary elements used in fertilizers; other macronutrients necessary for plant growth are calcium, magnesium, and sodium. Required micronutrients include sulfur, manganese, iron, boron, copper, zinc, and molybdenum. Symptoms of deficiencies in any of these elements may show up in the vegetation. However, the real problem may turn out to be the pH of the soil; at a given pH, some elements are not readily available in a usable form. For example, below a pH of 4.7, tree seedlings, particularly the more fastidious, deciduous species, suffer from a low availability of nitrogen, phosphorous, potassium, or other bases. An alkaline pH (above 7.0) may decrease the availability of phosphates, iron, boron, zinc, and manganese. If we consider both nutritional and biological needs, the desirable soil pH for coniferous species is around 5.0, although some healthy stands may have a somewhat lower pH. For deciduous species, the desirable range is nearer 5.7 to 6.5.[29]

Vegetation

Exotic vegetation can be used as a surfacing material, or to stabilize soil or improve aesthetics. Due to variations in climate and individual site conditions, there are no universally recommended species. State highway departments, agricultural experiment stations, and horticulture/gardening centers are usually good sources of information on local adaptability of species. For turf grasses, see Chapter 9.

Thinning

This will be discussed in more detail in Chapter 9. It is, however, important to recognize the potential for improving the growth and vigor of ground vegetation by removing shade and root competition. Usually this treatment, if needed, is done in conjunction with one or more of the above treatments.

MONITORING VISITOR EFFECTS ON THE SITE

You can use several techniques to monitor the effects of recreational use—line transects, milacre plots, and photo files. Always monitor from a permanent point so that you can obtain repeated measures over time. The line transect method is especially useful for measuring change not only in percentage of ground cover but also species composition. A more detailed discussion of this technique can be found in any applied ecology text.

The milacre plot method is commonly used to measure both the change in vigor and the percentage of ground cover. Permanent plots (6.6 feet square) are established in medium-to-heavy-use, light-use, and zero-use zones of sites and are measured at regular intervals. The zero-use zone is usually an isolated place located adjacent to the site and within the same vegetation type. This zone gives you an estimate of vegetative changes not directly influenced by recreational use— a form of ecological yardstick. In the medium-to-high-use zone (the primary recreational portion of the designed site), you can determine the extent of change in ground vegetation and thus plan needed management programs. Measuring the light-use zone should indicate overflow effects from the main portion of the site. Determine the number of sets of plots you need by the variability of site vegetation and use patterns. A set of plots is three—one for each zone.

The photo-file technique is merely photorecording vegetational changes from permanent photo points with a standard camera mount. The technique is extremely valuable in cases where you are primarily interested in changes in the percentage of ground cover at particular locations. With all of the techniques available, exercise care to protect permanent points from careless destruction by users or the data will not be comparable.

Look for indicator species to better understand what is happening to the site before actual loss of vegetation. This barometer can help in deciding on specific treatment and timing. Timing can be everything. Without knowing exactly when to start a treatment, it is probably better to implement such treatments as normal practices when the site is first opened to recreational use.

SELECTED READINGS

1. Beardsley, W. G., and Herrington, R. B. 1971. "Economics and Management Implications of Campground Irrigation-A Case Study." U.S. Forest Service Research Note INT-129.

2. Beardsley, W. G., and Wagar, J. A. 1971. "Vegetation Management on a Forested Recreation Site." *Journal of Forestry 69*:728.

3. Bockheim, J. B. 1990. "Forest Soils," Chapter 4 in R. A. Young & R. L. Giese, eds., *Introduction to Forest Science,* 2nd ed., New York, NY: John Wiley & Sons.

4. Burden, R. F., and Randerson, P. F. 1972. "Quantitative Studies on the Effects of Human Trampling on Vegetation as an Aid to the Management of Semi-Natural Areas. *Journal of Applied Ecology, 9*(2):439.

5. Carey, J. B. 1965. "The Use of Soil Surveys in Making Engineering Studies in Recreation Areas." Northeast Fish and Wildlife Conference. Harrisburg, PA

6. Cieslinski, T. J., and Wagar, J. A. 1970. "Predicting the Durability of Forest Recreation Sites in Northern Utah-Preliminary Results." U.S. Forest Service Research Note INT-117.

7. Cole, D. N. 1981. "Managing Ecological Impacts at Wilderness Campsites: An Evaluation of Techniques." *Journal of Forestry 79*(2):86-89.

8. Cole, D. N., and Ranz, B. 1983. "Temporary Campsite Closures in the Selway-Bitterroot Wilderness." *Journal of Forestry, 81*(11):729-732.

9. Cole, D. N., and Schreiner, E. G. 1981. "Impacts of Backcountry Recreation: Site Management and Rehabilitation-An Annotated Bibliography." USDA-Forest Service General Technical Report INT-121.

10. Echelberger, H. E. 1971. "Vegetative Changes at Adirondack Campgrounds 1964 to 1969." U.S. Forest Service Research Paper NE-142.

11. Feucht, J. R. 1988. *Landscape Management, Planning, and Maintenance of Trees, Shrubs, and Turfgrasses.* New York, NY: Van Nostrand-Reinhold.

12. Gangstad, E. O. 1988. *Recreation Resource Management.* New York, NY: St. Martin Press, Inc.

13. Harper, J. C., II. 1963. "Growing Turf Under Shaded Conditions." Pennsylvania State University Agricultural Extension Special Circular 149. State College, PA.

14. Hammitt, W. E., and Cole, D. N. 1987. *Wildland Recreation: Ecology and Management.* New York, NY: John Wiley & Sons.

15. Helgath, S. F. 1975. "Trail Deterioration in the Selway-Bitterroot Wilderness." U.S. Forest Service Research Note INT-193.

16. Herrington, R. B., and Beardsley, W. G. 1970. Improvement and Maintenance of Campground Vegetation in Central Idaho. U.S. Forest Service Research Paper INT-87.

17. Hendee, J. C., Stankey, G. H., and Lucas, R. C. 1990. *Wilderness Management* (Chapter 16). Golden, CO: North American Press.

18. Jemison, G. M. 1967. "Impacts of Recreation on the Ecology of Temperate North American Forests." Proceedings Tenth Technical Meeting International Union for the Conservation of Nature (Lucerne, Switzerland, 1966) 7(1):185.

19. Jolliff, G. D. 1969. Campground Site-Vegetation Relationships. Ph.D. Dissertation (unpub.). Colorado State University, Ft. Collins, CO.

20. Kuss, F. R., Graefe, A. R., and Loomis, L. 1985. "Plant and Soil Responses to Wilderness Recreation: A Synthesis of Previous Research." Proceedings National Wilderness Research Conference: Current Research USDA-Forest Service General Technical Report INT-212.

21. Kuss, F. R., Graefe, A. R., and Vaske, J. J. 1987. Visitor Impact Management (Vol. 1): A Review of Research. Washington, DC: National Parks and Conservation Association.

22. LaPage, W. F. 1967. Some Observations on Campground Trampling and Ground Cover Response. U.S. Forest Service Research Paper NE-68.

23. MacKie, D. K. 1966. "Site Planning to Reduce Deterioration." Proceedings, Society of American Foresters, p. 33.

24. Magill, A. W. 1970. Five California Campgrounds . . . Conditions Improving After Five Years of Rercreational Use. U.S. Forest Service Research Paper PSW-62.

25. Miller, R. 1988. *Urban Forestry: Planning and Managing Urban Vegetation.* New York, NY: Prentice Hall, Inc.

26. McEwen, D., and Tocher, S. R. 1976. "Zone Management: Key to Controlling Recreational Impact in Developed Campsites." *Journal of Forestry 74*(2):90.

27. Partain, L. E. 1966. "The Use of Soil Knowledge in Recreation Area Planning," Virginia Polytechnic Institute, Agricultural Extension Bulletin 301, p. 180.

28. Pigram, R. E. 1983. *Outdoor Recreation and Resource Management.* New York, NY: St. Martin Press, Inc.

29. Pritchett, W. L. 1987. *Properties and Management of Forest Soils,* New York, NY: John Wiley & Sons.

30. Ranz, B. 1979. "Closing Wilderness Campsites: Visitor Use Problems and Ecological Recovery in the Selway-Bitterroot Wilderness, Montana." MS Thesis (unpublished). University of Montana, Missoula, MT.

31. Reckman, R. W., Letey, J., and Stolzy, L. H. 1966. "Compact Subsoil Can Be Harmful to Plant Growth." *Parks and Recreation. 43*(2):334.

32. Ripley, T. H. 1962. "Tree and Shrub Response to Recreational Use." U.S. Forest Service Research Note SE-171.

33. Rudolph, P. O. 1967. "Silviculture for Recreation Area Management," *Journal of Forestry* 65:385.

34. Stevens, M. E. 1966. "Soil Surveys as Applied to Recreation Site Planning." *Journal of Forestry 64*(3): 14.

35. Tocher, S. R., Wagar, J. A., and Hunt, J. D. 1965. "Sound Management Prevents Worn Out Recreation Sites." *Journal of Forestry 63*(3):151.

CHAPTER 9

Turf Management

Too often we may overlook turf management because we feel it is applicable only in special situations, primarily in the modem portion of ROS. In reality, we all are involved in some form of turf management—whether stabilizing cut and fills, hardening a site for recreational use, or overseeing a special area such as a golf green (Figure 9-1). The objectives of a turf management program vary according to the needs of the particular recreational opportunity, but success depends on both analysis of local conditions and strategies that meet these conditions.

The basic systems that affect turf development are soil, climate, microclimate, and use. Soil is the medium in which grass seeds germinate, establish a root system, and grow through absorption of water and minerals. The physical properties (depth, texture, structure, organic matter) and chemical properties (exchange capacity, available nutrients, pH) of the soil determine the natural productivity of the site and thus its potential and limitations. It may be possible to adjust some of these factors to increase productivity and sod maintenance on a particular site.

Figure 9-1. Recreational turf management can involve golf course restoration and care. (Photo by B. W. Twight)

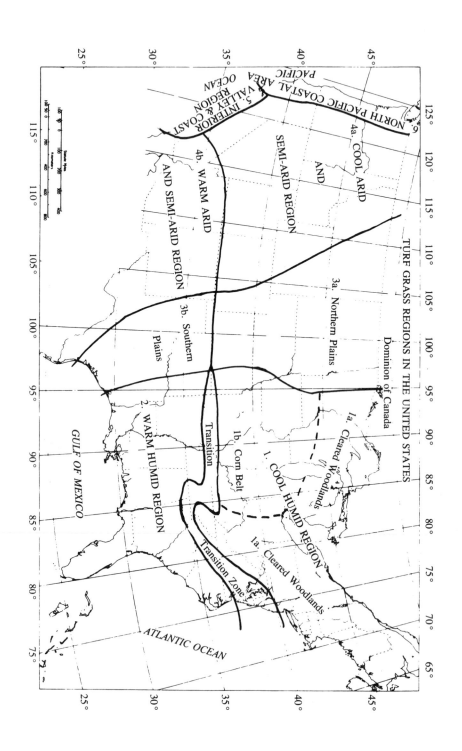

Figure 9-2. Major turf grass zones in the United States. (From Sprague, H. B. 1982. *Turf Management Handbook*. 3rd Edition. Danville, IL: The Interstate, p. 30)

Climate also affects the potential for turf development. Temperature and precipitation directly influence level of turf maturation, adaptability of species to edaphic conditions, and relative hardiness of a site after recreation use. Management recommendations for specific regions should be based on species adaptability and growth patterns. For example, if two grasses having different growth patterns are adaptable to a particular site, the one that ceases growth early might be more desirable in relation to a particular pattern of use.

You can alter soil conditions, species composition, and even cultural treatments to produce the desired turf. However, you must ask yourself the following: Is this what we really want to do in terms of particular recreational opportunity? Is it economically feasible? What are the probabilities that the program will succeed and how predictable is the outcome?

REGIONAL REQUIREMENTS

Turf grass species are generally adapted to particular climatic zones; but even within those zones, each species tends to adapt to specific microclimatic conditions. Recommended species and cultural treatments are based on zonal and microclimate variations. The different turf grass regions or zones are shown in Figure 9-2 (p. 118), and associated natural conditions are described in Table 9-1 (p. 121). General species recommendations for cool and warm regions are summarized in Table 9-2 (p. 122) and discussed in the following sections.

Cool Regions

Turf grasses which are best suited to cooler regions are: bluegrasses, bent grasses, fescues, and ryegrasses. Each species has its own particular characteristics, which you should attempt to match to the needs of the site. The following discussion is limited to a few important species, since new varieties are constantly being developed that are superior for specific turf uses. For example, new turf grasses for golf courses require less watering; this conserves the limited amount of water available for that function.

Bluegrasses (Poa). The bluegrasses are the most widely used of the cool-season grasses. They are best adapted for moist, fertile, fine-textured soils within a pH range of 6.0 to 7.0, and respond well to fertilization and irrigation. *Kentucky bluegrass (Poa pratensis)* grows well during cool weather but becomes less vigorous during warm periods. Not shade tolerant, it requires a soil with medium to high fertility, nearly neutral pH, and good water-holding capacity. It is not hardy enough to sustain medium to heavy recreational use without deterioration. *Roughstalk bluegrass (Poa trivalis)* has characteristics similar to those of Kentucky bluegrass, but it is more adapted to moderate shade, particularly in warmer conditions. *Canada bluegrass (Poa compressa),* although not aesthetically pleasing because of its coarse appearance, is drought-resistant and therefore generally used where there are poor soil and low-moisture conditions. *Annual bluegrass (Poa annua),* is shade-tolerant. Owing to its adaptation and profuse seed development, it can germinate and survive on compacted soils as long as the soil is not dry. However, since it tends to die-back during the summer, it is usually used only as a temporary site stabilizer or in a mixture of other grasses.

Fescues (Festuca). Chewing fescue (*Festuca* rubra commutala) is an improved strain of red fescue which adds bright green color to the turf grass mixture and improves wearability of the mixture in recreational areas. Also, it does well in a variety of environmental conditions. *Red fescue (Festuca elatior arundinacea)* is adaptable to a variety of soil-moisture and temperature conditions. It is suitable for sites maintained in a rough, rather than manicured, condition. Cuttings should be no less than four inches in height and then taken only at infrequent intervals. Fertilizing is necessary to maintain high productivity. *Meadow fescue (Festuca elatior)* is a fast-growing yet persistent species that can be valuable in a turf mixture used to establish new sod.

Bent grasses (Agrostis). Creeping bent grass *(Agrostis palustris)* can grow in a variety of environmental conditions except shade. Suitable for golf greens and other closely manicured sites that have regular top dressings, it is not generally effective for lawns. Colonial bentgrass *(Agrostis tenuis),* on the other hand, makes a suitable lawn grass when mixed with bluegrass and fescue. *Velvet bentgrass (Agrostis canina)* has important characteristics like shade tolerance, drought resistance, and ability to survive under varying temperature conditions. This makes it ideal for some specialized sites.

Ryegrass (Lolium). Perennial ryegrass *(Lolium perenne)* is probably the most widely used; in a seed mixture, it rapidly establishes a temporary sod until other grasses eventually take over and form the permanent sod.

Legumes. Although not classified as grasses, legumes are often used with them for site stabilization and soil improvement.

Herbaceous legumes have a taproot with nodules where bacteria fix free nitrogen from the air, enabling the legume and associated grasses to assimilate this nutrient.

Crown vetch (Coronilla varia L.). Crown vetch is a very competitive perennial, eighteen to twenty-four inches high but slow in initial establishment. Therefore it is usually mixed with grasses such as red fescue and ryegrass so that the grasses provide initial cover. Well-adapted to droughty, low-temperature sites, even in infertile, acidic areas such as road cuts, it is best suited for well-drained soils high in calcium, phosphorous, and potassium.[4]

Lespedeza (Lespedeza sp.). Planted on roadsides and other low-use areas for erosion control, Lespedeza is a legume that is primarily effective in the transition between cold and warm-season zones. It is adapted to acidic, low-fertility soils, and is drought resistant.

True Clovers (Trifolium sp.). Clovers, the most widely distributed legume, are suited to cool, humid areas on fairly fertile sites. They are sometimes used as a winter annual in warm humid climates. Drought tolerance is poor. Flowers are produced even at very low cutting heights.

Warm Regions

Most warm-region grasses are established by sprigging; only common Bermuda grass and carpet grass may be established with seeds. Consequently, although a monoculture may tend to be less attractive and less disease-resistant, a single species is generally preferable to a mixture of species. Since most

Table 9-1. Natural soil conditions in the principal turf grass regions.*

Region	Average Rainfall (inches yearly)	Natural Vegetative Cover	Natural Soil Characteristics	
			Topsoil (General Conditions)	Subsoil (General Conditions)
1. *Cool Humid Region*				
A. Cleared woodlands	30 to 50	Mostly forest	Thin, grayish-brown, acid	Yellowish or light gray, heavy textured, strongly acid
B. Corn Belt	30 to 40	Tall grasses	Dark brown, high in humus, slightly to strongly acid	Lighter brown, lower in humus, slightly to moderately acid
2. *Warm Humid Region*	30 to 50	Mostly forest	Thin, grayish to yellow, strongly acid	Strongly red or yellow, heavier textured, strongly acid
3. *Great Plains*				
A. Northern	12 to 30	Short to tall grasses	Brown to dark brown, humus stronger near surface, neutral to alkaline	Brown or lighter colored, little humus, lime nodules present
B. Southern	15 to 30	Short to tall grasses	Reddish brown (except Texas Blacklands), neutral to alkaline	Light reddish brown, heavier textured, lime nodules present
4. *Semi-arid and Arid*				
A. Cool, northern	3 to 12	Sparse grass and shrubs	Light grayish, alkaline	Light grayish, hardpan common, calcareous
B. Warm, southern	3 to 15	Sparse grass and shrubs	Light reddish brown, alkaline	Reddish brown, friable, highly calcareous
5. *California Coast and Interior Valleys*	10 to 20	Grass and shrubs	Dark reddish brown, neutral to alkaline	Reddish brown, some lime present
6. *North Pacific Coastal Area*	30 to 50	Mostly forest	Generally gray or grayish brown, thin, acid	Yellowish or light gray, heavier textured, strongly acid

Special soil conditions:
A. *Alluvial soils:* Found on the flood plains of rivers and lesser water courses. Formed from sediment deposited periodically by water. Often relatively rich in organic matter (if dark colored) and nutrients. Highly variable in texture.
B. *Excessively sandy soils:* Widely distributed. All sands are low in water-supplying power and subject to wind erosion. Generally low in nutrients, and easily leached by rainfall.
C. *Alkali and salty soils:* Occur locally throughout drier regions, wherever internal soil drainage is imperfect. Salty soils mostly occur on coastal plains, where sea or brackish water penetrates.

* From Sprague, H. B. 1982. *Turf Management Handbook.* 3rd Edition. Danville, IL: The Interstate, p. 15.

Table 9-2. Turf grass regions in the United States.*

1. Cool Humid Region
    Suited to cool-season grasses such as bluegrass, fescue and bent grasses. Soils generally acid, and often low in fertility. Sprinkler irrigation desired to supplement rainfall.
    1a. Transition Zone
        A difficult zone, where either cool-season or warm-season grasses may be grown. However, summers are too hot for desired growth of cool-season grasses, and winters are too long and cold for desired growth of warm-season grasses. Supplemental irrigation must be used carefully to encourage the type of grass desired. Soils are generally acid and low in native fertility.
2. Warm Humid Region
    Suited to warm-season grasses such as Bermuda grass and St. Augustine grass. Soils generally strongly acid, and may be relatively infertile. Sprinkler irrigation needed to supplement rainfall.
3. Plains Region
    3a. Northern Plains
        Suited to cool-season grasses, but artificial watering is essential for good lawns. Soils are not naturally acid, and may be well-supplied with mineral nutrients.
    3b. Southern Plains
        Suited to warm-season grasses, and sprinkler irrigation is indispensable for strong turf since it supplements uncertain rainfall. Soils are not naturally acid, but are less likely to be fertile than Northern Plains soils.
4. Arid and Semi-arid Regions
    Suited to cool-season grasses, but sprinkler irrigation must be provided throughout the growing season. Soils are not acid, and are generally well-supplied with mineral nutrients.
    4a. Warm Arid and Semi-arid Regions
        Suited to warm-season grasses, but sprinkler irrigation is imperative throughout the growing season. Soils are not acid, but are somewhat less fertile than regions to the North.
5. California Coast and Interior Valleys
    Suited to warm-season grasses, but sprinkler irrigation is imperative during the warm, dry, growing season. Soils are generally not acid, and contain moderate amounts of mineral nutrients.
6. North Pacific Coastal Areas
    Suited to cool-season grasses. Rainfall generally adequate except in midsummer when sprinkler irrigation is required. Soils are usually acid, and have fair-to-low mineral nutrient content.

* From Sprague, H. B. 1982. *Turf Management Handbook*, 3rd Edition. Danville, IL: The Interstate, p. 4-5.

warm-region species survive in any warm-zone area, it is imperative to select the one most suited to specific edaphic conditions and recreational use.

Common carpet grass (Axonopus affinis). This is common turf grass restricted to the sandy, low-fertility soils and high-moisture conditions of the southeast coastal plains. Carpet grass requires little care after initial establishment.

Common Bermuda grass (Cynodon dacrylon). This species grows well throughout warmer regions when moisture is not limited. It spreads quickly and lives long on any site with fertile, reasonably well-drained soil. As stated by H. B. Sprague,[16] common Bermuda grass has four weaknesses: it is not shade-tolerant; it turns brown with the first light frost; it has a high-fertility requirement and thus may be invaded by other species if not properly fertilized; and it is not very green. Although it has only a moderate tolerance for drought, it is probably the most drought-resistant of all the warm-region grasses.

Hybrid Bermuda grass. Several Bermuda grass hybrids have been developed that are superior to the common species as turf grass. They are usually more vibrant in color and more vigorous in growth, have fewer fertility requirements, and are more disease resistant.

Zoysia grasses (Zoyzia sp.). The zoysia grasses are best suited to warm, humid zones. They tolerate a wide range of soil conditions, except poorly drained areas. Slow to become established, zoysia grasses can nevertheless survive high levels of use once they take root.

St. Augustine grass (Stenotaphrum secundatum). This shade-tolerant grass is adaptable to a variety of soil conditions. It requires frequent fertilization and mowing to maintain vigorous growth. If soils are acidic, liming should be done to raise the pH closer to neutral.

Centipede grass (Eremochloa ophiuroides). This has characteristics similar to those of carpet grass. Centipede grass responds well to fertilization, and can he used to regenerate worn-out sites.

DEVELOPMENT OF TURF

There are two ways of establishing turf—seeding and vegetative planting. Choice of method depends on grass selected for use, site conditions, and anticipated patterns of use.

Seeding. Seeding is usually done in early spring or early fall when temperature and moisture conditions are good. In cool regions, early fall seeding allows reasonable establishment before dormancy. In warm regions, you can usually seed in early spring. However, if moisture is not limited, you can seed at any time.

Seed mixtures are usually planted in cooler regions. The exact mix depends on site conditions and specific recreational use, but it usually includes perennial ryegrass, which quickly occupies a site until the permanent grasses establish a sod.

Seed quality is important and therefore ensured through federal and state laws. Species, purity, and percentage of germination must he shown on the label along with percentage of weed seeds.

After you have obtained the seed, you must prepare a seedbed before planting begins. It is less expensive to install structures such as drain tiles or water bars at this time than after planting. If major reshaping is to be done to the landscape prior to planting, you should carefully remove the topsoil first and then replace it after the reshaping operation. You should also lime, fertilize, and add any organic matter to improve soil conditions prior to planting. Rototill these additives into the soil to a depth of about six inches. The organic matter not only improves soil fertility but also increases its water-holding capacity. For example, if sandy soils are a problem, you can add organic matter and fines to improve waterholding and cation exchange capacity. Since lime and fertilizer are translocated downward, not laterally, surface application of these materials should be uniform prior to rototilling.

Seed immediately after seedbed preparation. Seeding rates, expressed in pounds per acre or pounds per one thousand square feet, are based on species mixture, purity, and percent of germination, and seeds are broadcast evenly over the surface. The seeding technique recommended by Sprague is to divide the seeds into two equal portions.[16] One half is broadcast in one direction, the other half in a line perpendicular to the first half. Lightly rake the seeds into the seedbed, then roll the surface. Finally, lightly but evenly mulch the seedbed with straw.

Vegetative Plantings. You can plant vegetation by sprigging, spot sodding, or complete sodding. All these methods require the same ground preparation as seeding. Each has a preferred use, depending on circumstances, costs, and management objectives.

Complete sodding has often been overlooked because of the supposedly high cost of implementation. Yet cost analyses by a local park district indicate that on an area that is 2.5 acres or less, complete sodding is cheaper than other methods. This study takes into account the following local circumstances: high probability at high altitudes of at least partial failure of seeding; man-hours spent in maintaining constant attention prior to sod establishment; and short growing season.

Site stabilization on steeper slopes and the need to harden heavy-use portions dictate complete sodding. Management concerns should dictate the primary choice if there are sufficient monies to support the program.

In the sprigging method, separate the grass plant into sprigs or runners (pieces of stolons) that are planted to generate new sod. Spread the sprigs evenly over the area by means of a preplanned grid system; then push them into the soil until they approximately reach the root collar. You can use a notched dibble to push the sprigs into the soil. This minimizes damage to the sprig yet still maintains planting efficiency. Finally, press the soil down firmly with the heel of your boot.

You can also plant vegetation by the spot-sodding method, which involves planting small pieces of sod at regular intervals over an entire area. Lift the sod from the nursery and cut it into three-to four-inch squares, then lay them six to twelve inches apart. Make a hole for each piece of sod and plant them about one half inch below surface level, securing them by stamping down with your shoe. As the plant takes hold, it sends out runners.

Usually, spot-sodding and sprigging take a considerable time to root a dense sod. You must water and possibly mow carefully to enhance turf growth and establishment, then you must practice regular turf management.

MANAGEMENT OF TURF

Regular maintenance is essential for most grasses and particularly, for those located in areas of active recreational use. Here we will discuss two important aspects of turf maintenance: soil chemical treatments and cultural treatments of the sod.

Soil Chemical Treatments

Soil-acidity problems generally occur in areas of excessive precipitation or artificial watering. Although some grasses survive these conditions, all grasses grow better at a more neutral pH. One possible treatment to improve soil fertility is liming. For general recommendations on this method, consulting a person who is knowledgeable about local conditions, such as the county agent or soil conservationist, may suffice. In high precipitation areas, one to two tons of crushed limestone per acre should be sufficient to promote good sod development. However, soil analysis by a competent laboratory is the most accurate guideline since the relative acidity of soil can also vary according to texture.

After developing the sod, you should continue liming periodically to maintain a nearly neutral pH; this maximizes available plant nutrients. High soil acidity reduces decay of dead roots, thus decreasing humus breakdown. This in turn interferes with normal root development and percolation of water into the soil. Furthermore, highly acidic soils usually contain large amounts of certain elements such as soluble aluminum and manganese, which are toxic in large quantities, along with unusable forms of nitrogen. This is a result of acid-forming fertilizers that replace and leach calcium and magnesium from the upper soil layer. Correct this condition by applying crushed limestone.

Fertilizing is the other chemical treatment for improving soil fertility; however, it may create acidic soil conditions that must be corrected with lime if added nutrients are to be available for plant use. Again, you should fertilize only after a complete soil analysis has been made.

Fertilizers are usually labeled according to percentage by weight of available nitrogen (N_2), phosphate (P_2O_5), and potash (K_2O). These primary nutrients are necessary for vigorous plant growth. Thus one hundred pounds of a 10-5-5 fertilizer contains ten pounds of usable nitrogen, five pounds of phosphate, and five pounds of potash. As a general rule, an application of twenty-five to thirty pounds of a 10-5-5 fertilizer per one thousand square feet is advisable for seedbed preparation. Mix about two-thirds of the fertilizer throughout the soil and the remaining third into the upper inch. During the establishment of sod, you should also check the color of the young plants; for example, if the young leaves are pale green, additional nitrogen may be necessary.

Fertilize newly established sod with a 10-5-5 fertilizer applied at a rate of fifteen pounds per one hundred feet at least twice a year.[16] Watering aids in moving the fertilizer into the top inch of the soil, but sporadic light watering may also cause the germination of weed seed in the soil surface that competes with the grass seedlings.

In cool regions, apply fertilizer in the spring and fall. Fall applications accelerate the spring growth of the sod, particularly if the growing season is short. In warmer regions, applications are normally made in the spring and midsummer because of the lengthy growing season.

Cultural Treatments of the Sod

Managers should be familiar with the following cultural treatments:

Cleaning. This is the removal of tree leaves to maximize the amount of light reaching the ground cover. Cleaning promotes healthy growth of sod from spring through the early fall. It also reduces undesirable surface moisture and heating; these can be detrimental to grass blades and promote conditions that lead to disease.

Topdressing. Topdressing—i.e., spreading a thin layer (one-fourth inch or so) of fertile topsoil over the sod and lightly working it in—can improve soil conditions on poor sites, level small areas, raise a surface, cover a vegetative planting, and protect from winter kill. You can modify soil texture through coring (removal of soil cores) and topdressing.

A specific application of topdressing is mandatory to maintain golf greens. Perform this procedures by first scarifying and/or thatching the area to remove matted bentgrass, then top-dressing it to improve the fertility of the site and the vigor of the grass.

Scarifying. This means mechanically disturbing the sod cover and soil surface to improve water percolation and aeration, allowing penetration of less mobile fertilizers. You scarify by slicing into the soil with V-

Figure 9-3. Recreational turf management can also involve restoration of high elevation horse pastures. Wawona Meadow and Golf Course, Yosemite National Park. (Photo by B. W. Twight)

shaped knife blades on a circular wheel. The slicing penetrates deep into the soil at some predetermined interval.

Aeration. This process is the mechanical removal of sod-soil cores to improve soil aeration, increase water percolation and penetration of fertilizers, and reduce root competition. You can obtain some of these additional benefits through other treatments, but improved soil aeration is best achieved by removing small cores. Slicing, or similar scarification techniques that penetrate the sod, do not remove any soil or sod; consequently, the point of penetration is closed more quickly.

Thatching. Thatch is the layer of dead and living stems between the green tops and the surface of the soil. Some thatch is desirable as a cushion to reduce soil compaction and to insulate the soil.[3] Excessive accumulation increases disease and insect problems and localized dry spots, and increases susceptibility to mechanical injury. You can control thatch build-up biologically through proper scheduling of the previously discussed cultural treatments. Also avoid excessive nitrogen fertilization and/or irrigation since they stimulate too much stem growth and a build-up of thatch. Control thatch growth mechanically with vertical mowing or power raking. Thatch buildup tends to be more of a problem on poorly drained, fine-textured soils.

Mowing. This procedure can cause great damage to mature grasses if not done properly. Where recreation use is anticipated or adverse environmental conditions already exist (such as shading), grass should be mowed at greater heights than normal, up to two inches, and possibly at less frequent intervals. Longer grass has a greater photosynthetic

area and is consequently more hardy. Its "rougher" appearance may be a more desirable outcome than dead spots in the turf. Remember that the objective is to stimulate growth; if you mow at too short a height or too frequently, you may weaken rather than improve the vigor of the grass. Desired cutting height depends on the turf species; however, in recreation sites, other considerations such as aesthetics and playing conditions determine this. When those types of tradeoffs are made, you must alter the cutting schedule and increase other treatments to compensate. On more intensively managed sites, remove clippings to increase aesthetic appeal and reduce possible diseases.

There is a growing use for chemical turf growth regulators. Chemicals decrease shoot growth rate, but do not completely retard growth, reducing mowing expenses. Completely retarding growth eliminates the recuperative capacity of turf grass after recreational use, and weakens its ability to fend off possible diseases.

Watering. Water to supplement natural precipitation. In high-moisture areas, this may be necessary only during severe droughts. In dry areas, watering and irrigation systems can be very extensive. Water artificially to maintain turf growth for extended periods of time and at frequent intervals to get good penetration. Frequent intervals of light watering encourage weeds to germinate and grow in the sod.

Weeding. Weeding is important if you are to maintain a dense sod. This means you should perform all chemical and cultural treatments properly to foster good sod vigor after establishment. Any treatment not done properly can promote the growth of weeds, which should be checked. Once these weeds are established, you need selective herbicides to remove them. The use of the herbicides depends on local conditions and should be only undertaken by someone who is knowledgeable about the chemicals and E. P. A. certified to carry out their proper use.

If turf has not been maintained properly, you may have to renovate the sod. You must assess the problem and realign your maintenance program to improve the condition of the turf. You may even be faced with the decision to either revamp your program or start over with new turf! Such renovation should be carefully integrated with visitor management programs to protect the site during rejuvenation.

SEASONAL MANAGEMENT SCHEDULES

Some authors have offered specific schedules which they feel must be adhered to in order to properly maintain turf. We would suggest that there is sufficient variation in recreational use, environmental conditions, and species composition that local managers should develop their own seasonal schedules. This may mean separate schedules for each park or even for portions of a specific park that has different management programs.

Figure 9-4. Turf management is necessary in eastern state parks where summer rains generate lush growth. (Photo by Gordon Wissinger)

This chapter only gives an overview of turf management and the main variables and management techniques used by outdoor recreation managers. More detailed information can be found in turf-management books or through local agencies such as the Agricultural Extension Service, the Soil Conservation Service, and other related state organizations.

SELECTED READINGS

1.   Anonymous, 1990. "Fertilization Principles for Warm and Cool Season Turfgrasses," *Park and Grounds Management, 43*(4) Apr: 15.

2.   Barkely, D. B., Blaser, R. R., and Schmidt, R. E. 1965. "Effect of Mulches on Microclimate and Turf Establishment." *Agronomy Journal* 57:189.

3.   Beard, J. B. 1982. *Turfgrass Management for Golf Courses*. New York, NY: MacMillan.

4.   Beard, J. B. 1973. *Turfgrass: Science and Culture*. Englewood Cliffs, NJ: Prentice-Hall, Inc.

5.   Blaser, R. E. 1963. "Principles of Making Turf Mixtures for Roadside Seeding." Highway Research Records, No. 23, National Research Council, p. 79.

6.   Cattani, D. J., and Clark, K. W. 1991. "Influence of Wear Stress on Turfgrass Growth Components Visual Density Ratings," *Canadian Journal of Plant Science, 71*(1)Jan: 305.

7.   Curry, R. J., Foote, L. E., Anchrews, O. N., Jr., and Jakobs, J. A. 1964. "Lime and Fertilizer Requirements as Related to Turf Establishment along the Roadside." Highway Research Records, No. 53, National Research Council, p. 26.

8.   Emmons, R. D. 1984. *Turfgrass Science and Management*. Charlotte, NC: Delmar Co.

9.   Feucht, J. R. 1988. *Landscape Management, Planning and Maintenance of Trees, Shrubs, and Turfgrasses*. New York, NY: Van Nostrand-Reinhold.

10. Gross, C. M., Angle, J. S., and Welterlen, M. S. 1990. "Nutrient and Sediment Losses from Turfgrass," *Journal of Environmental Quality, 19*(4)Oct: 663.

11. Hanson, A. A. 1965. Grass Varieties in the United States. Agricultural Handbook No. 170. Agricultural Research Service, U.S. Department of Agriculture.

12. Ilnicki, R. D. 1991. "BAS 514 and Dithipyr for Weed control in Cool-Season Turfgrasses," *Weed Technology, 5*(3)Jul: 616.

13. Jones, S. B., and Foote, L. E. 1990. *Gardening with Native Wildflowers*, Portland, OR: Timber Press.

14. Mancino, C. F. 1992. "Irrigation of Turfgrass with Secondary Sewage Effluent: Soil Quality," *Agronomy Journal, 84*(4)Jul: 650.

15. Petrovic, A. M. 1990. "The Fate of Nitrogenous Fertilizers Applied to Turfgrass," *Journal of Environmental Quality, 19*(1)Jan: 1.

16. Sprague, H. B. 1982. *Turf Management Handbook*. 3rd edition. Danville, IL: The Interstate.

17. Triplett, G. B., and Sprague, H. B. 1986. *No-tillage and Surface-tillage Agriculture, the Tillage Revolution*, New York, NY: John Wiley & Sons.

18. Turgeon, A. J. 1985. *Turfgrass Management*, Reston, VA: Reston Publishing Co.

19. Vargas, J. M. 1981. *Management of Turfgrass Diseases*. Minneapolis, MN: Burgess Publishing Co.

CHAPTER 10

Management of Overstory Vegetation

The primary emphasis of this chapter is silvicultural treatments of overstory vegetation before, during, and after site development. Specific kinds of vegetation management are discussed, in addition to related visitor-management practices. The chapter also presents possibilities for site redevelopment, when vegetation reaches the point of biological maturity and you must decide to either abandon the site or regenerate the stand.

The timing of treatments can be extremely important. When done prior to development, they can reduce the shock of recreational use and increase the vigor of the trees, making them better able to sustain themselves. Successive treatments during and after development are based on need determined through monitoring.

SILVICULTURAL TREATMENTS PRIOR TO DEVELOPMENT

The three primary silvicultural treatments are thinning, sanitation cutting, and clear cutting.

Thinning

This practice requires coordination with long-range planning. Thinning prepares the site for development and improves the condition of vegetation prior to recreational use (see Figure 10-1, p. 132). Site preparation may precede site development by two to ten years, depending on how the vegetation responds. It may be done at regular intervals until an area is opened for visitors, particularly if the species is susceptible to windthrow.

Thinning opens up stands of trees to increase light and reduce root and crown competition, thereby strengthening the quantity and hardiness of both the ground cover and the remaining overstory vegetation. This also improves aesthetics, reduces dust, increases natural screening, and promotes desirable shading conditions. You should cut off trees at ground level, which may require you to dig a small trench around the base of the tree so that the chain saw operator can manipulate the saw. In thinning, you remove some of the dominant and codominant trees, along with all intermediate and suppressed stands. This should improve both crown size and general vigor of the remaining trees. In addition, it serves as an improvement cut that favors certain more durable species on the new site. In the process, the light reaching the ground should aid in improving species composition and add vigor to ground vegetation. Specific recommendations must be based on intended recreational use, the silvical characteristics of the tree species, and the requirements for improving ground cover.

For wind-firm, even-aged stands of trees, one thinning is usually needed three to five years prior to development and involves removing about one-third to one-half the crown density. For truly uneven-aged stands, which contain a mixture of size and age classes, do

Figure 10-1. Graphic illustration of the effects of thinning. (A) Nearly 100 percent overstory stocking with little understory; (B) thinning of overstory to improve growing conditions and ground cover; and (C) five years after thinning, the trees have bigger, more healthy crowns and well-established ground vegetation.

not thin prior to development since the desired conditions already exist in theory. However, you typically find only two or three size and age classes, which appear in clusters or multistory canopies. If size classes occur in clusters, thin each of these carefully to improve conditions for that portion of the site. If possible, put actual developments in the younger, more vigorous portions of the stand.

Multistory stands are generally in some stage of successional change—i.e., a less competitive (intolerant) species has been invaded by a more competitive (shade-tolerant) species. You can handle this in several ways, depending on species and type of recreational use. If the understory species is more desirable in terms of aesthetics and durability, you can remove the overstory species; thinning is then delayed until time of development. The new overstory should be well-stocked (fifty percent or more), thrifty in external appearance, and at least twenty-five feet high prior to site development. This height should encourage well-established trees with good canopy size, yet allow adequate room below the canopy for normal movement of people and vehicles. If the overstory is desirable and still in its biological prime, remove the understory where necessary and thin the overstory.

If the species are not wind-firm, predevelopment thinning should probably be done in two stages, starting five to ten years prior to development. The first thinning should remove approximately twenty to twenty-five percent of the crown canopy, and the second phase should open the canopy to the desired level.

Sanitation Cutting

Sanitation cutting is the removal of trees that have been affected by disease or insect attacks or have sustained mechanical injuries that would make them highly susceptible to these. Make such cuttings prior to development to improve the general health of the stand and reduce possible loss of live trees later on. If an insect or disease problem requires removing a significant number of trees, consider relocation. All fresh cutting, stumps, etc., should be removed, burned, or treated to eliminate any attractor of new insect infestations.

Give the stand a complete inventory to determine the degree of infestation; then individually mark each tree that you wish to remove. If the disease can be transmitted through root grafts, adjacent trees also have to be eliminated. In that case, it is advisable to burn all removed trees.

Clear Cutting

Clear cutting rights-of-way for major roads and minidevelopments must be staked out to determine the types of vegetation and microclimates the road will pass through. No predevelopment cutting may be necessary if microclimatic conditions are favorable, the species composition is acceptable and reasonably uniform, and species are wind-firm. In areas where the species is susceptible to windthrow because of a shallow root system, partial removal of the overstory in the right-of-way may be more desirable; you later perform total removal at the time of development. This also allows some minimum access prior to development of the site, and you can decrease the susceptibility of the remaining trees to windthrow by feathering the edges of the final clearcut.

The actual cutting of trees simply appears as thinning, and the partial cuttings can be used to improve the growth of the remaining stems. Select stems for actual removal based on their position relative to other trees, visible external signs of endemic insect and disease problems, potential for mechanical injury, or the necessary road access/mini-developments.

SILVICULTURAL TREATMENTS DURING DEVELOPMENT

Cuttings made during the development phase are similar to those made prior to it. Final thinning before development increases tree vigor, creates desired shade conditions, and improves aesthetics. The sanitation portion of the cutting removes any insect- and disease-promoting conditions. Remove up to fifty percent or more of the crown cover to allow sunlight into the site. Cutting may be uniform or variable, depending on your sun/shade requirements for specific portions of the site. For example, the campground unit may require an average amount of shade, whereas the comfort station and water-point areas may need more-than-average sunlight. When removing a high percentage of the crown cover, leave the remaining trees in clusters for mutual support from wind damage.

The final right-of-way cutting for the access road, including the shoulders of the roadbed, is done at the time of development. If there is a dense stand of trees, feather the edge of the right-of-way to improve aesthetics, reduce wind shear, and reduce shading along the shoulder for grass or other ground vegetation establishment.

On intensive-use portions of the site, prune the remaining trees along the bole from twelve to sixteen feet high after all other development cuttings have been made. This is an expensive procedure that requires close attention to detail in order to minimize mechanical damage to trees; timing and technique are important. Pruning is often criticized because it opens the tree to insect and disease attacks. On the other hand, pruning removes dead limbs and those that are injured by recreationists. Prune in the spring so that trees have an opportunity to form callous tissue over wounds immediately. If you prune in late summer after growth has ceased or during the fall, trees are more susceptible to insect attack through open wounds. In the fall, insects deposit their eggs in wounds for overwintering.

Proper technique for removal of tree limbs is to undercut the limb with a pruning saw and then remove it with a flush-out along the bole. The undercut keeps the limb from tearing the bark below. Limbs up to two inches in diameter should heal naturally without being sealed artificially; those over two inches should he sealed immediately. To encourage rapid healing of the larger wounds, light scarification with the saw around the wound may help.

The last treatment during the development phase is called minidevelopment. This involves preparation of such areas as an open play space at a group picnic area or a guard station at a campground. Make a small clear cutting where the minidevelopment is to be located, and remove all trees. You should also remove those trees that may interfere with the facility, and give consideration to the effects of root systems on foundations and sewers.

POSTDEVELOPMENT TREATMENTS

Schedule periodic surveys, using specific data collection forms, to assess the condition of the overstory vegetation. This fulfills your legal as well as professional obligation to reduce hazardous conditions due to dead or dying trees and reduce risks of further insect and disease attacks while maintaining desirable, natural aesthetics (also see Chapter 18). The survey should focus on the following:

1. disease- and insect-infected trees;
2. mechanical injury to tops from ice or wind;
3. mechanical injury from recreational use, primarily from cutting on the bole and trampling around the root collar;
4. stagheading (die-back of tree top), which may indicate severe soil compaction or biological overmaturity of species; and
5. general vigor and coloration of the crowns.

Not all trees with negative signs must be removed. Those away from developed facilities and other public use areas, and of no danger to persons on established trails or roads, probably should be left in place as habitat for cavity dwelling birds and various mammals. Old snags, in addition to providing wildlife habitat are also highly scenic and photogenic, providing diversity and contrast in the forest and other wild settings. Near developed public use areas, solid trees (not rotten or apt to fall soon) may be left for a time, if regularly checked for rot and broken or hanging limbs (be sure to document each regular inspection in the files, including dates, times and photos).

Classify such negative-condition trees left standing near public use areas as either *cut,* or *watch* trees and put them on a schedule for regular safety inspections. Remove the ones classified as *cut* because they are probably a hazard to visitors or the general health of the other trees. Flag *watch* trees and observe them during subsequent surveys to determine whether or not their condition is stable. If individual trees are important in the landscape design of the site, specific treatment such as tree surgery may be recommended by an arboriculturist. The individual employed in seasonal site maintenance should also receive instructions on making and reporting casual observations while working on any site. This provides some periodic observations in between surveys.

Postdevelopment cuttings are designed to maintain the general health of a stand of trees, to remove public hazards through the use of sanitation cutting and hazard-tree removal, and to possibly thin, though thinning is generally not necessary except on better sites. Since the crowns grow at a rate proportionate to the root system, they cannot expand very fast if the system becomes restricted by compacted soil.

One postdevelopment treatment that has not been given sufficient attention is site expansion. If a site has been chosen to allow for future expansion, the cycle of treatments may be repeated, starting with predevelopment on each new expansion; however, these treatments must be coordinated with the existing site, since the area is simply an expansion of that site. In sum, this means you must consider the overstory vegetation management program in initial site planning so that all management activities can be coordinated.

SITE REGENERATION

Ultimately, managers must concern themselves with regenerating overstory vegetation to redevelop sites. After trees have reached their biological maturity, they begin to deteriorate. At some point, you must decide to regenerate the site or abandon it. Not much consideration has been given to this problem because most developed sites are relatively new and trees have not yet reached the point of massive deterioration. Also, little research is available about techniques for regenerating vegetation on recreational sites. A discussion of some theoretical possibilities for regenerating overstory vegetation follows.

Option 1: Relocate

If there is a minimum investment involved and if several potential sites are available, relocation seems to be the most logical choice. It causes less inconvenience to the user, it is possibly less expensive to develop, and it offers an opportunity to update the design of the site.

Option 2: Close and Regenerate

Probably the least desirable alternative is to close the site so that the overstory can be regenerated. This is inconvenient for users since the site must be closed for a number of years. Also, other sites have to absorb user demand for the seven to ten years required for vegetation to reach a sufficient height (at least twenty to twenty-five feet). Any vegetation that is smaller tends to be damaged by visitors, even with normal use.

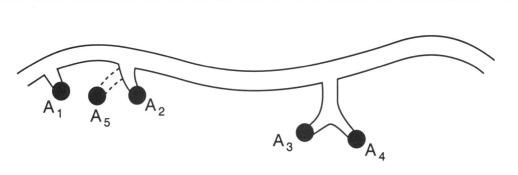

The operation is as follows:
1. In one cut, remove all competing and undesirable understory, along with approximately fifty to sixty percent of the overstory.
2. Plant older nursery stock, possibly 2-1 or 2-2 stock.* The root system is larger and therefore better able to survive and grow quickly; the remaining overstory provides protection to the to the seedlings during the reestablishment period (about three years).
3. After establishment, the remaining overstory is removed. In another four to ten years, the seedling will have grown to sapling size—the minimum necessary prior to reopening the site. Possibly fertilization and irrigation can reduce reestablishment time.

_____

* 2-1 refers to two years in the seed bed and one year in the transplant bed at the nursery.

Figure 10-2. Rotation of similar types of sites during regeneration. A_5 is the new site that is being used to replace A_1, while it is being regenerated, and so on. This is possible only in cases where age and site variability will allow rotation over an extended number of years, possible decades.

If there are several similar sites in the area, you may only need one new site so that regeneration can be done by rotation. For example, in Figure 10-2, A_5 is the newly developed site. It replaces A_1 during the regeneration period; A_1 then replaces A_2 during the next regeneration; A_2 replaces A_3, and so on.

The regeneration method should be compatible with silvical requirements of the forest types being regenerated and with local site conditions. Natural regeneration typically takes too long to reestablish; therefore planting is the most logical choice. For some more shade-tolerant species, a two-cut shelter wood might be desirable though it appears as a three-cut shelter wood. You remove the undesirable understory and slightly open the overstory, and then plant nursery stock. After establishment of the understory, the overstory is removed.

Option 3: Redesign and Reestablish

In this alternative, the entire site is not closed; however, individual units such as those in a forest campground are permanently closed and intermediate areas are then opened (see Figure 10-3). The steps are as follows:

1. Vegetation for proposed new units is reestablished in a sufficient amount of time to grow to a minimum height of twenty to twenty-five feet prior to designing, developing, and opening new units. These must be "patch" or group selection cuttings and require a great distance in between existing units.[13] Some barriers have to be developed to minimize casual trampling.
2. The old units are regenerated—perhaps as discussed in Option 2.

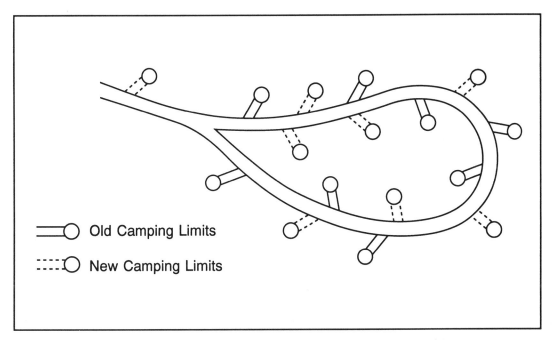

Old Camping Limits

New Camping Limits

Figure 10-3. Diagram showing option to reestablish or redesign site.

The arguments against this option are strong. People question why units are not developed since demand generally outstrips supply in most recreational areas. The public also decries destruction of portions of the site through timber harvesting. At the same time, the situation dictates that smaller units (openings) be regenerated one at a time rather than across the entire site, and small openings may not meet the biological requirements of the particular species for adequate regeneration. Finally, Option 3 is only possible on low-density occupancy sites in which individual units are adequately separated so that they can be relocated in intermediate zones.

In sum, Option 1 (relocate) appears to be a more logical and economically efficient management strategy. However, on heavy-use sites where available open space is at a premium, the only choice may be to regenerate the site. The challenge is how to make that happen.

"CREATING" A NEW RECREATIONAL ENVIRONMENT SILVICULTURALLY

Most of us tend to think in terms of how to maintain the status quo, to increase the health and vigor of what is already present. Rarely do we think of creating something new—a different environmental setting. This can be done by using the right silvicultural technique to convert from one forest type to another—enhancing the appeal of the site for particular recreational opportunities, increasing visual variety, and encouraging specific activities. We could go from a dense spruce forest to a spruce-hardwood mixture to increase landscape variety and allow more snow

to reach the ground so the site is suitable for cross-country skiing. Or we can create natural-appearing openings to appear as forest meadows. Forests can also be converted to more pastoral-like landscapes with large, open green spaces, and you can dam small streams to create a stronger interface between the forest and water.

Such changes can be expensive, and we give up something to get something else. Long-term management costs may also be associated with the new status. But technology is available to create these environmental settings. The question, then, is not can we, but under what circumstances should we? And the costs may not be as high as we think, particularly if we receive the revenue from the forests removed during the stand conversion, or when the benefits to the using public are greatly enhanced.

METHODS OF REGENERATION

There are three methods of regenerating trees: natural seeding, artificial seeding, and planting. Natural regeneration, even when associated with cultural treatments, is generally not as desirable as the other two methods for the intensive-use sites. However, natural regeneration is probably the only viable choice in dispersed use areas because of both cost and the aesthetics of maintaining the normal character of the landscape. At a number of smaller, heavily used locations in dispersed areas, some cultural treatments encourage rapid regeneration to quickly stabilize a site. However, you must also shift patterns of recreational use during the regeneration period to minimize disruption of the process. You can obtain exact natural regeneration requirements from the United States Department of

Agriculture's Woody Plant Seed Manual,[15] or the U.S. Forest Service publications on silvical characteristics for each species.[16]

Machine planting is generally not a viable alternative since the areas to be planted are usually small. If the need arises because of area size and gentle terrain, you can usually contract a local operator to do the machine planting.

Seeding can be done by either broadcasting over large openings or spot seeding. Again this method has limitations where recreation use occurs; it takes longer to regenerate the trees, and there is always the possibility of failure because of unusual environmental conditions. You can determine exact seeding requirements by using the sources that were suggested above.

For natural areas, you have no other choice but to regenerate naturally. If a species has been extirpated locally within a natural area and you wish to reintroduce the same species, collect seeds close to the point of introduction and on sites similar to that point. This is expensive but essential if you are to maintain maximum genetic integrity—just any local seed source will not do.

Of more concern to the outdoor recreation manager is an artificial means of regenerating trees—direct seeding or planting. You should base your selection of species not only on site conditions but also on intended use; i.e., the site plan may require shade trees, wind-firm trees, wildlife food, and so forth. Choose species that have those characteristics but are also adaptable to local site conditions.

The last and most important regeneration method is hand planting. Selecting and handling plant stock are important to the success of your planting program. You should obtain your stock from a local, nursery-grown, certified seed source, a seed source whose location features environmental conditions similar to those of your planting site. It is often advisable to buy transplant stock (stock that is transplanted from the seed bed) because it has a larger root system and is thus more resistant to the shock of being transplanted.

Once you obtain the seedlings, heel them in until you are ready for planting. This requires digging a V-shaped trench in a shaded moist location, making sure that the sides of the trench are approximately three to four inches longer than the root systems. Open each bundle of seedlings and then spread them out along one side of the ditch. Place loose soil, with some additional organic matter, back into the ditch and water it heavily. Tamp the seedlings gently with your foot, taking care to minimize root damage.

When it is time to plant, lift the seedlings out and place them in an open container filled with sufficient water to cover their roots. The soil opening for the seedling should be large enough to accommodate the root system without bending or changing natural root conformation. Depth is also extremely important; ideally you should plant the seedling approximately one-half inch below the depth at which it grew in the nursery; planting it too deep or too shallow increases the chance of mortality.

After planting, you may need temporary fencing to protect the young seedlings from rodents, deer, etc. Additional cultural treatments such as weeding to eliminate competition from less desirable species may also be necessary, particularly on the better sites.

There are two types of planting tools—the dibble (or planting bar) and the mattock (see Figure 10-4, p. 140). Either method is satisfactory; however, mattock planting is necessary on hard, heavy soils or when you're using transplant stock with large roots.

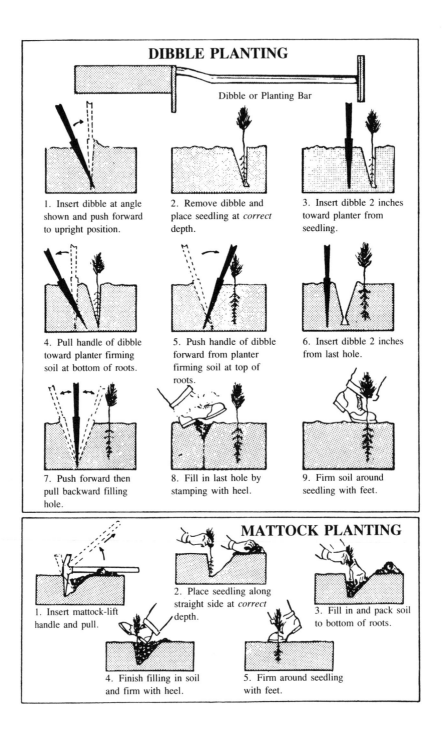

Figure 10-4. Planting methods. (From *Forestry Handbook*. 2nd Edition. K. F. Wenger, ed. 1984. New York, NY: John Wiley & Sons)

INTRODUCTION OF EXOTICS

"Exotic" simply refers to a species that does not naturally grow on a particular site. Up to this point, a good rule of thumb has been to avoid exotics. Though this is not always possible, it is a legal requirement in National Park Service natural areas and in units of the National Wilderness System. Some exotics have very desirable characteristics, and you may wish to take advantage of these species. Careful review of species within a region, discussion with local experts, and trial plantings may help you identify the best exotics for your planting program. A list of those that are suitable for intensive-use sites and adaptable to specific regions is shown in Table 10-1 (p. 142) and Figure 10-5 (p. 144).

INSECTS AND DISEASES—A CONTINUED PROBLEM

Insects and diseases are endemic in most areas, but rarely do they reach epidemic proportions. The best preventive measure is to keep trees healthy, at reasonable growth rates with minimum mechanical damage. Obviously trees are not as healthy as they could be if a site is not used for recreation; however, the strategies outlined in the beginning of this chapter should help to promote healthy trees and reduce high risks. Some individual trees may be valuable enough to receive special treatment, e.g., fertilizers and water, infected limb removal, or spraying.

You should institute some control measures when you detect certain insects or diseases. Unfortunately, since trees are not in an optimal growing environment on a recreational site, they may rapidly deteriorate and die after any insect or disease attack. The other consideration is that an insect or disease problem, if not checked, may spread to areas outside the immediate site.

In sum, the best approach is to maintain healthy trees. Periodically inspect for any insect or disease problem. If a major problem emerges, use the specific, recommended control and warn other residents and agencies of the potential problem. Ripley, through a synthesis of his considerable research, prioritizes eastern species of trees based on their ability to withstand the impact of recreation use[16] (see Table 10-2, p. 143).

RELATED MANAGEMENT PROGRAMS

Management of overstory vegetation is not complete until it has been integrated with visitor-management programs:

Area Planning

Area planning (see Chapter 17) can reduce direct management costs after site development if you evaluate potential sites for particular kinds of development. Then the site you actually choose provides the desired recreational opportunity with minimum capital *and* operational costs. When you choose a less stable or less productive site, you also commit yourself to higher operational costs

Table 10-1. Trees suitable for an urban environment.*

SPECIES			GROWTH RATE	GROWING CONDITIONS	HARDINESS ZONES
PIN OAK *QUERCUS PALLUSTRIS* 20 to 25 METERS			MODERATE TO FAST	FULL SUN. RICH LOAMY,WELL-DRAINED, SLIGHTLY ACIDIC SOIL.	4-8
WILLOW OAK *QUERCUS PHELLOS* TO 18 METERS			MODERATE TO FAST	FULL SUN. RICH, WELL-DRAINED, ACID SOIL.	5-8
UPRIGHT GINKGO *GINKGO BILOBA* "FASTIGIATA" TO 18 METERS			SLOW	HIGHLY TOLERANT OF URBAN CONDITIONS.	4-8. INCLUDING CALIFORNIA
GREEN ASH. *FRAXINUS PENNSYLVANICA* "MARSHALL'S SEEDLESS" TO 20 METERS			FAST	FULL SUN. LOAMY, WELL-DRAINED, NEARLY NEUTRAL SOIL.	3-8. INCLUDING CALIFORNIA AND PACIFIC NORTHWEST
MODESTO ASH *FRAXINUS VELUTINA* VAR. GLABRA TO 20 METERS			FAST	TOLERANT OF DRY, ALKALINE SOIL.	5-8. PARTICULARLY CALIFORNIA AND SOUTHWESTERN DESERT AREAS
NORWAY MAPLE *ACER. PLATANOIDES* 12 to 30 METERS			MODERATE TO FAST	FULL SUN. TOLERANT OF POOR SOIL	3-10. EXCEPT SOUTHERN CALIFORNIA AND SOUTHWESTERN DESERT AREAS
JAPANESE PAGODA *SOPHORA JAPONICA* "REGENT" TO 20 METERS			SLOW TO MODERATE	TOLERANT OF POOR SOIL. DOES BEST IN NEARLY NEUTRAL WELL-DRAINED SOIL.	4-7
THORNLESS HONEY LOCUST *GLEDITSIA TRIACANTHOS* VAR. INERMIS "SHADEMASTER" TO 25 METERS			FAST	FULL SUN OR PARTIAL SHADE. TOLERATES DROUGHT AND RANGE OF SOIL CONDITIONS.	4-10
SERVICEBERRY *AMELANCHIER CANADENSIS* OR *A. LAEVIS* 7 TO 12 METERS			MODERATELY FAST	PARTIAL SUN. MOIST SOIL.	4-8
GRECIAN LAUREL *LAURUS NOBILIS* TO 10 METERS			SLOW	FULL SUN. WELL-DRAINED ACID OR ALKALINE SOIL.	7-8. INCLUDING PACIFIC NORTHWEST, NORTHERN CALIFORNIA AND SOUTHERN STATES

Table 10-2. List of Eastern conifers and hardwoods

Hardwoods		Conifers
1. Hickories	12. Red maple	1. Shortleaf pine
2. Persimmon	13. American holly	2. Hemlocks
3. Sycamore	14. Sourwood	3. White pine
4. White ash	15. Black birch	4. Pitch pine
5. Beech	16. White oaks	5. Virginia pine
6. Sassafras	17. Black walnut	
7. Buckeye	18. Red oaks	
8. Yellow-poplar	19. Black locust	
9. Dogwood	20. Magnolia	
10. Blackgum	21. Black cherry	
11. Yellow birch	22. Blue beech	

Note: The above conifers and hardwoods are listed in order of decreasing ability to withstand the impact of recreation use as gauged by disease infection, insect infestation, and decline. (From Ripley, T. H. 1962. "Tree and Shrub Response to Recreational Use." U.S. Forest Service Note SE-171, p. 2.)

in managing overstory vegetation. To commit yourself to less than that decreases intended benefits of the recreational opportunity.

Consequently area planning must not be viewed, as indicated in Chapter 17, as a site development process but as a total management process that includes all relevant programs for a particular activity. In terms of overstory management, that undertaking starts prior to development, committing you to a continual program both *during* and *after* visitor use.

One other thought is that overstory trees are what people see and equate with the generalized landscape. In some cases they are even the primary attractors, e.g., giant sequoias and ponderosa pines—the medicine trees of the Northern Rockies. Based on this perspective, managing overstory vegetation is a much higher priority, and the process starts with area planning.

Site Planning

Site planning is as much an outgrowth of area planning as any other program. Facilities such as architectural barriers, elevated walkways, etc., can direct use to minimize soil compaction and physical damage to trees. Barriers may be vegetative or constructed of appropriate materials, and used to simply avoid zones of sensitive vegetation and soils. Just make sure that the facilities you provide reduce the impact on the overstory vegetation and are appropriate to the opportunity.

Information Programs

Much visitor damage to vegetation is done out of ignorance. People often don't understand the consequences of their actions. They tie their horses to trees while they fish. They peel the bark from around the birch trees.

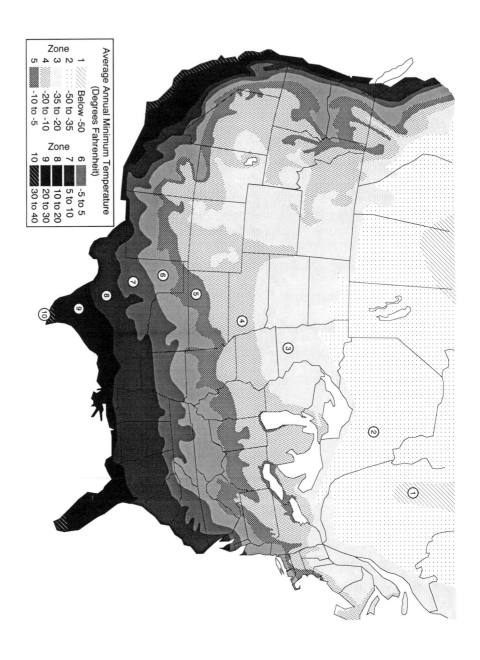

Figure 10-5. Hardiness zones of the United States and part of Canada reflect differences in the average annual minimum temperature and thus differences in the species of trees that can be expected to flourish in each zone. The map is based on a compilation and prepared at the Arnold Arboretum of Harvard University. Table shows the range of minimum temperatures. (From "Urban Trees," by Thomas S. Elias and Howard S. Irwin. Copyright © 1976 by Scientific American, Inc. All rights reserved.)

They cut off limbs for hot dog-sticks or bough beds. There is no end to the possible list, but the damage is not done to deliberately destroy the tree. It is done out of ignorance. Information programs, if properly developed, can reach many of these people and improve the quality of use of the site. Even with these, you may not reach some people or change their behavior.

What is needed is a better understanding of nonverbal barriers to encourage certain kinds of behavior, yet remain unobtrusive. Beyond that, we need to search for creative answers that simply can't be pulled out of a textbook. The example of indiscriminate tree-hacking is a good one. In one park, nothing seemed to work completely. Verbal communication reduced some. Patrolling and regulation enforcement helped. Then one employee suggested "hack trees," and workers "planted" 16-foot logs at each camp unit with a sign "Please hack on me—not my live brothers and sisters." Indiscriminate hacking of live trees was reduced to a negligible amount. Hack trees? It worked.

BIODIVERSITY

Through various land use practices we can favor one forest type over another. Typically we have favored commercial species over noncommercial ones. In some places a monoculture of pines has significantly reduced the presence of hardwood species, the genetic diversity of the remaining plants, and the variety of associated vertebrate and invertebrate animals. We know that biodiversity—at the genetic, community, or general landscape levels—is important to the health of the environmental setting, and is a required consideration on lands governed by the National Environmental Policy Act and the National Forest Management Act of 1976.

Probably no lands are more important in this regard than our dedicated parks, natural areas, and wilderness areas. In essence, these are the vanguard areas for biodiversity. Without them, some areas in the United States would have lost many species and the associated genetic variability. What we need is a planning process that ensures maintenance of this diversity into the future—if necessary, even to the point of significantly altering present plant associations to restore the natural biodiversity.[12,20,22] We must become stewards of this concept and set the example for other agencies and landowners. Associated management programs include fire (ecosystems) management and natural history interpretation.

Biodiversity efforts do not negate any of the previous discussion in these chapters. It will always be important to harden sites that receive heavy use; introduction of exotics remains a viable option. Even favoring one species or another associated with the site for good reasons is acceptable. However, on the larger acreages, and even smaller ones with unique contributions to the genetic pool, we should adopt biodiversity protection and restoration as a guiding resource management concept. Public support and understanding of the importance of this effort will only come about if we also do a first rate job of incorporating this into our natural history interpretive programs.

SELECTED READINGS

1. Blandon, R. R. (ed.). 1990. *Forestry Resources Management.* White Plains, NY: Quality Resources.

2. Elias, T. S., and Irwin, H. S. 1976. "Urban Trees," *Scientific American, 235*(5):111.

3. Feucht, J. R. 1988. *Landscape Management, Planning, and Maintenance of Trees, Shrubs, and Turfgrass.* New York, NY: Van Nostrand-Reinhold.

4. Gangstad, E. O. 1988. *Recreation Resource Management.* Fresno, CA: Thomson Publications.

5. Grey, G. W., and Deneke, F. J. 1978. *Urban Forestry.* New York, NY: John Wiley & Sons.

6. Haller, J. 1957. *Tree Care.* New York, NY: MacMillan Publishing Co.

7. Harris, R. 1983. *Arboriculture: Care of Trees, Shrubs, and Vines in the Landscape.* Englewood Cliffs, NJ: Prentice-Hall.

8. Howard, C. S. 1972. "Plants for Problem Areas of the Western States." *Yearbook of Agriculture,* p. 154.

9. Knight, F. B. and Heikkenen, H. J. 1980. *Principles of Forest Entomology.* New York, NY: McGraw-Hill Book Co.

10. Kuss, F. R., Graefe, A. R., and Vaske, J. J. 1990. *Visitor Impact Management, Vol. 1: A Review of Research.* Washington, DC: National Parks and Conservation Association.

11. Leuschner, W. A. 1984. *Introduction to Forest Resource Management.* New York, NY: John Wiley & Sons.

12. McNeely, J. A., Miller, K. A., Reid, W. V., Mittermeier, R. A., and Werner, T. B. 1990. *Conserving the World's Biological Diversity,* Washington, DC: World Bank Publications.

13. Miller, R. 1988. *Urban Forestry: Planning and Managing Urban Vegetation.* Englewood Cliffs, NJ: Prentice-Hall.

14. Neeley, D. and Himeleck, E. B. 1962. "Fertilizing and Watering Trees." Circular 52, Urbana, IL: Natural History Survey, University of Illinois.

15. Pigram, J. J. 1983. *Outdoor Recreation and Resource Management.* New York, NY: St. Martin Press.

16. Ripley, T. H. 1962. "Tree and Shrub Response to Recreational Use," U.S. Forest Service Research Note SE 171.

17. Rudolph, P. O. 1967. "Silviculture for Recreation Area Management." *Journal of Forestry* 65:385.

18. Settergren, C. D., and Cole, D. M. 1970. "Recreation Effects on Soil and Vegetation in the Missouri Ozarks." *Journal of Forestry* 68:231.

19. Smith, D. M. 1986. *The Practice of Silviculture.* 8th edition. New York, NY: John Wiley & Sons.

20. Soule, M. E. (ed). 1986. *Conservation Biology,* Sunderland, MA: Sinauer Assoc. Inc.

21. Spurr, S. H. 1980. *Forest Ecology.* 3rd edition. New York, NY: John Wiley & Sons.

22. U.S. Congress, Office of Technology Assessment. 1987. *Technologies to Maintain Biological Diversity,* OTA-F-330, Washington, DC: U.S. Government Printing Office.

23. U.S. Department of Agriculture. 1948. *Woody Plant Seed Manual.* Misc. Publ. 654.

24. U.S. Forest Service. 1965. *Silvics of Forest Trees of the United States.* Agriculture Handbook 271.

25. Wagar, J. A. 1965. "Cultural Treatment of Vegetation on Recreation Sites." *Proceedings of Society of American Foresters,* p. 37.

26. Wenger, K. F. 1984. *Forestry Handbook,* 2nd Edition. New York, NY: John Wiley & Sons.

27. Westveld, R. H. 1958. *Forestry in Farm Management.* New York, NY: John Wiley & Sons.

28. Young, R. A., and R. L. Giese (eds.). 1990. *Introduction to Forest Science,* (2nd Edition). New York, NY: John Wiley & Sons.

CHAPTER 11

Management of Natural Ecosystems

In Chapter 10, we suggested altering ecosystems to produce desired new environmental settings. This chapter looks at the other perspective—maintaining the natural ecosystem. An ecosystem is an association of plant and animal populations living together in dynamic equilibrium. In an open system of the natural setting, as with recreational opportunities in Chapter 3, we find an equilibrium not only internally affected by the interrelationships of the natural populations, but externally by changes in the environment such as climate and weather, chance introduction of exotic species, natural disasters, and modern man's activities.

Biodiversity, as discussed in Chapter 10, applies here also. When the primary agents of change are removed, vegetative succession continues toward the ecological climax. The climax vegetation offers little diversity of species and interrelationships, reducing the available habitats, gene pool, and the ability to resist major catastrophes. Paradoxically,

Figure 11-1. A natural wildfire in Grand Park, Mt. Rainer National Park. (Photo by Glenn Powell)

then, in a natural ecosystem the primary agents of change are important to the long-term *stability* of the dynamic system. In this chapter, the focus is on fire as the really significant agent of change and as such a protector of biological diversity.

While probably no ecosystem has not been affected by modern man in some way (the ones preserved through legal designations are usually only partial, with some disruption of energy flows, etc.), we typically divide them into those that are manageable as such and those that are not. Manageable ecosystems appear essentially intact, without the major disruptive forces of modern man, and large enough to allow the natural forces of fire, insects, disease, flood, etc. to maintain it in some less-than-climactic stage.

Few of these are left, and most are probably found in the state of Alaska. Even these are not inviolate because of their legal status; on the contrary, they often suffer encroachment because of artificial boundaries or because we eliminate or modify the natural forces that maintain them.

What we typically classify or are called upon to manage as natural ecosystems are vestiges that are nearly impossible to maintain as such. Worse yet, many of these are anomalies or freaks of nature such as a disjunct colony of boreal forest left when the boreal forest retreated northward after the last glacial period.

This discussion is not intended to diminish the role of management in natural ecosystems; it is only intended to point out the difficulty and complexity of striving to reach such a lofty goal. Unfortunately, such management is often equated with protecting the setting against the evils of man the recreationist, ignoring the forces of nature which shape the ecosystem and previous management actions which have encouraged existing use patterns. Recreational use typically causes only local aesthetic impact.

In sum, management of natural ecosystems is probably best summarized as:

1. protection against *external* influence of modern man's activity, i.e., keeping the landscape intact;
2. protection against internal influences of modern man's activities such as recreation, range use by livestock, etc.; and
3. maintenance or introduction of forces that maintain or reestablish the dynamic equilibrium.

The first two items are essential to any outdoor recreation management program, although most of us would agree that the threshold of acceptable impact lowers when we try to maintain visual as well as ecological intactness. Other chapters may reflect somewhat on those types of management programs; however, this one focuses on the third step.

NATURAL ECOSYSTEMS

There are two main parts of the ecosystem: the physical and the biological. The physical environment provides the energy, raw materials, and living space for use by the biological component. The biological component uses energy and raw materials to assimilate and produce biomass. Energy is passed through an ecosystem in a hierarchy of trophic levels, from green vegetation to herbivores (plant eaters) to carnivores. Eventually it is completely returned through decomposers to the soil/water. The passage of energy and nutrients through an ecosystem is a cycling process. Some plants, or parts, and some animals simply die and are decomposed; others are consumed by the next higher trophic level.

The dynamic equilibrium, in theory, is created by recycling, when raw materials and energy are maintained within the ecosystem. Remove the raw materials and/or some level of energy from the system and you have an altered ecosystem. That altered ecosystem can be natural in that it was caused by a natural disruption such as a volcanic eruption, rechannelization of a river, etc. Or it can be man-caused, like the removal of raw material or energy stored in the various trophic levels.

Here we will focus on the first trophic level—green vegetation—because all succeeding trophic levels are dependent upon it. Green vegetation fixes energy through photosynthesis, takes up almost all necessary minerals, and acts as a modifier of the environment, indirectly determining which organisms can live here. From a management perspective, the emphasis falls on agents of change in the dynamic equilibria that characterize particular ecosystems. While probably no natural ecosystem is free of the influence of modern man, these agents of change maintain the natural processes that cumulatively distinguish one ecosystem from another. Some small ecosystems are uniquely adapted to particular microclimatic conditions and are maintained with minimum influence from agents of change. These should almost be considered as climax systems.

There is, or should be, for a given ecosystem, a natural diversity in plant and animal species and successional stages. This is brought about by many natural conditions such as poorly drained soils, level of solar radiation, precipitation patterns, and numerous others. But, wholesale successional changes at the ecosystem or landscape level, which help to shape the biodiversity, are the major agents of change. These agents include disease, fire, insects, floods, tectonics and altered climates. The one force that has the predictable potential for recycling nutrients and energy and maintaining biological diversity for large areas over time is fire. However, this is not to insinuate that fire is the primary force in all cases.

HISTORY OF FIRE MANAGEMENT

A knowledge of the historical role of fire is important if we are to properly use fire to manage natural ecosystems. Fire has always been a primary force in shaping vegetation patterns, subsequently affecting the total ecosystem, including flora, fauna, soil, and water. During early times, fires were caused by weather cycles, particularly in places where natural fuels had built up during the intervening years between blazes. If not intense enough to kill, these fires usually caused some reshaping of vegetative structure, opening it to insect and disease attacks. A fire could completely destroy a stand of trees or create a die-back that resulted in a large fuel buildup, leading to an even more destructive wildfire.*

There is some disagreement as to the extent that American Indians used fire as part of their culture. According to Brown and Davis' forestry textbook on fire management, these native Americans may have started fires that destroyed forests and plains, but

---

* Wildfires are defined as having started naturally and burned a normal course without outside interference.

only accidentally. These authors suggest fire was primarily used by Indians for cooking, heating, signaling, and occasionally for driving game or waging war against an enemy tribe. Brown and Davis acknowledge that the Indians' use of fire as well as the accidental starting of wildfires (mostly by lightning but also from campfires) did affect ecosystems, but they argue that:

> "... firsthand testimony of old Indians of Western tribes indicates that they had great fear of conflagrations and a high respect for fire's destructiveness ..."

and

> "... It is at least a fair assumption that no habitual or systematic burning was carried out by the Indians."[8]

However, it is well-known that the "Smokey the Bear" fire prevention campaign twisted official forestry fire policy for years, and part of this policy was to downplay and even deny any beneficial or natural purpose for wildfires (see Schiff[44]). A reading of the Tall Timbers annual *Fire Ecology Conference Proceedings,*[26] Pyne's *Fire in America,*[42] and Biswell's *Prescribed Burning*[7] suggest a much higher level of fire usage by the native Americans. Despite the somewhat self serving claims of the foresters, Pyne, for example, thoroughly documents that:

> "... Through the use of fire ... Indian tribes created an environment favorable to their existence ... the lush wildlife that provided subsistence to early vanguards of frontiersmen depended on a habitat created and sustained by the Indian pattern of broadcast fire ..."[42]

Dendrochronology studies of the giant sequoias of California as well as pollen grain studies in bogs also have shown that fire has influenced native flora for thousands of years.[17,18] During the nineteenth century, white men began to invade and settle the Midwest, the Upper Plains, the Northern Rockies, and then the West Coast. The use of fire changed drastically—abuse would be a more correct term. Forest and prairie vegetation became an obstacle to westward expansion and settlement. Native vegetation had to be cleared for farming and community development, and later for industrial development. The easiest and cheapest means of clearing a forest was to start a fire and allow it to burn until a change in weather extinguished it. Also, settler-caused fires were thought to be an encouraging sign of progress since people felt that the forest was inexhaustible and that agriculture was part of a "manifest destiny." Unless they threatened personal property or accessible "firewood" stands, conflagrations were regarded with indifference.

In the late nineteenth and early twentieth centuries, the size, intensity, and frequency of fires greatly increased with the rise of settlements and logging. Many of the great fires in American history occurred during this time. Then the permanent reservation of land in public ownership, the introduction of German forestry, and the creation of agencies to administer lands and resources changed the official policy on forest fires. Experts agreed that forest fires destroyed valuable timber and should therefore be eliminated. Action was initiated by many states and also received presidential support at the federal level.[8]

As the benefits of increased timber production were realized, a basic fire-protection philosophy also became accepted as the proper means for maximizing timber production and protecting other resource values, including recreation. This policy has changed in recent years, particularly in designated wilderness, specific wildlife habitats, etc. As fires were once considered destructive, the policy was to immediately suppress them. Early fire education programs served primarily to prevent or reduce the number of man-caused fires. Agencies primarily used hand tools in the early limited-suppression programs. Later, power equipment, even heavy equipment and bomber aircraft, helped to suppress almost all fires, regardless of origin or potential effects.

Since immediate elimination was the sole objective, the policy on forest fires excluded fire as a natural force in the dynamics of the ecosystems for more than three-quarters of a century. By eliminating one of the primary forces of change, we created unnatural conditions in the wildlands of the United States. However, we felt this to be necessary in the overall management of land and valuable resources, even in so-called natural areas. Public educational programs instituted in the l940s promoted a fire prevention policy. Today we still feel the effects of the "Smokey the Bear" concerted antifire campaigns. Indeed, the criticism resulting from the 1989 Yellowstone conflagration shows that unfortunately many in the public still perceive only the need to prevent and suppress fires. Much more educational and interpretive efforts are still necessary in regard to fire's important natural role in ecosystems.

Be that as it may, back in 1963, one of the first attempts to overcome "Smokey" was made by a "blue ribbon" committee appointed by then Interior Secretary Stewart Udall and headed by A. Starker Leopold, which reviewed the ecosystems management programs of the National Parks. They concluded that the elimination of fire had drastically altered the natural parks' ecosystems.[27] The dynamic succession of vegetation had been disrupted. Fire climax communities had been eliminated, and vegetation succession was moving towards the climatic climax. There was reduced availability of nutrients, little dynamic recycling of successional stages, and no attempt at maintaining a diverse age/species structure. We were attempting to stabilize the natural structure of the ecosystem through fire prevention and suppression rather than allowing normal dynamics to take place. The committee's primary recommendation was to return the ecosystem to "pre-European man" conditions, so the public might be able to experience "vignettes of primitive America."[27]

This did not imply that a fire prevention policy is always absolutely wrong, but that in the case of parks and wilderness it is seldom valid—particularly in the most natural areas and where the effects of fire can be relatively easily contained. While many professionals recognize the positive role of fire in the natural ecosystem, it has also been found that higher administrators, as well as the public, often do not readily accept this philosophy. Managers have regularly been reluctant to take a forward look in our approach to the role of fire. Although we now recognize this need, we have not been very effective in implementing fire management plans in natural areas because of public criticism. Indeed, the 1989 Yellowstone conflagration set back these efforts politically for many years.

At the other extreme, some overzealous managers have attempted to implement a policy of fire management through the controlled use of fire without any knowledge of its historical role in their particular ecosystem. In fact, fire prevention and suppression have reduced the diversity of life forms, particularly in preparation for replanting clearcuts and in wilderness areas which are theoretically dedicated in maintaining the diversity and dynamics of a natural ecosystem. Technological advancements have also made it easier to reach isolated fires and suppress them.

Two decades ago, from his campsite in the Bob Marshall Wilderness, the senior author witnessed a fire suppression operation on Cardinal Mountain. Two large helicopters of equipment and men were flown in, and small, motorized equipment secured a fire line. The crew mopped up inside the line and the fire was quickly suppressed.

Ironically that fire, which had been burning for two days, covered less than fifty acres. Even if allowed to burn, the fire would probably have covered only one hundred to one hundred fifty acres before it reached natural boundaries that would have contained it. A walk through the burned area a few days after the suppression operation revealed that the deterioration of the site by men and equipment far surpassed fire damage—and all this occurred in an area "dedicated to the maintenance of the natural ecosystem." The same scene was repeated in 1985 on Nimrod Peak, Yukon-Charlie National Preserve, Alaska—in a zone officially designated as a "let-burn" zone in the regional fire plan.

Has the fire suppression program become a self-perpetuating juggernaut? Can we continue to afford that type of land management? Do our management strategies concerning fire fit the objectives for the area? Do we really understand the long-term effects of our management policies? Should we attempt to zone for fire management based on specific objectives? How do we properly "reintroduce" fire to the ecosystem? These questions and perhaps others are the ones we should be seeking responses to if we are to maintain fire as a primary force in shaping our natural ecosystems.

THE EFFECTS OF FIRE

This section focuses on effects so that we may have a better understanding of the natural role of fire. Predicting the behavior of wildfires is difficult because of the tremendous variation in the conditions under which they take place. Fire behavior on the same site may differ from day to day because of changing environmental conditions. Consequently, even the fire researcher has difficulty evaluating field data because many significant factors do not remain constant. According to Brown and Davis,

> "Fires respond to fuels, weather, and topography, with so many variables operating that it is nearly impossible to exactly duplicate fires in outdoor test plots, even where measured samples give assurance of reasonably uniform fuels and weather conditions and topography—carefully selected."[8]

Nevertheless, managers should attempt to understand the potential effects of a given fire, if they are to manage that fire. New computer simulation models can aid in understanding the probable behavior of a given fire.

Effects On Overstory Vegetation

The effects of fire on overstory vegetation are significant to our discussion because the overstory tends to have a pronounced influence on the microclimate. So, too, is the relative resistance of certain species to fires of less than lethal temperatures. Lethal fires cause a complete loss of vegetation and a change in microclimate. Fires that cause extensive change through the "partial kill" are more important to managers because they are more common than lethal fires, and cause the typical ecological changes associated with earlier wildfires.

Susceptibility to Fire Damage

According to Brown and Davis, the following factors determine the amount of damage that fire can do to wooded areas:

1. *Initial temperature of the vegetation.* Foliage temperatures of over 100 may occur naturally, and to 80°F is common. The higher the initial temperature, the less additional heat is necessary to bring about lethal temperatures and the more quickly they can develop. This point is of importance in prescribed use of fire, since initial temperatures can be controlled by selecting the time of burning.

2. *The size of the critical tree portion exposed and its morphology.* Young trees, leaves, and small branches are easily killed because they can quickly be heated to a lethal temperature. Buds are particularly important, and their resistance to heat damage is directly related to size.

3. *The thickness and character of the bark.* Of all the protective mechanisms of the tree, the bark is the most important. This is especially true near the ground surface where most fires occur. Bark is an excellent insulating material; "bark structure, in general, is a natural design for insulation board."

The insulating capacity of the bark layer depends on its structure, composition, density, moisture content, and thickness. It is known that these things vary widely by species, growth habitat, and possibly by seasons to some degree, but complete information is not available.

4. *Branching and growth habit.* Other things being equal, trees that self-prune readily and develop high and open crowns are more successful in escaping fire damage because they are less susceptible to crown fires and they accumulate less litter close to the stem.

5. *Rooting habit.* Roots have thin cortical covering and, if near the surface, are easily damaged by fire. Shallow-rooted species, like the spruces and most of the true firs, are frequently damaged by ground fires through root injury, even though the stem and crown are not affected.

6. *Organic material covering the mineral soil.* The depth and character of the organic mantle on the ground may largely control damage by surface fires to the roots, especially of the more shallow-rooted trees. If the mantle is fairly thick and the lower part does not burn, its high insulating ability will protect roots from damage. If, however, the organic mantle burns, it becomes a source of heat rather than of protection, and damaging soil temperatures are likely to result.

7. *Flammability of foliage.* Evergreens as a group, and conifers especially, are more flammable than deciduous

hardwoods. There are significant differences between conifer species, though these are not of critical importance in damage susceptibility. There are wider differences within hardwoods. The differences are least in times of severe drought, and at such times some species of both groups, mostly occurring in scrub or brush vegetative types, will burn furiously. In general, however, green hardwood foliage will not carry a forest fire except when abnormally dry.

8. *Stand habit.* Because of their greater liability to crown fires, coniferous trees that grow in dense stands or are commonly associated with abundant subordinate vegetation are more subject to fire damage than those occurring in sparsely canopied open stands with scanty subordinate ground cover. Canopy density is of little importance in hardwoods because the foliage is relatively nonflammable. Damage is controlled mostly by the flammability of subordinate vegetation and surface fuels. The volume and vertical distribution of available fuels, affecting crown-fire incidence, and the duration and intensity of the fire are closely related to stand habit.

9. *Season and growth cycle.* The seasonal stage of growth affects net damage in three ways. First, it greatly affects the total moisture content of the crown, which in turn affects its flammability. Second, new succulent growth is much more susceptible to fire damage. So growing tips and cambium are more easily damaged during the active growing stage than during the dormant state. Third, the ability of the tree to recover is affected by the food reserves in the roots, which fluctuate with the season. Fortunately, the rapid growing stage, when food reserves are low, is also the period of lowest susceptibility to crown fires.[8]

Natural Fire Resistance

The relative fire resistance of tree species is determined by basal bark thickness of mature trees, character of the individual tree crown and forest stand, and rooting pattern (see Table 11-1, p. 156, and Table 11-2, p. 157). Typically, the less intense fires are ground fires that may cause damage to the lower bole. Mature trees, which have thick bark on the lower bole, are more resistant to fire injury than younger trees, which have thinner bark and more succulent tissue. The character of the individual tree crown is important since low, dense crowns are more susceptible to crown fires than higher, less dense tops. Similarly, stands of trees that grow in a very dense pattern, such as spruce or fir, are more prone to devastating crown fires than those growing in open stands, such as ponderosa pine. Rooting patterns (deep versus shallow) obviously determine susceptibility of roots to injury.

Physical Damage

A fire that causes partial damage to an area usually leaves some basal injuries on standing trees that heal over and form scars. Since these indicate previous fire damage, you can determine the history, frequency, and intensity of fire in the existing stand from older, living trees. These scars also make trees more susceptible to insect and disease attacks due to increased ease of entry and decreased vigor of the tree.

Effects on Microclimate

The microclimate is the summation of local site factors that create a unique climate for a specific site and distinguish it from adjacent sites by factors such as soil, water, vegetation, and solar radiation. These interact to produce local air temperatures, relative humidity, soil moisture regimen, and air movement. Probably the greatest single factor in maintaining existing microclimate is overstory vegetation. If it is destroyed, temperatures rise, moisture is lost, humidity decreases, and air movement increases, accelerating the drying effect.

The degree of change in microclimate determines plant succession on the site. If the change is too drastic, plant succession is extremely slow, with potential dramatic effects on soil, air and water conditions.[8] Some other effects may be temporary loss of wildlife and bird habitat, change in water flow and chemistry of nearby streams, and so forth. The microclimate is a complex and dynamic system that can affect large areas outside the fire's perimeter. This requires monitoring the effects of a fire on all aspects of the microclimate as well as surrounding influence areas.

Effects on Soil

The effects of fire on soil include loss of unincorporated organic material, change in physical conditions through erosion and possibly aggregation of soil particles, change in soil chemistry, and loss of soil organisms by heating.

Unincorporated organic material forms a layer over the mineral soil and, as it breaks down, becomes soil nutrients. It protects the earth from heating and allows water infiltration without compaction.

Physical conditions of the soil are changed by compaction and erosion of exposed mineral soil. The force of raindrops directly hitting the ground causes compaction of the heavier soils. Fire seals the surface, causing runoff and subsequent erosion, or bakes soil particles to form larger aggregates, reducing pore space, aeration, and nutrient exchange. In addition, fire produces charcoal, which is black, durable, and high in heat-absorptive capacity.[8] This creates higher-than-normal surface soil temperatures that may have a lethal effect on natural reproduction of ground cover. Fire produces chemical changes in the soil through combustion of organic material. The immediate effect of this process is the release of mineral elements into the earth, increasing available plant nutrients. The surge of nutrients stimulates revegetation of the site unless the soil is very sandy—in which case, nutrients soon become completely leached out away from the root zone. In heavier soils, the increased nutrient supply can last several years.[8] Leaching may affect the total ecosystem, including lakes and rivers within the system.

After a fire, the pH of the soil becomes more basic in the primary root zone area. This decrease in acidity causes an increase in nitrification by the immediate invasion of light-seeded, nitrogen-fixing organisms that are more adaptable to the higher pH levels. Even small changes in pH can cause significant changes in the growth of vegetation.[46]

The significant biological effects of a fire are often equated only with changes in flora and fauna. Yet other, less apparent biological effects occur in the soil. Fires that destroy the protective humus layer often reduce the number of beneficial soil organisms. In nonlethal fires, either increased soil temperatures or a change in soil chemistry may actually stimulate the productivity of soil organisms.[8]

Table 11-1. Relative fire resistance of selected conifers of the Western United States. (after Starker [1934] and Flint [1925])*

Species	Basal Bark Thickness of Mature Trees	Character of Tree Crown	Character of Stands	Rooting Habit	Associated Lichen Growth
Extremely resistant: (old trees only): Redwood (Sequoia sempervirens)	Extremely thick	High and moderately open	Dense	Not a factor	
Western larch (Larix occidentalis)	Very thick	High and very open	Moderately open	Deep	Medium
Highly resistant: Ponderosa pine (Pinus ponderosa)	Very thick	Moderately high and open	Open	Deep	Light
Douglas-fir (Pseudotsuga menziesii)	Very thick	Moderately high and dense	Dense	Deep	Heavy
Moderately resistant: White and grand fir (Abies concolor and grandis)	Thick	Low and dense	Dense	Moderately shallow	Heavy
White pine and sugar pine (Pinus monticola and lambertiana)	Medium	Moderately high and dense	Dense	Medium	Medium
Lodgepole pine (Pinus contorta)	Very thin	Moderately high and open	Open	Deep	Medium
Low resistance: Western red cedar (Thuja plicata)	Thin	Low and dense	Dense	Shallow	Moderate to heavy
Western hemlock (Tsuga heterophylla)	Medium	Low and dense	Dense	Shallow	Heavy
Engelmann spruce (Picea engelmanii)	Thin	Low and dense	Dense	Shallow	Heavy
Sitka spruce (Picea sitchensis)	Thin	Moderately high and dense	Dense	Shallow	Heavy
Very low resistance: Alpine fir (Abies lasiocarpa)	Very thin	Very low and dense	Dense	Shallow	Heavy

* From Brown, A. A., and Davis, K. P. 1973. *Forest Fire: Control and Use*, 2nd Edition. New York, NY: McGraw-Hill Book Company. pp. 52-53.

Table 11-2. Relative fire resistance of selected conifers of the Eastern United States, (after Starker [1934] and others)*

Species and Resistance Group	Basal Bark Thickness of Mature Trees	Character of Tree Crown**	Character of Stands	Rooting Habit
Highly resistant:				
Longleaf pine (Pinus palustris)	Thick	High and open	Open	Very deep
Resistant:				
Pitch pine (Pinus rigida)	Medium	Moderately high and open	Moderately open	Medium deep
Pond pine (Pinus serotina)	Medium	Moderately high and open	Moderately open	Medium
Red pine (Pinus resinosa)	Medium	Moderately high and dense	Moderately open	Deep
Slash pine (Pinus elliottii)	Medium	Moderately high and open	Moderately open	Medium deep
Shortleaf pine (Pinus echinata)	Medium	Moderately high and open	Moderately open	Medium deep
Loblolly pine (Pinus taeda)	Medium	Medium height and density	Moderately dense	Medium
Moderately resistant:				
Chestnut oak (Quercus montana)	Thick		Moderately dense	Medium
Yellow poplar (Liriodendron tulipifera)	Medium		Moderately dense	Medium
Black and post oak (Quercus vetulina, stellata)	Medium		Moderately open	Medium
Eastern white pine (Pinus strobus)	Medium	Medium height and density	Medium dense	Medium
Jack pine (Pinus banksiana)	Medium	Medium height and density	Moderately open	Medium
Of intermediate resistance:				
Red oak (Quercus rubra)	Medium		Medium	Medium
Hickory (Carya spp.)	Medium		Moderately dense	Medium
Sweetgum (Liquidambar styraciflua)	Moderately thin		Moderately dense	Medium
White oak (Quercus alba)	Moderately thin		Moderately dense	Medium
Of low resistance:				
Sugar maple (Acer saccharum)	Moderately thin		Dense	Medium
Scarlet oak (Quercus coccinea)			Dense	Medium
Yellow birch (Betula lutea)	Moderately thin		Dense	Medium
Black cherry (Prunus serotina)	Moderately thin		Dense	Medium
Spruces (Picea spp.)	Thin	Low and dense	Dense	Shallow
Aspens (Poplus tremuloides and grandidentata)	Thin	High and open	Medium	Medium
Cedars (Thuja and Juniperus spp.)	Thin	Medium height and density	Dense	Shallow
Firs (Abies spp.)	Very thin	Low and dense	Dense	Shallow

* From Brown, A. A., and Davis, K. P. 1973. *Forest Fire: Control and Use*, 2nd Edition. New York, NY: McGraw-Hill Book Company
** Not considered significant for hardwoods since fires seldom burn in crowns.

A BASIC APPROACH TO ECOSYSTEM MANAGEMENT

Management must answer several questions. Where is a given natural area in the scheme of ecological succession? Where should it be? And what kind of management strategies move succession from where it is to where you want it to be? From a practical perspective, is such a move achievable?

In response to these questions, managers must consider several steps.

Inventory of Present Conditions

An inventory of present soil and vegetative conditions is an important first step. This tells you what stage of succession the system is in, which you then use as the baseline for judging the effects of either naturally or artificially introduced change. You should sample all components to determine the present condition of the vegetation (overstory and ground cover), fauna (vertebrate and nonvertebrate), water (open bodies and ground water), and soil (soil profile and chemistry). However, as we pointed out earlier, this sampling should focus on the first trophic level—green vegetation. Possibly a single small representative drainage can be singled out for intensive sampling.

Ecological Modeling

In step one, you determine existing conditions; in this step you want to predict the ideal—what the area should look like without the interference of modern European man. There are many computer models dealing with specific regions which could be used to project the normal ecological stage of a given ecosystem, assuming agents of change need not be suppressed. Even if computer models are available for your situation, generally enough is known about a given ecosystem to qualitatively and quantitatively describe the normal ecological succession from agents of change.

The mosaic pattern of vegetation associated with a given terrain will not only reflect the effects of agents of change, like fire, but also reflect local microclimatic conditions which mitigate the impacts. Certainly soil moisture, air mass flows, lightning storm patterns, natural fire breaks, fire history, understory vegetation, etc. can be used to characterize the expected vegetation pattern. With modern geographic information systems (assuming the data are easily obtainable), and with or without ecosystem computer models, one can estimate the probable vegetative patterns brought about by fire regimes. This is essential for comparison with the present situation with fire removed.

Reconstruction of Recent Ecological History

In this step you are trying to determine how best to move from the present to the ideal. Essentially what you are looking for are the tools, techniques, and applications that nature used before European man came on the scene. Thus, to trace the history of an area, you must first determine the *baseline* conditions during the most recent period prior to the intervention of European man. One pinpoints these primarily by the alteration or elimination of significant agents of change— fire, flood, insects/diseases, etc. You then link together successional changes and the agents of such changes for the period under study. In the case of fire, it is not sufficient to simply reconstruct historical trends without some indication of their effects on vegetative succession. Reconstruction of recent ecological history should give you an indication of not only the vegetation types one can encourage, but also the primary agents nature uses to do so, the periodicity of change, and the size/shape of the areas within which dynamic equilibria were achieved. In theory, specific policy is adopted to move present conditions to the ecological "norms" for a particular area without the interference of modern man. Those ecological "norms" vary over a large area based on differences in microclimatic conditions. You must also adopt a strategy to maintain dynamic equilibrium once the "ideal" is achieved.

Reconstruction of fire history utilizes fire dating, historic records, and interviews. Fire dating is done by dendrochronological examination of fire scars on living vegetation or by carbon-dating charcoal layers in the soil.

Standing trees can be living testimony of a natural catastrophe such as a wildfire. You can date fire scars on living trees by counting tree rings from tree cores (see Figure 11-2). However, using fire scars to date fire history has its limitations. Logging, mining, and biologically disruptive land uses have eliminated most of the older, virgin trees that could have provided a chronological fire record over several hundred years. Without these older trees, it is difficult to reconstruct the natural cycle of fire since recent fire history has been directly affected by fire suppression and other management activities. Except for isolated tracts of old timber, generally only wilderness areas and dedicated natural areas offer good chronographs of fire history.

However, even most of these areas have typically been included in the universal policy of modern fire suppression. Also, destructive fires may have eliminated older trees for fire

Figure 11-2. Fire dating using old fire scars in the annual rings. (From Heinselman, M.L. 1969. "Diary of the Canoe County's Landscape." *Naturalist 20*(1): 13.)

dating. This means you may have to search harder for the remaining clusters of trees that escaped the destructive fires. Even then, geographic boundaries of individual fires may be difficult to determine if only clusters of older trees remain instead of the original, expansive forests.

The history of fire in a particular area should be limited to geographic boundaries so that you can focus your fire-management plan on when and where fire has been a major force in the ecology of the particular area. Also, base your procedure for reintroducing a fire artificially on specific geographic boundaries and the cycles from previous fire history. Researchers are finding many areas in which fire has played only an insignificant ecological role.

Carbon dating can also help you to compile a fire history, and if you locate large enough pieces of charcoal, you can determine the species involved in the fire. Carbon dating of burned stump/logs can also be used to reconstruct fire history. A more sophisticated technique is to first make a pollen analysis of lake sediments to determine the dynamic successional changes and then to date each layer of sediment, using carbon dating.[17]

Historical records, from newspaper clippings to trappers' diaries, are useful in dating fires for a particular locale. They can help verify tree-ring counts from old, fire-scarred trees as well as establish a fire history for locales where no living vegetation exists to serve as evidence. In that case, you should search for other written accounts, such as paintings, hospital records, and other local historical accounts, to verify the date and location of the fire. If the fires occurred within the last seventy-five years, personal interviews with early residents of the area can assist in reconstructing a detailed fire history.

Establishment of Policy

Based on a comparison of present conditions and projected ecological norms, you must establish a policy to move the existing situation toward the conditions represented by anticipated norms. In fire management, this is often called the "burn or no burn" decision. Accepted policy for areas to be burned has been that all natural fires are allowed to burn and all man-made fires are suppressed. This has moved agencies away from the "all-fires-are-bad" policy to one where natural fires are "good" and "man-caused" fires are bad. If we had good natural fire breaks and wildfires had not been suppressed in the past, perhaps such a distinction between good and bad would be an appropriate policy. However, the fire suppression policies of the past have caused significant vegetative changes and a build-up of fuel wood on the ground. Now any fire, natural or man-caused, has the potential to be a bad one because, under the right conditions, it can become so destructive or severe that in its aftermath the uniform, mature pattern of vegetation is replaced by a younger cover offering no more ecological diversity than the original one. On the other hand, any fire has the potential to be beneficial if it produces the desired pattern of ecological diversity.

Often land-use goals conflict. When these conflicts arise, you must establish a goal priority system to determine which decision takes priority. In areas where intensive development priorities exist, like housing, recreation, and quality-timber sites, the policy must be no burn. In other areas this distinction is not so clear. However, if the decision is to burn, then you must also determine which method to use—to let natural fires burn or to prescribe burn by introducing fires artificially in order to achieve the same objectives. These are all priority decisions that must be made a part of the fire management plan. If such policies are not established, you may choose a less desirable course of action under pressure from the public, other agencies, or higher headquarters when a major fire erupts.

A "burn or no burn" decision is the first order, and a base map can delineate no-burn zones. This means that any fire within the no-burn zone or any outside the zone that can affect it should be suppressed. Here there is no question that the proper course of action is to eliminate fire as an agent of change. However, before that decision is made a part of the fire management plan, it is advisable to enumerate the opportunity costs (values lost from the effects of wildfires foregone when the decision is not to burn). In fact, the last management step mentioned in this chapter, interpretation of the natural role of the fire, is to direct such enumeration to the public so they, too, understand the trade-offs.

Burn zones are delineated based on the historic role of fire in maintaining the ecosystem, their relationship to the no-burn zones, and the agreement among landowners that this is the proper management course. You must further separate burn zones into "let burn" and "prescribe burn." Prescribe burn subzones are so designated because there are typically insufficient natural fire breaks to guarantee that a natural fire stays within the subzone boundary. Fires within these subzones are started by management under conditions that predictably produce the desired diversity, yet are easily contained within the boundaries through appropriate management actions. By definition, wildfires are suppressed in these subzones because they are typically not containable within set boundaries. Prescribed burn subzones may never be burned because the right combination of terrain, fuel moisture, and atmospheric conditions

cannot be achieved to guarantee containment. Under these conditions, some agencies have resorted to mechanical disturbances to create some diversity. Wood is shredded mechanically and allowed to rot, returning the nutrients to the soil slowly; or it is piled and burned.

Let-burn subzones pose the greatest challenge to management. Any fire predicted to be a threat to a no-burn zone must be suppressed. Under present modern policy, we suspect that all other wildfires should be normally allowed to run their courses with one stipulation: that the effects of all fires be predicted and, based on those predictions, fires are allowed to run their course or are stopped. Those that produce desired diversity should be the only ones allowed to burn.

Using Alaska as an example, we can envision large areas of let-burn subzones because of the isolation, natural firebreaks, and lack of competing land values. However, when applied to other regions, it becomes very difficult to delineate let-burn subzones. Some areas obviously fit the policy requirements. Others may fit with close monitoring while being prepared for a major suppression effort if necessary. At least these areas can be recognized as part of the burn zone that requires fire as the primary element of change. Whether this is achieved through natural or man-caused activities is probably not important. The let-burn policy should simply be viewed as the least costly solution to achieving desired ecological norms, assuming that you can predict that a given wildfire will produce those results and be contained within specified boundaries.

Coordination of Fire Management

The key to fire management planning is coordination. With the mixture of landownership and thus diverse and often competing land management goals, it is essential that all affected parties work out an agreement on how to handle fires on wildlands. Negotiations on a proper course of action must take place before the fire starts, not after. These should produce a fire management plan that establishes a basic policy for handling fires on all affected lands.

The plan should not only delineate policy direction for each zone but also agency roles/responsibilities in carrying out that plan. One of those roles is monitoring implementation to ensure compliance with policies. The state of Alaska, for example, has been divided into five fire management regions with separate fire management plans. A coordinating team consisting of representatives from all affected agencies and the private sector develops policy direction to meet goals for specified geographical areas. Primary suppression responsibility rests either with the U.S. Bureau of Land Management or the Alaska State Department of Natural Resources. Managers of individual parcels of land within the region monitor the implementation of plans for their own lands. Once a plan is agreed upon by the agencies, it is then distributed for public input. Unfortunately public sentiment, fostered by earlier agency programs that suppressed all fires, is often against letting any fires burn. This adds to the agency's responsibility to increase the public's understanding of the benefits of fire.

Interpretation of the Natural Role of Fire

Interpretation of the natural role of fire in the scheme of wildland management is one of the keys to the successful development and implementation of any fire-management plan. This means that agencies are going to have to work with the public on a continuous basis to inform them about the natural role of fire well before any plan is presented for their comments. Without some understanding of the role of fire and the benefits to be derived, as well as being forced by time constraints to get a plan approved, the public understandably rebels at accepting the idea that fires, which used to be bad, are now good. This does not mean that everyone is going to agree and accept the plan; however, it should give the interested public a better foundation for judging a plan's merits.

A SUMMARY

Use of fire as a management tool is controversial, but where education is well-handled, support replaces controversy. The acceptance of fire-management planning appears to be directly linked to public understanding of goals such as maintaining the habitats of critical wildlife and fisheries and using wildfires in achieving that. Even then, because the system is out of kilter due to previous decades of fire suppression, all man-caused fires as primary agents of change are not necessarily bad and all wildfires good. If we had already attained a natural balance, perhaps we could make that statement. Probably a more realistic way of solving the problem is to establish "let burn" zones and monitor any new fires. If it appears that these create or help create the desired mosaic of vegetative patterns—similar to a "pre-Columbian" state—then let them burn. If not, put them out.

Severity is a term which refers to how severe or destructive a fire is. Very severe fires will likely replace the lack of diversity of vegetation with a new uniform carpet that shows a similar lack of diversity. By monitoring fuel build-up, fuel moisture, relative humidity, and wind conditions, you should be able to project the severity of a given fire just like it is done in a prescribe-burn situation. Prescribed burns are carried out where conditions do not allow natural fires to run their courses. Ecological diversity in wilderness/natural areas is important to the well-being of the ecosystem and also provides a diversity of environmental settings and thus diversity in recreational opportunities. Where other significant land values exist, the obvious course of action is to suppress all fires.

A critical link to the acceptance and implementation of fire management plans is public education. On-site information/ interpretive programs are beneficial; however, it is important to use the mass media to reach large audiences potentially affected by the plan.

Cost-benefit analysis is also important. Costs are high for fire suppression, and many administrative units spend a goodly portion of their budgets on fire suppression while other program areas go lacking. On the benefit side, you can estimate benefits even for foregone market and nonmarket values like wildlife and recreation based on the predicted outcome of the fire and cost of suppression. While estimating the benefits and costs of a particular fire may not be easy and cheap, the fact remains that the large sums of money for fire suppression should be spent efficiently to achieve public goals. It would not be unusual in Alaska, for example, to spend one to two million dollars on suppressing a single fire that protects, say thirty to fifty thousand dollars of public/private values. In the process, other public values such as improved moose browse may be foregone. We suspect that many fires in smaller natural areas can easily be handled with the cost benefit technique.

The key to ecosystems management in natural areas probably has less to do with understanding the ecological process taking place there and delineating a boundary where primary forces of nature can run their courses than resolving the conflicts between competing land uses and thus agreeing on a course of action.

SELECTED READINGS

1.   Agee, J. K., and Johnson, D. R. (eds.). 1989. *Ecosystem Management for Parks and Wilderness.* Seattle, WA: University of Washington Press.

2.   Agee, J. K. 1974. "Fire Management in the National Parks." *Western Wildlands 1*(3):27.

3.   Aldrich, D. F., and Mutch, R. W. 1972. "Wilderness Fires Allowed to Burn More Naturally," U.S. Forest Service *Fire Control Notes 33*(1): Washington, DC: U.S. Government Printing Office.

4.   Anderson, H. E. 1983. Predicting Wind Driven Wildland Fire Size and Shape. USDA-Forest Service Research Paper, INT-305.

5.   Andrews, P. L. 1986. BEHAVE: Fire Behavior Prediction Model and Fuel Modeling System BURN Subsystem, Part I. USDA-Forest Service General Technical Report, INT-194.

6.   Barney, R. J. 1979. Fire Control in the 80's Symposium. Missoula, MT: Intermountain Fire Council and Society of American Foresters.

7. Biswell, H. H. 1988. *Prescribed Burning,* Berkeley, CA: University of California Press.

8. Brown, A. A., and Davis, K. P. 1973. *Forest Fire: Control and Use,* 2nd Edition. New York, NY: McGraw-Hill Book Co.

9. Brown, J. K. 1982. Fuel and Fire Behavior Prediction in Big Sagebrush. USDA-Forest Service Research Paper, INT-290.

10. Carey, A., and Carey, S. 1989. *Yellowstone's Red Summer.* Flagstaff, AZ: Northland Publishing.

11. Connally, E. H. 1982. *National Parks in Crisis.* Washington, DC: National Parks and Conservation Association.

12. Cushing, E. J. 1969. "The Changing Landscape: Clues from the Canoe Country's Lakes." *Naturalist* 20(1):18.

13. Dottavio, F. D., et al. (eds.). 1990. Protecting Biological Diversity in National Parks: Workshop Recommendations. Atlanta, GA: National Park Service Science Publications.

14. Douglas, G. W., and Ballard, T. M. 1971. "Effects of Fire on Alpine Plant Communities in the North Cascades, Washington." *Ecology* 52:1058.

15. Gill, A. M. 1974. "Towards an Understanding of Fire Scar Formation: Field Observation and Laboratory Simulation." *Forest Science* 20:198.

16. Hall, C. A. S., and Day, J. W., Jr. 1977. *Ecosystem Modeling in Theory and Practice.* New York, NY: John Wiley & Sons.

17. Hansen, H. P. 1955. "Postglacial Forests in South Central and Central British Columbia," *American Jour. Sci.* v.253: 640-658. (also see Fig. 11-2 in C. B. Schultz & H. T. U. Smith (eds.).

1965. INQUA, VIIth Congress Guidebook, field conference J, Aug-Sep., Lincoln: University of Nebraska Press.)

18. Hartesveldt, R. J. et al. 1975. *The Giant Sequoia of the Sierra Nevada,* Washington, DC: U.S. Government Printing Office.

19. Heinselman, M. L. 1966. "Vegetation in Wilderness Areas." *Trends* 3(1):23.

20. Hendrickson, W. H. 1962. "Fire in the National Park Symposium." *Tall Timbers Fire Ecology Conference, Proceedings,* No. 2., Tallahassee, FL: Tall Timbers Research Station.

21. Houston, D. B. 1973. "Wildfire in Northern Yellowstone National Park." *Ecology* 54(5):1111.

22. Howe, G. E. 1975. "The Evolutionary Role of Wildfire in the Northern Rockies and Implications for Resource Managers." *Tall Timbers Fire Ecology Conference, Proceedings,* Volume 14.

23. Hunter, M. L. 1990. *Wildlife, Forests, and Forestry: Principles of Managing Forests for Biological Diversity.* Englewood Cliffs, NJ: Prentice-Hall.

24. Kilgore, B. M. 1975. "Restoring Fire to National Park Wilderness." *American Forests* 81(3):16,57.

25. Kilgore, B. M. 1984. "Restoring Fire's Natural Role in America's Wilderness." *Western Wildlands,* 10(2):2-8.

26. Komarek, Sr., E. V. 1966. "The Use of Fire: A Historical Background." *Tall Timbers Fire Ecology Conference, Proceedings,* Volume 6. Tallahassee, FL: Tall Timbers Research Station.

27. Leopold, A. S., Cain, S. A., Gabrielson, I. N., Cottam, C. M., and Kimball, T. L. 1963. "Wildlife Management in the National Parks." *The Living Wilderness* 83:11.

28. Loope, L. L., and Wood, R. P. 1975. "Fire Management in Grand Teton National Park." *Tall Timbers Fire Ecology Conference, Proceedings,* Volume 14. Tallahassee, FL: Tall Timbers Research Station.

29. Lunan, J. S., and Habeck, J. R. 1973. "The Effects of Fire Exclusion on Ponderosa Pine Communities in Glacier National Park, Montana." *Canadian Journal of Forest Research,* 3:574.

30. McLaughlin, J. S. 1972. "Restoring Fire to the Environment of the National Parks." *Tall Timbers Fire Ecology Conference, Proceedings,* Volume 12. Tallahassee, FL: Tall Timbers Research Station.

31. McNeeley, J. A., and Meller, K. R. (eds.). 1984. *National Parks, Conservation and Development: The Role of Protected Areas in Sustaining Society.* Washington, DC: National Parks and Conservation Association.

32. Mitchell, R. S., Sheviak, C. J., and Leopold, D. L. 1988. *Ecosystem Management, Rare Species, and Significant Habitats.* Albany, NY: Proceedings, 15th Annual Natural Areas Conference.

33. Mutch, R. W. 1970. "Wildland Fires and Ecosystems: A Hypothesis." *Ecology* 51(6):1046.

34. Mutch, R. W., and Aldrich, D. F. 1973. Wilderness Fire Management: Planning Guidelines and Inventory Procedures. U.S. Forest Service, Region 1, Missoula, MT.

35. National Park Service. 1975. The Natural Role of Fire: A Fire Management Plan. Yellowstone National Park, Wyoming.

36. National Parks and Conservation Association. 1988. *Investing in Park Futures: A Blueprint for Tomorrow.* Vol. 1, To Preserve Unimpaired: The Challenge of Protecting Park Resources. Washington, DC: National Parks and Conservation Association.

37. Peek, J. M. 1981. "Thoughts on Preservation." *Western Wildlands,* 7(1):13-15.

38. Peterson, D. L., and Flowers, P. J. 1984. Estimating Postfire Changes in Production and Value of Northern Rocky Mountain and Intermountain Rangelands. USDA-Forest Service Research Paper, PSW-173,

39. Polunin, N. 1986. *Ecosystem Theory and Application.* New York, NY: John Wiley & Sons.

40. Pritchett, W. L. 1987. *Properties and Management of Forest Soils.* New York, NY: John Wiley & Sons.

41. Pyne, S. J. 1984. *Introduction to Wildland Fire: Fire Management in U.S. History.* New York, NY: John Wiley & Sons.

42. Pyne, S. J. 1982. *Fire in America, A Cultural History of Wildland and Rural Fire,* Princeton, NJ: Princeton University Press.

43. Rundel, R. W. 1973. "The Relationship between Basal Fire Scars and Crown Damage in Giant Sequoia." *Ecology* 54:210.

44. Schiff, A. L. 1962. *Fire and Water: Scientific Heresy in the Forest Service,* Cambridge, MA: Harvard University Press.

45. Sellers, R. E., and Despain, D. G. 1974. "Fire Management in Yellowstone National Park." *Tall Timbers Fire Ecology Conference, Proceedings,* Volume 14. Tallahassee, FL: Tall Timbers Research Station.

46. Spurr, S. H. 1980. *Forest Ecology.* 3rd edition. New York: John Wiley & Sons, Inc.

47. Sweeney, J. R. 1967. "Ecology of Some Fire Type Vegetation in Northern California." *Tall Timbers Fire Ecology Conference, Proceedings,* Volume 7. Tallahassee, FL: Tall Timbers Research Station.

48. Taylor, D. L. 1973. "Some Ecological Implications of Forest Fire Control in Yellowstone National Park, Wyoming." *Ecology 54*(6):1394.

49. USDA-Forest Service. 1985. Fire's Effects on Wildlife Habitat: Symposium Proceedings. USDA Forest Service General Technical Report, INT-186.

50. USDA-Forest Service. 1983. Proceedings, Symposium and Workshop on Wilderness Fire. USDA-Forest Service General Technical Report, INT-182.

51. Van Nao, T. 1981. Forest Fire Prevention and Control: Proceedings. Timber Committee of the United Nations, Economic Commission On Europe.

52. Vogel, C. G. 1990. *Great Yellowstone Fire* (Vol.1). Boston, MA: Little, Brown & Co.

53. Waring, R. H., and Schlesinger, W. H. 1985. *Forest Ecosystems: Concepts and Management.* Corpus Christi, TX: Academic Press, Inc.

54. Wright, H. E., Jr., and Heinselman, M. L. (eds.). 1973. "The Ecological Role of Fire in Natural Conifer Forests of Western and Northern America." *Quaternary Research* 3:317.

CHAPTER 12

Visual Resource Management

Plan in full awareness of nature's forces, forms, and features—the sweep of the sun, the air currents, the peaks and hollows of the earth, rock and soil strata, vegetation, lakes and streams, watersheds and natural drainage ways—and this awareness should obviously entail planning in harmony with the elements of nature. If we disregard them, we will engender countless unnecessary frictions and preclude those experiences of fitness and compatibility that can bring so much pleasure and satisfaction to our lives.[24]

Approximately eighty-seven percent of our perception of the landscape is based on sight. If we are to enjoy the aesthetic beauty of the environment, we must protect these important visual elements. Where possible, we can also manipulate viewing distance, lighting, and vertical position, so that the observer's enjoyment of the landscape is enhanced. Too often, planners interpret this approach in the context of the superlative view and forget the typical one. Unfortunately, most people participate in recreational activities on typical, regional landscapes. If we agreed with the planners' interpretation, we would be remiss in our jobs as recreation managers since very few superlative landscapes exist and we are already protecting many of those. At the same time, we are rapidly losing the typical landscape to incompatible and often destructive changes. This in turn lowers its quality and desirability as a place for living as well as for recreational activities. We do not mean to imply that all incompatible land uses must cease. However, to protect the treasured beauty of our surrounding landscapes, we must alter many existing land use practices. In some instances, this may mean renovating the landscape to produce an acceptable visual environment.

In most cases, there are no simple answers. Innovative approaches are necessary because of the conflict in public interest, from aesthetic to economic, over existing and proposed land uses and the potentially high cost of maintaining or renovating landscapes. But with a minimal investment, a Midwest city was able to turn "eyesores" (i.e., old gravel pits) into beautifully landscaped, open-space areas for water-based recreational activities. The municipal government even bought up gravel reserves outside its jurisdiction so that, as the city expands, water-based parks can become an integral part of any new neighborhoods—at zero cost.

Therefore, visual resource management is a term that refers to the way in which the visual qualities of a landscape are handled to produce the maximum aesthetic response. This is only achieved by first understanding what people are responding to in the landscape, and then mitigating the impact of man's activities on those elements.

---

*Parts of this chapter have been adapted from *National Forest Landscape Management,* vol.1, 1973, U.S. Forest Service, and "The Visual Management System," *National Forest Landscape Management,* Vol. II, 1974, Washington, DC: U.S. Department of Agriculture.

AESTHETIC RESPONSE TO THE LANDSCAPE

Several models attempt to describe how people respond to the landscape (see Selected Readings). Many of these focus on landscape elements and simply disregard the observer. Other models are based on personal biases without any theoretical reasoning as to relationships or predictability. Some researchers have translated peoples' responses to the landscape into quantitative terms. However, the basic model of aesthetic response is more than a function of a static, unchanging landscape; it is a response based on the dynamic relationship of many classes of variables, from environmental to social. The following equation describes this response:

$$VP = f (BO, E, OLR, CO),$$

> VP =   the aesthetic response of
>   the observer,
>
> BO =   the background of the observer,
>
> EC =   the environmental conditions
>   under which the observation
>   takes place,
>
> OLR = the observer/landscape
>   relationships, and
>
> CO =   the character of the object
>   being observed.

How people respond to their visual perception of the landscape depends on the background of each individual, i.e., previous learning experiences to which that individual has been exposed. These experiences shape attitudes toward certain environmental stimuli. For example, people who live in high-density areas may perceive gateway towns to national parks as desirable settings that accommodate their needs; whereas, someone who wants to aesthetically experience and enjoy the unmodified landscape of a natural park may see these towns as man-made disasters. The haze in the valley from the cement processing plant may be perceived as an aesthetic disaster by one person and economic prosperity by another. We respond not just based on conditioning from previous experiences, but also on our motivations at the time. It is only after more mundane needs are met, such as the financial survival of the family and perhaps the community, that we are able to view the haze from the cement plant as potentially harmful or aesthetically undesirable.

Environmental conditions for observation can vary considerably, often during the course of a single day. Perception of the landscape is affected by these changes, from the obvious such as direct sunlight or fog to the more subtle, such as temperature inversions which trap smoke and smog but are only visible above the inversion layer.

Observer/landscape relations are further discussed by Litton.[11] He claims that the relationship of the observer to the observed is important to visual resource management. The landscape is more than just a state of mind; it is an array of environmental stimuli bombarding the individual. Each person reacts to this stimuli according to his or her state of mind and the conditions under which the observation takes place.[12] Thus, to be effective in management prescription, managers must be able to describe the landscape—both its physical aspects and the observer's response—in tangible terms. Doing this should provide a firmer grasp of the effects of landscape manipulation on the aesthetic experience of the user. If a response is predictably negative, the project can be redesigned, relocated, or eliminated in order to maintain the appeal of the landscape.

Sometimes environmental manipulations enhance the aesthetic appeal of an altered landscape, depending on existing conditions from past land uses and the state of mind of the observer. Removing offensive sights like junkyards, or removing vegetation to create natural-appearing openings in a mundane forest landscape, are examples of enhancing aesthetics.

Lastly, the character of the object being observed affects how we perceive the natural landscape. While the uniqueness of the object in comparison to its surroundings attracts our attention, it is the contrast between the object and its surroundings that enhances the object and thus our ability to perceive it. There are three categories of variables that interplay to create our perceptions of landscapes: dominance elements, principles of dominance, and environmental factors.

DOMINANCE ELEMENTS

Four elements that compete for dominance in any landscape are form, line, color, and texture. It is important to analyze their relative strengths in an existing landscape and the possible effects proposed developments may have on them. Developments should generally complement, or at least not detract from, more dominant elements. If alterations supplant them, they may destroy the natural harmonious appeal of the landscape or, worse, create a landscape that people react to negatively.

Form

Form is the mass of an object or of a combination of objects that appears unified. When viewed in two dimensions, it is referred to as shape.

Line

Line is the intersection of two planes. In nature, it occurs in shorelines, timberlines, meadow edges, avalanche paths, vegetation boundaries, ridge lines and tree trunks.

Color

Color patterns of landscapes are important in differentiating objects. Your perception of color often depends greatly on your position; distant colors appear muted while foreground colors seem stronger and more dominant. This contrast is especially obvious when you view the same color from varying distances. Color can be described in terms of hue, such as blue and green, and value such as the tonal quality between light and dark. Value tends to dominate hue, except in very close viewing; however, a detectable variation gives greater clarity to the elements of a landscape—the golden yellow of a dandelion meadow in contrast with the brilliant blue of a mountain lake, for example.

Texture

The dominant texture, or grain, of a landscape varies with distance. From short distances, individual trees or leaf patterns may show more than the rough texture of bark or clusters of leaves. From greater distances, stands of trees may be dominant and appear to have a medium texture. From extreme distances, the texture of the entire viewing area may appear homogeneous and relatively smooth.

PRINCIPLES OF DOMINANCE

Six principles affect the visual dominance of form, line, color, and texture in a landscape:

Contrast

Contrast is important in discriminating form. In areas dominated by heavy texture and little variation, any change in the landscape produces a sharp contrast and is quickly recognized by any observer.

Sequence

There are two aspects to sequence: sequential landscapes and sequential experiences. Sequential landscapes are those in which the dominant elements of form, line, color, and texture are repeated in the specific area. Potential developments or activities for an area should thus be evaluated according to their visual effect on the continuity of these elements. Any development or activity imposed on a specific area should complement its landscape sequence. Otherwise, the development will most likely appear incongruent or out of sequence.

Sequential experiences are also important: "A well-planned sequence of visual experiences can enrich viewer appreciation."[29] Since most people travel by developed transportation systems such as roads or trails, we might try to maximize a hiking or driving experience by utilizing sequence. Perhaps the focus of a trail is St. Mary's Peak. Exposing the peak to hikers at given distances through trail location and/or vista clearings should heighten their anticipation of the next exposure as well as increase their appreciation of this dominant feature. With constant exposure to the peak, however, change may be so continuous and gradual that it is difficult to really appreciate.

Axis

Axis is the main line of focus created by converging lines toward some central point. Observers focus secondary attention on the lines of approach to a focal point. An axis can be natural, such as a river, an elongated ridge, or a narrow valley; or man-made, such as a road, a fence line, or a bridge. It can also be used intentionally to focus attention on natural or man-made objects of interest. For example, the tunnels on the road through Mt. Rushmore National Memorial Park form the axes which focus attention on Mt. Rushmore. In identifying axes and focal points for visitors, managers should try to maintain the continuity of the axis, the immediate landscape around the axis, and the background of the particular landscape. If this continuity is disrupted, attention may be directed away from the primary object, diminishing visual aesthetics for visitors.

Convergence

In convergence, several axes meet at a single focal point. Regardless of which axis you focus on, all ultimately lead to a focal point. Thus the area around a point of convergence is a dominant part of the landscape, and any development in this area should blend with the character of the landscape. Even then, development in these locations should serve as a backdrop to activities and/or facilities such as visitor centers.

Multi-dominance

Multi-dominance is created by two or more similar features in a landscape view. This may occur naturally in something like a series of rock outcroppings, but occasionally results from man-made activities such as timber harvesting or mining exploration. If the series of objects are competing for landscape dominance, they can distract the viewer and create an inferior view.

Enframement

Enframement occurs when vertical axes such as rock walls or timber edges intercept a flat plane such as a valley, road, or lake. It often reinforces other dominance principles.

ENVIRONMENTAL FACTORS

Eight environmental factors influence the way in which we perceive dominant elements. These often can be indirectly controlled by manipulating the observer. In analyzing the influence of these variable factors, it is important that you choose environmental conditions which create the greatest contrast between the land use activity and the characteristic landscape. Although these factors may vary considerably, their occurrence and influence are generally predictable. The motion of water plummeting over a waterfall is breathtaking in early summer; by fall, this motion may be reduced to a trickle of water. Knowing that when the motion of the water is

high and the visual experience is more intense gives the manager a level of predictability that he or she can incorporate into management planning.

Motion

Motion can be influential in capturing the visual interest of the observer. Water is probably the most important source of motion in the natural landscape, followed by wind, rain, snow, and avalanche. Motion can attract and hold the attention of observers and draw their attention to or away from various land use activities. In some places, it may be difficult to control the negative effects of land use or to screen these effects with intervening topography or vegetation. Possibly the natural motion in the existing landscape can divert attention away from a negative scene.

Light

All objects reflect sunlight to some degree. Natural light varies daily and seasonally, producing a contrast that affects visitors' visual perception of a landscape. We know that variety is important in producing an aesthetic response; we also need to understand how light can enhance this response by emphasizing or masking particular landscape elements.

For a scenic road corridor, we may choose light conditions that maximize contrast in the landscape and increase visual perception of forms, lines, colors, and textures. We can also choose reduced light intensity and reflection; this subdues the elements of the landscape so that the more negative land uses are less apparent along a corridor.

Determined by the time of day, the season of the year, and the position of the observer relative to its source, the direction of the light is also important. Backlighting—

i.e., facing into the light—obscures details so that only a general outline is discernible. Frontlighting—facing away from the light—tends to produce less contrast and consequently less interest in the scene. Shadows tend to be shorter and fall away from the observer, and more surface tends to lay in direct sunlight.

Sidelighting generally produces the greatest contrast; thus it is usually best for evaluating scenes for visual acuity or man-made activity (visitor centers, road layouts, and so forth). This information can aid us in selecting overlooks, trail locations, etc. that maximize visual experience. Consider the time of day the observation would normally take place, and remember that the angle of the sun and the intensity of the light vary with each season.

Atmospheric Conditions

These often have a masking effect on dominance elements. The visual impact of a scene is reduced by cloud cover, fog, or precipitation, so you should not evaluate the landscape under those conditions. Some atmospheric phenomena can accent landscape form, line, color, texture. Water on the opposite side of a mountain peak may affect the creation of a fog or a cloud bank that can serve as a backdrop to accent particular elements. An impressive scene that is usually obscured by fog or clouds may become even more dramatic to the observer when seen in the abrupt contrast of gleaming brilliant sunlight. Mount McKinley is an example of this type of effect. Although we personally visited Mount McKinley National Park several times in the 1960s, our only glimpse of the peak was from a commercial jetliner at 27,000 feet. As the clouds abruptly parted, the peak was exposed. Then, just as quickly, the clouds again covered the mountain. We remember it as being one of the greatest visual experiences we have ever had, yet it lasted only a moment.

Distance

Color value affects the visual qualities of the landscape. As distance increases, color value decreases because of the scattering of light rays. At great distances, the landscape is reduced to uniformity of both color value, usually blues or grays, and relief, or less-perceived vertical change. The distance at which an object can no longer be identified depends on two factors: the size of the object and the degree of contrast with its surroundings. Sample viewing zones were established with criteria that included an overlap of distances (see Figure 12-1, p. 173). These zones and their characteristics are shown in Table 12-1, p. 174.

Observer Position

Observer position is the vertical location of the individual in relation to the object being observed. The three positions are normal (at the same level as the object observed), inferior (below the object observed), and superior (above the object observed). Superior and inferior positions are only important in areas having reasonable topographic relief. The superior position offers opportunities for maximum viewing orientation to the total landscape. Also, more surface area of a given object is exposed here than in the normal position. The least surface area is exposed in the inferior position, and that is easily screened by intervening vegetation.

For example, you can locate an interpretive center in a superior position so that visitors can see entire plant communities and interpret the total ecosystem.

Figure 12-1. Distinctive foreground, middle ground, and background. Lamar Valley, Yellowstone National Park. (Photo by B. W. Twight)

Scale

Scale means measuring the relative size of an object, and viewing distance affects scale relationships. Objects viewed closely are often measured in proportion to the human figure. In intermediate and distant viewing zones, an object is seen in proportion to the total scene. When a person looks at a pipeline corridor from a one quarter mile distance, the irregular feathered edge of surrounding vegetation may be visually acceptable to him or her. But when the same scene is viewed from several miles away, the corridor becomes lost within the general texture of the landscape.

Time

This refers to the length of time in which observers view a point of interest. The longer the time, the more detail they see. "Seeing takes time—up to three-tenths of a second is needed for the eye to fixate." [28] This means that the auto driver, as speed increases, concentrates his or her vision on fewer objects at greater distances. The time factor primarily pertains to visitors who are in their automobiles. When on foot visitors generally concentrates on the landscape, thus increasing their perception of detail. Visual cones and minimum fixation distances are shown in Figure 12-2, p. 175.

Table 12-1. Viewing zones.

Foreground Characteristics	Middleground Characteristics	Background Characteristics
• Presence—the observer is in it • Maximum discernment of detail—in proportion to time and speed • Scale—observer can feel a size relationship with the elements • Discernment of color intensity and value seen in maximum contrasts • Discernment of other sensory experiences—sound, smell, and touch are most acute here • Discernment of wind motion • Aerial perspective absent	• Linkage between foreground and background parts of the landscape • Emergence of overall shapes and patterns • Visual simplification of vegetative surfaces into textures • Presence of aerial perspective—softens color contrasts • Discernment of relation between landscape units	• Simplification—outline shapes, little texture or detail apparent, objects viewed mostly as patterns of light and dark • Strong discernment of aerial perspective—reduces color distinction, replaces them with values of blue and gray • Discernment of entire landscape units—drainage patterns, vegetative patterns, landforms • Individual visual impacts least apparent

	Foreground	Middleground	Background
Distance	0 to half-mile	1/4 to 5 miles	3 to 5 miles—infinity
Sight capacity	Detail	Detail and general	General—no detail
Object viewed	Rock point	Entire ridge	System of ridges
Visual characteristics	Individual plants and species	Textures (conifers and hardwoods)	Patterns (light and dark)

From U.S. Forest Service. 1973. *National Forest Landscape Management,* Vol. I. Washington, DC: U.S. Department of Agriculture, p. 57.

Seasons

Season of use is important because the contrasts that accent landscapes vary considerably through weather changes. In the summer when leaves are fully developed, landscapes may offer little variety because the heavy texture of the trees predominates. The colors of newly emerging leaves in the spring or frost-colored leaves in the fall may break up the monotony of a landscape; they can also decrease the visual impact of a development and cause the line, color, form, and texture of man-made structures to blend in more naturally with the surrounding area.

Snow tends to strengthen form and line through maximum contrast; thus winter is often the best time for evaluating potential visual impact.

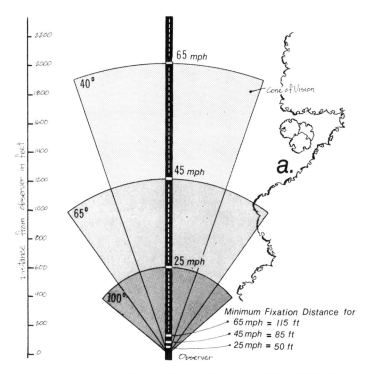

Figure 12-2. Visual cones and minimum fixation distances. (From U.S. Forest Service. 1973. *National Forest Landscape Management,* Vol. 1, Washington, DC: U.S. Government Printing Office, p. 63)

MANAGING THE VISUAL RESOURCE

Basic Concepts

You must understand three terms to manage a visual resource. All geographic areas have *characteristic landscapes* with a normal amount of *variety* or natural variation. Man's activities cause *deviation* from that characteristic landscape. With a firm understanding of these three terms, you should be able to synthesize a workable visual-resource management model.

Characteristic Landscape. Each landscape, regardless of the size or segment being viewed, has an identifiable character created by its unique combination of visible features such as land, vegetation, water, and structures. To classify a landscape you must describe its physical elements in terms of their visual effects. A recommended classification is:

$$\text{Characteristic} = f \begin{cases} \text{Dominance Elements} \\ \text{(Primary Descriptors)} \\ \text{Principles of Dominance} \\ \text{(Secondary Descriptors)} \\ \text{Perception Variables} \\ \text{(Context of Observation)} \end{cases}$$

Variety. Variety in the landscape is a desirable visual quality. Monotonous landscapes are not pleasing to the user and discourage the observer, creating a minimal perceptual response to existing environmental stimuli. The question is, how much variety is enough? For a given area, it can range from zero (low appeal) to an acceptable level. Beyond this level, appeal may decrease until it again reaches zero. Planting trees on an open hillside may increase variety and visual appeal, but at some point adding more may in fact reduce the effect of both qualities. Planting could continue until the hillside is entirely covered with trees, creating a new monotonous landscape.

Deviation. Deviation refers to man-made alterations in the characteristic landscape. Most land has been subjected to some use and/or development. Thus deviation, including that created by recreational developments, occurs and will continue to occur on the landscape. Deviations that emulate the elements of the natural landscape or create desirable variety may be acceptable to the observer. Unfortunately in the past, decisions about these matters have often been made without considering landscape aesthetics. Nevertheless, more people are becoming aware of the appeal of the landscape, and although they realize some modification is necessary to provide needed goods and services for our modern society, they still feel that deviations should affect visual qualities as little as possible. Often, too little attention has been paid to visually disruptive land use, allowing unacceptable deviations to occur. Given proper concern, we can make alterations acceptable, even enjoyable, for users.

Landscape Types

The above variables manifest themselves in four primary and three secondary landscape types. The primary types—panoramic, feature, focal and enclosed—are the generalized area landscapes to which people respond. By categorizing them, we can better understand and appreciate the strengths (and weaknesses) of particular landscapes. The secondary landscape types—canopied, detail, and ephemeral—simply occur at specific points within the generalized landscape and can be used managerially to enhance the visual experience.

1. Panoramic Landscape. A panoramic landscape features a 360-degree view limited by the continuous line of the horizon, such as you might find on a flat, continuous surface like a large body of water. On land, the panorama is often limited to 180 degrees or less because of changes in landscape composition, limits of peripheral vision, or natural side screening. The basic dimension is horizontal, with little feeling of boundary or visual restriction. This landscape stimulates the greatest feeling of distance and openness, with no single dominant feature.

2. Feature Landscape. This landscape is visually dominated by a singular or closely related group of features, natural or man-made. There is a great diversity in the types of dominant features, scale (relative to other items around it), configuration (shape), orientation (vertical or horizontal), and position relative to the observer and other potentially dominant elements. You must consider all of these variables if you plan to feature a given element for the observer. If you feature too many elements, the dominance you hope to present may be obscured. Similar shapes, orientation, and other factors may confuse the observer. Also, objects in the near-viewing zone may appear larger than the high mountain peak in the distant-viewing zone—the item you might have wanted to emphasize in the landscape.

3. *Enclosed Landscape*. In this landscape type, vertical sides enclose a base plane. Sides in a natural landscape are formed by either vegetation or topographic features, and the base generally approaches a horizontal plane. The water's edge can form a conspicuous junction with vertical walls composed of vegetation or steep topography and a horizontal base composed of flat water. The enclosure is then created by well-defined limits of space; if the base (body of water, meadow, etc.) is enlarged to the point that vertical walls become insignificant or even visible, then the feeling of enclosure is lost. The landscape then approaches the panoramic type.

4. *Focal Landscape*. This type of landscape is structured by a series of parallel lines, or aligned objects, which converge or tend to converge on a focal point in the landscape. According to R. B. Litton, both point convergence and feature terminus may occur with or without side enclosures; that is, either may be overlaid on an open panoramic landscape or can occur as corridors on a flat plane. Portal or self-enclosure compositions can occur only in the context of enclosed landscape . . . A stream course or a road tangent are the most likely places to look for the focal landscape. Perhaps the most commanding or effective focal composition occurs when a landscape feature is present as a visual terminus.[12]

5. *Secondary Landscape Types*. These are part of the basic landscape types, are smaller in scale, and generally have more detail because of their closeness to the observer:

a. CANOPIED LANDSCAPE

Vegetative canopies tend to limit viewing and are relatively small scale. Thus the landscape is easily seen and observed by the pedestrian, but the vehicle operator, because of his closeness, speed of travel, and focus on the road, is not able to grasp the detail. Roads within a canopied situation may be the closest contact that many auto visitors have with the out-of-doors. These rapidly moving observers can sense three sources of contrast in the canopied landscape: changes in general vegetation types, marked changes in size, class and condition of vegetation, and spatial definition of the canopied enclosure. There are three basic canopied postures: broad open corridors of major highways; medium closure corridors of secondary, moderate-speed roads; and small corridors or completely enclosed vegetative tunnels on slow-speed, minimally improved roads. We can create a feeling of contact with the natural landscape by bringing the edge of the road to the forest edge and minimizing or lowering road cuts and fills. On the other hand, we can create a feeling of detachment by separating the road from the forest edge and increasing cuts and fills. We can also increase vegetative contrast by running roads or portions thereof somewhat perpendicular to major topographic features, since changes in topography generally reflect changes in vegetation. As Litton states:

> Transferring the characteristics of the lower-speed road to high speed roads has little chance to succeed. Lane division and use of broad median areas can help maintain contact with forest stands. But we should recognize that each road type imparts a different scenic quality to the stand—more

light or less; more enclosure or less. One is not better than the other. Each offers a difference which should he retained for variety and contrast.[13]

b. DETAIL LANDSCAPE

A detail landscape is part of a basic landscape that focuses on specific detail close to the observer. The detail requires pedestrians to proceed at a slow pace to seek out the natural, artistic amenities in the detail. Patterns, forms, and symbolism the observer perceives can offer personal satisfaction. These may he unique, symbolic, or merely reflective of the total landscape composition. Such detail may be composed of plants, rock deposits, water, and other features; however, the position of the observer in terms of background, lighting, and changing weather can cause him or her to focus attention on specific detail while creating a sense of changing landscape through small changes in light, weather, and other conditions. Thus observers may want to return again and again to receive the full continuum of visual opportunities from the specific detail landscape. Also, this type of landscape can be used as a relief and transition from one observer position to another in a given basic landscape, or between basic landscapes. This situation is similar to using foreground detail as a transition scene in a play while the larger background scene is being changed.

c. EPHEMERAL LANDSCAPE

The ephemeral landscape depends on temporal or transitory effects that may last a few seconds or perhaps several days. Five types of influences affect ephemeral detail in the landscape: atmospheric conditions, projected and reflected images, displacement, signs, and animal presence. Produced by cloud and fog formation, precipitation, changing light, and wind motion, atmospheric conditions are the most extensive effects. Projected and reflected images are secondary images created by light shadows or reflections on water. Reflections are more conspicuous than shadows because they mirror the image of a real form even though the color may be somewhat darker. With suitable conditions, a secondary image can be complete and can enhance recognition of objects. Signs are indications of former life or occupancy by animals or plants. Animal tracks, bird nests, spider webs, chewed trees, feathers, or bubbles from feeding fishes indicate that animals were recently present. Animal presence has a transitory influence on the landscape, generally in the near-viewing zone of subtle secondary landscapes available mostly to pedestrians. Although impossible to control, the ephemeral landscape is important and extremely stimulating to many observers who seek out subtle transitory natural elements. Timing is often important and observers should be made aware of its importance to these elements.

Summary of Landscape Classification

The following examples summarize the analysis of landscape character, giving you an opportunity to apply the above information on landscape classification.

Figure 12-3 is a feature landscape characteristic of the alpine zone as viewed from fore- and middle-ground zones. It has tremendous visual variation, which makes it attractive to observers. This land has strong form in the granite outcropping, strong line in the ridges and shoreline of the lake, and excellent textural variation in vegetation, snow, and rock outcroppings.

Figure 12-3. Landscape character of the alpine zone, Summit Lake, Yosemite National Park. (Photo by B. W. Twight)

Any management practice should consider the strong line, texture, and form. Trails should be located so as not to detract from the ridgeline on the horizon or along the lake. Primitive campsites should complement texture and form and avoid disrupting the strong lines around the lake. All development should be avoided at the focal point—the upper reach of the lake.

Figure 12-4 (p. 180) is an enclosed landscape dominated in the foreground by the line of the lake, the interface of forest and meadow, and the variation in texture. Management practices should consider the strong lines and the strong attraction of the water; the lake should be made visually accessible for the enjoyment of the casual user since any kind of intensive use or development would be too distracting. Intensive developments such as roads, trails, and campgrounds should be screened within the spruce-fir forest. There are also ecological factors to consider in these types of decisions.

The best features of the landscape in Figure 12-4 fall completely in the foreground and are dominated by the shoreline and the texture of lakeside vegetation. Any management action should preserve the existing line and texture if visual integrity is to be preserved for those using the lake. Campgrounds and picnic stops should be located away from the lakeshore.

Any intensive land-use development is better located in middle ground where it can be screened and blended with vegetation. Any development in the foreground should blend with the texture and not disrupt the dominance of the mountain range.

Figure 12-4. Enclosed landscape along the lakeshore of Tilden Canyon Lake, Yosemite National Park. (Photo by B. W. Twight)

APPLICATION OF VISUAL RESOURCE MANAGEMENT

This discussion covers scale of application, the visual resource management model, and mapping techniques.

Scale of Application

In visual resource planning, scale of application is divided into three major levels—regional, area, and site.

Regional Landscape. The regional landscape is delimited by physiographic provinces. For example, the major physiographic provinces in southeastern Wyoming (from east to west—the eastern plains, the Laramie Mountains, the Laramie Basin, the Medicine Bow Mountains, the Platte River Basin, and the Sierra Madres—describe the characteristic regional landscapes. Major developments such as transportation and utility systems should be evaluated in terms of their general affect on the regional landscape. Properly locating developments ensures minimal visual impact at the regional level.

Area Landscape. The area landscape is delimited by the visual corridor, or the envelope of space enclosed by land forms.[13] Detailed

Figure 12-5. A national forest scenic road built before the actual practice of Forest Service landscape management began. Note how it fails to "lay lightly on the land." Monongahela National Forest, WV. (Photo by B. W. Twight)

visual resource management planning is usually done at the area level. At this level you make judgments about the specific effects of a given development on the visual experiences of visitors. Most recreational use occurs along roads, trails, water courses, or at specific sites. Managers should give priority to any portion of a landscape readily viewed by visitors, but this should not be interpreted as a "green light" to exploit the remaining areas.

The primary application is at the area level and made either a part of the area plan or an addendum to it. After all, the *area* represents the generalized landscape within which the recreational use occurs. While that use may be focused on specific environmental attractors, maintenance of the generalized landscape is essential to the overall satisfaction one receives from the experience.

Visual resource management is predicated on developing visual quality objectives (VQO's) for every acre, not just what can be seen from a road, travel corridor, or developed site. This is not designed to preclude specific land uses, but to insure that whatever visual impacts that occur conform to the standards for the particular visual quality objective. Plus, by developing VQO's for contiguous acreage that cannot be seen from the present travel route or site development, we maintain future options for expansion of sites, trails, roads etc., to expand the recreational opportunities.

If you do not preserve those future options, then the area is destined to remain at the present mosaic pattern of recreational opportunities with little hope of expanding to meet future demands. If you do expand, there is no guarantee for maintaining the visual quality of the generalized landscape that the clientele have come to associate with the particular recreational opportunity.

Without going into great detail, there is one other area-level concept you should understand—visual corridor or "seen" area. This is what you can actually see from the travel route or recreational site. There are several computer graphics programs that will plot the "seen" area; all that is needed are map coordinates and elevations along the axes from the potential viewing points. Typically along a travel route, the viewing points might be arbitrarily assigned at 1/2 mile intervals, with the axes around each point set first at right angles, and then 45 degrees to each side of the right angle. Next the data points, map coordinates, and elevations, are collected along all axes and fed into the computer to plot the "seen" area.

The "seen" area concept does not negate the need for VQO's on all acres; it merely highlights or emphasizes the zone which requires more intensive management under the present regime. The "nonseen" areas are managed on an extensive basis, using the VQO's to ensure compliance with the standards.

Site Landscape. Site landscape refers to the area on which you locate a recreational development. It is important to maintain a visually pleasing environment throughout the site, and this is generally accomplished during the site-planning phase. The visual effects of site development on casual observers passing through the area should also be considered under area-landscape management.

All site developments should conform to the requirements of the stated visual-quality objectives, which are covered in the succeeding section.

At the site level, scenes that have strong contrasts in the primary descriptors are more desirable, because the characteristics of the particular landscape are more discernable. The contexts in terms of observer-landscape relationships are also important, if we are to enhance the features important to the observer. We can go beyond that and suggest specific resource elements that enhance attractiveness to the recreationist—presence of water, natural motion in the landscape (wind, running water, etc.), rock outcroppings, and so on. Much of the actual site selection based on the above discussion would be subjective, taking into account some generic features one should look for.

Others have developed statistical models to isolate specific variables and estimate their contribution to the viewer's satisfaction. Each study has been somewhat unique and the findings applicable within the specific context or locale. The Kamler study was particularly unique in that it was conducted using the photo-choice technique for an area that had not previously been open to the driving public—the Brooks Range and North Slope along the Dalton Highway, Alaska.[9]

Visual Resource Management Model

The basic visual resource management model is illustrated in Figure 12-6. Here a visual resource is inventoried according to the character, variety, and affect of the landscape. Note the feedback loop which suggests that we should periodically test the professional judgments made in the VRM plan against the

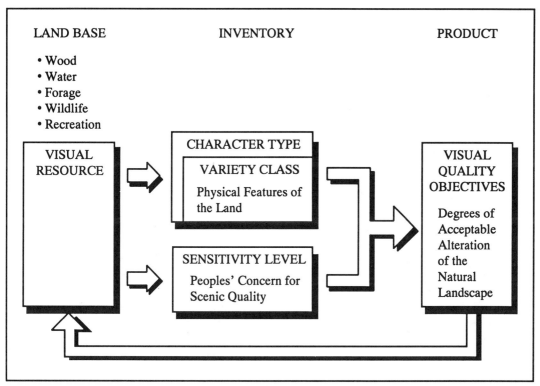

Figure 12-6. Visual resource management model. (From U.S. Forest Service. 1974. "The Visual Management System." *National Forest Landscape Management,* Vol. II. Washington, DC: USGPO, p. 9.)

preference/perceptions of the clientele. Ultimately, a resource's ability to absorb development must be coordinated with the sensitivity of observers to establish visual-quality objectives. These objectives affect the location, type, and level of development allowed in an area.

Landscape Character. First, character type and subtypes of the resource must be identified and mapped. The Laramie Mountains in southeast Wyoming are one example of character type. Subtypes are areas of significant size with visual differences that distinguish them from others within an overall character type.

Next, you should establish the variety classes of each subtype, of which three are recognized: 1) distinctive—those landscapes having outstanding visual qualities such as a mountain peak, a deep gorge, or a glacial field; 2) common—those having a variety of basic landscape elements but no outstanding features; and 3) minimal—those having little variety in basic elements such as an unbroken canopy of lodgepole pine or a grain field.

Finally, you should draw up a chart that classifies the basic features of each subtype into distinctive, common, or minimal. To illustrate this idea, an example is shown in Table 12-2 (p. 184), which uses the Western Cascades as a landscape character type and steep mountain lands as a subtype. You can

Table 12-2. Chart of landscape features of resource area—Western Cascades character type, steep mountain slope subtype.*

	CLASS A Distinctive	CLASS B Common	CLASS C Minimal
Landform	Over 60 percent slopes which are dissected, uneven, sharp exposed ridges or large dominant features.	30-60 percent slopes which are moderately dissected or rolling.	0-30 percent slopes which have little variety. No dissection and no dominant features.
Rock Form	Features stand out on landform. Unusual or outstanding, avalanche chutes, talus slopes, outcrops, etc., in size, shape, and location.	Features obvious but do not stand out. Common but not outstanding avalanche chutes, talus slopes, boulders, and rock outcrops.	Small to nonexistent features. No avalanche chutes, talus slopes, boulders, and rock outcrops.
Vegetation	High degree of patterns in vegetation.\n\nLarge old growth timber. Unusual or outstanding diversity in plant species.	Continuous vegetative cover with interspersed patterns. Mature but not outstanding old growth. Common diversity in plant species.	Continuous vegetative cover with little or no pattern. No understory, overstory, or ground cover.
Water Forms, Lakes	50 acres or larger. Those smaller than 50 acres with one or more of the following: (1) Unusual or outstanding shoreline configuration, (2) reflects major features, (3) islands, (4) Class A Shoreline vegetation or rock forms.	5 to 50 acres. Some shoreline irregularity. Minor reflections only. Class B shoreline vegetation.	Less than 5 acres. No irregularity or reflection.
Water Forms, Streams	Drainage with numerous or unusual changing flow characteristics, falls, rapids, pools and meanders or large volume.	Drainage, with common meandering and flow characteristics.	Intermittent streams or small perennial streams with little or no fluctuation in flow or falls, rapids, or meandering.

* From U.S. Forest Service, 1974. "The Visual Management System." *National Forest Landscape Management,* Vol. II. Washington, DC: U.S. Department of Agriculture, p. 13.

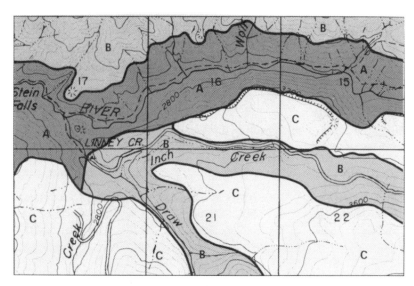

Figure 12-7. Mapping landscape variety classes A, B, and C. *Top,* vertical photos, particularly in stereo pairs, are an excellent tool in judging the broad variety classes. *Bottom,* Prepare a detailed base map at the same scale as those currently being used for Multiple Use planning units. Prepare an overlay as shown to illustrate the variety class determination. Information on the base map will be used for all aspects of the Visual Management System process and should include but not be limited to: Topographic data (best available); land ownership boundaries; existing and proposed (within 10 years) travel routes, and bodies of water. (This would include but not be limited to roads, trails, low-level commercial air routes, passenger rail routes, etc.) Information can be obtained from local, state and national route studies and transportation plans. (From U.S. Forest Service. 1974. "The Visual Management System." *National Forest Landscape Management,* Vol. II Washington, DC: U.S. Government Printing Office. p. 9.

use vertical aerial photos in conjunction with the criteria established in the variety class chart to delineate distinctive (A), common (B), and minimal (C) classes. Then you can transfer the information to a base topographic map (see Figure 12-7, p. 185).

To obtain the necessary detail needed at the subtype level, managers may be forced to establish a priority system, phasing in the visual resource management program over several years. Typically, distinctive landscapes are recognized and visual aesthetics protected. This is as it should be; however, we should also devote more attention to the common landscape, which is where most people participate in recreational activities. Most landscapes fall into the common category; therefore, we should give more attention to managing the common landscape if we are to provide adequately for aesthetic and recreational needs. Minimal landscape may absorb intensive developments because of dense overstory vegetation; however, some prairie and desert lands which are classified as minimal cannot absorb any development without maximum disruption of landscape elements.

Viewer Sensitivity. Viewer sensitivity is a composite of attitudes and viewer distance. Ideally, you should survey the attitudes of those who use the specific management area to evaluate their level of sensitivity. In the absence of such information, use Table 12-3 as a guideline. Now combine your survey with viewer distance—foreground (FG), middle ground (MG), and background (BG), shown in Table 12-1 (p. 174)—to determine the overall level of viewer sensitivity. At level 3, it is not necessary to divide into foreground, middle ground, and background because of the low sensitivity level.

Table 12-3. Summary of sensitivity levels.*

Summary Table for all Sensitivity Levels:

Use	1	2	3
Primary travel routes, use areas and water bodies	At least 1/4 of users have MAJOR concern for scenic qualities	Less than 1/4 of users have MAJOR concern for scenic qualities	
Secondary travel routes, use areas and water bodies	At least 3/4 of users have MAJOR concern for scenic qualities	At least 1/4 and not more than 3/4 of users have MAJOR concern for scenic qualities.	Less than 1/4 of users have MAJOR concern for scenic qualities

Level 1 - Highest Sensitivity
Level 2 - Average Sensitivity
Level 3 - Lowest Sensitivity

* From U.S. Forest Service. 1974. "The Visual Management System." *National Forest Landscape Management,* Vol. II. Washington, DC: U.S. Department of Agriculture, p. 21.

For mapping viewer sensitivity, prepare an overlay of all viewable areas for all travel routes using areas and bodies of water. This can be done with a large-scale topographic map since all you need is the distance and elevation from the potential viewing point. Plot foreground, middle ground, background, and viewer sensitivity in terms of attitude for each road, trail, recreational development, and body of water, including streams. In the past, only roads have been given consideration in relation to viewer sensitivity; however, travel on water and trail is increasing and should therefore be given equal consideration. Overlays for all travel/use areas should then be superimposed to produce a composite overlay (see Figure 12-8, p. 188).

Note the multiple classifications for most zones since many are viewable from more than one distance zone or viewer sensitivity level as classified in Table 12-3. For zones in which multiple classifications occur, the more

restrictive sensitivity classification should always be used. To determine which classification is most sensitive, refer to the matrix shown in Table 12-4.

Visual Quality Objectives. Viewer sensitivity and landscape variety must be integrated into visual quality objectives. Do this with the matrix in Table 12-5 (p. 189); you can see the result in Figure 12-9 (p. 190). Visual quality objectives are as follows:

1. PRESERVATION (P)

The intent is that only natural, ecological changes are allowed since some local impact from recreational use may occur. These are roadless areas where the main development is the trail system and possibly some primitive campsites; all should be designed to blend with the visual resource.

Table 12-4. Chart for determining most restrictive sensitivity level.*

	fg1	mg1	bg1	fg2	mg2	bg2
bg2	fg1	mg1	bg1	fg2	mg2	bg2
mg2	fg1	mg1	mg2	fg2	mg2	
fg2	fg1	mg1	fg2	fg2		
bg1	fg1	mg1	bg1			
mg1	fg1	mg1				
fg1	fg1					

fg1 - Foreground Level 1
mg1 - Middleground Level 1
bg1 - Background Level 1

* From U.S. Forest Service. 1974. "The Visual Management System." *National Forest Landscape Management,* Vol. II. Washington, DC: U.S. Department of Agriculture, p. 25.

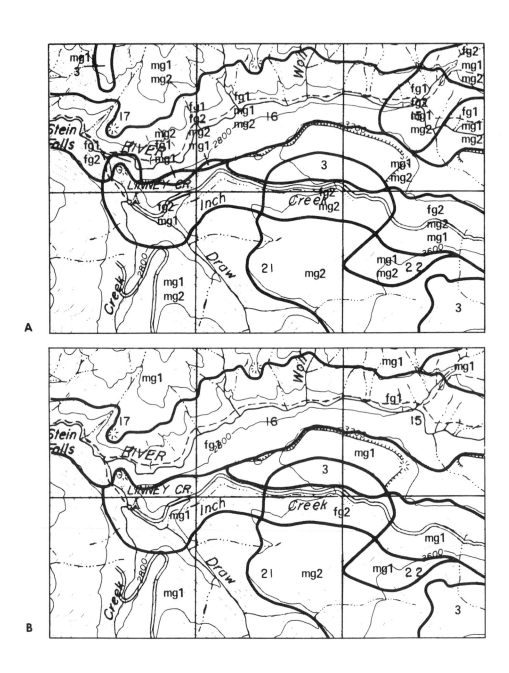

Figure 12-8. Composite overlay of viewer sensitivity based on general visitor attitudes (Table 12-3) and viewing distance zones (Table 12-1). A is a composite overlay before adjustments have been made, B is the final overlay showing the most restrictive sensitivity levels as in Table 12-4. (From U.S. Forest Service. 1974. "The Visual Management System." *National Forest Landscape Management,* Vol. II. Washington, DC: U.S. Department of Agriculture.)

Table 12-5. Visual quality matrix.**

Variety Class		Sensitivity Level						
		fg1	mg1	bg1	fg2	mg2	bg2	3
	Class A	R	R	R	PR	PR	PR	PR
	Class B	R	PR	PR	PR	M	M	M* MM
	Class C	PR	PR	M	M	M	MM	MM

SYMBOL	OBJECTIVE
R	Retention
PR	Partial Retention
M	Modification
MM	Maximum Modification

* If a 3B area is adjacent to a *Retention* or *Partial Retention* visual quality objective, select the *Modification* visual quality objective. If adjacent to *Modification* or *Maximum Modification* objective areas, select *Maximum Modification*.

** From U.S. Forest Service. 1974. "The Visual Management System." *National Forest Landscape Management*, Vol. II. Washington, DC: U.S. Department of Agriculture, p. 43.

2. RETENTION (R)

Retention refers to planning developments so that they are not evident to the casual observer. You should maintain existing form, line, color, and texture in the landscape as viewed from the same point(s) where most people casually observe.

3. PARTIAL RETENTION (PR)

To achieve partial retention, make developments subordinate to characteristic landscape features. Try to imitate landscape elements, but realize that no development can completely blend into the background. The goal is to make the view acceptable for observers by preserving or complementing the landscape.

4. MODIFICATION (M)

With modification, man's activities may visually dominate the characteristic landscape, but even these activities should borrow as much as possible from the elements of form, line, color, and texture so that it appears congruent with the setting.

5. MAXIMUM MODIFICATION (MM)

Man's activities, including alteration of land forms by timber harvesting or major development, may dominate the landscape and seem somewhat incongruent within foreground or middle ground viewing distances. Yet when viewed as backgrounds, these forms should blend in. Viewing distance is therefore

Objective Map

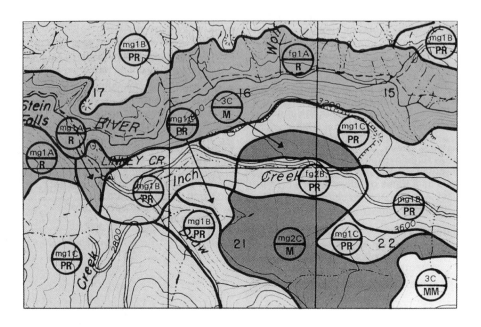

CODE

Symbol Objective

R   Retention
PR   Partial Retention
M   Modification
MM   Maximum Modification

Preservation does not appear on the chart but is indicated by:

P   Preservation

Assign Preservation Objective to all existing and proposed (within 10 years) Specify Classified Areas.

Figure 12-9. The application of visual quality objectives, integrating landscape variety and viewer sensitivity. Note those areas in need of either rehabilitation or enhancement by the appropriate symbol beside the quality objective, *e* for enhancement and *reh* for rehabilitation. Rehabilitation should be noted when management activities in a particular area do not conform to an agreed upon quality objective. Enhancement notation should come from a detailed landscape management plan for a particular area. The Visual Resource Management System thus produces an area map showing visual quality objectives. (From U.S. Forest Service. 1974. "The Visual Management System." *National Forest Landscape Management,* Vol. II.

important, and the duration of the visual impact should be minimal through either rehabilitation or enhancement (secondary objectives).

There is also such a thing as unacceptable modification that does not blend with the character of the landscape regardless of viewing distance. Activities such as contour strip mining and large symmetrical clearcuts often have a lingering effect that cannot be mitigated. Modification or enhancement may improve the visual quality of the activity, but the activity often remains unacceptable. In any situation, you should not tolerate unacceptable modification. Note the amount around you. If you recognize it on the ground, the picture is more vivid than any photo could reproduce.

Rehabilitation is a secondary, short-term, visual-quality way to improve the landscape. Enhancement, another secondary, short-term objective, is aimed at increasing visual appeal by creating variety in a monotonous vista.

Visual Absorption Capacity (VAC). VAC is the relative ability of the landscape to absorb a given land use without visual impact. When you implement a given Visual Quality Objective (VQO), adjust the prescription to achieve it within the constraints of the VAC.

There are *no* absolute absorption values in management decision making. It is, however, important to recognize the need to adjust land-use developments according to the relative absorption of a given landscape. This relative absorption is a function of landscape character—primarily topography and vegetation. The adjustment in management prescriptions must also reflect proposed land use/development because some of it may not be absorbable, even though a particular landscape has a high VAC. Two other factors affect relative absorption—distance from the viewer and user perception or sensitivity. However, these are already accounted for in the basic visual resource management model.

VISUAL RESOURCE MANAGEMENT—AN INTERPRETATION

We have just discussed a system used by an agency whose interest in land management is multifaceted. Some modification of the system may be necessary at the local level, depending on the perceptions of the user population. User perceptions have sometimes differed from professional ones. Also, the legislative mandate, agency goals, and complexity of programs may determine the visual quality objectives that you select. Regardless of agency or situation, what is presented is a basic model that managers can use to arrive at the specific objectives for visual resource management prescriptions. If you understand the underlying concepts of characteristic landscape, variety, and deviation, then specifics within a model can be modified to suit an individual manager's needs or a new model can be developed.

SELECTED READINGS

1.   Alexander, C., and Chemmayeff, S. L. 1964. *Notes on Synthesis of Form.* Cambridge, MA: Harvard University Press.

2.   Amheim, R. 1974. *Art and Visual Perception.* A Psychology of the Creative Eye. Revised edition. Berkeley, CA: University of California Press.

3.   Appleyard, D., Lyncy, K., and Myer, J. R. 1964. *The View from the Road.* Cambridge, MA: M.I.T. Press.

4. Birren, F. 1982. *Light, Color. and Environment.* Revised edition. New York, NY: Van Nostrand Reinhold Co.

5. Brown, T. C., and Daniel, T. C. 1984. *Modeling Forest Scenic Beauty: Application to Ponderosa Pine.* USDA-Forest Service Research Paper RM-256.

6. Chenoweth, R., and Gobster, P. H. 1986. "Wildland Description and Analysis," *Foundations for Visual Project Analysis.* R. C. Smardon, J. F. Palmer, and J. P. Felleman (eds.). New York, NY: John Wiley & Sons.

7. Ekbo, G. 1969. *The Landscape We See.* New York, NY: McGraw-Hill Book Co.

8. Elsner, G. H., and Smarden, R. C. (eds.). 1979. *Proceedings of Our National Landscape: A Conference on Applied Techniques for Analysis and Management of the Visual Resource.* USDA-Forest Service General Technical Report PSW-35.

9. Kamler, J. W. 1991. "Predicting Landscape Preferences: A Modeling Application to the Dalton Highway Alaska." M.S. Thesis (unpublished). University of Alaska Fairbanks.

10. Kellomaki, S., and Pulskala, T. 1989. "Forest Landscape: A Method of Amenity Evaluation Based On Computer Simulation." *Landscape and Urban Planning 18*(2):117-125.

11. Litton, R. B., Jr. 1973. Landscape Control Points: A Procedure for Predicting and Monitoring Visual Impacts. U.S. Forest Service Research Paper PSW-91.

12. Litton, R. B., Jr. 1968. Forest Landscape Description and Inventories: A Basis for Land Planning and Design. U.S. Forest Service research paper, PSW-Forest Exp. Sta.

13. Litton, R. B., Jr., and Twiss, R. H. 1967. "The Forest Landscape: Some Elements of Visual Analysis." *Proceedings of Society of American Foresters.* Portland, OR: Society of American Foresters, p. 212.

14. Lynch, K. 1984. *Site Planning.* 3rd Ed., Cambridge, MA: M.I.T. Press.

15. Lynch. K. 1976. *Managing the Sense of A Region.* Cambridge, MA: M.I.T. Press.

16. Mitchell, W. J. (ed.). 1972. *Environmental Design: Research and Practice.* Los Angeles, CA: University of California at Los Angeles.

17. Nighswonger, J. J. 1970. A Methodology of Inventorying and Evaluating the Scenic Quality and Related Recreational Values of Kansas Streams. Topeka, KS: Kansas Department of Economic Development, Planning Division.

18. Olmsted, F. L., Jr., and Kimball, T., (eds.). 1973. *Forty Years of Landscape Architecture: Central Park,* by Frederick Law Olmsted, Sr., Cambridge, MA: M.I.T. Press.

19. Peterson, G. L., and Neamann, E. S. 1969. "Modeling and Predicting Human Response to the Visual Recreation Environment." *Journal of Leisure Research, 1*(3):219-237.

20. Reed, H. H., and Duckworth, S. 1967. *Central Park; A History and A Guide.* New York, NY: C. N. Potter.

21. Rudis, V. A., Gramman, J. H., Ruddell, E. J., and Westphal, J. M. 1988. "Forest Inventory and Management-Based Visual Preference Models of Southern Pine Stands." *Forest Science 34*(4):846-863.

22. Rutledge, A. J. 1986. *Anatomy of A Park.* 2nd edition. New York, NY: McGraw-Hill Book Co.

23. Shafer, E. L., Hamilton, J. L., and Schmidt, E. A. 1969. "Natural Landscape Preferences: A Predictive Model." *Journal of Leisure Research 1*(1):1.

24. Simonds, J. O. 1983. *Landscape Architecture*. Revised edition. New York, NY: McGraw-Hill.

25. Steintz, C., and Way, D. 1970. "A Model for Evaluating Visual Consequences of Urbanization on Shoreline Landscapes." U.S. Army Corps of Engineers. Washington, DC: U.S. Government Printing Office.

26. Stevenson, E. 1977. *Park Maker, A Life of Frederick Law Olmsted*. New York, NY: Macmillan.

27. Tunnard, C. 1978. *A World With A View, An Inquiry into the Nature of Scenic Values*. New Haven, CT: Yale University Press.

28. U.S. Forest Service. 1974. *National Forest Landscape Management*, Volume I. Agriculture Handbook 434. Washington, DC: U.S. Government Printing Office.

29. USDA-Forest Service. 1974. *National Forest Landscape Management*, Volume II, Chapter 1, (The Visual Management System), Agriculture Handbook 462. Washington, DC: U.S. Government Printing Office.

30. USDA-Forest Service. 1975. *National Forest Landscape Management*, Volume II, Chapter 2, (Utilities), Agriculture Handbook 478. Washington, DC: U.S. Government Printing Office.

31. USDA-Forest Service. 1977. *National Forest Landscape Management*, Volume II, Chapter 3, (Range), Agriculture Handbook 484. Washington, DC: U.S. Government Printing Office.

32. USDA-Forest Service. 1977. *National Forest Landscape Management*, Volume II, Chapter 4, (Roads), Agriculture Handbook 483. Washington, DC: U.S. Government Printing Office.

33. USDA-Forest Service. 1980. *National Forest Landscape Management*, Volume II, Chapter 5, (Timber), Agriculture Handbook 559. Washington, DC: U.S. Government Printing Office.

34. USDA-Forest Service. 1987. *National Forest Landscape Management-Recreation*, Vol. 2, Chapter 8.

35. Vernon, M. D. 1962. *The Psychology of Perception*. Baltimore, MD: Penguin Books.

36. Vining, J., Daniels, T. C., and Schroeder, H. W. 1984. "Predicting Scenic Values in Forested Residential Landscapes." *Journal of Leisure Research, 16*(2):124-135.

37. Wurman, R. S., Levy, A., and Katz, J. 1972. *The Nature of Recreation, A Handbook in Honor of Frederick Law Olmsted, Using Examples From His Work*. Cambridge, MA: M.I.T. Press.

38. Zube, E. H., Brush, R. O., and Fabos, J. G. 1975. *Landscape Assessment: Values, Perceptions, and Resources*. Stroudsburg, PA: Dowden, Hutchinson, and Ross.

39. Zube, E. H., Sell, J. L., and Taylor, J. G. 1982. "Landscape Perception: Research, Application, and Theory." *Landscape Planning 9*(1):1-33.

PART III

Visitor Management

To reiterate what was presented in Chapters 2 and 3, the total management program is the combination/interaction of three sub-systems—resource, visitor, and service. The particular combination of all programs for a given area constitutes the recreational opportunity being provided. Part II focused on the resource management programs, or the resource management subsystem. Part III covers the visitor management programs. These are aimed at directly or indirectly manipulating visitors to protect/enhance their recreational experiences and/or to protect, enhance, or rehabilitate the resource base. Thus, as stated before, no one program can be summarily or arbitrarily judged good or bad, appropriate or inappropriate, a success or a failure by itself. It must be judged in relation to the opportunity being provided.

Included in Part III are discussions about the following programs: distribution of use, information, interpretation, and public safety. Redistribution is a perennial problem that exists because we have not understood the linkage between specific management programs and the resulting user response, macro-behavioral patterns. In other words, the need to redistribute use is often created by failing to achieve a given equilibrium, described in Chapter 3, or overestimating the ability of a resource to sustain that equilibrium over time. The chapter on distribution of use deals with

the principles and techniques, not on how to achieve a given equilibrium.

Information programs have three functions: 1) to provide visitors with sufficient information to make a rational choice between competing recreational opportunities; 2) to manage visitor use patterns by clearly establishing norms of behavior and warning of potential hazards; and 3) to explain the necessity for specific management actions. The first two are obvious, but the last is often overlooked. If the public does not understand the need for a given program, such as the value of fire in maintaining a given ecosystem, it may react very negatively to a new program and thwart or negate your efforts.

Interpretive programming deals with translating the history or natural history of the landscape into something that is meaningful to visitors. The goal is simply enhanced appreciation of the historical or natural setting, which should also enhance the recreational opportunity for the typical visitor. Principles, methods, and media for doing so are presented here.

Public safety is an important consideration, and the character of the program reflects its relative location along ROS. Safety is often an implied goal or simply seen as a constraint on management; however, it should be realistically viewed as an integral part of any recreational opportunity. As such, public safety goals should become part of the written management prescription.

CHAPTER 13

Distribution of Visitor Use

How to obtain a reasonable distribution of use over existing recreational areas and sites has always been a management concern. However, as suggested in Chapter 3, people tend to concentrate at particular attractions within a landscape—sometimes to the exclusion of the rest of the landscape. Other managerial and user input also affects points of visitor concentration, so this chapter focuses not only on techniques of dispersal but also on conditions that make each one most effective. The common ideal of spatially and temporally redistributing use is also appraised.

PRINCIPLES OF DISPERSAL OF VISITOR USE

You can disperse use on a local, area-wide, or regional basis. Local or area-wide programs are easiest because land typically falls under the jurisdiction of one agency and programs can often be implemented without the approval of higher authority. Typically, road

Figure 13-1. "No Camping Within 300 Feet of Road"—A distribution of use technique requiring regular enforcement. Monongahela National Forest, WV. (Photo by B. W. Twight)

and trail access can be controlled or redirected in local zones, and, as shown in Chapter 3, access is the primary managerially-influenced attribute which affects users' perceptions of the opportunity.

Figure 13-2 shows the three principles of visitor dispersal in ascending order. If you want to change existing use patterns, you should first try voluntary dispersal through either information programs or changes in the physical design of the setting. Changes in physical design are most effective. Limiting parking space, erecting physical barriers, etc. are nonconfrontational compared to permit or regulation enforcement. When these programs fail to achieve your objective, you may still have to limit use to protect the recreational opportunity and the environment in which it takes place. When you begin to limit use, you may also be detracting from the very opportunity you are trying to preserve. As suggested in Chapter 3, voluntary dispersal through physical design should generally not detract from the opportunity, but implementing a confrontational limited-entry system to redistribute use may have a negative impact on perception of the opportunity and on public support for your agency. It may also attract a new clientele group while causing

some of the current clientele to go elsewhere. Even in the most carefully considered and empathetically introduced program, you may have to offend some longtime clientele—by closing a certain locale to recreational use allowing it to recover, or to protect, on a long-term basis, its unique, fragile environment.

Dispersion is considered a voluntary redistribution of recreation use over an area. This should really be the manager's first alternative when overuse occurs on some sites while others remain underused. Assume that there are planned, physically available substitutes and that you are simply publicizing them. Note that crowding, or density of use, is not targeted as a justification for dispersal from the visitors' perspective. Density should reflect the opportunity to be provided, and it is better and more naturally achieved by altering access, facilities, and services.

As shown in Chapter 3, people who want certain density levels choose opportunities which have the greatest probability of providing them. Even within those limits, management can use some sort of feedback mechanism, such as a report card, to enhance recreational opportunities for the existing clientele.[16] That is the reason this chapter is entitled "Distribution of Visitor Use" rather

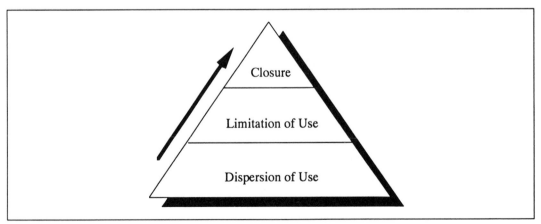

Figure 13-2. Principles of visitor dispersal, in ascending order of implementation.

than "Redistribution." Management tries to create certain recreational opportunities and to stabilize these over time. If they do not become stable over time, you end up with constant social succession rather than simple adjustments to achieve and maintain the desired balance. Under those conditions, management constantly confronts the public it is trying to service.

To maintain public confidence, stability of recreational opportunities is essential. The agency also has some self-interest in stability because developed supportive clientele who are satisfied with the present and who are likely to support the budgetary commitment of the legislature to keep it that way.

A program should disperse use voluntarily through information services. This may be very effective where there is a lack of information and/or the networks through which people seek information affect existing use patterns (see Chapter 14). Better information may not achieve optimal dispersal from the manager's perspective, but it may provide sufficient redistribution to reduce problems of overuse on specific sites. Through this approach, you cause minimal disruption to normal visitor participation patterns. Visitors do not feel forced into changing their itineraries, yet may find other sites more enjoyable. In fact, providing more information on available recreation opportunities allows users more variety.

Such a technique may also help to eliminate "off-site" users. For example, suppose some horsemen drive two to three hours from the Butte, Montana area to the Anaconda-Pintlar Wilderness to go horseback riding. They have been assured that there will be no encounters with noisy trail bikes during their ride because of the wilderness designation. They do not seek a wilderness opportunity; they only desire a respite from trail bikes.

You can possibly eliminate these "off-site" users and simultaneously enhance their experience by providing information on bridle paths or trails zoned for horse use only that are within easy driving distance of Butte.

Limitation means restricting the number of people who may participate in a particular activity at a particular location. It involves determining a site-capacity limit beyond which use cannot be permitted. Such limits are often arbitrary, based on managerial judgment, but they can also take very specific criteria like water-quality standards into account. There are several ways of limiting use; the most desirable is one closely aligned with normal visitor-use patterns that minimizes disruption. Perhaps this may seem a somewhat idealistic approach, but by using it you can often discover the existing social mechanisms that tend to separate users into compatible patterns.[26]

Closure is usually the last alternative for changing recreational use patterns, and it may be either temporary or permanent to protect the resource base. Attempt permanent closures only when no other means are available for protecting a valued resource. The size of the area involved should be no larger than necessary when you do this.

Under certain circumstances, closure may logically be your first alternative. For example, perhaps you have located a pair of nesting bald eagles along the river in your park. You may wish to close the general area to recreational use and not allow people to get out of their boats along this stretch. You also may want to limit the number of people or the size of the craft on this portion of the river. Through your information program, you may even attempt to direct people voluntarily to other rivers and streams or to other portions of the same river. In other words, you can simultaneously employ all levels of visitor redistribution for a specific problem in a recreation area. As the preceding example illustrates, the problem for management becomes much more complex when you try to incorporate resource and social variables into your decision; therefore it is important to follow the hierarchy to redistribute recreational use.

Technique—Dispersion

There are three general techniques for obtaining voluntary dispersal: regional and area planning, regional information management, and area information systems.

Regional and Area Planning. On a regional or area basis, patterns of use are primarily determined by transportation systems like roads and trails. Since nearly all recreational use is associated with road or trail access, the type, character, and location of either or both generally determine the type and amount of recreational use a given place will receive. Use is concentrated on environmental attractors associated with these transportation systems.

The type and character of roads or trails encourage or discourage certain recreational uses and patterns of use. For example, a scenic road can be designed to slow people down so that they enjoy the view of the surrounding landscape. If we design the scenic road for high-speed through traffic, we may encourage undesirable behavior and create conflict between users. Even if the road has been properly designed in terms of speed, its character must still be considered. The presence of large cuts and fills or widely cleared areas for rights-of-way may detract from its character and discourage sightseeing. Location can also influence use—whether a road features a wide variety of scenery or masks negative sights like dumps and junk yards.

As indicated in Chapter 3, the above example suggests that macro-patterns of use are directed by the location and character of access. Hopefully we encourage certain uses and patterns of use through a positive process rather than discourage use through negative means like unpleasant landscapes or poorly designed road or trail systems. Or we can improve access and services and then simply allow use to increase to a point where the site is no longer desirable for social or environmental recreation. People then move on to other sites that have not yet been overused or, we arbitrarily regulate it at that point.

This scenario is reminiscent of the early days of farming in this country. When the soil was worn-out, farmers simply moved onto new lands. Today, while there may be a scarcity of truly unique recreational opportunities and/or a disparity between where people live and the location of public lands, space *per se* is still generally not limiting. However, there may be limits or shortages of unique natural attractors or budgets for certain types of opportunities. We should try to optimize existing space *within the constraints of the dedicated recreational opportunity,* which requires a positive approach to the distribution of people over the landscape. In sum, there is a limit to the amount of land and facilities the public is willing to maintain for intensive recreational use. Thus, if we wish to maintain or improve the quality of opportunities provided at these dedicated intensive use areas, dispersal of use is necessary.

Given a particular transportation system, the character of the adjacent landscape and the type, character, and location of specific site developments determine patterns of recreational use. While more valued portions of the landscape attract and concentrate users, who is actually attracted is often determined by the type of site development associated with the means of access. Everyone has different preferences for specific site developments. For example, campers must choose between primitive auto campgrounds versus modern ones. Character is really the quality that distinguishes one development from another, given a specific type of site. Thus, it can encourage or discourage certain types of uses.

The location of a development can also directly affect use patterns.[14] If location adversely affects normal visitor behavior, substitutes may be sought. For example, a transient campground located away from the main through route will not be used for the purpose it was originally intended. And informal, transient camping often occurs near the access to a through route because dedicated sites are not available.

Regional Information Management. After development, the most effective management tool for obtaining voluntary dispersal is an information system that reaches visitors before they arrive at their destination. Ideally, you should reach the recreationist in the planning stage so that he or she has sufficient information on which to make the best personal choice. By the time you contact visitors on the site, it is often too late to better disperse use since plans are less flexible at that point. It is critical that people know the alternatives available, and also understand why you are attempting to disperse use away from the deteriorating site or deteriorating social experience.

Area Information Systems. Area distribution or redistribution can be accomplished through specific visitor information programs.

Information programs at the area level can be aimed at direct visitor contact through signing, information centers, on-site contact, and brochures.[4,14] By making specific information available to users, managers do influence the distribution of people over an area and may also affect redistribution of visitor use by making information available on existing patterns, points of overuse, and conflicts (see Figure 13-3, p. 202). However, information is most effective during the trip planning phase.[13,15,20] You may cause some on-site redistribution through information programs, but such programs may also increase impact by attracting new users. Intensive on-site contact has been found to improve redistribution.[18] Many people feel that socially this is a more desirable approach to redistribution than limitation or closure programs.

Technique—Limitation

Limitation of use is *not* predicated on determining the carrying capacity of a site. It is a matter of discovering at what point the impact of recreational use becomes unacceptable. Laws and regulations may establish these limits sometimes. At others, professional judgments do. Such judgments should reflect the opportunity being provided. Too often, as suggested by F. E. Boteler, the manager who needs to limit use has searched for some "magic" capacity to justify his or her decision.[1] There is no good substitute for professional judgment in terms of limiting use. Probably as important is the decision on *how* to limit it. Once you decide to steer visitors away from an area, you should try to understand those factors—particularly those under your control—which have created the existing recreational pattern. Knowing them, you can judge the reversibility of such patterns with regional and area planning. If it is not

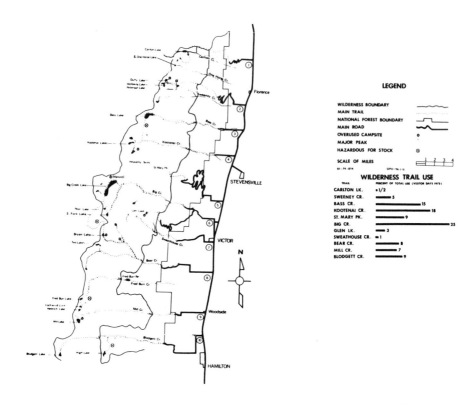

Figure 13-3. Informational map showing existing use patterns on the Stevensville District of the Selway-Bitterroot wilderness area. (From a U.S. Forest Service brochure)

feasible to reverse the process, then look at some sort of limited entry system or simply live with the new equilibrium created.

Recreational Use Zoning. This is probably the most common method of limiting use—and also one of the most appropriate.[18] It consists of clustering compatible recreational activities in selected zones to limit them within an area. This type of zoning has been employed successfully on large bodies of water to separate activities like motorized and nonmotorized boating, boating and swimming, and fishing and water-skiing. Perhaps zoning should be your first step since this is essentially what is meant by area planning— i.e., allocating space for specific recreational uses and locating that space, based on some pattern or system, within a given area.[14] If existing physiographic features such as waterfalls on rivers, lack of road access, or steep topography constrain recreational use, you can incorporate these into the area recreation plan so that desired patterns of use are encouraged without having to actually zone and enforce zoning regulations.

Time Limitation. Time zoning is a means of controlling use during peak periods, reducing conflicts between users, and ensuring adequate turnover rates so that opportunities are available for everyone. The actual time limit can be daily, weekly, seasonal, or annual. The time frame you choose depends on the activities, the season of use, the concentration during certain periods, and the efficiency level that you wish to attain in redistributing use over the area. Where competition for open space is high, time zoning can assist in redistribution by limiting visitor stays. This forces some users who want to stay longer to seek other alternatives or change their use patterns on that particular site. If the program is to be reasonably successful, visitor-use alternatives must be available because time zoning often forces some users to abandon a particular opportunity in favor of alternative ones.

Ideally, time zoning fits the normal behavioral patterns of users as closely as possible. For example, a small lake near the coast of North Carolina was being used by fishermen and water-skiers. Conflict occurred between users because the lake was oval-shaped and not large enough to handle both types. An observational study showed that the fisherman typically used the lake from daybreak until about 9 a.m., returning around 5 p.m. until dark. Water-skiers usually arrived around 10 a.m. and stayed until 4 p.m. Conflict arose over the times when the fisherman stayed late and/or the water-skiers arrived early. The final policy decision limited the fisherman to a period from daylight to 9 a.m. and from 5 p.m. until sunset; water-skiers were allowed on the lake from 9 a.m. to 5 p.m. Minimal monitoring of transition times was all that was necessary to ensure a successful program.

Most situations are not that simplistic but regardless of the problem you should consider existing user behavior. Time zoning is better adapted to shorter time frames like days or weeks. Seasonal or annual periods are usually too long to effectively redistribute use for either ecological or sociological purposes. You should also consider specific time frames as different recreational opportunities and managerially treat them as such. Since the basic management model is an open system, responsiveness to public input or changes in other social factors can create different opportunities at different times on the same site—summer versus winter, a three-day Fourth of July weekend versus any other summer weekend, etc. A good example is a newly designated wild river in Alaska. Heavy use concentrates around the Fourth of July weekend, which also coincides with the peak of the salmon runs. If one avoids that time frame, very few people are on the river. However, management has decided to try to redistribute use over the entire summer. Bon chance!

Space Limitation (Use per Unit Area). Space limitation, or density zoning, is a relatively new concept that has been applied to surface waters and roadless areas.[2,12] Desirable density levels are functions of the type of opportunity to be provided, the durability of the resource, and the perception of users, and are established as the upper limit for various management zones. Once these densities are reached, use is shifted to less-populated zones. To be effective, this measure requires a well-supervised limited-entry permit system.[26]

Quota or Service Limitation. Quota limitations are established for developed sites based on their capacity to handle a given number of people at any one time. Capacity may be limited by the size of the facility, by the service loads of supporting facilities, or by legal criteria such as fire codes. Often the quota system is referred to as a "bed count" (for overnight facilities) and a "head count" (for day-use facilities). If no overflow camping is allowed, service limitation is the total number of camping units located in developed sites. Camping is usually regulated on a unit basis rather than by number of individual campers.

Technique—Closure

Closure simply means closing an area to recreational use. No matter what the reason behind its use, managers need to identify closure as temporary or permanent since these are entirely different programs.

Temporary Closures. Temporary closures are implemented on a particular site for specific objectives and for a given amount of time. Their primary purpose is to renovate a worn-out site or to protect the resource during periods of maximum vulnerability—such as high precipitation periods in areas with heavy clay soils, nesting times for particular bird species, or gathering seasons for grizzly bears or other large mammals.

Obviously you should employ other techniques to reduce visitor concentrations before attempting a temporary closure program. Seasonal closures generally relieve pressure on a resource from visitors during critical periods. Many times, the situation is a self-correcting one. For example, times of heavy rain, when soil compaction is highest, also discourages visitor participation, though some activities such as four-wheel driving and hunting may not follow this trend.

Ultimately, managers may have to make unpopular decisions to close areas or sites during a particular season. In doing so, they realize the need to sustain resources over time rather than having them depleted by visitor use for short periods. When you use this approach, a concomitant information program is also mandatory so that people understand what you are attempting to do and become aware of available alternative sites. Without this program, you may face a greater, long-term problem—visitor dissatisfaction with any new management program because of a lack of confidence in management that stems from poor communications.

Temporary closures do not necessarily have to be obtrusive. For example, the road leading to a campground located in a sub-alpine zone was snow plowed during the early camping season so that people could use the site. Because of the semi-open forest cover, the campground was freed of snow but the soil was saturated by snow melt. Early use was causing problems such as soil compaction, loss of vegetation, and sheet erosion of the soil surface. The decision was made to discontinue plowing since the timing of the natural snow melt on the road would allow the site to dry out before campers could get into it. This was less obtrusive than continued plowing with a sign stretched across the entrance to the campground stating that no camping would be allowed until after July 1.

After reviewing many impact studies, D. N. Cole concludes that regardless of the site, the greatest cumulative impact is from limited initial use.[9] Thus in backcountry areas, rest and rotation are not very effective because management tends not to be intensive (people may continue to use a closed site) and deterioration is typically faster than recovery. More and more sites have to be allocated under such a system. The other consideration is the attributes of these alternatives in terms of natural attractors. Simply closing one and opening another does not guarantee that people will obey the rule and shift to the new site(s). If use does not shift, resource allocation costs increase because the closure has to be stringently enforced.

Permanent Closures. Permanent closures may be needed to protect people from environmental hazards or to protect a very sensitive resource from any recreational use. Determine the need for such a measure during the area planning process. Generally, problems requiring closure are more easily handled by not locating roads, trails, or sites near suspect areas. Locating the new sites, roads, and trails away from problem points creates more of a psychological barrier than a physical one. More significant problem locations such as sink holes or rare or endangered vegetation, may still need physical barriers to deter the public from general recreational use.

APPRAISAL OF DISPERSAL MANAGEMENT

Much consideration has been given to dispersal of use. Often defined as the redistribution of use over a given geographical area or time period, or both, neither are ideal goals. Recreational use tends to concentrate naturally at more valued portions of the landscape—the natural attractors—whether they be a Mount Denali or a small midwestern lake. Society also makes particular time periods attractive for visits—Memorial Day weekend, summers after schools close, work weeks that become four 10-hour days, or whatever.

You might argue that access to Mount Denali or the midwestern lake should not be allowed to the point where attractiveness or the quality of the resource is significantly reduced. We would all agree on that point. But the answer is not trying to redistribute use over an entire geographical area; it is in designing management actions, particularly the access transportation system, to maintain a level of use commensurate with the capability of the resource to sustain that use, and to maintain the desired recreational opportunity.[14]

You could make the same argument for attempting to redistribute times for use. Many factors beyond management control affect chronological distribution, such as flexible work schedules, designation of holidays as three-day weekends, internal allocation of family vacation time, and so on. On the other hand, resource attributes themselves often determine visitation times—like the spring Chinook salmon run, the changing of the leaf colors in the fall, etc.

The newly designated wild river example used earlier points to the problem of trying to redistribute use which coincides with the summer king salmon run, around the Fourth of July weekend. The river is accessible via road, but once you get on the river it takes three days to float back to the road system. Many Alaskans are given three-day weekends for the Fourth of July celebration. Thus the concentration of people on the river during that period is a product of circumstances not directly controlled by a managing agency. Yet the agency has expressed a desire to redistribute river use because it exceeds social carrying capacity. From a social standpoint, we would doubt that very many people are disappointed with their Fourth of July float/fish trips, unless the fishing is lousy. Since fish stocks have not been affected by the "pressure," it may not be possible to cause a voluntary movement to other rivers or other time periods on the same river.

Perhaps limiting use would cause some redistribution, but this would also require an expensive enforcement program. Such action may be unjustified if the resource is not being measurably affected and users are satisfied with the recreation opportunity they are experiencing. Ironically, management's perceived need for redistributing use fails to account for the unique circumstances that cause such concentrations, including a previous management action that improved access to the upper river after it was designated a wild river.

While the literature on distribution of use is limited, Jubenville and Becker suggest that visitors naturally concentrate at natural attractors within the generalized landscape, because the level of use and type of user attracted result from the management norms influencing developed access and facilities.[14] To suggest that we can redistribute use voluntarily, without modifying the development norms already in place, implies that visitors are choosing recreational opportunities under maximum uncertainty that they are not aware of what they are getting into and/or alternative choices, or that they are not looking for a particular set of resource attributes.

Studies by E. E. Krumpe and P. J. Brown in the backcountry of Yellowstone National Park,[13] R. C. Lucas in the Selway-Bitterroot Wilderness,[17] and J. H. Schomaker[23] indicate that two factors must be present to effectively redistribute use voluntarily: 1) novice users, *inexperienced* at either the activity or the geographical area; and 2) people who can be reached at the point in their planning process where they can incorporate such information into their decisions. J. W. Roggenbuck and D. L. Berrier feel that some redistribution can be accomplished through intensive on-site contact programs, but these can be very expensive.[21] They also caution against impact from the program itself.

In summation, voluntary redistribution of use based on an information program would probably not be very successful unless the circumstances are similar to those outlined above. The redistribution of use through regulation, probably a limited-entry permit system, is not very effective unless monitored and enforced. A. Plaeger and P. Womble,[20] and J. W. Van Wagtendonk and J. M. Benedict[26] found that over fifty percent of those who received a backcountry permit deliberately violated its provisions because there was no monitoring. You could close an area permanently or temporarily, but such a move would likely come under close public scrutiny. Justification would have to be overwhelming and generally related to the protection of the resource.

From a more pragmatic viewpoint, the dispersion technique is a tool of modern management. This technique is used regularly to maintain the potential for a particular experience via equal opportunity, protection of desired social or resource attributes, or pressure from existing user groups to maintain the status quo. However, unless circumstances are similar to those cited previously, you should not invest much in *voluntary* redistribution.

Rather than viewing the above as redistribution of use, we prefer the term "distribution." The geographical pattern of use is really a response to the total attributes of a recreational opportunity. Thus, if there is a problem with current distribution, it is most likely the result of some previous management action creating those attributes. A logical management direction would be to examine the link between present use and past management actions, then seek the least costly solution that maintains the desired pattern of use.

Because of equity issues, some opportunities may be artificially supported by increasing access, yet regulating numbers and patterns of use. Developing trails for the physically handicapped is an example of this. Social equity is also the main justification for not charging the full per capita costs for recreational use of public resources. Yet many managers have become interested in charging users full fares, or at least more of the base cost. The neoclassical economist would consider this the appropriate direction, letting the signals from the marketplace direct the allocation of resources and thus the distribution of recreational use. Probably some compromise will be established for public lands where less-than-fair-market-value fees are charged, but users will be expected to supply many needed services such as trash disposal, firewood, etc.

For the more primitive user, "sweat equity" will likely be touted as a substitute for price. With "sweat equity," rather than charge a hard-to-collect fee and then provide facilities such as footbridges, trail maintenance, etc., users are provided minimal access and expected to reach their destinations within roadless areas through their own physical effort. Some people create their own trails, bridges, campsite developments, etc. in order to reduce or average the amount of "sweat equity," particularly if they use an area more than once. This is simply a cost averaging. Unfortunately the ideals of such a "sweat equity" program may not be achieved unless we closely monitor such activity in relation to the impact on the opportunities being provided, which in turn increases the cost of the program.

SELECTED READINGS

1.   Boteler F. E. 1984. "Carrying Capacity As A Framework for Managing Whitewater Use." *Journal of Park and Recreation Administration,* 2(2):26-36.

2.   Brooks, L. 1963. "Zoning as a Step in the Planning of Natural Parks." Second Federal-Provincial Parks Conference Proceedings, Ottawa: Canadian National and Historical Parks Branch.

3.   Brockman, C. F., and Merriam, L. C., Jr. 1979. *Recreational Use of Wildlands.* 3rd Edition. New York, NY: McGraw-Hill Book Co.

4.   Brown, P. J., and Hunt, J. D. 1969. "The Influence of Information Signs of Visitor Distribution and Use." *Journal of Leisure Research,* 1(1):69.

5.   Bureau of Outdoor Recreation. 1966. National Conference on Policy Issues in Outdoor Recreation. Washington, DC: CD: U.S. Department of the Interior.

6.   Canon, L. K., Adler, S., and Leonard, R. E. 1979. "Factors Affecting Dispersal of Backcountry Campsites." USDA Forest Service Research Note NE-276.

7.   Cowgill, P. 1971. "Too Many People on the Colorado River." *National Parks and Conservation Magazine,* 45(11):10.

8.   Cole, D. N. 1981. "Managing Ecological Impacts At Wilderness Campsites: An Evaluation of Techniques." *Journal of Forestry,* 79(2):86-89.

9.   Douglass, R. W. 1983. *Forest Recreation.* New York, NY: Pergamon Press.

10. Godfrey, E. B., and Peckfelder, R. L. 1972. "Recreation Carrying Capacity and Wild Rivers: A Case Study of the Middle Fork of the Salmon." Western Agricultural Economic Association Annual Meeting, Proceedings.

11. Hammitt, W. E., and Cole, D. N. 1987. *Wildland Recreation: Ecology and Management*. New York, NY: John Wiley & Sons.

12. Jackson, R. 1971. "Zoning to Regulate On Water Recreation." *Land Economics 45*(4):382.

13. Krumpe, E. E., and Brown, P. J. 1982. "Redistributing Backcountry Use through Information Relating to Recreational Experiences." *Journal of Forestry, 80*(5):360-362.

14. Jubenville, A., and Becker, R. H. 1983. "Outdoor Recreation Management Planning: Contemporary Schools of Thought." *Recreation Planning and Management*. S. Lieber, and D. Fesennaier (eds.). State College, PA: Venture Publishing, Inc.

15. LaPage, W. F. 1968. The Role of Fees in Campers' Decisions. U.S. Forest Service Research Paper NE-118.

16. LaPage, W. F. 1983. "Recreation Resource Management for Visitor Satisfaction." *Journal of Park and Recreation Administration, 1*(2):37-44.

17. Lucas, R. C. 1981. Redistributing Wilderness Use through Information Supplied to Visitors. USDA Forest Service Research Paper INT-277.

18. McEwen, D., and Tocher, S. R. 1976. "Zone Management: Key to Controlling Recreational Impact in Developed Campsites." *Journal of Forestry, 14*(2):90.

19. McGill, A. W. 1974. "Dispersal of Recreationists on Wildlands." Outdoor Recreation Research: Applying the Results. U.S. Forest Service General Technical Report NC-9.

20. Plaeger, A., and Womble, P. 1981. "Compliance with Backcountry Permits in Mount McKinley National Park." *Journal of Forestry, 79*(3):155-156.

21. Roggenbuck, J. W., and Berrier, D. L. 1981. "Communications to Disperse Wilderness Campers." *Journal of Forestry, 79*(5):295-297.

22. Roggenbuck, J. W., and Berrier, D. L. 1982. "A Comparison of the Effectiveness of Two Communication Strategies in Dispersing Wilderness Campers." *Journal of Leisure Research, 14*(1):77-89.

23. Schomaker, J. H. 1975. "Effect of Selected Information on Dispersal of Wilderness Recreationists." Ph.D. dissertation (unpublished). Colorado State University.

24. Shelby, B., and Heberlein, T. A. 1986. *Carrying Capacity in Recreational Settings*. Corvallis, OR: Oregon State University Press.

25. Stankey, G. H., and McCool, S. F. 1985. Proceedings of the Symposium On Recreation Choice Behavior. USDA-Forest Service General Technical Report INT-184.

26. Van Wagtendonk, J. W., and Benedict, J. M. 1980. "Wilderness Permit Compliance and Validity." *Journal of Forestry, 78*(7):399-401.

27. Wagar, J. A. 1964. *The Carrying Capacity of Wild Lands for Recreation*. Forest Science Monograph 7, Society of American Foresters, Washington, DC.

28. Wilson, G. T. 1969. Lake Zoning for Recreation: How to Improve Recreation Use of Lakes. American Institute of Park Executives, Washington, DC.

CHAPTER 14

Information Services

From a management perspective, information programs ensure the success of all other programs. Their primary purpose is to inform visitors of available recreational opportunities, behavioral norms, and explain *why* certain actions are necessary. Explanation is essential to understanding the problem and supporting the agency.

Information *per se* is not a stand-alone program; it is the binder that pulls together the total recreational opportunity. As such, it links other visitor management programs. Making particular recreational opportunities available, closing backcountry zones to protect a resource, warning of hazardous water conditions, improving wilderness user etiquette, and so on are management actions that require information programs. We think it is safe to state that public support for recreation programs is often affected by associated information programs.

By giving visitors adequate information on which to make rational choices and using the information program to protect the quality of the recreational opportunities provided, agencies build a committed clientele who

Figure 14-1. Information is important both for management of the recreational opportunity and improved decision making by visitors. (Photo by Alan Jubenville)

support them in the long run. In essence, this program is a marketing strategy that insures an agency's survival and growth.

In sum, information programs serve visitors. They provide information that improves personal decision making, promotes general welfare, and protects the resource where the activity takes place. Information is essential to the success of most agency programs. Informing visitors and encouraging feedback to management provides cues to keeping those programs on target.

There is no guarantee that any particular information program will be an instantaneous success. Understanding applied communication can obviously help, but we must recognize that communication is a two-way street. You must offer some type of feedback mechanism to determine if a program meets visitors' needs and presents your message clearly. If they do not understand or you do not reach them, you can make adjustments. Too many management programs fail to satisfy the public because they lack a proper feedback mechanism or management fails to make adjustments after receiving visitor feedback.

Think about your own experiences. Have you ever visited a park where you were handed a four-page, single-spaced brochure and told to read it because you must abide by the rules? Observe other users under those circumstances. How many pull their auto over to the side of the road and read the brochure? How many stop at the first coffee shop to read the brochure? Simply handing out information is no guarantee of success. If you are sincerely interested in guiding resource use and enhancing visitor experiences, then you must become more sophisticated at designing, implementing and monitoring information programs.

APPLIED COMMUNICATION THEORY

People seek information for two reasons: 1) as an end in itself to increase their knowledge about some particular subject of interest and 2) as a means to an end. In this situation, people seek specific information to help make personal decisions. While they may accept information about some natural feature such as a thermal pool, what most visitors need is assistance in choosing a form of recreation. In the broadest sense, people want information about recreational opportunities so they can maximize their outdoor experience. This is an ongoing process for anyone before, during, and after participation. Getting information before participation is obviously preferable. However, most people continually accept and respond to information while engaged in an activity to conform to rules and norms and to adjust to situational conditions. Future decisions are affected not only by this stored information, but also new data received later on.

The form the information takes—verbal or nonverbal—is extremely important. Our formal programming often focuses on verbal communications, yet much of what we communicate to users is nonverbal. In fact, some of our nonverbal communications are so strong as to override the verbal ones. For example, a sign can say "No Motorized Use" but the design of the trail head and trail can say "Trail bikes and three-wheelers welcome!" These are typical causes of constant conflict, where additional dollars are required to enforce a no-motor policy and solutions are rarely lasting. When you design access facilities, you nonverbally communicate the nature of the recreational opportunity for that particular setting. As R. A. Hinde states, nonverbal stimuli may be so strong that people either miss any verbal message or dismiss it as a mistake or inappropriate.[6] In sum, the strength of an information program lies in proper nonverbal communications and alignment of the verbal message with the nonverbal.

You must also consider what information people seek and how they seek it. Styles of participation affect what people need to know and how they try to obtain this knowledge. Most RV campers want information on camping facilities, but the local RV'er already knows about these. This individual has a greater interest in the condition of the access road, whether the fish are biting, the anticipated weather pattern for next weekend, or the marauding black bears that sometimes patrol the campground. The nonlocal RV'er may want to know about the types of environmental settings, the local attractors within each, and the RV facilities available to enjoy those things. Perhaps, if a particular activity is of interest, such as lake fishing, he may want to know what particular lakes are available within a given distance of camp or along a given travel route.

The nonlocal may choose Site A because it offers fishing, is accessible by RV, has RV camping facilities, and falls within limits of distance. The local user may choose Site A for all of the above reasons but utilize additional, more refined information to, as much as possible, eliminate the uncertainty of not catching good-sized fish at the lake. Nonlocals tend to seek the more general information already available to locals and choose recreational opportunities based on that information. If they participate and find the fishing poor, the reason may be timing. If they need to arrive a month earlier, they use this information for future trips to the lake. Perhaps

you can locate a local resident to find out fishing conditions, such as a marina owner. After a sufficient number of "trial and error" trips, you may gather much more detailed information about Site A that the locals use. Thus what you seek and how you seek it depend on what you already know.

As suggested in Chapter 5, *how* we seek information is based on sources that are known to us and how familiar and trustworthy we perceive those sources to be. People perceived as "experts" are trusted, and the more familiar we are with an individual, the more willing we are to trust his or her information. If we find no experts on available sources, familiarity with the source may become the overriding factor in accepting the message.

The *how* is probably best described by the term "networking." To choose a type of recreational opportunity, you may use a single network or a whole series of networks, depending on how important your decision is to you, the networks available, and how much uncertainty you are willing to live with. For generalized participation decisions, people typically use formal information networks supplied by the agency which manages the resource base, or some affiliated group such as a RV association or sport-fishing group. For more specific information, people typically rely on informal networks: friends, acquaintances, or mutual friends.

Standing or acceptance within a network is essential to getting desired information. In the formal networks, you may already have standing as a member of the general public (public sector) or association (private sector). In the informal networks, you obtain standing through familiarity and trust. You can often penetrate a network through a mutual friend who is already involved. The senior author faced that very problem trying to gather information about bighorn sheep hunting in a particular drainage in Idaho. He drew a once-in-a-lifetime permit and used formal networks to obtain all the generalized information available. However, to get detailed information, he needed to communicate with the local hunters, taxidermists, etc. who are knowledgeable about bighorn sheep habits and patterns in that drainage. Mutual friends either sought this information or legitimized entrance into their networks.

Dividing users into locals and nonlocals is a classic illustration of networking. Other divisions based on participatory style include guided and nonguided visitors, groups and individuals, etc. What management must recognize are formal and informal networks. The agency's formal network is only one source of information, and for many users not the most important, particularly for more detailed, refined participation decisions.

Next you must consider when people seek information. Clawson's five stages of the recreational experience suggest that stage one—the Planning Stage—is when people use information to make decisions. The plan can be very abbreviated, like one based on a comment by the "Dean of the Bass Fishermen" who says, "The big ones are biting in the north arm," or very involved, like the one for the RV camper-fisherman who lives a thousand miles away and invests considerable time and expense to catch a "big one." The "when" is important to management, as suggested in Chapter 12, because it affects the type of information needed and how visitors seek/accept that information.

To put it into context, local users are already knowledgeable about an area and tied into informal networks. A formal information program is probably of no use to this individual unless some recent change has been introduced by either management (change of regulations, rerouting of the road)

or some exogenous input such as a flood. Consequently, management should rely on local informal networks and nonverbal communications to inform locals, then use on-site verbal communications to encourage proper use patterns where nonverbal communications and local informal networks are not sufficient. Management can take advantage of these networks simply by "passing the word" to a few key links—the postmaster, the bait-shop owner, the bartender, etc.

Most people are ethical and respond to verbal messages from management.[3] For those who are not, the only effective communication appeals to their sense of moral costs and benefits. What is the probability of getting caught, and what is the cost if they do? Off-site communications, if desired, can also be accomplished through other formal networks that locals might use, such as the Valley Sportsman's Association or an area chapter of an RV association, or perhaps even a nearby radio or television station. Where use is rationed and monitored closely by an agency, local users may take advantage of a formal information program to obtain detailed news. Where such contacts become routine, an agency may use a recorded phone message which can be quickly updated. Mass media such as newspapers, radio, and television also help reach local users on either a regularly scheduled basis to announce the latest information on local conditions or on a periodic basis to warn users of abrupt changes in local conditions or impending regulatory changes.

Nonlocals use formal information programs more because they do not possess all the general data known to locals. If this group constitutes a considerable portion of the user population, your off-site program becomes more important. Printed material, particularly maps showing activity sites and written descriptions called recreational opportunity guides (ROGs), are an essential part of the program. Potential local users, if they take advantage of the formal program, have needs similar to nonlocals. They may, however, seek information differently—by calling on the phone or stopping at the office. Some agencies try to improve this effort by conveniently placing ROGs in the local library or other public areas. Nonlocal nonusers are people who may travel to an area for a given purpose and seek information about available opportunities. These individuals confront the same problems as local nonusers, finding it difficult to enter a formal network because of uncertainty of public and private ownerships in a given area and difficult to locate agencies and access their information programs. Many states and multistate regions have established specific informational programs, including regional visitor centers, to help this type of person make decisions and to increase access to specific agency-information programs.

REGIONAL INFORMATION SYSTEMS

There are two potential planning stages in individual decision making: 1) the macrolevel, region or general zone of participation, and 2) the microlevel, the specific recreational opportunity within a general zone or area information program.

Some people choose a region or general zone, travel to that zone, and then select specific opportunities. While it may appear that such a planning process leaves much uncertainty, people typically choose a region because it offers a number of *desired* recreational opportunities. They go prepared with sufficient skills, equipment, and information about the area in order to take advantage of what the region has to offer.

Others choose a region and a given opportunity simultaneously. They select the specific activity and focus all of their additional planning and trip preparation on that activity. Thus they need maximum information because they are likely to have less flexible schedules and locations if some problem arises. Still others focus all their planning on the specific activity or microlevel.

Regional Programs

The regional informational network is designed to enhance macrolevel decision making by providing base data on available recreational opportunities and an agency contact for obtaining more detailed information. Regional information systems can be holistic and offer an entire gamut of opportunities, public or private, within a region. Under those conditions, the information has to be relatively general so people can assimilate it quickly and make choices. The state or some private company typically provides this type of publication/service.

Or the regional system can focus only on one agency. Parks or recreation areas under its jurisdiction are identified, and the information program describes only recreational opportunities within these units. A system can also delineate a theme such as colonial history, trout fishing, or wilderness hiking, then build a regional program around that theme. Typically the private sector offers this type of service.

Regionalization

It is important to gather and disseminate information on a regional level to minimize discrepancies due to variation in data collection methods, units of analyses, and models of actual participation. Many people agree on this point; however, the problem becomes one of defining regional boundaries. Some feel that each state should be divided into regions, but this is not a large enough geographic area to describe normal visitor travel and behavioral patterns and disseminate this information to the using public. The geographic area should be larger—much larger. Since use patterns and demands for information often exceed state and even multi-state boundaries, these regional boundaries should cover an area as large as six to ten states, and the regions should be interconnected for information exchange. Probably the best way to delineate boundaries is to base them on the primary physiographic areas of the United States that have been adjusted to the political boundaries of the states (see Figure 14-2). Alaska and Hawaii, not shown, would be separate regions.

Probably as important as any single phase of a regional information system is actual operation. Other systems are usually limited to a single agency that does not show visitors the total spectrum of available opportunities. Consequently, visitors often have limited options but sufficient information with which to make a choice. Increased information helps people make better choices.

Figure 14-2. The major physiographic provinces in the United States (excluding Alaska and Hawaii). These represent general recreational opportunities.

This requires constant updating of information if the system is to be effective. Every agency should use the same data collection methods, the same units of measure, and so forth to feed new data into the system. Such an operation is ideally computer-based because of volume and the need for constant updating.

Some broad-range systems are already in operation, such as that used by AAA; however these simplified information systems generally inform people about limited opportunities/services. A more sophisticated, nationwide operation might be devised where individuals go to their local branch offices, plug in their computer cards, and obtain all the information needed for visits to southern Florida during December or the North Slope of Alaska in July.

There are many drawbacks to a regional information system, including the following:

1. information overload at the macrolevel of decision making,
2. lack of participation by agencies and organizations,
3. current availability of much of the information, often in fragmented form,
4. competition from existing private endeavors,
5. lack of acceptance by the public, and
6. attempts to reduce uncertainty when it is really a part of the recreational experience.

Many agencies are looking closely at the regional information system for communicating with the public. This is a contemporary concept and very controversial. Though it is worth considering, we should proceed slowly. People do need information to make decisions. However, if it requires an extensive new infrastructure, data collection and updating, and/or long-term commitment from agencies already experiencing severe budget reductions, then one has to question the desirability of such a system. We suspect that many people who have to travel long distances to get *to* a region will only rely on an agency for general information and that other sources, including formal networking and literature through clubs, organizations, etc., will supply the detailed information. However, detailed information about areas *within* a region or specific opportunities *within* a given area are the function of an area information program. Thus, while most agencies continue to search for ways of reaching people at the macrolevel, the microlevel continues to be the primary focus of agency programs.

AREA INFORMATION SYSTEMS

Area information systems are designed to focus on microlevel decision making. As previously indicated, they offer more refined information in greater detail so participants can make more informed choices. But managers must remember that timing the receipt of information and networking through associations other than the agency are important to the participants. Rather than repeat the concepts discussed with regional information systems, we will summarize the ones applicable to area information systems during the actual participation period:

1. While part of the program aims at assisting people in macro decision making, much of it is directed at the microlevel.
2. Nonverbal communication is important to convey the type of recreational opportunity participants should expect.

3. Verbal communication must be aligned with nonverbal so no mixed signals confuse participants.

4. The on-site information program is a simple reminder of what to expect or what rules govern participation. Simplicity is the key.

5. Types and level of information provided should reflect where that activity falls on the recreational opportunity spectrum. The more primitive the opportunity, the less specific the information. Under these conditions, risk, uncertainty, and self-reliance become more essential to the experience. Thus the area information program becomes an important management tool, much more so than the regional one.

Information Media

Since the area information program is directed toward specific opportunities with specific geographical boundaries, necessary information is more easily identified, updated, and transmitted. Media for transmitting these verbal communications are as follows:

1. Visitor Centers. Probably the most traditional means of transmitting information to visitors is through on-site contact at a visitor center. The visitor center is usually located at the main access point of the area so it is easily identifiable and accessible to visitors entering the area. Or it is located at some critical point in the visitor's path, like near a mountain pass, where he or she can seek information about several surrounding areas.

Figure 14-3. Ohanapecosh visitor center. Mt. Rainier National Park. (Photo by B. W. Twight)

Cost efficiency depends on user population and the users' need for that type of detailed information. In sum, there have to be a relatively large number of recreation participants, primarily nonlocals, who use the visitor center. Capital and operating costs for any center should reflect the concern for getting information to visitors as cost efficiently as possible. From a design perspective, visitor centers should be stationary, easily accessed, and readily available. They should not be disruptive to visitors who are not interested in using them. Site planning should not create traffic problems or facilities that are visually incongruent with the landscape. Based on observations it is amazing how auto and pedestrian traffic flows and the appearance of centers affect visitor participation. A center that is properly located along main access routes, has easy ingress/egress, and fits the surrounding landscape is more casually and continuously used than one that does not possess these characteristics. Thus the original plan has tremendous effect on a visitor center's success. Facilities should fit the situation. They may be very simple or complex, yet we often provide expensive facilities at visitor centers. A simple, one-room building with parking is sufficient in some situations; others may call for a major complex to handle high visitor loads. You can also offer additional services and information like comfort stations, emergency phones, interpretive programs, overnight accommodations, and reservation systems. This improves the availability of all services by increasing accessibility. Housing them together in a single facility is also more economical, offering a combination of services.

2. Area Signing. Use signing to provide visitors with information as they travel through the area. An area sign or a map showing road and trail systems, available recreational opportunities, and developed facilities should be strategically placed at major access points to quickly familiarize visitors with the area (see Figure 14-4, p. 218). This type of area information sign is becoming more popular in relatively large areas where there is no visitor information center. Ideally visitors can understand the message with minimum time and inconvenience. Post additional signs in an area for information, education or warnings, but carefully scrutinize use and location. Below are some rules of signing that you should remember:

a. Do not overload the visitor with informational signing.
b. Identify need at specific location.
c. Convey only one message per sign, and make the message as simple as possible.
d. Where possible, use international symbols which have been adopted by most major park systems.

3. Publications. Publications are important sources of information; however, you should follow the basic rules of signing and not overdo them. Consider conducting follow-up studies to determine the effectiveness of publications, particularly those that are not sold at publication cost. Often we spend considerable amounts of money on brochures that are used very little by visitors, reach the wrong audience, or are misunderstood.

Brochures passed out at entrance stations are often wordy and difficult to read, so visitors just scan and discard them. Therefore such publications are frequently an ineffective information medium because people are not interested in reading extensively while pursuing outdoor leisure activities. They prefer a minimum of inconvenience and a format such as a newspaper that they are familiar with.

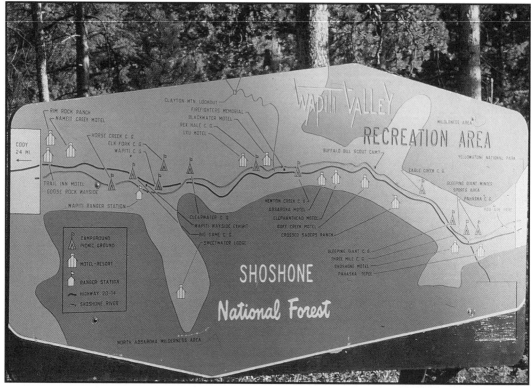

Figure 14-4. An example of an area information sign. Wapiti Valley, Shoshone National Forest. (Photo by Alan Jubenville)

Assuming this is true, managers must seek more innovative means of getting necessary information to visitors. Sometimes agencies are more concerned with meeting legal and administrative requirements in their publications than communicating with visitors, as discussed in the beginning of this chapter. Thus, as previously indicated, you shouldn't oversell the role of publications.

At the same time, a brochure that is done well can be very effective. When developing one, consider the following variables beyond specific managerial goals:

a. OVERALL APPEARANCE

The overall appearance should invite the user to read (see Figure 14-5). Too often, we will be more concerned with the technical aspects of the message rather than whether it will be read. Packaging is as important as the product.

b. ATTRACTIVE COVER

The cover creates the initial impression. If done well, it may encourage visitors to open the brochure and read further. The title should clearly state the subject presented. Remember that you never get a second chance to make a good first impression.

c. PROPER SIZE AND SHAPE

Proper size and shape can encourage continued use. For the backpacker to refer to a brochure during a trip, it should easily fit into a shirt pocket; otherwise it will not be convenient to use. If it is to be mailed to visitors prior to arrival, it should be the right shape for mailing.

d. CONCISENESS

Use as few words as possible in your message. People at their leisure are generally unreceptive to lengthy messages.

e. PICTURES AND DIAGRAMS

Pictures and diagrams can clearly convey a message with minimum distortion, regardless of audience. In addition, you reduce the amount of time needed to read and understand.

f. ELIMINATE AGENCY RHETORIC AND BIAS

Don't try to impress others with technical jargon and artificial eloquence. Also try to be factual, eliminating agency bias and personal values.

g. LOCAL CONTACT

Provide a local contact if desirable. Too often, we attract people's interest only to frustrate them by not including an address, phone number, or schedule for those who want more information.

FLOATING THE SNAKE RIVER IN GRAND TETON NATIONAL PARK

THE NATIONAL PARK SERVICE
U.S. DEPARTMENT OF
THE INTERIOR

MILEAGE LOG AND TRAVEL TIME. The following chart gives the river mileage between all major landings. The location of these landings is shown on the Snake River map.

Major Landings	Jackson Lake Dam	Pacific Creek	R. K. O. Site	Deadmans Bar	Lower Schwabacher
Jackson Lake Dam	0				
Pacific Creek	4.5				
R. K. O. Site	8.5	4.0			
Deadmans Bar	15.0	10.5	6.5		
Lower Schwabacher	20.0	15.0	11.5	5.0	
Moose	25.0	20.0	16.5	10.0	5.0

Travel time on the river is highly variable depending on many factors, such as rate of water flow, type of craft, speed and direction of wind, and rate of rowing and paddling. Suffice to say that the entire 25 mile trip from Jackson Lake Dam to Moose can be made in one day under all but the most unfavorable conditions.

Figure 14-5. A simple but effective brochure. (National Park Service brochure, illustrations by Scott M. Coburn)

h. MANAGEMENT PROBLEM

If your brochure focuses on a management problem, mention the regulations designed to alleviate it, but don't dwell on the subject. Also indicate the reasons for these actions and rewards for the user.

4. *Radio Gadgetry.* Special radio programs can provide information to visitors. The mobile visitor may receive a signal on an auto radio from a remote, short-distance transmitter usually within a one-mile transmitting radius. A foot traveler receives it through a headset receiver. Remote radio transmitting is done with a continuous taped program easily changed at the site. Usually a short and concise presentation works best because of time limitations as people pass through the transmitting radius.

For walking visitors, headset receivers operate from a very short distance—sometimes less than one hundred feet. Usually these gadgets work best in well-developed, controlled areas like historical sites or museums. On-call radio transmitters, on which you push a button to receive information over an open speaker or headset, may also be available.

5. *On-site Contact.* On-site visitor contact is a very personal and often very necessary means of transmitting information—information that is an integral part of a visitor-safety program, for example. However, as a general program, on-site contact, tends to be ineffective and inefficient unless large numbers of visitors converge on a developed site. For dispersed use, the cost of such a program typically far exceeds the benefits; however, personnel who are actually performing other on-the-ground services may contact people informally.

6. *Mass Media.* Mass media such as radio, television, and newspapers are a legitimate means of disseminating information to large numbers of people. Too often this is deplored as being impersonal and consequently is not used. However, the media may be the only means to reach large numbers of people, who do not consider this method impersonal at all since we receive much daily information in this manner anyway. Whenever mass media are used, listeners should be made aware of direct communication channels for follow-up.

7. *Group Contact.* Continuous contact with groups—conservation, recreational, business, or otherwise—is an excellent means of communicating. Today more people belong to various recreational organizations and special-interest groups who participate together. It is important to maintain open communications with such groups to understand their motives and concerns. At the same time, you can express the concerns and contemplated actions of your agency. The contact between agency and groups simply provides a forum for open discussion.

Group contact is often spurned by the politically naive as having no real benefit for the agency or is envisioned as "consorting with the enemy." If such contacts are to be made, they should be done on a continuous basis with a variety of organizations to maximize information exchange and maintain the groups' confidence in management. Being extremely selective in choosing groups for contact is self-defeating because, in doing so, you lose the attention and respect of other organizations. It appears that you are listening only to those groups whose values you personally agree with.

8. Public Hearings. Public input into decision making has been covered in Chapter 6. It should be emphasized that public hearings are excellent opportunities for communication; however, too often managers treat them as one-way information flows rather than exchanges of ideas. If handled correctly, these sessions can enable you to clear up unfounded concerns and any misinformation. As indicated in Chapter 6, people are often polarized because they don't understand the views of others or are suspicious of their motives. Public hearings, if handled properly, can alleviate some of this with objective information and discussion.

SUMMARY

Sometimes we forget that information management involves communications—a continuous interchange of information. Both agencies and visitors must reassess and adjust their own programs, modes of behavior, and so forth. Management adjusts the prescriptions for a particular area to obtain the desired equilibrium, as discussed in Chapter 3, or to enhance an already stable opportunity. This communication can be formal and informal, verbal or nonverbal. Unfortunately such programs are sometimes undertaken without any regard for public reception and response. When this happens, channels of communication often become restricted and the public loses confidence in management. These channels can only be reestablished after the public agency has done something to redeem public confidence.

The following are types of communication that agencies should encourage:

1. information to users on available recreational opportunities and feedback from users on the quality of the experience,

2. information to users on existing activity patterns and feedback,
3. information and feedback on major problems or proposed plans being considered by agencies, and
4. open channels for continuous interchange of information.

Item number four is vital to any organization and the public. As indicated in Chapter 6, projects or programs can often be delayed or stopped when there is no *interchange of information.* An uninformed public loses confidence in an agency and subsequently withholds support—even for a very sound, rational program. It is important that all people feel they can use open channels; otherwise we may discourage the interchange that we wish to encourage. We already have too many people talking to those who agree with them and not enough people talking to those who do not.

SELECTED READINGS

1. Brown, P. J., and Hunt, J. D. 1969. "The Influence of Information Signs On Visitor Distribution and Use." *Journal of Leisure Research,* *1*(1):79-83.

2. Donaghy, W. C. 1980. *Our Silent Language: An Introduction to Nonverbal Communication.* New York, NY: Cambridge University Press.

3. Dustin, D. 1984. "To Feed or Not to Feed the Bears," *Parks and Recreation, 20*(10): 54-57.

4. Eisenberg, A. M., and Smith, R. R., Jr. 1971. *Nonverbal Communications.* New York, NY: Bobbs-Merrill Co., Inc.

5. Fazio, J. R., and Gilbert, D. L. 1990. *Public Relations and Communications for Natural Resource Managers.* Dubuque, IA: Kendall-Hunt.

6.   Hendee, J. C., and Burdge, R. J. 1974. "The Substitutability Concept; Implications for Recreation Research and Management." *Journal of Leisure Research,* 6:155.

7.   Hinde, R. A. (ed.). 1972. *Nonverbal Communication.* New York, NY: Cambridge University Press.

8.   Howard, C. J., and Tracz, R. F. 1984. *Contact: A Textbook in Applied Communications.* Englewood Cliffs, NJ: Prentice-Hall.

9.   Huffman, M. G., and Williams, D. R. 1987. "The Use of Microcomputers for Park Trail Information Dissemination," *Journal of Park and Recreation Administration.*

10.   Kasschau, R. A. 1982. *Information Technology and Psychology: Prospects for the Future.* New York, NY: Praeger Publishers.

11.   Lucas, R. C. 1981. Redistributing Wilderness Use Through Information Supplied Visitors. USDA-Forest Service Research Paper INT-277.

12.   McAvoy, L. H., and Dustin, D. 1983. "Indirect Versus Direct Regulation of Behavior." *Journal of Park and Recreation Administration,* 1(4):12-17.

13.   Manfredo, M. J. 1989. "An Investigation of the Bias For External Information Search in Recreation and Tourism," *Leisure Sciences,* 11:29-45.

14.   Rapoport, A. 1982. *The Meaning of a Built Environment: A Nonverbal Communication Approach.* Beverly Hills, CA: Sage Publications.

15.   Roggenbuck, J. W., and Berrier, D. L. 1982. "A Comparison of the Effectiveness of Two Communication Strategies in Dispersing Wilderness Campers." *Journal of Leisure Research,* 14(1):77-89.

16.   Ross, T. L., and Moeller, G. H. 1974. Communicating Rules in Recreation Areas. U.S. Forest Service Research Paper NE-297.

17.   Searle, M. S., and Jackson, E. L. 1985. "Recreation Non-participation and Barriers to Participation: Considerations for the Management of Recreation Delivery Systems," *Journal of Park and Recreation Administration,* 3(2):23-35.

18.   Schramm, W. L. 1982. *Men, Women, Messages, and Media.* 2nd edition. New York, NY: Harper & Row, Inc.

19.   Surronson, I., Huber, J., and Payne, J. 1988. "The Relationship Between Prior Brand Knowledge and Information Acquisition Order." *Journal of Consumer Research,* 14(3):566-78.

20.   Wagar, J. A., and Twight, B. W. 1983. "Communication and Public Involvement." Section 23, *Forestry Handbook.* 2nd edition. Wenger, K. F. (ed.). New York, NY: John Wiley & Sons.

21.   Williams, D. R. 1988. "Measuring Perceived Similarity Among Outdoor Recreation Activities: A Comparison of Visual and Verbal Stimulus Presentations." *Leisure Sciences,* 10:153-166.

CHAPTER 15

Interpretive Services

It is not so much what we see in nature but how we interpret what we see

—John Burroughs

Interpretation may have many meanings. In park management, it is essentially the act of stimulating curiosity about, and understanding and appreciation of, meaningful relationships among the natural phenomena around us. F. Tilden considers interpretation to be more than mere communication of information; it is "an educational activity which aims to reveal meanings and relationships through the use of original subjects, by first-hand experience, and by illustrative media . . ." He further states that:

"the chief aim of interpretation is not instruction, but provocation."[35]

These citations summarize the role of interpretation. Through it, we can reveal the meaning of natural phenomena to visitors on a first-hand basis with common, easily understood examples that illustrate the interrelationships of various phenomena. In addition, it is hoped that our examples motivate readers into searching for greater meaning and understanding in nature.

Interpretive services must adequately tell the story of a specific park, ecosystem, or historic/cultural artifact. A total program designed to portray a whole story, interpretation usually breaks the event into parts intended to reach a variety of audiences. Variety is a key word; we must use many different methods and media to reach a variety of users since they have diverse interests and ways of using parks. Most failures in interpretive programs result from a lack of understanding about the role of interpretation and a lack of sufficient variety within the total program.

G. W. Sharpe lists three objectives for interpretation programs:

> The first or primary objective of interpretation is to assist the visitor in developing a keener awareness, appreciation, and understanding of the area he or she is visiting. Interpretation should help to make the visit a rich and enjoyable experience.

> The second objective of interpretation is to accomplish management goals. It can be done in two ways. First, interpretation can encourage thoughtful use of the recreation resource on the part of the visitor, helping reinforce the idea that parks are special places requiring special behavior. Second, interpretation can be used to minimize human impact on the resource by guiding people away from fragile or overused areas into areas that can withstand heavier use.

> The third objective of interpretation is to promote public understanding of an agency and its programs.[31]

Figure 15-1. The third objective of interpretation is to promote public understanding of an agency and its programs.[31] Olympic National Forest, WA. (Photo by B. W. Twight)

Many agencies have developed their interpretive programs around these objectives. If you look at the umbrella program called interpretation, you find that it includes not only history and natural-history interpretation but also public information, behavioral modification (manipulation through information), and public relations. While all these programs are certainly important, the original meaning of interpretation in terms of history or natural history is sometimes lost or at best relegated to a position of lesser importance.

Our concern is to maintain the purity of programs that interpret natural history and contribute to our national and international park heritage by not becoming confused with visitor management and related public relations programs. We are *not* saying that other aspects under the general umbrella are not as important, but rather that they should not be confused with interpretive programs. Others have stated a similar view most eloquently:

> Our interpretive efforts must be designed to complement an area, to tell its story, and at the same time utilize the purpose and values of the area to stimulate better understanding and the appreciation of this place—earth—our home.[34]

—Tom D. Thomas

To excite curiosity, to open a person's mind—there is a challenge for anyone who seeks to communicate ideas. I know of no one more sensitive to the challenge than the interpreter, for he is a teacher in the purist sense of the word. He works with people who are at leisure, at the special places of beauty and history which have been dedicated and set aside. He seeks to translate, vividly, the language of the earth, and of the earth's inhabitants.[35]

—Freeman Tilden

When technology has nothing more for man, then nature will go on showing him her wonders.[2]

—Eduardo Arango

There is the world around us, the complex society in which we live, and our increasing detachment from nature. Then there are interpreters. For them to tell a story that we can appreciate and understand is a real challenge.

BASIC INTERPRETIVE MODEL

The basic interpretive model is presented in Figure 15-2, p. 226. The park is the microcosm in which interpretation takes place, and it is hoped that the effects of the program extend beyond that microcosm. Interpretation is necessary for people to appreciate natural phenomena, and from this need the principles of interpretation evolve. Certain methods facilitate the art of interpretation—personal services, self-guiding programs, and now electronic gadgetry. The media associated with these methods has also become more sophisticated, including the modern interpretive center, the interpretive trail, and radio and television. The special programs aim at children, environmental education in public schools, junior rangers, urban awareness, and so forth. The ultimate goal is that the visitors can relate this information to the world in which they live.

While we all tend to glorify idealism, to want to have some impact on the world beyond our park, it is awfully naive to think of our efforts as saving or even having a meaningful impact on that world. Rather than dwelling on the grandiosity of the interpretive model, then, it is better to go back to the basics of history/natural history interpretation.

People personally grow through the experiences that they have with other people, situations, and even the natural wonders of the world. That growth evolves in three stages: appreciation, understanding, and knowledge. Certainly we cannot expect people to grow much in understanding and knowledge if we offer a fairly simplistic explanation of a very complex phenomenon presented over a very short period of time. What we should expect interpretive programs to cause is greater appreciation of that phenomenon. Maybe the intellectual arousal stimulated by the program leads you to more detailed readings, perhaps even formal courses to fully develop your knowledge. But hopefully what most people leave with is simply a heightened appreciation of a particular part of nature.

As part of the basic model, we would like to explore the concept of appreciation from a managerial perspective. Appreciation means to recognize, be sensitive to, and enjoy. Assume that people are at a given location to

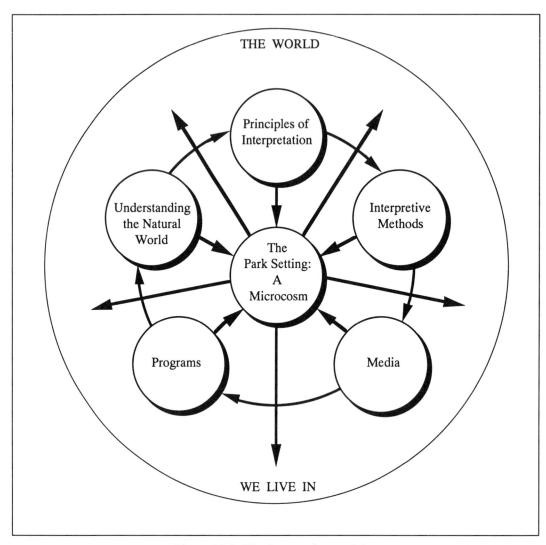

Figure 15-2. The interpretive model.

participate and enjoy a particular recreational opportunity. The activity could be an auto tour of Banff National Park or a wilderness backpack trip in the Arctic Wildlife Refuge. Now, from the users' perspective, classify the recreational perceptions they receive as a "larger experience." Within that "larger experience" may be several smaller exposures to particular natural phenomena—a view of a glacier-covered mountain, a moose feeding on aquatic vegetation, or perhaps the rich bouquets of Alpine flowers. These informal contacts with the full force of nature, though usually viewed and enjoyed in the abstract, are really informal interpretive programs because they promote appreciation of nature, reach more people, and reveal more in reality than our formal programs.

From a managerial perspective, we should, within limits, offer more opportunities for "larger experiences" because visitors are better able to find suitable recreational niches to enjoy. In the process, they can find more suitable and varied "smaller experiences" to heighten their appreciation of nature, to awaken curiosity, and perhaps to seek more formal programs, if desired, to satisfy that curiosity. Through design we can help visitors capture these smaller experiences.

We put much emphasis on the formal, concrete program; yet, as suggested by Tilden, enjoyment of the landscape in the abstract may be more rewarding and stimulating.[34] If we recognize the goal of interpretation to be appreciation, perhaps we can, and already do, reach and stimulate many more visitors than we actually count in formal programs. The way to make this happen is to emphasize the larger experience, to let people find their own stimulating smaller ones, and to be prepared through a well-publicized formal, concrete interpretive program to enrich this appreciation.

The best example of such planning is the road between Banff and Jasper in two Canadian national parks. It passes through some of the most spectacular scenery in North America and attracts people from all over the world. One subtle design feature, a paved parking lane on each side of the road, allows visitors to stop and enjoy a myriad of "smaller experiences" along the way—a gnarled lodgepole pine, a lazy riffle in a brook, a colorful rock outcropping, or a coyote stalking a vole. Everyone can find something in the landscape that tingles their imagination and causes them to linger and reflect, which in turn may lead to increased appreciation. Some of those "smaller experiences" may actually inspire people into searching for deeper understanding, but certainly that should not be our goal. Possibly formal programs directed at improving observational skills would be of benefit in this appreciation game.

Many people recognize historic interpretation as a pure form because the story to be told is well-delineated, involving a period of time, an event, a building, etc. What actually happens is that, to the participant, the "larger experience" and "smaller experience" become essentially inseparable. You visit a historic site because of the associated history for which it was dedicated, and not generally for other activities. Even then, if allowed to browse, you may find numerous "smaller experiences" on which to cogitate.

PRINCIPLES OF INTERPRETATION

Tilden summarizes these principles as follows:

1. Any interpretation that does not somehow relate what is being displayed or described to something within the personality or experience of the visitor will be sterile.
2. Information, as such, is not interpretation. Interpretation is revelation based on information, but they are entirely different things. However, all interpretation includes information.
3. Interpretation is an art which combines many arts, whether the material is scientific, historical or architectural. Art is in some degree teachable.[34]
4. The chief aim of interpretation is not instruction, but provocation.
5. Interpretation should aim to present a whole rather than a part, and must address itself to the whole, rather than any phase.

6. Interpretation (say up to age twelve) should not be a dilution of the presentation to adults, but should allow a fundamentally different approach. To be at its best, it will require a separate program.[34]

These principles are as meaningful today as when they were written, and the fourth one best summarizes the intent of interpretive programming: as an attempt to stimulate curiosity, awareness, and appreciation for an environmental setting. Program planning pulls it all together to present the whole, the total, picture. Individual interpreters may add to this picture, but there are many concepts and skills you need to become a bona fide interpreter of the environment. Probably none is more important than the basic philosophy of interpretation developed in the first two sections and summarized in the above principles.

PROGRAM PLANNING

As a process, interpretive planning is probably not much different than other planning. You inventory what you have, select pertinent environmental themes, establish specific programs and activities to fully capture themes and develop necessary infrastructure, hire personnel to conduct programs, train them, and then monitor their presentations. Simple? Not really, but those are the basic steps.

Typically, overseers of the individual park or recreation area first develop an overall *resource management plan* which includes an inventory of natural or historical resources. Then they compose a *statement of interpretation* which identifies the basic interpretive

themes from the inventory and the amount of programming the agency intends to do. This is a very concise document that simply establishes scope. The actual *interpretive plan* comes next, identifying necessary facilities, activities, and locations for presenting themes and making them meaningful to the public. The annual *activity plan* is what the staff interpretive specialist prepares, within budgetary limits, for the logistics of annual interpretive activities. Thus what visitors enjoy as an interpretive program is really just the tip of the iceberg. R. K. Grater offers a detailed outline of the total interpretive prospectus.

Methods

There are three methods of interpretation:

1. Personal services, which include talks, demonstrations, and walks.
2. Self-guiding, by which the visitor is directed through the program with special self-guiding materials and facilities.
3. Gadgetry, by which the interpreter uses electronic devices to communicate to the public.[15]

Personal Services. Communicating directly with visitors is important; these contacts may be formal or informal. Informal interpretive programs are conducted by all park personnel—from the information specialist to the law enforcement officer. Visitors expect all park employees to be able to answer questions about an area, and so even maintenance personnel should be able to respond to these questions, and thus should receive training. If they are unsure, they should refer visitors to a place where questions can be answered. Informal contacts usually occur on a one-to-one basis at points of visitor concentrations. Point duty generally consists of answering questions, but you can also interpret surrounding wildlands in the process.

Formal personal-service programs include:

1. TALKS

As indicated by G. W. Sharpe, interpretive talks involve the . . . translation of technical and often complex language of the environment into nontechnical form, with no loss in accuracy, so as to create in the listener sensitivity, awareness, understanding, enthusiasm, and commitment.[31]

These talks should accommodate the level of understanding of the audience and are usually more effective when you add illustrations or real examples. For example, it is much more effective to show a weathered replica of an early horse-drawn wagon that depicts life on the trail during westward expansion than to merely describe it.

2. DEMONSTRATIONS

Demonstrations enhance appreciation with minimal verbal communication. They can inform by recreating history. For example, suppose a living-history program illustrates the lifestyle and hardships of early settlers. When using this technique to show a natural ecosystem, you should display a model so that the audience can see the entire system and any changes in the system that you wish to demonstrate.

3. WALKS

Guided interpretive walks are what we consider the classical interpretative approach. They are probably most interesting and motivating for visitors because they can learn through first-hand experience and ask questions about what they see. Personal interactions are greater on interpretive walks because of the informality and the small group size. Also, a capable interpreter is reassuring to people who visit a new and strange environment for the first time. At ease, they can focus more attention on the environment around them.

Self-Guiding. Self-guiding refers to unattended, interpretive programs that are usually designed to interpret a particular landscape, environmental variable, or unique species. Self-guided programs are propelled by printed brochures or signs. On the long walks, a brochure is typically provided to interpret natural phenomena for the visitor. For point-specific opportunities such as an overlook, interpretation is usually conveyed through signs and displays.

Gadgetry. Interpretation has reached the age of advanced communications. We now use radio contact from remote stations, short-distance radio contact requiring headsets, electronically controlled moving displays, and educational television. This type of gadgetry has made it easier to reach more people. The questions to ask are how far do we go, and at what price?

Interpretive Media

Although some of these have been mentioned previously, this is an appropriate place for enumerating and discussing the various media available to managers.

Interpretive Centers. Interpretive centers should be relatively accessible to all park visitors and generally connected with a variety of other services such as information areas, rest stops, possibly a special permits center, or transportation centers. It is listed as a prime medium in which interpretation takes place because, as a complex, it is usually one of the focal points of visitors' itineraries.

Interpretive Trail. The interpretive trail facilitates the nature walk. If a trail is purely interpretive, its design enhances the interpretive program so that each stop along the way tells part of the story. By the end of the walk, visitors should have received the entire message that you wished to convey.

Signs and Displays. Signs and displays can reach visitors along the road, trail, or water routes. They can very effectively present simple ideas to visitors, particularly at points where it is difficult or inefficient to have an interpreter (see Figure 15-3). The only word of caution here is to keep the message simple since there is no one to answer any follow-up questions about the phenomenon.

Publications. Brochures and lengthier publications have been used as primary media since the beginnings of interpretation. Possibly millions of dollars are spent annually on printing information related to the use of our parks, recreation areas, and open spaces; yet little effort goes into evaluating these programs.

Too often, we immerse ourselves in the natural history of an area without effectively communicating our ideas to visitors. First, we need reliable communication techniques in our publications; second, we should periodically evaluate how well the public is receiving and using this information.

Radio, Television, and Other Special Devices. These are being used more and more as interpretive media because they can reach large numbers of people quickly and efficiently. Radio and television have some limitations. Usually the receiving range is limited; at times you may have to restrict this range even further to reduce possible overlap during transmission.

There also are some legal concerns involving overlap with commercial frequencies. With more public education channels, these concerns are minimized.

Special devices may include a tape series that visitors use while driving through the park or a battery-operated headset that picks up short-distance, continuously playing radio programs as one passes from one point to another on a trail or historic site. New gadgetry is continuously being developed, especially for interpretation purposes. Watch the market in the next few years as we proceed through the space age of communications.

A FINAL THOUGHT

This chapter focuses on developing interpretive programs—*not* presenting them. There are four managerial concerns:

Evaluate the Total Interpretive Program

Typically, interpretive programs start out as a few presentations and limited facilities and grow from there. Evaluation occurs incrementally as additional presentations are proposed. Periodically evaluate the total program to ensure that the entire story and the themes within the story are adequately covered.

You should also evaluate how effectively your message is received and understood. Baseline data on the use of any program are essential to a long-term evaluation. However, these only indicate patterns of visitor

Figure 15-3. Interpretive facilities should be designed with the user in mind. Siuslaw National Forest, Oregon. (Photo by B. W. Twight)

use. You need more to determine the effectiveness of communication and visitors' reaction to it.

Quality control of presentations is also important. This starts with your procedures for hiring seasonal employees—who conduct most of the presentations—and the training you provide them. Quality control continues through periodic review of individuals.

Assess Effort Versus Reward

Bucy and Bucy[5] offer a novel criterion for effective interpretation—effort versus reward. To the well-informed participant it is the benefit cost analysis of interpretive services. If the effort is high, such as having to tediously read some detailed message in small print, most people will be unlikely to read the sign. The only way they would, would be if the reward were perceived to be so great that reading the message was imperative. Let's face it, imperatives are rare for people enjoying their leisure in a park or recreation area. Thus, ideally whatever message you want to give to the visitor, regardless of the medium, you must present it so that it can be easily consumed by the visitor and has some perceived benefit. Benefits can be enhanced awareness of some unique natural phenomena, or simply awareness of how long the trail is. In sum, think of effort first—how to reduce the effort without losing the message. Then assess the potential rewards in terms of the *typical* visitor.

Don't Overdo the Formal Interpretive Program

Too often we feel that we must reach visitors with our programs, yet many may wish to have minimal "interference" in their leisure activities and rebel at being overtly "forced" into enjoying nature. As suggested earlier, you should emphasize the informal interpretive program where people can be exposed to something in the landscape that touches each personality and stimulates each individual. The formal program becomes a focal point for enhancing appreciation acquired through informal contact with nature.

Maximize Budgetary Efficiency of the Formal Program

By first emphasizing informal programs and then capturing increased interest at critical points, you should be able to provide more for visitors at less cost. These critical points, dubbed Optimal Interpretive Opportunities (OIO's), are where people normally concentrate within the landscape. An OIO consists of a combination of unique natural attractors and improved access, such as the road to the scenic vista overlooking the falls of the Grand Canyon of the Yellowstone River. They may also be strategically located facilities such as visitor centers near park entrances. By identifying OIO's, you can maximize participation in your formal program at some fixed cost because these are points where visitors would normally concentrate and seek information about the environmental setting.

We think that through the combination of emphasizing the informal program, emphasizing OIO's, and utilizing electronic media such as videos and computers, more people can be reached at lesser cost. If anything, our interpretive programs have not been very successful because we managers try to be "eyes, ears and noses" for the visitor. What is needed is to help the visitors to utilize *their* senses so they become better observers. They can then capture more of what the landscape has to offer (the informal programs) and see greater benefits from the formal programs. People will benefit more, participation should be greater, and costs can be contained.

Lastly, and perhaps most importantly, the interpretive program is a system component, a very special way of communicating with system "customers"—whom Etzioni might describe as casual or indifferent visitors, having little or no moral *commitment* to their source of outdoor recreation products and services.[11] Such casual visitors *often do not know or care what agency is providing them with their recreation opportunity.* They take the recreation opportunity for granted.

In this situation interpretation provides the outdoor recreation manager with a method of converting "customers" into loyal "clients" by stimulating them—via a higher more positive involvement—and by provoking curiosity and interest in the resource opportunities provided by the management agency.

Visitors who have a more positive involvement with the agency and its special products and services, develop a stronger level of commitment to the agency and its products, and thus have more performance obligations to it (in Etzioni's terms). This means not only can they be counted on to return again and again, but some of them will provide *both political and monetary support* to the program and the agency. This commitment is created in much the same way as parishioners, members and devoted adherents of a church are involved and normatively influenced. The agency's interpretive program has met some of the visitors' internalized needs. If the agency interpretive action is conceived of by the visitor as both legitimate and gratifying, or what Koteler terms the action of a "fully responsive organization," then the consumer has become "a voting member of the organization."[19] The interpretive action is

viewed as an exchange relationship and thus a commitment is generated—to the program, the park or recreation area, and the provider agency.[11]

SELECTED READINGS

1. Agee, J. K., and Johnson, D. R. (eds.). 1989. *Ecosystem Management for Parks and Wilderness.* Seattle, WA: University of Washington Press.

2. Arango, E. 1982. "Interpretation Around the World." *Interpreting the Environment.* Ed. G. W. Sharpe. New York, NY: John Wiley & Sons.

3. Bates, M. 1990. *The Nature of Natural History.* Princeton, NJ: Princeton University Press.

4. Boulanger, F. D., and Smith, J. A. 1973. Educational Principles and Techniques for Interpreters. U.S. Forest Service General Technical Report PNW-9.

5. Bucy, D. and Bucy, M. 1991. *Plan for Success: the Interpretive Planning Resource.* Corvallis, OR: D. & M. Bucy and Associates.

6. Brooks, P. 1980. *Speaking for Nature, How Literary Naturalists from Henry Thoreau to Rachel Carson have Shaped America.* Boston, MA: Houghton Mifflin.

7. Catlin, D. T. 1984. *A Naturalist's Blue Ridge Parkway,* Knoxville, TN: University of Tennessee Press.

8. Comstock, A. B. 1986. *Handbook of Nature Study.* Ithaca, NY: Cornell University Press.

9. Danilov, V. J. 1992. *A Planning Guide for Corporate Museums, Galleries and Visitor Centers,* New York, NY: Greenwood Press.

10. Dick, R. E., Myklestad, E., and Wagar, J. A. 1975. Audience Attention as a Basis for Evaluating Interpretive Presentations. U.S. Forest Service Research Paper PNW-198.

11. Etzioni, A. 1975. *A Comparative Analysis of Complex Organizations.* Rev. Ed., New York, NY: The Free Press.

12. Ewan, J. A. 1981. *Biographical Dictionary of Rocky Mountain Naturalists.* The Hague: Scheltema & Holkema, distributed by Kluwer Boston, MA.

13. Food and Agricultural Organization. 1976. *Planning Interpretive Programs in National Parks.* Rome: United Nations.

14. Gibson, W. H. 1897. *Eye Spy: Afield with Nature among Flowers and Animate Things.* New York, NY: Harper and Brothers.

15. Grater, R. K. 1976. *The Interpreter's Handbook.* Globe, AZ: Southwest Parks and Monuments Association.

16. Ham, S. H. 1992. *Environmental Interpretation: A Practical Guide for People with Big Ideas and Small Budgets.* Golden, CO: North American Press.

17. Herman, S. G. 1986. *The Naturalist's Field Journal, A Manual of Instruction.* Vermillion, TX: Buteo Books, 200 p. illus.

18. Hudson, K. 1975. *A Social History of Museums, What The Visitors Thought,* Atlantic Highlands, NJ: Humanities Press.

19. Koteler, P. 1982. Chapter 2 in *Marketing for Non-Profit Organizations,* 2nd Ed., Englewood Cliffs, NJ: Prentice Hall.

20. Lewis, W. J. 1981. *Interpreting for Park Visitors,* Philadelphia, PA: Eastern Acorn Press.

21. Machlis, G. E. (ed.). 1986. *Interpretive Views, Opinions on Evaluating Interpretation in the National Park Service.* Washington, DC: National Parks & Conservation Association. 178 p., illus.

22. Machlis, G., and Field, D. R. v1984. *On Interpretation: Sociology for Interpreters of Natural and Cultural History.* Corvallis, OR: Oregon State University Press.

23. Mackintosh, B. 1986. *Interpretation in the National Park Service, A Historical Perspective.* Washington, DC: National Park Service, U.S. Department of the Interior, 117 p., illus.

24. Mahaffey, B. D. 1968. "Interpretation: The Missing Ingredient?" *Trends* 5(3):9.

25. McCurdy, D. R., and Johnson, L. K. 1967. *Recommended Policies for the Development and Management of State Park Systems.* Southern Illinois University Agric. Pub. No. 26. Carbondale, IL: Southern Illinois University Press.

26. Mills, E. A. 1911. *The Spell of the Rockies.* Boston, MA: Houghton-Mifflin.

27. Motts, P. H. 1983. An Assessment of Visitor Interests and Evaluation of Conducted Interpretive Programs at Everglades National Park, unpublished MS Thesis, Pennsylvania State University, University Park, PA 16802.

28. National Parks and Conservation Association. 1988. *Investing in Park Futures-the National Park System Plan: A Blueprint for Tomorrow.* Vol. III. *Parks and People: A Natural Relationship.* Vol. IV. *Interpretation: Key to the Experience.* Washington, DC: National Parks and Conservation Association.

29. Pile, J. 1962. "Enjoyment and Understanding." First World Conference on National Parks. Washington, DC: U.S. Government Printing Office.

30. Royal Ontario Museum. 1976. *Communicating with the Museum Visitor, Guidelines for Planning,* Toronto, Ontairo, Canada: The Museum, 498 p. illus.

31. Sharpe, G. W. 1982. *Interpreting the Environment.* New York, NY: John Wiley & Sons.

32. Shiner, J. W., and Shafer, E. L., Jr. 1975. How Long Do People Look at and Listen to Forest Oriented Exhibits? U.S. Forest Service Research Paper NE-325 .

33. Smith, P. W. 1986. *A Naturalist in the Environmental Crisis.* New York, NY: Carlton Press.

34. Thomas, T. D. 1968. "The Challenges of Interpretation." Proceedings, Recreation Management Institute, College Station, TX: Texas A&M University.

35. Tilden, F. 1967. *Interpreting Our Heritage.* Chapel Hill, NC: The University of North Carolina Press.

36. Waddell, G. 1984. *Collecting, Preserving, Exhibiting, A Theory of Museum Work.* Easley, SC: Southern Historical Press.

37. Wagar, J. A. 1974. Interpretation to Increase Benefits to Recreationists. U.S. Forest Service General Technical Report, NC-9.

38. Wauer, R. H. 1980. *A Naturalist's Big Bend, An Introduction to (flora & fauna).* College Station, TX: Texas A & M University Press.

39. Webb, E. J. 1971. *Unobtrusive Measures: Nonreactive Research in the Social Sciences.* Chicago, IL: Rand McNally and Co.

40. Wiley, E. A. 1951. *John Burroughs' America.* New York, NY: Devin-Adair.

CHAPTER 16

Public Safety

Broadly defined, public safety means using public lands without harm or risk. Too often, managers adopt a paternalistic approach, attempting to eliminate all potential safety problems and control participant behavior to prevent accidents; examples include requiring ranger approval of participants and gear for permission to climb Mount Rainier, or by refusing permission for midwinter cross-country ski travel in Yosemite's backcountry so that no rescue will be needed. By this approach we assume that man is not rational and cannot make reasonable choices when faced with personal risk. In some instances this may be true. However, this attitude creates a very sterile environment for recreationists because free choice is taken away. Such an attitude may even modify visitors' perceptions of a setting so much that it is no longer desirable to pursue activities there. Many activities are undertaken because of the risk involved and the challenge they present.

Public safety also involves protection of visitors and their property from other visitors who may be thoughtless or perhaps have had a little too much to drink. It involves protection of visitors and their property from the predatory or other illicit actions of both professional and amateur criminals. Many outdoor recreation areas can have crime problems similar to those of towns and small cities of equivalent population size to the temporary visitor population. Burglary of autos, drug use and sales, theft from campsites, auto theft, burglary of cabins and lodge rooms, thefts of sleeping bags and backpacks, sex crimes, aggravated assaults, disorderly conduct, even minor riots, occur far too often, particularly in heavily used outdoor recreation areas. Persons with mental disorders have even been occasional problems in some areas.

Operating autos or boats while intoxicated and investigation of traffic accidents are other events requiring attention. Occasionally a case of murder or manslaughter occurs, as has occurred, for example, on the Appalachian Trail, at Yosemite, and at Point Reyes National Seashore. Outdoor recreation managers are generally the first to learn of and to investigate such problems in their

Figure 16-1. Directing traffic is an important part of public safety in Yosemite National Park. (Photo by B. W. Twight)

areas and often are the only law enforcement officials to take any action in regard to the violations or accidents.

As land managers we are responsible for public safety and thus we must develop reasonable and professionally competent programs to ensure this. While our personnel must be adequately trained to carry out law enforcement and search-and-rescue activities, and some areas even require staff specialists (e.g., Yosemite, Grand Canyon and Yellowstone National Parks), these programs must balance the safety of visitors with their level of sophistication, the type of activity, and the potential consequences of a decision. An overbearing, overzealous law enforcement or accident prevention program can detract greatly from the recreation experiences sought by users. Such enforcement and accident prevention programs that are utilized, must be carried out with the utmost politeness and courtesy. We can be firm if necessary but we must remember that users come to outdoor recreation areas to get away from the regimentation and control existing in their urban or suburban communities where they live.

Thus, the activity itself should dictate the need for a general safety program. Law enforcement and safety programs must be the *minimum necessary under the circumstances* and always carried out with the maintenance of the atmosphere of the particular type of user's experience in mind. Certain activities require maximum safety standards; others, such as wilderness recreation, require only a minimum (usually information). One should also consider the level of knowledge or experience required for a particular activity. Visitors with less experience should be encouraged to participate with those who have more until they develop the necessary skills. Interpretive programs can even be developed where inexperienced visitors can gain experience

and appreciation of outdoor skills. Possibly, in potential life-threatening situations, only those individuals possessing requisite skills should be allowed to participate. However, it is often difficult to define that level of expertise with any accuracy. More commonly, programs feed up-to-date information to users and allow them to make their own decisions.

Nevertheless, managers *must be trained and competent* so that whatever action is taken or deemed necessary under the particular circumstances, can be performed in a professionally credible manner, reflecting well upon their agency. Indeed, in the law enforcement activity area, agencies like the National Park Service and U.S. Forest Service require their law enforcement personnel to receive 200 or more hours of special course work, and/or to attend the Federal Law Enforcement Training Center in Georgia, for three months of special training. This must be done before agency personnel may make arrests or carry sidearms. A number of National Park Service officers have also graduated from the FBI Academy at Quantico, Virginia. A number of state agencies, such as the California State Park System, send their law enforcement personnel to their state highway patrol or state police academies for lengthy special training.

However, personnel with such special training must generally be debriefed and reindoctrinated with the recreation agency goals after such education, as too often they pick up a "zealous cop" attitude at these training programs. Such law enforcement personnel must be reminded that 95 percent or more of their visitors are not deliberate violators or criminals and require only friendly polite reminders or warnings. *Most infractions are inadvertent violations and most transgressors should be treated as potential friends and political supporters of the agency.*

Often public safety activities are handled cooperatively with other agencies, or are turned over to them as soon as they arrive on the scene, particularly activities like more serious crimes or major search-and-rescue actions. These may be turned over to the state police, county sheriff, Federal Bureau of Investigation or Drug Enforcement Administration for example, depending on the offense and the jurisdictions involved. However, it should be remembered that on outdoor recreation lands, both the visitor's experience and the protection of the resource are the paramount concerns of the outdoor recreation manager, and cooperation with outside agencies and organizations must be coordinated with these paramount concerns. Getting another agency to carry out law enforcement or other activities in an outdoor recreation area (as the U.S. Forest Service does in some areas) can be detrimental to visitor experiences, akin to the potential problems with overbearing and overzealous personnel on your own staff.

Paying the sheriff's office can put the onus of the tough cop on another agency and provide trained readily available police patrol, but also can create unpleasant experiences for the recreation area user who are seeking to get away from the regimentation and gruff police attitudes in their home towns. By not using its own personnel for any necessary law enforcement, the Forest Service misses an opportunity to sell its programs and agency to visitors, and it may unnecessarily create an undue police presence when circumstances don't warrant strict paternalistic supervision of behavior.

In addition, remember that programs must also focus on protecting the resource from deliberate abuse and destruction by visitors. And safety is really a two-way street. We try to provide a risk-free, enjoyable experience for visitors, but must also protect the natural resource base and developed facilities from overuse and abuse.

Furthermore, in small areas or small agencies, public safety, as a management objective, is often implied and consequently not delineated as a separate program. To ensure adequate safety control, it is sometimes better to state objectives for public safety and develop specific safety programs that eventually are integrated into all other agency programs.

PUBLIC SAFETY AND ROS

Public safety fits very well into the ROS concept. As stated in Chapter 3, all programs should be aligned with a chosen anchor point on the recreational opportunity spectrum. As you move toward the modern portion of the spectrum, your public safety program becomes more intensive and sophisticated. Barriers are erected, regulations increased, and rules enforced to increase visitor safety. On the other hand, as you move toward the primitive end, programs become more simplistic, relying on information programs and subtle design features such as with few or primarily primitive trails from which fallen trees are not removed. Visitors must assume a greater burden of the risk and deal more personally with the uncertainty of this kind of environmental setting.

At the extremely primitive portion of the ROS, visitors assume complete responsibility for their own welfare. L. H. McAvoy and D. L. Dustin suggest that we have a no rescue zone to accommodate such visitors.[25] Participants should rely strictly on their own skills to cope with hazards and extricate themselves from dangerous situations. Many feel that this is appropriate, but that "no rescue" is unacceptable. Probably the best way to philosophically deal with the primitive end of the recreation continuum is to maximize potential uncertainty—leave the area totally undeveloped, minimize public information flow, and sever the umbilical cord connecting users with management via two-way radio monitoring and schedule registration.

Obviously we are all human enough to respond to distress calls. Thus, where warranted, we should maintain our ability to respond with search-and-rescue operations. We should not simply pass by an injured climber, ignoring the plea for help, because he or she is responsible for his or her own actions. Neither should we try to make every area safe by eliminating hazards (see Chapter 18) and the uncertainty of the environmental setting. However, to improve user decision making and preclude lawsuits, risk-takers must be adequately warned about "the hazards inherent" in pursuing activities within a particular area.

As you read above, this chapter focuses on law enforcement and search-and-rescue operations. Keep in mind that the type of program, intensity, and sophistication are functions of the opportunity being provided. Failure to align public safety programs with this opportunity either alters the activity or has dire consequences for naive, unsuspecting visitors.

LAW ENFORCEMENT

As a visitor management program, law enforcement is purposely included under the category of public safety since it is a primary activity of any public safety program. (Hazard management is handled in the succeeding chapter.) As managers, we try to reduce safety violations and improve the ways in which visitors treat the landscape. These efforts not only utilize information programs, but must be backed up by law and the authority to enforce it. It may be wiser to use the term "public safety" here; too often people are turned off by "law enforcement" because they associate the words with police action after a crime has been committed. Public safety is more acceptable because it connotes a genuine interest in visitors and the protection of those values that originally attracted them to a site.

Each park or recreation area generally has its own public safety problems. The actual number of law-enforcement programs reflects its particular needs. Therefore, several types or levels of law enforcement may operate within a given management structure. In some areas, the park supervisor or naturalist may be able to handle all the violations or other problems occurring in the outdoor recreation area, with an occasional assist from the local deputy sheriff. In other areas, such as Yosemite, Grand Canyon or Yellowstone, full-time law enforcement specialists, with their own staff of detectives (e.g., Yosemite), are maintained, along with jails with several cells, and even jailers.

In these areas, as in most other large national parks, a full-time federal magistrate is in residence to handle the judicial decisions resulting from arrests made by rangers and law enforcement personnel. U.S. Forest Service special agents, U.S. Bureau of Land Management Rangers, U.S. Fish & Wildlife Refuge Managers and Wardens, and Army Corps of Engineers Reservoir Rangers also use federal magistrates, United States Attorneys, and the federal court system for the enforcement of the federal laws and regulations pertaining to their lands. In state agencies, rangers and park police use the regular local justice courts and county prosecutors and courts to enforce the state laws and regulations pertaining to their areas, or they turn the cases over to the county sheriff's office or state police for prosecution.

Scope

There are really two basic guidelines for law enforcement in parks/recreation areas:

1. Protect the resource from the visitor. Assuming that the system is designed so that overuse cannot occur, vandalism causes the most harm even though some site impact results from visitor ignorance. Information and education eliminate ignorance. Vandalism, a real management concern, is covered in more detail later in this chapter.

2. Protect the visitor from the visitor. This means high-profile law enforcement, from traffic control to criminal investigations. In this chapter, we address the issue primarily from the management planning perspective, not that of normal daily operations. You can find material on daily operations in various books on police patrol, rules of evidence, enforcement tactics, etc. (see selected readings at end of chapter).

Both guidelines are important in any park operation. Certainly the welfare of the visitor is paramount; however, as suggested previously, how you actually provide for that welfare is a function of the recreational opportunity. In the process, you must protect the resource base and make realistic trade-offs between the two. Again, if we were to look at the extreme positions on the ROS, trade-offs would be easy. The difficult ones fall in the

intermediate positions along the spectrum where we deliberately permit large numbers of people to use an extremely sensitive resource. There are no simple answers, but under these circumstances you must consider trade-offs in the planning stage and account for all factors and their impacts in relation to your overall goals for an area.

Levels of Law Enforcement

The three primary levels of law enforcement for park and recreation agencies consist of the following:

High Profile. High-profile programs enable you to supervise and enforce existing laws and regulations. This may involve highly visible monitoring, e.g., road and trail patrols, facility surveillance during periods of visitor use, and a two way radio communications network for receiving and responding to distress calls. As note above, it also may include investigation, apprehension, and prosecution of criminals. While the public equates such programs with the typical police action of most cities, it is absolutely necessary in light of the many law and regulation violations in most park and recreation areas. Because of highly specialized requirements, actual investigation and follow-through on major crimes like felonies and high misdemeanors are usually handled by a staff specialist or an outside law-enforcement agency—depending on who has legal jurisdiction.

Managers frequently assume that this type of program requires the regularly visible presence of emergency flashing lights, special law-enforcement vehicles, special training, and sidearms. Where required by law, as in the National Park Service, this may be warranted, but in others it may not be necessary or even desirable. Agencies must uphold law and agency regulations, but too much identification with law-enforcement programs creates false fears of crime and an impression of regimentation, reducing the overall effectiveness of the general public safety program as well as the quality of visitors' experiences. There is a fine line between the two, and one that varies according to the particular agency and its legal and administrative mandates. But it is not a trivial matter to consider when planning an effective program.

Low Profile. In low-profile programs, we try to either encourage or discourage certain types of visitor behavior by design, continuous monitoring and improvement of safety conditions, or information aimed at improved visitor cooperation. If we can anticipate problems in visitor conduct during the planning phase, we may be able to design a road, a trail, a recreation site, or even an entire system, such as a river system, so that it promotes the intended types of use and discourages others. In this respect, we are often our own worst enemy. We create a lot of management problems when we, for example, develop a poorly designed site with many access roads and no entrance control, then implement an intensive, high-profile law enforcement effort to alter the use patterns created by the design. To even a casual observer, this appears a rather expensive way to make a poor design actually work. On-site enforcement is very expensive and often difficult to implement without good facility design.

For instance, a number of trails and trail heads led into certain wilderness and backcountry areas where considerable illegal and uncontrollable vehicle use was taking place, along with vandalism. Typically, the agency attempted to catch the culprits. When

that proved nearly impossible, they asked nonvehicular travelers to report any violations (the agency would follow up any reports). When this approach also did not work, the agency gave up on the problem. In most cases, the real problem was poor design. Widened trails, low gradients, removal of barriers, and casually placed occupancy sites had been located adjacent to the trail head. They encouraged casual trail bike use that could have been discouraged by natural barriers, steep grades, and fencing.

We can also manipulate the social environment to deal with problem situations. We can separate conflicting and competing uses to reduce tension, such as limiting horseback riding and hiking to separate trails. Possibly, we can also limit the size of parties, require them to register, and work with interest groups to plan their itineraries for a more manageable situation.

Visitors can even police themselves. For example, a state park was having trouble with large motorcycle gangs abusing the parkscape and harassing other users. The park agency developed a plan whereby all large groups were required to register twenty-four hours in advance so that facilities could be reserved. In addition, a group member had to register as a trip leader. Problems from the gangs diminished drastically because of these reasonable controls exercised by the manager. Ultimately the gangs began to police themselves.

Continuously monitoring potential problems and developing mutual-aid agreements, contingency plans, and up-to-date training for law enforcers help managers maintain law and order in parks. This type of planning was exemplified by training Yosemite National Park's road crews, trail crews, and other normally nonlaw enforcement personnel in the use of riot-control tactics in the 1960s and 1970s. Such training proved most helpful in the famous "Battle of Stoneman Meadow" in 1970, when more than two hundred drug-using unlawful meadow campers were arrested and jailed.

Educational. The educational approach improves quality of use by making people aware of important park values and the individual's role in protecting these values. For example, the very survival of the grizzly bear in Glacier National Park may depend on educational programs to reduce the number of undesirable encounters between man and bear. In such an encounter, the bear ultimately loses to man. We can issue citations for camping in the wrong area, leaving food to attract the bears, etc., or we can relocate trails and campsites to reduce the probability of an encounter. Beyond that we still must educate users, or the program is not effective. All levels of law enforcement must be operable in order to have a total program; however, to protect the parkscape, we must work with visitors before they commit violations—with a positive approach that emphasizes education and environmental design.

Consider establishing other related public safety programs for emergencies and search-and-rescue. Both are important and require good management, good planning, and regular training to be effective; facilities, well-maintained equipment, skilled personnel, good communications and cooperative mutual-aid agreements with other agencies are all necessary for programs to succeed. These must be considered in a management plan so that you know how to respond before a problem situation arises. It is easier to be logical and objective in decision making without the tension and pressures of an emergency situation.

Organizational Framework

You manage the way you are organized for management; this axiom is especially true in law enforcement. You have to be prepared to respond to specific law-enforcement problems rather than just react to particular circumstances. The organizational framework is the first step in management planning. If you are not organized properly, you are not very effective no matter what you do. Your plan should be thought-out well in advance. Then you should practice by carrying out realistic training operations with serviceable equipment and sufficiently trained personnel to see if the plan is properly organized.

Problems caused by a poor organizational framework are shown in the following example. A state park division is part of the state's Department of Natural Resources. It is organized into seven districts, each with a district supervisor. The conservation law enforcement division of the department is not organized into districts but small areas in which a conservation law-enforcement office reports directly to the division chief at the state level. If a problem arises, the park superintendent has to call his district supervisor, who then relays the problem to the park division chief at the state office. The chief then asks the law enforcement division chief to respond to the problem by calling the local field officer.

Needless to say, there is much inefficiency here, and many problems receive no response. In fact, the situation has become so frustrating that the state park division chief has armed and trained his own personnel in some of the troublesome parks. Because of the difficulty in getting the proper authority to respond, these park personnel, with limited training and experience, have taken over the primary law enforcement program. Some poorly trained park personnel have become so "gun-happy" that many of the charges they bring against violators are dismissed, and people have become upset and angry. Because of the officials' behavior, all management programs suffer.

In delegating responsibility within your organization, you should consider separating areas of responsibility as follows:

Crime (Felonies and Major Misdemeanors). Felonies are crimes punishable by *more* than a year in prison and more than a $1000 fine. Major or high misdemeanors are punishable by six months to a year in jail, and from a $500 to $1000 fine. Felonies require "probable cause" to believe a person committed a crime or a warrant signed by a judge in order for a ranger to legally arrest them. Misdemeanors, punishable by six months in jail or less, or a $500 fine or less, require that the officer either witness the offense or have a warrant signed by a judge or magistrate for the arrest. Normally a warrant must be served by a sheriff or a U.S. Marshal, depending on whether it is a state or federal violation.

Commissioned National Park rangers and FBI agents also have legal authority to serve warrants. Other federal and state officers may have this authority by virtue of special legislation or by being designated deputy U.S. Marshals or deputy sheriffs. Arrested persons must be taken before a magistrate as soon as possible for a hearing. However, making arrests for misdemeanor violations is generally felt to be poor policy, and only necessary when the violator is intoxicated or otherwise a threat to him or her self. Misdemeanors are generally handled by giving the violator a notice to appear in court at a particular place and time, otherwise known as a citation. Then the officer signs a complaint and presents sworn testimony to the magistrate in regard to the offense. If the defendant fails to appear as notified, the magistrate then issues a summons or a warrant for an arrest, and gives it to the sheriff or marshal to implement.

In the case of major misdemeanors (e.g., drunk driving) and felonies, a person in a staff position should investigate, arrest, and assist in the prosecution of these major crimes that have occurred within the park. He/she needs to complete all the training and experience required to handle this type of law enforcement and generally be the liaison person with the county or federal prosecutor's office. Where there is shared legal jurisdiction, this role is often handled by the other legally authorized law-enforcement agency—state troopers, the sheriff's office, the FBI, etc.

Traffic Accidents, Minor Misdemeanors, and Rule Violations. This should be the responsibility of the management staff assigned to patrol duty, where the emphasis is on reducing accidents, investigating park violations, and handling emergency situations as well as educating the using public. Investigating traffic accidents and issuing citations is secondary but necessary in certain situations.

As we mentioned above, park staff members are typically the first officials at the scene of a crime or an accident. Although they may not directly handle the problem, they should still supervise (e.g., obtain witness statements, record potential witness license numbers, take pictures, seal off the area, and detain violators) in a legally proper fashion until the staff law-enforcement officer or the other agency sharing jurisdiction arrives. Thus all management personnel should have at least minimal training in law enforcement practices and be familiar with the standard operating procedures of the agency.

General Safety Management Problems. All staff members, including those in the lowest positions, should have some public-safety training in general law enforcement, first aid, and public relations. Many times the maintenance worker or similar technician is present when a problem arises. He or she needs minimal training to handle the situation, quietly and firmly, *without being officious,* until other assistance arrives on the scene. While some organizations are large enough to have staff diversity in public safety, you should generally consider the above three levels of law enforcement and try to organize your agency to respond accordingly. Furthermore, you must understand the legal responsibilities involved and attempt to maximize your legal role while cooperating with other agencies that may have specific law enforcement functions within park boundaries.

For the major national parks, these functions are defined in enabling legislation that describes the jurisdiction of the federal government and state law enforcement agencies. In the case of the federal government, these laws appear in United States Code Titles 16 and 18. If all responsibilities for law enforcement are delegated to the federal agency, the agency has what is called *exclusive jurisdiction.* If the states have not ceded their jurisdiction back to the federal government, which is not necessary if the park predates the establishment of the state, then the jurisdiction may be either *concurrent* or sometimes only *proprietary.* Note however, that . . . "the description 'proprietorial' is no longer appropriate since the (Supreme) Court in Kleppe v. New Mexico (1976) found that "federal power under the Property Clause (of the Constitution) far exceeds that of a proprietor" . . . (Coggins & Wilkinson, 1987). The Court later reaffirmed the supremacy of federal law

over state laws on federally owned lands, when in conflict (Calif. Coastal Commission v. Granite Rock Mining Co., Coggins & Wilkinson, 1990).

A Conceptual Program

Based on the previous discussion, a law-enforcement program should respond to two kinds of behavior—crime and park violations. Crime is an important part of a total program, particularly in our larger parks and recreation areas. Some of these areas have tremendous crime problems that have been difficult to combat. Thus, much of their management budget has gone toward crime-prevention efforts. However, the law enforcement staff must still be made aware of and properly trained for several related programs.

Crime Prevention. Crime prevention is very important and includes roving and point patrol, installation of building and recreation-site security equipment, and public information/ education efforts. Through information and education, visitors can help discourage or report suspected crime to a degree.

Detection and Arrest Procedures. Detection is best accomplished by direct observation, electronic surveillance, and reports of violations by visitors. This requires the manager to identify and concentrate on potential crime areas, yet respond to crime in all portions of the park or recreation area.

Arresting someone requires special training and a knowledge of proper procedures. It involves 1) personally witnessing the crime, 2) having probable cause to believe a felony has been committed, or 3) having an arrest warrant for the subject from a judge. It also involves informing subjects of the violation they are being charged with and advising them of their rights. By law, the manager making an arrest is not allowed to use excessive force; at the same time, he/she should be extremely cautious about personal safety. Don't try to be a hero and do it alone; control yourself, be a good observer and get a backup car or some other additional help first. FBI policy is to only make arrests of a potentially dangerous person when you have overwhelming odds in your favor. With good descriptions the criminal who gets away can be more safely apprehended later. "Heroes" can easily end up dead or maimed for life.

Criminal Investigation. Successful prosecution of a crime depends on good investigation. This begins as soon as the first park staff member arrives at the scene. Seal off the area immediately and record the names, addresses, location, and auto license numbers of all potential witnesses. If you do not take these steps, evidence may be destroyed or testimony lost. Only qualified investigators should handle evidence and interview witnesses. Investigations may take weeks or even months; thus the staff investigator or outside law enforcement agency must have time to examine the problem.

Assistance in Prosecution. An investigation is not finished until the prosecution is completed. Management personnel and investigators must work with the local prosecutor or United States attorney, understand court procedures, and be able to properly present testimony in court.

Coordination with Other Agencies. Coordination with other law enforcement agencies and the prosecuting attorney is essential to developing a viable program, and must be planned so it can immediately be implemented at the local level. That way criminals can be apprehended and prosecuted with minimal delay. Sometimes federal, state, or local statutes, or written cooperative agreements outline parameters for coordination, but at no time should it be merely implied or assumed. Get acquainted with and get the trust of the prosecuting attorney and judges before you have to make an arrest and go to trial.

Park Violations. Three subprograms involve park violations and types of protection:

PROTECTING PEOPLE FROM PEOPLE

We should try to maximize the enjoyment of each visitor. This often requires rules that reduce conflict between users. Through management, we minimize harassment and confrontation, and this is becoming more important as the number of visitors increases. With more people there is more social contact and greater diversity of interest. Crowding leads to social conflict if we try to provide too much variety in too small a space, and a feasible area plan and site design can reduce tension between user groups.[11,39] Enforcement of rules is still necessary to minimize social tension. In addition, many recreation areas are prime targets for predation by professional thieves, so park authorities must be constantly alert and warn the public about them.

PROTECTING PEOPLE FROM THE PARK

We can encourage or discourage certain types of use patterns in order to minimize potential harmful effects to the visitor—whether from grizzly bears, hot springs, or automobiles.

PROTECTING THE PARK FROM THE PEOPLE

An important, traditional role of law enforcement, this kind of protection requires a set of rules for visitor conduct and a means of making visitors aware of these rules. If the rules are broken, many of the features for which the park is established and maintained are destroyed.

Try to remain objective and respond according to the actions of visitors, the consequences of their actions, and causal relationships. Intentions are often not as significant as you first imagine, and people may act out of ignorance or at least a lack of awareness. Don't overreact. Don't be hasty or harsh. Do be firm in your handling of the individuals involved. Remember that this is an opportunity to informally educate visitors on the effects of their behavior. If you can change someone's behavior, you also increase the future treatment of the landscape. Often nothing more than a verbal warning and explanation are necessary. The mere act of stopping adult visitors is generally quite embarrassing, and a few friendly "words to the wise" make a lasting impression and a park supporter.

Vandalism—A Special Problem

As pointed out by Sharpe, Odegaard, and Sharpe, vandalism means malicious or ignorant destruction of public or private property.[40] Vandalism is thus seen from the perspective of the property owner or manager. Whether it detracts socially or environmentally, any act of destructive or malicious behavior obviously affects users' perceptions of a recreational opportunity and ultimately the experiences they derive from it. Most problems and managerial responses are logically covered by the umbrella of public-safety law enforcement, so why does vandalism have to be treated separately? Probably because it is one of the significant budget items of most park and recreation agencies, and its allocation has increased while budgets decrease. Consequently, while it has always been a problem, the percentage of operating budgets allotted for correcting vandalism has reached alarming proportions.

Now managers are asking what they can do. How do you deal with these acts? How can you reduce budget impact to a more acceptable level?

Figure 16-2. Some national parks have large law enforcement problems requiring their own jails. Yellowstone National Park. (Photo by B. W. Twight)

Management Programming. Consider three areas of programming when dealing with vandalism:

1. OBJECTIVES

Your goal is to reduce the costs of vandalism, to free up declining budget dollars, to enhance existing opportunities, or to add new ones. Objectives, then, are specific statements of what you propose to achieve for a given recreational opportunity, site, or facility. These can be a reduction in the number of incidents, actual dollar costs, or percentage of budget.[11] The important thing to recognize is that while it may be philosophically desirable to eliminate vandalism, it may not be practicable or cost-efficient to actually do so. Vandalism occurs in many forms and has no universal solution. Therefore, managers need to isolate significant forms of vandalism within parks or recreational areas, analyze what is happening and the probable perpetrators, and direct management programs where the greatest budget savings can be realized.

At the same time, you should also look at vandalism in a holistic manner. What is its impact on the recreational opportunity? Minor acts that cost little may have a dramatic effect on users' perceptions of the opportunity and ultimately the value of that opportunity. In other words, you can greatly increase net benefits to society but spend very little on repairs. Perhaps early morning fishermen have been cleaning their fish on picnic tables. The smell has driven away many afternoon picnickers. A few simple signs may solve the problem at very little cost. For more money, perhaps a fish-cleaning facility can enhance the opportunity. There are no savings; only expenditures. Strategy can solve problems and enhance the recreational experience for family picnickers and fishermen.

In terms of ROS, there are obviously greater potential budget consequences at the modern end of the spectrum. Here there are more facilities, more intensive management, and more people, particularly casual users. However, the impact of vandalism on the perception or opportunity can be great over the entire spectrum. Consequently, specific program objectives that deal with vandalism should be a part of your total recreational planning process. From a more positive perspective, the effectiveness of any vandalism program starts with initial planning of specific opportunities—What facilities are needed? What about location? Design? Vandalism control does not begin after the act, and management program objectives should reflect this.

2. ANALYSIS

Some authors recommend trying to analyze the motivations for specific acts of vandalism so that programs can eliminate causes rather than simply reduce effects. This may work well in small park districts or isolated regional parks used on a regular basis by local constituents. For larger units with more dispersed use and fewer oversights in operations, designers must focus on immediate behavior at the site and ways of mitigating the impact of that behavior.

Christiansen[11] categorized acts of vandalism into eight categories:

1. breakage
2. surface graffiti
3. disfigurement
4. disassembly or removal
5. burn
6. blockage
7. vegetative damage or loss
8. miscellaneous

Inventory or inspect the entire park or recreation area on a regular basis to document particular acts and their locations. You should also establish a system to report any incidents as soon as possible. Timing may be critical to minimize additional damage, e.g., graffiti on rocks should be removed as soon as possible. If possible, incident reports may help in analyzing target groups by category, location, and frequency. If particular groups of users can be isolated, then you can better tailor the actual program for a particular situation.

From a programmatic perspective, it would also be appropriate to categorize acts according to the intent of users—ignorance versus malicious intent. Those done out of ignorance may be correctable with a softer, low-profile approach—improved design, an informational program, etc. Others typically require a much more high-profile approach to oversee operations, apprehend offenders, and warn potential offenders of legal consequences. Even then management must continually remind itself that there are two generalized consequences of vandalism: increased costs and decreased benefits.

The final step in analysis is to set priorities according to need. Below is a list of general concerns:

a. Safety (any act which creates unsafe or potentially unsafe conditions).
b. Recreational opportunity (any act which affects user perception of the quality of the experience).
c. Increased costs of operation.
d. Other (such as socially offensive acts).

3. CONTROL STRATEGIES

The following are program strategies you can use to mitigate impact:

a. Area Planning

Proper location can help to reduce vandalism. Typically, extensive facilities in more secluded areas are vandalized to a greater degree and more frequently.[39] This is particularly true when casual (nontargeted) users are allowed or encouraged.

b. Site Design

Proper design and use of more resistant materials can reduce the impact of certain types of vandalism. Even architectural barriers can discourage certain behavior such as driving cars over ground vegetation.

c. Surveillance

The visible presence of uniformed personnel reduces the probability of destructive acts.

d. Law Enforcement

Enforcement of regulations, apprehension and prosecution, and published results are also important.

e. Information and Education

These programs are aimed at preventing acts committed through ignorance and at those users who are typically at the preconventional and conventional stages of moral decision making.[17]

f. Creative Responses

Many acts require creative responses, and analyzing these can help you respond to future problems. One example is using "hack" trees in campgrounds. Place sawn logs on the ground with signs that say "if you need to hack, do it here." Indiscriminate hacking essentially disappeared when this was done at a large park. Elsewhere an agency included representatives of four-wheel drive clubs on a planning team to eliminate indiscriminate four-wheeling. Up to that point, no control strategy had worked. Once the final strategy was agreed upon, the clubs not only abided by the agreement but also became on-the-ground enforcers of the rules.

A Final Thought

The five DO's in developing a park or recreation law enforcement program are as follows:

1. Do emphasize management by design. If we can alter the physical environment and/or informational programs to encourage or discourage certain behavior, we need less direct control through law enforcement.

2. Do emphasize the need to have the program requirements correspond to those of the general recreational opportunity.

3. Do maximize education and information efforts that increase visitor awareness and consequently the quality of use. If we are to improve user etiquette to protect prime park values, we must educate visitors about these values and how their behavior affects them.

Figure 16-3. Rescuing a hiker from a crevass, Mt. Rainier National Park. (photo by B. W. Twight)

4. Do delineate staff and other agencies' roles and responsibilities. These roles must be outlined and coordinated so that you can create an effective, total program.

5. Do maintain immediate response capability for both crime prevention and emergency treatment. You must be able to respond to any emergency on a twenty-four hour basis. This may only dictate a coordinating or liaison role for some management units, particularly smaller ones. Others may require full staffing on-site.

SEARCH-AND-RESCUE

Search-and-rescue are two separate but coordinated operations. They may involve a single party or separate parties. Both operations require planning, team skills, and coordination. Setnicka (1980), whose book is probably the best comprehensive single source for search-and-rescue planning and techniques, divided search-and-rescue operations into four phases: locate, reach, stabilize, and evaluate.[39] Depending on the situation, search involves the locate and reach phases, and stabilization may simply be reassurance for "found" person(s). This section primarily focuses on search operations because they are the essential first steps, are often a function of the land manager, and can often be accomplished with sufficient leadership and volunteer help (see Figure 16-3).

Many local searches involve little rescue. They are simply matters of finding people who have wandered away from campgrounds or other sites, and who are in no real danger other than from the psychological damage of being lost for a short period of time. However, searches for lost children can take several days, hundreds of personnel, aircraft, and dogs. Sometimes they have sad endings, too.

On the other hand, rescue operations often require very specialized skills such as mountain helicopter flying, mountaineering, scuba diving, etc. in conjunction with EMT or specialized first-aid training. In those cases where very specialized skills are needed, search-and-rescue operations are usually handled by the same team. At other times, a search team may comb an area only to locate the missing person down a rock slide or other hazardous area requiring special rescue. This does not alleviate the need for normal rescue skills among park personnel.

Preventive Programs

Many search-and-rescue efforts would not be necessary if resource managers and participants had assumed greater responsibility prior to the incident. Participants should become accountable for their own behavior—develop necessary skills, acquire proper clothing and equipment, check on weather patterns, and plan and organize specific trips sufficiently to accommodate the unusual and the unexpected. They should also notify a nonparticipant of their particular itinerary and expected return date in the event that something does happen. Managers can assist this process and avoid liability through information programs, but the responsibility is still the individual's.

Typically, planned trips are not a problem unless the unusual happens—bad weather, flooding, an accidental fall, or whatever. Often the problem occurs because of a spontaneous decision—a child wanders away from a campground, a mountain-goat hunter gets stuck on a ledge, and so on.

Preventive programs include:

Information. If you can predict the types of use and users of an area, and have a good inventory of potential hazards, then you should be able to project potential hazards. Information programs devised to reach users prior to participation can officially warn them of risks and potential danger, and show how to properly prepare for a trip into the area. Visitors should understand that they must file a travel schedule with a friend so someone anticipates their return.

Design. Through planning and design, you can attract certain types of user groups, and encourage/discourage specific behavior. Transportation systems are a primary tool for directing use and encouraging given activities at particular nodes along the transportation ribbon. If there are some unique natural/cultural attractors along that ribbon, use concentrates there. Types of activity and users reflect types of associated facilities and services. If hazards occur at these points, design access and facilities to capture natural values yet minimize risks to users. Even wilderness trail planning should consider designs that encourage particular behavior, especially when risk is involved.

Regulation and Enforcement. Even with good design and information programs, you often need to establish regulations, particularly if there is high risk and a high proportion of novice users. It in unconscionable, however, to create a rule and never enforce it. Whatever technique you use—from the continuous presence of personnel to periodic patrols, it is important to generally enforce regulations first to protect visitors and second to preclude potential liability. Otherwise people begin taking regulatory warnings less than seriously, both encouraging visitors to take foolish chances and creating a legal indication of agency negligence.

Planning

Management, even if preventive programs work well, must still develop contingency plans for search-and-rescue operations. The role the individual agency plays depends on legal jurisdiction. Regardless of this role, you must devise a plan for search-and-rescue operations that explicitly states the responsibility of every party and how each should respond to a call for help. The plan should include:

Delineation of Responsibilities. Is there a mutual agreement in effect? Who is to do what? When? How?

Communications. Communications are essential for any search-and-rescue. They start with teaching participants about conditions they might encounter and properly preparing them for such. This includes designating someone to notify authorities if they do not return. Once an agency is alerted, it must notify team members and other cooperating organizations, collect all possible information about the missing party, establish a plan of attack, and provide mobile and portable two-way radios to maintain communications with all team members. Often radios must be exchanged with cooperating agencies so as to maintain interagency communications in the search-and-rescue or other emergency effort.

Coordination. Coordination is essential so that voids and duplication of search efforts are minimized and response is as rapid as possible. Coordination is even more important when several agencies, volunteers, or related groups all participate in the search. For larger, more complex operations, a radio communications center, a special radio net and portable radio relay stations are essential to maintain contact and direct operations.

Manpower. Usually the plan specifies what manpower and mutual aid is locally available, along with how it will be used and under what conditions. Cooperative agreements for manpower should be worked out ahead of time with nearby law enforcement agencies, fire departments and military posts. The latter also may be a source for rescue helicopters, although the Coast Guard and USAF Air Rescue Service are generally better trained and experienced.

Special Needs: Trackers and Dogs. For searches, a source of persons skilled in tracking should be obtained and an agreement made, *ahead of the time* when they might be needed. Also, a similar arrangement should be made for the services of competent trained tracking dogs, such as bloodhounds. Sometimes it will be necessary to contract with an agency or company with dogs which are some distance away, requiring air travel or other special arrangements for emergency transportation. This is particularly important when a search for a lost child, in conditions where hypothermia is a problem, must be planned for in your worst-case scenarios. Thus, prior planning and contractual arrangements for tracking dogs are a must. Always have an article of the child's or other person's personal clothing (such as underwear) preserved in a sealed container, ready for the dog handlers when they arrive.

Equipment. The plan should indicate what equipment is available, who is responsible for its maintenance, where it is located, and whom to contact to get the equipment. Agencies with rescue responsibility should participate in the planning and should purchase and maintain adequate stocks of equipment (packs, sleeping bags, emergency food rations, flashlights, batteries, climbing ropes,

Stokes rescue litter, etc.) in rescue caches, available for most all types of rescues which may be anticipated. Sufficient equipment should be on hand or on call from other sources to adequately handle a worst-case situation.

Rescue equipment (such as wheeled trail evacuation litters) can sometimes be manufactured by an agency machine shop, using old bicycles and Navy surplus Stokes basket litters. Stokes litters can be purchased from Western Fire Equipment Co. in San Francisco and Denver, or from Ben Meadows Forestry Suppliers in Atlanta. They may be available from other fire equipment suppliers such as American LaFrance Co. and from the U.S. Navy. Some other types of equipment such as bullhorns and large first-aid kits can also be obtained from police supply companies, such as the F. W. Darley Company in Chicago, IL, and the George Cake Co. in Berkeley, CA. Mountaineering equipment (ropes, safety harnesses, carabiners, chocks, bolts, pitons, avalanche locator radios, headlamps, rock helmets, freeze-dried meals, mountain stoves, clothing, sleeping bags, packs, canteens, water purification filters, special clothing, etc.) is available from Recreational Equipment Inc. in Seattle or its other stores throughout the country.

High quality Austrian and Swiss mountain rescue equipment, such as cable winches, akjas (aluminum boat-shaped snow litters w/ detachable trail wheel and brake), avalanche probes, high test lightweight pulleys, harnesses for lowering victims, body bags, and wheeled trail litters (gebirgstrage) are available from Herbert G. Schwarz Imports, Box 49959, Los Angeles, CA 90049. They can be ordered directly from Gebr. Koellensperger, Abt. Tyromont, Franz-Fisherstrasse 7, A-6010, Innsbruck, Austria, tel. 43-05222-29731, Telex 05/3408 (for best results have a

German speaking person call). The search-and-rescue office of the National Park Service in Yosemite National Park, California, tel. (209) 372-4605, may be a good source of information, if you can catch them during a lull in emergencies.

Annual cooperative training should be carried out in conjunction with cooperating organizations and agencies, practicing search-and-rescue techniques. Call lists of telephone numbers for all cooperating agencies, with night and weekend numbers for several of the agencies' *current* decision-making officials, should be maintained on plastic covered wallet cards and kept by all officials who have any responsibility for rescue work. Lives may depend on such thorough preplanning.

Training should also include the use of specialized equipment and manpower such as that used in mountaineering rescues, helicopter rescues, whitewater rescues and searches for lost persons. Helicopters should be obtainable on an annual basis, preferably with rescue trained personnel, through cooperative agreements with the U.S. Coast Guard, U.S. Air Force Air Rescue Service, state police units, or commercial helicopter contracts. Cooperative arrangements should also be made *ahead of time* with large hospital "Lifeline" helicopter evacuation services.

Budget. Create a policy that delineates who pays for what. This is important so that all concerned can anticipate certain costs and budget for them. If the participants being rescued are expected to pay the costs or some portion thereof, then they should be reminded of this prior to their trip into the area. Incidentally, such a policy reduces calls for search-and-rescue considerably. Some people abused the system in the past because they had aching backs or "saddle sores." At all times, make rescues first and then submit bills after the fact.

Training. All potential search-and-rescue operations that involve equipment and tactics should be regularly practiced. Even real operations should be critiqued afterwards to determine if there are ways of improving future response.

Conduct of Operations

Initial response depends on the information received. If there is a call for rescue from a credible source, like one of the team members or other reliable source, and the location is pinpointed, then plan and execute a search-and-rescue operation. On the other hand, if you are notified of a lost or missing person without any indication of injury, then emphasize search operations to locate that individual first. Possibly no real rescue will be needed once the person is located.

What we traditionally envision in search-and-rescue are people lost in a general location and known or anticipated to be in trouble, such as a climbing party caught in a major storm. The actual search can be conducted in the air or on the ground. If the area to be searched is large, an initial aerial effort may turn up clues or discover the missing parties. Aerial searches require tremendous coordination and pilot discipline. If they check a few key areas in the initial search and find no clues, then you must organize a sustained aerial search. Such an effort generally requires pilots to fly some sort of grid pattern to ensure adequate coverage.

Make ground searches the initial and sustained method if the area is relatively small, the overstory vegetation is dense enough to minimize aerial viewing, or the weather is so bad as to preclude flying. Since weather may be adverse, a ground search must always be planned for. Ground efforts may not be very fruitful in large areas unless you find clues to isolate the likely location of the missing parties. Some well-trained ground crews may be used in conjunction with aerial searchers to uncover clues. Do not commit ground-search parties wholesale unless they have discovered sufficient clues to isolate the probable location. Use volunteers, the military, or other less skilled groups only after the search area has been narrowed, if the lost party is in immediate danger such as hypothermia, and if deploying such people under the supervision of skilled personnel poses no danger to themselves.

It is important to distinguish between summer and winter search-and-rescue operations. All operations require skilled personnel, but winter efforts are extremely dangerous and require team members to have special survival skills. Without proper field equipment and prior training, winter operations can be disastrous.

Timing is important, but managers must weigh the information they receive against the manpower and equipment available. If the information is sketchy, or the probability of someone being in danger is not known, or the geographical area is very large, your best initial response is to gather as much information as possible, verify all possible leads, and probe all details. Under these circumstances, it is prudent to determine if someone is actually lost, in immediate danger, and within identifiable geographical boundaries. Unless you can determine this, any field operations are likely to be fruitless and expensive.

For example, a man was flown into a mountain area in Alaska to stake a homesite under a state land program. He had told his neighbor that he would then walk out to a nearby village and return in about a month. After this period of time had passed, his neighbor reported him missing. The agency decided to wait four or five days to see if he showed up. He didn't.

The potential search area covered several million acres. Agency managers sent out a couple of reconnaissance planes and instructed the pilots to fly two possible routes to the village from the homesite area, buzzing any trapper cabins or other structures along the way. The missing person turned up at one of the cabins, out of food, but no worse for his adventure than a fifteen-pound weight loss. The agency did the right thing to wait, and then to initially probe the area with reconnaissance aircraft.

Did they get lucky in finding this man? Not really. Early ice breakup on intervening streams had kept him from reaching the village, so he sought shelter in a cabin that was easily identifiable from the air. Most importantly, he notified his neighbor of his trip plans, making the search-and-rescue operation much easier. Even if he had not been located during initial reconnaissance, the sustained search would have been conducted from the air because of the size of the area and the difficulty in ground travel due to ice breakup.

Suspending an operation, although difficult, is an important decision. It usually rests on two factors—the probability that the person still lives and the clues uncovered during the search. If there are sufficient clues—even though probability dictates that the person is already dead—then in all likelihood the search should continue until the body is recovered. You must also contend with the possibility that a body is not recoverable, as in an avalanche.

Throughout the entire ordeal, the agency should maintain contact with relatives and friends, and keep them informed. But you should also follow your own plan, using common sense about conditions without undue influence from the family. Public relations are ever so important, but you should never forget your responsibility to those members of the search-and-rescue parties who endanger themselves in the process of helping others.

SELECTED READINGS

1.   Allen, S. 1981. "No Rescue Wilderness—A Risky Proposition." *Journal of Forestry,* 79(3): 98-100.

2.   Alpert, G. P. and Dunham, R. G.   1990. *Police Pursuit Driving, Controlling Responses to Emergency Situations.* New York, NY: Greenwood Press.

3.   Anonymous. 1955-to date. *Accidents in American Mountaineering,* yearly, New York, NY: American Alpine Club.

4.   Anonymous. 1972 to date. *Emergency Medical Services: The Journal of Emergency Care and Transportation,* bimonthly, North Hollywood, CA: Emergency Medical Services.

5.   Bard, M., and Shellow, R. 1976. *Issues in Law Enforcement: Essays and Case Studies.* Englewood Cliffs, NJ: Reston Publishing Co.

6.   Beckman, E. 1977. *Law Enforcement in a Democratic Society: An Introduction.* Chicago, IL: Nelson-Hall Co.

7.   Brockman, C. F., and Merriam, L. C., Jr. 1979. *Recreational Use of Wild Lands.* 3rd Ed. New York, NY: McGraw-Hill Book Co.

8.   Budassi, S. A., and Barber, J. 1984. *Mosby's Manual of Emergency Care, Practices and Procedures.* 2nd Ed. St. Louis, MO: Mosby.

9.   Campbell, F. L., Hendee, J. C., and Clark, R. 1968. "Law and Order in Public Parks." *Parks and Recreation, 3*:28, 51.

10. Chandler, J. T. 1990. *Modern Police Psychology, for Law Enforcement and Human Behavior Professionals.* Springfield, IL: C. C. Thomas.

11. Christiansen, M. L. 1983. *Vandalism Control Management in Parks and Recreation.* State College, PA: Venture Publishing, Inc.

12. Cliff, P. 1987. *Ski Mountaineering,* Seattle, WA: Pacific Search Press.

13. Coggins, G. C., and Wilkinson, C. F. 1990. *Federal Public Land and Resources Law, 1990 Case Supplement.* Westbury, NY: Foundation Press.

14. Coggins, G. C., and Wilkinson, C. F. 1987. *Federal Public Land and Resources Law.* 2nd Ed., Mineola, NY: Foundation Press.

15. Das, D. K.   1987.   *Understanding Police Human Relations.* Metuchen, NJ: Scarecrow Press.

16. Davis, C. 1966. "Legal Problems and Liability in Outdoor Recreation." *Park Maintenance 19*(12).

17. Dustin, D. 1984. "To Feed or Not to Feed the Bears." *Parks and Recreation 20*(10):54-57.

18. Epp, M., and Stephen Lee. 1987. *Avalanche Awareness, for Skiers and Mountaineers,* London: The Wild Side.

19. FAO, Forest Resources Division, 1985. *Avalanche Control,* Rome: Food and Agricultural Organization of the United Nations.

20. Fazio, J. R., and Gilbert, D. L. 1981. *Public Relations and Communications for Natural Resource Managers.* Dubuque, IA: Kendall-Hunt Publishing Co.

21. Frakt, A. N., and Rankin, J. S. 1982. *The Law of Parks and Recreation.* Medford, NJ: Brighton Publishing Company.

22. Hewitt, M. H. 1989. *Rural Emergency Medical Services,* Washington, DC: Office of Technology Assessment, USGPO.

23. Klockars, C. B. 1985. *The Idea of Police,* Beverly Hills, CA: Sage Publications.

24. LaValla, R., and Fear, G. 1978. *Resource Guide for Search and Rescue Training Material.* Tacoma, WA: Survival Education Association.

25. MacInnes, H. 1972. *International Mountain Rescue Handbook.* New York, NY: Scribners.

26. McAvoy, L. H., and Dustin, D. L. 1985. "Regulating Risks in the Nation's Parks." *Trends,* 22(3):27-30.

27. More, H. W., and Shipley, O. R. 1987. *Police Policy Manual—Operations.* Springfield, IL: C. C. Thomas.

28. The Mountaineers. 1992. *Mountaineering, The Freedom of the Hills: The Classic Climbers Handbook.,* 5th Ed., Seattle, WA: Seattle Mountaineers, Inc.

29. National Assn. of State Emergency Medical Services Directors. 1988. *Emergency Medical Services Transportation Systems and Available Facilities.* Lexington, KY: National EMS Clearing House.

30. National Park Service. 1975. "Law Enforcement Program." Grand Canyon National Park, Arizona: Horace M. Albright Training Academy.

31. National Recreation and Park Association, 1971. *Manual and Survey for Public Safety.* Management Aid Series No. 20.

32. National Recreation and Park Association. 1973. *Park Police.* Management Aid Series No. 32.

33. National Recreation and Park Association. 1975. *Litter Control.* Management Aid Series No. 53.

34. Perla, R. I., and Martinelli, M., Jr. 1976. *Avalanche Handbook,* USDA-Forest Service, Washington, DC: U.S. Government Printing Office.

35. Poynter, M. 1980. *Search and Rescue: The Team and the Missions.* New York, NY: Macmillan.

36. Risk, P. H. 1983. *Outdoor Safety and Survival.* New York, NY: John Wiley & Sons.

37. Salkeld, A. (ed.). 1987. *The Climber's Handbook,* San Francisco, CA: Sierra Club Books.

38. Sansone, S. J. 1987. *Police Photography,* 2nd Ed., Cincinnati, OH: Anderson Publishing Co.

39. Setnicka, T. J. 1980. *Wilderness Search and Rescue.* Boston, MA: Appalachian Mountain Club.

40. Sharpe, G. W., Odegaard, C. H., and Sharpe, W. F. 1983. *Park Management.* New York, NY: John Wiley & Sons.

41. Turner, D. M., and Lesce, T. 1990. *Watercraft Patrol and Survival Tactics.* Springfield, IL: C. C. Thomas.

42. Urban, J. T. 1973. *A White Water Handbook for Canoe and Kayak.* Boston, MA: Appalachian Mountain Club.

43. Washburne, R. 1989. *The Coastal Kayaker's Manual,* Seattle, WA: The Mountaineers.

44. Yarmey, A. D. 1990. *Understanding Police and Police Work, Psychosocial Issues.* New York, NY: New York University Press.

45. Zulawski, D. E., and Wicklander, D. E. 1992. *Practical Aspects of Interview and Interrogation,* New York, NY: Elsevier.

PART IV

Service Management

Providing facilities and services to accommodate visitors is an essential role of management, particularly where visitors must travel long distances or simply wish to enjoy a given setting. Even when facilities are "extras," managers should ensure that these services and accommodations are accessible.

While you might think that environment alone creates satisfactory recreational opportunities, your programs affect how your clientele receive these experiences. If targeted clientele enjoy their activities, then you can judge your efforts successful. Satisfied visitors support good programs, not dissatisfying ones. Thus, in service management, it is important to monitor users' responses to particular programs so that you can adjust them over time to meet the needs of various groups.

At the same time, you must recognize that all services and accommodations need not be provided within a park or recreation area. In fact, if you can appropriately and conveniently offer them outside site boundaries, do so. This maximizes the potential of the private sector without undue regulations from the public sector, and minimizes the immediate impact on the environment that attracts people to the area.

Included in Part IV are chapters on concessions, maintenance, hazards, and area planning. Concession management focuses on planning, developing, and overseeing those facilities and services that are essential to the public's enjoyment of the environment. The chapter on maintenance is not a "how to" process but instead brings together important elements and procedures. Hazard management is included here because of the emphasis on providing necessary facilities and services to ensure a reasonably safe environment within the constraints of the activity offered.

CHAPTER 17

Recreation Area Planning

INTRODUCTION

Recreational area planning is also called unit planning, master planning, and management planning. Actually it is the planning level sandwiched between regional or subregional and the individual site. Typically it is a land management plan for recreational land uses where all the acreage within the plan is under one agency's jurisdiction and the physiography and access are distinct enough to separate it from other areas in the same location under the auspices of the same agency. Even large conservation units such as a national park or wildlife refuge may be divided into several distinct *areas* for planning purposes. The overall conservation unit plan acts as a regional resource allocation vehicle—establishing guidelines (for coordination between areas), possibly priorities, policies and regulations, and area plan formats. *However, the specific resource allocation decisions are made at the AREA level.* The area plan does this by describing the desired recreations use patterns within the area, and then creates

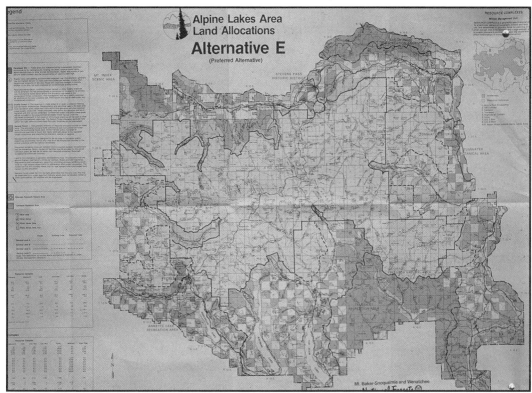

Figure 17-1. Recreation area planning involves the integrated planning of resource allocations for an entire unit or regional resource. Alpine Lakes plan, Mt. Baker—Snowqualmie National Forest, WA. (Photo by B. W. Twight)

those patterns on the ground by mixing the various inputs into the recreational opportunities. As shown in Chapter 3, the idea is to establish a particular recreational opportunity (biophysical inputs plus managerially-determined attributes) which in turn produces the desired general recreational use pattern. This becomes an equilibrium, as long as managerial inputs and external inputs remain constant. The recreational opportunities should be provided within identified constraints, by specifying the desired access and associated facilities and their locations, and describing the concomitant management programs to maintain those opportunities over time.

In sum, it is *the* resource allocation process. If an agency has a legal or regulatory mandate to provide for recreation as a land use, then it must focus on efficiently allocating the limited resources it has in accomplishing that mandate. The *recreational area plan* is the vehicle for accomplishing this task. Just like any other land use, it can be intensive or extensive. Assuming that a given piece of land/water is reasonably attractive, the relative intensity of use is determined, in the main, by the intensity of management—not the other way around, unless access is extremely easy, not controlled by management, and the user population is extremely large and demanding easy access.

To fully appreciate the need for area planning we must understand what happens without it. Let us take a look at an example:[3]

• 1890

Big and Little Kachess Lakes, alpine lakes on the east side of the Cascades, were accessible via game trails.

• early 1900s

U.S. Bureau of Reclamation dammed the drainage creating the 11-mile long Lake Kachess.

• through 1930s

The road used to construct the dam and new logging roads were developed and periodically updated. More people showed up at the natural attractors, such as the lake. People camped, fished, and hiked around the lake, and also created impacts. The 'old-timers' were gone, replaced by those who were happy with the new conditions.

• 1940s

Several informal camping areas became evident—lots of fire pits, trails, human waste, and solid waste.

• 1950s

Agency develops several heavily-used sites. Roads were improved, and tables and outhouses installed. Signing and regulations were posted. More people came. The site now looked more modern than ever before.

• 1960s

In response to growing use and increasing impact, the area was furthered 'improved,' roads paved, water wells added and newer campgrounds developed.

• 1970s

As use increased, more campsites were added and facilities upgraded to more modern standards.

This is not an unusual scenario. Wilderness, near and dear to many Americans, typically shows this evolution, albeit without roads, from essentially no access to trails, to modern trails with trailhead facilities, wide, easy treads, and footbridges over all creeks. Use simply increased every time a new enhancement was added.

The message is *not* one of what went wrong in the above examples, but at what point along the continuum (now called ROS) do we want to operate—establishing objectives in terms of what kinds of opportunities, and then allocating our resources to achieve that operating point. If management is to be effective, it must recognize the linkage between what they do and how the visitor responds in terms of use patterns. Without that recognition, no planning will ever be very effective in achieving stated goals. What people are responding to is not only the natural resource base but also how that opportunity has been modified by management programs of access and facility development and related services.

To date, management has not recognized the significance of this linkage and, thus, has continually moved the individual sites toward the developed end of the continuum. Ultimately someone officially decries the situation. The recreationists have befouled their nest. We must teach them a lesson through regulation and enforcement, or the ultimate management option will be to limit these wretched souls through a limited entry system.

What management must recognize is that a specific opportunity is a product of the natural resource that attracts people and the managerially determined attributes. This puts the manager squarely in charge of the recreation opportunity and the desired recreational use pattern. It is actually achieved by allocating resources (natural and fiscal) through the area planning process to create and stabilize the specific opportunity over time. Without that commitment to stability, you will continually run the gamut of examples such as those shown earlier, even if you do this thing called planning—where management is reactive rather than proactive.

PLANNING AS A PROCESS

Area planning has many characteristics of any other planning process:

1. Based on Objectives. Following the thought developed in Chapter 3, area planning should focus the objectives on outcomes on what you ultimately hope to produce—*recreational use patterns.* Do you want river floating or motorized boating, or both? Do you want a low-density, primitive setting, or a high-density, modern setting? Or do you want a low-density, modern setting? An oxymoron? You bet! But we do this all the time because we are not careful in stating our objectives. There are many national wild rivers with high-density access, yet trying to achieve low-density on-water use. The low-density is contrived through an *ex post facto* decision to use a limited entry permit system. Or was it an *ex post facto* decision? Was the need for such low density predictable before the fact? You bet it was.

Area planning must be carefully stated in terms of the desired recreational use patterns. Be as specific as possible. If you want something to happen, then state it as an objective. In a recent case, an agency could not state upfront what type of use pattern it wanted on a newly-designated national wild river; yet, management "knew" when they had exceeded "carrying capacity" (density of use). Why didn't they state the desired density of river floaters and then develop (or not develop) the access to achieve it? Ironically, they did just the opposite. They put in a $250,000 high density access to within 1/4 mile (allowed by law) of the water. It makes you wonder if the agency had any feel for why the river was designated wild in the first place.

Even in the more modern portion of the spectrum, you must state your desired outcomes in terms of types of recreational use patterns. Then in the process of designing transportation systems and individual sites you can control the generic outcome (recreational use pattern), realizing that some regulations and enforcement may be necessary.

We like to think of the desired outcome in terms of the anchor point along the Recreation Opportunity Spectrum. It is simply a way of visualizing where you want to operate on a continuum. This would reflect the level of development, level of use, and subsequent level of commitment of managerial resources to achieve that anchor point.

How do you decide where this point should be on the continuum? The economist would say for a given parcel of public land the point should be where the net benefits to society are maximized. The exact point then becomes an empirical problem. In reality, there is typically neither the data, the money, nor time to solve the empirical problem. Sometimes they are solved for us—such as designating an area through the legislative process. In fact, those legislative bits do not define the anchor, only a segment of the continuum with lots of room for making mistakes. If there wasn't, we wouldn't be pushing roads to within a 1/4 mile of a new wild river with the intent of keeping it wild.

We think a more rational approach would be to define the constraints on the options for the anchor point. Refer to Figure 3-3, p. 37. Look at legislation, policy, operating budgets, the lay of the land, and sensitivity of the resource as defining the constraints under which the area will be operated. These constraints will limit your options, or viable alternatives, to a truncated continuum (a narrow segment) and sometimes to almost an identified point (few options). Then take the

constrained choice set to the public for their input. The assumption is that whatever decision is arrived at is actually acceptable because it falls within the constraints. See Chapter 6 on public involvement. Too often the choice set presented to the public as Plan A, Plan B, Plan C, and Plan D are not all viable because of one constraint or another and are not implementable. A review of a recent agency planning document found that Plans A, C, and D (we prefer the term Options) were not viable. Consequently most of the public input was not useful ("Those damned recreationists never give us anything we can use"). The Options presented in this case should have been $B_1, B_2, B_3 \ldots B_n$.

No, defining constraints and following through with public involvement does not guarantee you will be operating at the point of maximizing net benefits to society. However, it is a good proxy for efficiency because you will not have to spend large sums of money to overcome major constraints if you operate within them. As expenditures go up, you have the potential for greatly reducing net benefits (benefits minus management costs), unless such expenditures greatly enhance benefits. Plus, if you make the public aware of the constraints on options, then their input becomes more useful in selecting the exact anchor point. Your clientele will have greater confidence in you and the planning process. There should be less challenges to the selected option.

Now that we have said all that, there is another cross you must bear—the realization that there are events, activities, or acts (ignoring acts of God) that may affect your plan that you have little or no control over. The system is an open one, meaning things can happen over which you have no control, which completely change the plan. A new highway may be built right to the boundary, a bedroom community associated with energy development springs to life 10-miles down the road, or the rancho condos begin to hover above the low-density trail system. All bets are off. It's a new ballgame, requiring the revision of objectives, or at least a rethinking of the how to best achieve the original objectives.

2. Achieving objectives. The desired recreational use pattern is achieved through how we choose the mix of inputs into the recreation opportunity. As discussed in Chapter 3, an equilibrium is set up between the Recreation Opportunity and the Recreational Use Pattern. The RO determines the general use pattern and the use pattern has some impact on the RO until an equilibrium is reached. Assuming that the external inputs to the open system are stable and the managerial inputs into the RO are stable, the equilibrium should be stable, except for the periodic vagaries of the exogenous inputs of weather.

Jubenville, Matulich, and Workman suggest that the recreationists respond to inputs into the recreation opportunity in a hierarchical fashion.[13] The direct attributes are environmental attractors (places in the landscape that are more valued than others), the visual continuity of the landscape through which the participant passes (plus those lands surrounding the attraction), and the access development with associated facilities. For the participant, these represent the inherent characteristics of the opportunity. Why access development? Because it represents a stable part of the opportunity (at least in most people's lifetime) that determines *who*—the mix of clientele who are willing to participate. The attendant facilities almost always correspond to the character and scope of the access transportation system.

The indirect attributes of visitor services, resource management, and regulations, while not the primary reason for participating, may ultimately determine which RO people actually choose and participate. Resource management programs that people recognize as enhancing the environmental setting may be considered as direct attributes. If the resource management program is significant to the stabilization of the RO over time, then it becomes a direct attribute. For example, the stocking of fish as a continual supplement to the native population, or even on a "put and take" basis, are essential to the continual maintenance of the opportunity. The reintroduction of a species that has been extirpated, as long as it maintains itself afterwards, is simply a part of the environmental setting and a direct attribute.

The stability of the indirect attributes are important to the stability of the equilibrium achieved. Since indirect attributes affect peoples' choices of ROs, continually changing a single, simple service can change the mix of people actually attracted. This continual change means that there are many dissatisfied customers, a distrust in the goodwill of the agency, and general confusion as to the "real" RO.

The original Lake Kachess example shows what happens when you do not state in the beginning the desired use pattern and then try to maintain desired equilibria through the use of access and facility development. The same can happen when services are also changed, except the change in clientele is more subtle. On the surface, everything appears intact because the environmental setting and development norms have not been altered; yet, people still are displaced to other RO's that better meet their interests, or continue to participate but with lowered expectation and thus lowered value.

To guarantee this stability, all indirect attribute programs must be stated as part of the original resource allocations in the area plan. You cannot continually add programs over time without considering the impacts on the desired recreational use pattern. As an analogy, the forester commits to specific cultural treatments at the beginning of the forest plan, not months nor years later. The same holds true for the recreation manager, unless (as restated from Chapter 3):

1. The desired equilibrium, based on monitoring, was not being achieved, and some micrometer adjustments are needed.
2. The external inputs had changed drastically, causing a rethinking of the desired recreational use pattern or at least the inputs into the present RO.
3. The original recreational use pattern was no longer desired.

Furthermore, all inputs must be vertically aligned with the chosen anchor point on the recreational opportunity spectrum. You cannot operate one program such as facility development at one anchor point and public safety at another. You give mixed signals and confuse the prospective participants, and create a less-than-efficient allocation of resources. As an example, suppose you develop a very primitive trail 20 miles up to a lake. The development norm would be close to the end of the primitive portion of the spectrum. Then you implemented a public safety plan which included trailhead and lakeside signing of the dangers of cold, clearwater lakes, brochures at the trailhead about hypothermia treatment, emergency equipment for dealing with the problem cached and signed at the lake, and an emergency telephone located near the lake at the end of the trail. The service norm would probably approach the central part of the continuum, obviously much more than needed. Because the norm is out of alignment, the facility costs soar and possibly encourage people to attempt swimming since help seems so near (even though they are 20 miles from the trailhead). Possibly a warning in the informational brochure and trailhead sign would have sufficed.

Another factor should be considered—functional relationships associated with the development of access and facilities. Functional relationships are usually associated to the individual facilities in a given site at so they are placed at their "right" locations within the site.[7] This process is even more important at the area level. Assume that three specific sites have been allocated in the area to promote the on-water use of a particular lake—a marina, a picnic (day use) grounds, and a campground, plus a concession operation for fuel and campstore. If you place either the picnic grounds or campground too close to the Marina, you could create confusion of traffic, hazardous use patterns, and general queueing problems. You can put the campground too close, even without the attendant problems suggested above, because people tend to seek more privacy and less noise and less mixing of user groups in their outdoor bedroom (loosely their individual campsite). Plus, the day use sites and overnight sites need to be separated so as not to overlap and mix the two use patterns. The functional relationship, in this case, might look like Figure 17-2.

As indicated by the diagram, both day use and overnight boaters focus their activities on the lake, primarily through boating out of the marina. The overnighter has greater needs for boat fuel and food supplies than the day user. Thus, although the concession is at the

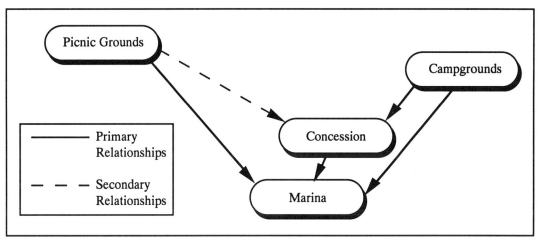

Figure 17-2. Possible functional relationships in an area plan.

marina, it is located to favor the overnighter, and to minimize the safety problems of the people going to the concession stand. In sum, it is the tool for placing complementary sites adjacent to one another, and separating conflicting ones.

In this case, the primary attractor is the lake; the diagram indicates this and focuses water-based use patterns through the marina. The day-use and overnight sites are then developed around that central focus, yet separating potentially conflicting uses.

A practical way of fitting those functional relationships to the area is to have a large-scale topographic base map with boundaries delineated. Use paper cutouts to represent each site. Write the name on each cutout and move them around on the map, while maintaining the desired relationships. In the above example, you first locate suitable locations for the marina and then put the other sites in perspective shown by the function relationship diagram. Then you could actually reverse the day-use and overnight sites and still maintain the desired relationships.

Finally you need to concern yourself with protecting visual quality in the area plan. You do not wait until site planning to consider visual quality, even though one can and should do a lot through micro-site location and individual site design to minimize visual impacts. You need to account for potential impacts at the area level by developing visual quality objectives (VQO's), delineating and analyzing "seen areas" for all probably access routes, taking advantage of unique views and reducing impacts through visual absorption (Chapter 11).

3. Coordination. Rarely does an agency have exclusion jurisdiction, well-defined, natural external boundaries, and activity patterns that do not impinge on the rights of their neighbors. There is always a need for coordination of planning. The specifics of coordination need to, first, be negotiated between affected parties and then explicitly stated in the area plan. This way one can ensure that all necessary programs that are integral to a given RO are in place, vertically aligned, and agency/landowner responsibilities are clearly spelled out. Excellent examples of management activities requiring coordination are wildfire management, public utilities, public road systems, law enforcement, environmental protection, migratory species, endangered species, access to private inholdings, search and rescue, emergency medical response, fire protection, and protection of visual resources.

One of the worst examples of coordination was at a major reservoir in the Midwest. All of the campgrounds were designed for the modern RV'er—wide, paved roads, pull-through camp units (reduces the need for backing up), and flush toilets. Unfortunately all of the county roads that led to these campgrounds were only about 1 1/2 vehicles wide with drainage ditches right at the edges of the road. Guess what? Only a few hardy souls showed up for the grand opening!

A new term, co-management, is a true shared management program where one agency owns specific resource rights but another agency(ies) owns other specific rights— to the point that each must work in a co-equal partnership to provide for specific outcomes that are acceptable to all.

Examples where co-management seems desirable include subsistence activities, mining, ownership of submerged lands, private inholdings, and wildfire control. The typical situation is where one's rights to do certain things can measurably impact the rights of others such that the offended party can effectively preclude the particular activity, or at least reduce the full implementation of a program. Certainly one agency needs to act as the lead agency, but the negotiated management pact would clearly spell out roles and responsibilities and establish framework for co-management.

4. Public Safety. Public safety is always a concern and thus such programs should be explicitly stated. Too often they are implied but rarely stated. While public liability and the need to reduce the risk of loss to the firm are important reasons to incorporate a *risk management* program into the area plan,

the real reason for such is to guide management in their responsibilities toward the using clientele. Those responsibilities are generally based on the six criteria under Evaluation of Hazards (Chapter 18).

5. Partnerships. Development of partnerships seems to be a contemporary concept where we attempt to forge voluntary relationships to get the job done. In reality we have always fostered such relationships. We have just reaffirmed those efforts. Examples include maintenance of outlying public-use cabin by a voluntary group, trail maintenance by a private contractor, or overnight accommodations by a concessionaire. The reasons can be as varied as the need to have local people with a vested interest in providing the best possible service within the requirements of the RO, stretching limited budget dollars, or having the participant pay the full cost in unusual and expensive services. Thus, partners can be other agencies, volunteer groups, entrepreneurs, or active user groups.

6. Emphasis on Design. Through good design of the access transportation systems, facilities, and good information programs to foster public stewardship, the manager can *build* on a setting that, while probably not maintenance-free, vandal-proof, and guaranteed totally safe to public use, will capture the essence of a self-regulatory system. No system is any better than the well-thought-out design of its access, facilities, and services, realizing that some regulations, law enforcement, and other oversight will be necessary. Operationally this is the heart and soul of the equilibrium concept.

7. Quality. Quality is dealt with only because it is often a misused concept. Quality is a nebulous term that often crops up in plans and tends to reflect the density of use. Low density is equated to high quality; and high density, low quality. Nothing could be further from the truth unless our goal was to keep people from using public recreational resources, i.e., pragmatically the lowest achievable density. Quality from a management perspective has to be more cosmopolitan than that; it has to be achievable at any anchor point along the continuum. Thus, we propose that *quality* from a management perspective is achieving the desired equilibrium at the chosen anchor point on the recreation opportunity spectrum, producing the desired recreational use pattern. While we may conclude that, based on monitoring, we have generally achieved such equilibrium, there is always room for improvement. One way of assessing needed improvements is the *Report Card* system suggested by LaPage, where survey questionnaires are used to judge how well we are doing in our existing services, but not to make wholesale changes to the point of causing social succession to occur, i.e., moving the anchor point and achieving a new equilibrium.[15]

   8. *Review and Revision*. As suggested above, we need to monitor how well we are doing and be willing to make micro-adjustments to improve. However, we also need to monitor external factors to determine if external changes warrant reallocation of resources (inputs to RO) to continue to achieve the desired equilibrium. If you think a new equilibrium may be in order, then the area planning process must start anew. Constraints and assumptions must first be reexamined to determine the realm of possible options, and then the desired recreational use patterns must be stated.

BENEFIT-COST ANALYSIS

Achieving the desired equilibrium is the theoretical least-cost solution because a given set of benefits are captured at the least cost—i.e., long-term impact on your operating budget. What people are valuing or demanding in a given package of attributes is probably no different than buying a new car. We choose the package of attributes that best suits our needs and is within our personal economic constraints. Recreation, not unlike the car, is an experience where the manager provides a certain amount of input, but the remaining inputs to the experience are provided by the recreationists themselves. They take the particular RO, and add their own touches to produce unique outcomes or experiences. The previous example of a primitive 20-mile trail into a lake serves the point. Some families may visit the area so parents can pass on the values of independence and self-reliance in the wild settings to their children. Some groups may come strictly for the good fishing, ignoring the wilds of the landscape. Still others may come for photography adventures to capture the wilds on film. So on and so on. Yet, they all used the common RO to capture this. The point is that it is important to respond to mass demand and not try to individualize the particular opportunity to the point of only being attractive to a small part of the potential market. People can and will create their own individual experiences as long as the general RO is acceptable. In that regard, the participant becomes his/her own quality control as long as management has done their job.

   From the demand side of the ledger, it is important to recognize that unique natural resources have inherent value without the added physical development and related services. In fact, the demand curve is an inelastic one for unique resources such as a wild river, mountain peaks, a waterfall, etc.—that is, the curve will be a steep gradient where all of the supply will be completely consumed regardless of price. As we add development to the RO, there is the potential to change the demand curve from inelastic to elastic—people focus as much on the facilities and services as the resource base, if not more so. When this happens, the RO begins to look like many other ROs (substitutes) which means people are now willing to pay less because they can find similar ROs elsewhere at a competitive price. Under these circumstances, the demand curve flattens, or becomes less steep, and people will seek alternatives if the price becomes too high. The point is that you can actually lower the net benefits to society at some point in development. Certainly Yosemite Valley is a great place to play golf because of the pleasant backdrop for the game. But if prices rise too much the golfer may shift to another course where the golf challenge is still the same, even though the general landscape is much more mundane.

How do you estimate benefits associated with a particular RO? Federal guidelines recommend *willingness to pay* as the appropriate economic measure of the benefits of using public resources for recreation. There are three ways of estimating these benefits: 1) *unit day value,* which uses expert opinion on average willingness to pay; 2) *travel costs,* which use out-of-pocket expenses to indirectly measure consumer surplus; and 3) *contingent valuation,* which uses simulated markets in an interview process to estimate willingness to pay. In the contingent valuation method (CVM), a sample of the affected population are asked their maximum willingness to pay contingent on hypothetical change

in existing recreational opportunities. R. G. Walsh describes each of these approaches in detail.[20]

Typically, at present, market values are measured directly and then compared to descriptions of recreational opportunities and public concerns. At best, this can only be described as a subjective decision-making process which most managers give greater credence to than, say, the CVM estimate of those values.

One thing for certain is that the present practice of using participation levels as an estimate of the value of a given opportunity is a poor one because it assumes that all users value the resource equally. If that were the case, all one would have to do to capture more net benefits is somehow increase use. Sufficient case studies indicate that in various conditions a given resource may provide greater net benefits under low-density rather than high-density use. In that case, either the total benefits are high because users value the opportunity highly or costs soar under high-use conditions, or both.

Estimating Costs

The Recreational Opportunity Spectrum (see Figure 3-1, p. 32) shows the management intensity to be a straight-line function with a low gradient. In most cases it would probably be a curvilinear relationship, the gradient increasing rapidly with increasing intensity of recreational use. Unfortunately we really do not have good supply curves, relating how much of a given management input do we need for a given level of use. If we need two river rangers on a river where there is 2,000 tubers on any Saturday in June, how many do you need for 10,000 tubers? Recreational supply curves have not been of interest to the economic researcher; there are almost no articles in the literature addressing these. The economist has been more interested in the demand issues dealing with nonmarket goods such as recreation. Obviously there is more challenge, both theoretically and empirically, to understanding demand, but that does not lessen the need for understanding supply.

The best solution is obvious—your experience factors. Based on experience, how many river rangers do you need for 10,000 tubers? Still there is a lot of uncertainty, particularly in your initial allocation decisions.

Decisions Without Numbers

Nonmarket demand data are very expensive to collect, analyze, and put into a useful form for management. Many people are hoping for a table of numbers where you can match up your situation with the table and read off average benefits per user. Then all we need is an estimate of the number of users. Certainly that will give you an estimate, but you will not know how good that estimate is. Besides, it may take decades to accumulate such, even then it can only be loosely applied. It seems to us that the best alternative would be for resource agencies to form regional consortia, identify important general ROs for the region and then hire an economic team to develop the demand curves, and supply curves too!

Absent such curves, how do you make the incremental decisions about managing an area. A classical, yet contemporary, problem is the implementation of a limited entry permit system. What are benefits? Costs? Is the decision viable—do benefits exceed costs? Let's look at an example:

In 1980, 1,000 people float the upper 25 miles of the Smith River. In 1981, a new access road was developed to

within 1/4-mile of the river. The access trail was upgraded and a canoe rack was installed at the 1/8-mile point. Use jumped by 50 percent the first year, and was up to 3,000 people by 1985. Some complaints were being received about too many people on the river. The river rangers indicated some of the more popular camping spots are showing loss of ground vegetation and some slight sheet erosion, plus solid waste build-up. Your inclination is to implement a limited entry permit system. Do you want to bring back the good old days and have 1,000 people per year? Reduce enough to minimize impact—say 2,000?

To justify implementing such a program, you would have to assume that the reduction from 3,000 to 1,000 users would cause the average net benefits to the user to increase from $11.67 per person to $60 per person. Hardly a reasonable assumption! But, it is empirically testable. If the RO was to be a low-density one, approximating 1,000 people per year, then the appropriate decision would have been to leave the access as it was in 1980 because it was essentially self-regulating. This would keep the system within the established tolerances at some minimum management costs. To increase access and then to reduce use to the good-old-day's level could probably only be justified through an insanity plea. This further emphasizes the need to make primary management decisions at time zero (when formulating the plan). Later, incremental decisions have a way of coming back to haunt you.

Benefits-Cost Calculation

Present

1. Assume an average benefit or use your regional estimate:

    3,000 visitors x $20 benefits/person = $60,000 Total Benefits.

2. Costs are:
    a. Periodic River Ranger patrol and cleanup $10,000
    b. Upkeep of access   15,000
                                                    $25,000

3. Net benefits are:

    Net Benefits = $60,000 - 25,000 = $35,000
    Average Net Benefit = $35,000 , 3,000 users = $11.67

Reduce to 1,000 Users

1. Decision choice must exceed present net benefits:

Present Net Benefits	No. of Users		
$35,000,	1,000	=	$35 average per user benefit

    x = $35 average net benefit. The average net benefit from reducing the number of users must now be equal to this for at least a break even point (B/C ratio of 1:1), assuming no increase in management costs.

2. Cost of management does increase:

    a. Part-time clerk to issue permits $7,000
    b. Add one more river ranger   8,000
    c. Increased upkeep of access   10,000
                                            $25,000

3. Average net benefit must be:

    1000 x = $35,000 + 25,000
        x = $60

Figure 17-3. Calculation of reducing visitation via a limited entry permit system.

SUMMARY

The area plan is the manager's tool for allocating resources—natural resources (land and water) and fiscal resources (dollars for the managerially-determined attributes of access/facilities, and services). It must emphasize the resource values because, in wildland recreation, these are the direct attributes that are central to people's choices to recreate. Indirect attributes such as service may ultimately affect those decisions but are not (or should not) be the primary reasons they choose a particular RO in the wildlands.

Area planning for wildland recreation fits with the Recreation Opportunity Spectrum very nicely:

1. Modern portion of the spectrum.
The modern portion emphasizes physical development—aesthetic, functional, and comfortable. The expectation is for maximum service with some minimum effort on the part of the participant. Generally this is interpreted as providing a specialized service for a very specific, identifiable clientele. In general, these types of facilities and/or services tend to be provided by the private sector at full cost to the client. These may be administered on public lands through a concession lease (usually long-term) or a special land-use permit (usually a small business and short-term). Or they may be encouraged through partnerships on private lands outside of the park or recreation area without any agency control. It is the pay-as-you-go segment of ROS, at the modern end of the continuum. There are some exceptions.

2. Primitive portion of the spectrum.
This portion generally represents the 'fuzzy' notion of wilderness. It is fuzzy because it can mean all things to all people—from the 400-acre Fire Island Wilderness to the 8-million-acre Gates of the Arctic Wilderness National Park. In essence, wilderness covers the entire roadless segment of the spectrum. This leaves the definition of wilderness and any other primitive opportunities up to the imagination of the particular manager. Anything goes as long as we couch everything in terms of protecting the resource and don't allow engineered roads. This practice is untenable.

We offer a new approach, not uniquely our own; divide the roadless portion (primitive) of the spectrum into subunits, call them $P_1, P_2, \ldots P_n$. Define the limits of the subunits, or subsegments, by the direct inputs of the development norms (acceptable level and character of development, particular access). Once an area is dedicated to wilderness, most likely the best one can hope for is to stabilize at its present anchor point, unless you establish objectives with full knowledge of the public to move it to a less primitive subsegment of the roadless portion of the spectrum. Even if you wanted to make a roadless RO more primitive, you will probably find it nearly impossible because of the clientele that have been attracted over time. They like it just the way it is—no changes please and they know how to say that through pressure group politics. If you want to change to more primitive, you need to accept small changes as successes—realizing that it took a myriad of small changes over decades to get it to the existing less primitive state.

3. Intermediate portion of spectrum.
This is where you as a public land manager do or should spend the bulk of your time, talent, and dollars. The intermediate portion covers the central part of the recreational opportunity spectrum—the less primitive and the less modern. This is where the vast majority of

users will participate, assuming that you have some environmental attractors within the area you are responsible for. Delineate the subsegments (say M_3, M_4, and P_1 and P_2) by development and service norms and allocate resources according to the requirements of the subsegment. The challenge is to design the area such that recreational use patterns are essentially self-regulating, realizing that some regulations and enforcement will be necessary. While we do not fully understand the nuances of behavioral response to management inputs, we believe that with proper design you can create those desired equilibria

$$\text{RO} \quad \rightleftharpoons \quad \text{RUP}$$

even in the intermediate portion of the spectrum. What is needed is to recognize the unique features of an area as the primary value to be captured, and the way these values are captured for a given mix of clientele is through recognizing the cause-effect relationship between management action (and in some cases inaction), a careful attempt to design the system to create a particular recreational use of pattern, a smidgen of creativity, and a willingness to monitor and adjust as needed.

Bonne chance!

SELECTED READINGS

1. Becker, R. H., and Jubenville, A. 1990. Forest Recreation Management (Chapter 20), *Introduction to Forest Science* (2nd edition). R. A. Young and R. L. Giese (eds.). New York, NY: John Wiley & Sons.

2. Bealeschki, M. D., and Henderson, K. A. 1988. "Constraints to Trail Use." *Journal of Park & Recreation Administration, 6*(3):20-29.

3. Clark, R. N., and G. H. Stankey. 1979. The Recreation Opportunity Spectrum: A Framework for Planning, Management, and Research. USDA-Forest Service Publication GTR PNW-98.

4. Crawford, D. W., Jackson, E. L., and Godbey, G. "A Hierarchy Model of Leisure Constraints." *Leisure Sciences, 13*(4):309-320.

5. Driver, B. L. 1985. "Specifying What Is Produced by Management of Wildlife By Public Agencies." *Leisure Sciences, 7*(3):281-295.

6. Driver, B. L., Brown, P. J., Stankey, G. N., and Gregoire, T. G. "The ROS Planning System: Evolution, Basic Concepts, and Research Needed." *Leisure Sciences, 9*(3):201-212.

7. Espeth, R. D. 1988. *Site Planning*. North Central Regional Extension Publication 290, University of Illinois-Urbana-Champaign.

8. Fogg, G. E., and Shiner, J. W. 1989. *Management Planning for Park and Recreation Areas*. (3rd Printing) Alexandria, VA: NRPA.

9. Fridgen, J. D. 1987. "Use of Cognitive Maps to Determine Perceived Tourism Regions." *Leisure Sciences, 9*(2):101-118.

10. Graefe, A. R., Kuss, F. R., and Vaske, J. J. 1987. *Recreation Impacts and Carrying Capacity: A Visitor Impact Management Framework*. Washington, DC: Nat. Parks & Cons. Assn.

11. Hammitt, W. E. and Cole, D. N. 1987. *Wildland Recreation: Ecology and Management*. New York, NY: John Wiley & Sons.

12. Heywood, J. L. 1991. "Visitor Inputs to Recreation Opportunity Spectrum Allocation and Monitoring." *Journal of Parks & Recreation Administration, 9*(4):42-58.

13. Jubenville, A., Matulich, S. C., and Workman, W. G. 1986. *Toward the Integration of*

Economics and Outdoor Recreation Management. Station Bulletin 68. Ag. & For. Exp. Sta., Univ. Alaska Fairbanks.

14. Kelly, J. 1987. Recreation Trends Towards the Year 2000. Champaign, IL. Management Learing Laboratories.

15. LaPage, W. F. 1983. "Resource Management for Visitor Satisfaction." *Journal of Parks & Recreation Administration,* 1(2):37-44.

16. McAvoy, L. H., Schatz, C., and Lime, D. W. 1991. "Cooperation in Resource Management: A Model Planning Process for Promoting Partnerships Between Resource Managers and Private Sector Providers." *Journal of Parks & Recreation Administration,* 9(4):42-58.

17. Miller, P. T. and Mutter, L. R. 1988. "The Language of Strategic Planning." *Journal of Parks & Recreation Administration,* 6(3):59-65.

18. National Recreation and Parks Association. 1992. NRPA *Pacific Risk Management School Handbook.* Western Regional Office, NRPA, Sacramento, CA.

19. Shelby, B. and Heberlein, T. A. 1986. *Carrying Capacity in Recreational Settings.* Corvallis, OR: Oregon State Univ. Press.

20. Walsh, R. G. 1986. *Recreation Economic Decisions: Comparing Benefits and Costs.* State College, PA: Venture Publishing, Inc.

CHAPTER 18

Hazard Management

Hazard management is the purposeful action taken by management to reduce the probability of injury, loss of life, or loss of property occurring to the participant from known or suspected, natural or man-made hazards within the recreational environment.

Some people refer to this as "risk management;" however, risk management is an entrepreneurial term that means minimizing the risk of loss to the firm. The role and responsibility of the public land manager, however, is to provide a given recreational opportunity. Part of that opportunity typically involves hazards, so management has a responsibility to deal with those hazards to reduce the probability of injury or loss of property. The course of action taken reflects many situational variables, such as the type of activity, anticipated participants, need to preserve the environment and where on the ROS the particular opportunity is located. Individual participants are still in charge of their own behavior, and if they conform to special management programs they should minimize risks to themselves. In sum, participants are in charge of themselves; managers provide hazard management programs to warn visitors or otherwise reduce unnecessary and undesirable dangers.

Figure 18-1. Removing rotten tree limbs in a heavy public use area. (Photo by Gordon Wissinger)

INTRODUCTION

Peril is part of today's lifestyle—the automobile, the hurried approach to life, the attractive nuisances, and the last-minute decisions. Life may seem more rushed, decisions more complex, and problem issues more numerous, but this does not mean we should merely accept associated hazards as part of modern life. On the contrary, they should be enumerated, evaluated, and managed. This task should he a primary goal in any activity, but particularly those associated with park and recreation settings.[4] When you participate in any leisure activity, you often lower your guard to potential jeopardy. Perhaps you do not understand or appreciate the possible hazards, or you feel that management has minimized the danger, or your attention is diverted by an enjoyable activity, or you accept the risk and are possibly attracted by it.

As managers of parks and recreation areas, we should feel some obligation to identify and effectively reduce known hazards. How far should we carry this obligation? Do you, as recreation manager, make your area completely free of danger? Do you selectively choose certain hazards for specific management action? If so, which ones? If complete removal is unwarranted or perhaps even impossible, how do you manage risk?

Hazard management requires the following four steps:

1. *Establishment of objectives.* Managing any hazard must measurably contribute to the recreational objectives for an area and the legitimate mission of the agency. Determine how you can do this.

2. *Identification of hazards.* Identify all known or potential hazards and locate them on a base map.

3. *Evaluation of hazards.* Evaluate all hazards within the framework of your area's specific recreational objectives and the degree to which they meet established standards.

4. *Development of management strategies.* Adopted strategies should reflect the previous steps and be continually validated by positive feedback. Do they improve the quality of visitors' experiences? Positive feedback might include a decline in injury rates, tort claims, complaints, etc.

ESTABLISHMENT OF OBJECTIVES

Managers should determine where the anchor point or recreational opportunity of an area falls on the spectrum. Specific hazard management programs should be aligned with requirements for this opportunity. Consider expert opinion and public involvement when you develop your hazard management program. Develop specific program objectives that address risk reduction in a specific zone for specific identified hazards within the constraints of the ROS classification.

Management assumes greater responsibility for the safety of visitors at the more modern end of the ROS. Many primary natural attractors are also natural hazards. When management deliberately exposes visitors to these dangers through improved access, the hazard management program must be sophisticated enough to accommodate novices participating in low-risk activities in high-risk zones. At the other end of the ROS, visitors assume greater responsibility for their own behavior in the face of specific risks. Even then management has a responsibility to inform or enlighten participants of known hazards. It is in the intermediate portions of the spectrum that responsibility and subsequent program objectives become hazy.

While this text does not pretend to provide legal advice, you should consider the legal implications of most program decisions.* Programs dealing with public safety issues such as hazard management are obviously more controversial and have greater legal implications (also consult Chapter 5 on Administrative Law).

Several interrelated legal concepts relate to program planning, including establishment of objectives. A *public trust doctrine* means that real property—the natural resource base—is held and administered by a trustee for a third party. The particular legislative body imposes legal constraints to administer that resource. These constraints are typically very broadly defined, and leave much discretion to the individual agency. The *discretionary function* of governments exempts them from public liability for broad, policy-oriented decisions that primarily deal with resource allocation, e.g., designation of a four thousand acre area as a backcountry zone.

In order to help encourage this designation, you might put in an intensive trail system with large-capacity parking lots on the periphery of the zone to expose the visitors to the beautiful river gorge for which the area was originally preserved. (In Chapter 3, we discussed how this resource allocation created the Smith Gorge backcountry hiking opportunity). To fully develop and maintain your area, you must align *operational decisions*—like those dealing with the Smith Gorge hazards—with the selected anchor point, or recreational opportunity. These

operational decisions are not exempt from public liability. The best defense against liability is to show *due care;* that is, to be aware of inherent risks and take appropriate action, within the limits of a particular opportunity, to prevent or at least decrease the dangers. In the case of Smith Gorge, participant risk could be appropriately reduced through proper trail design, construction of barriers at critical points, installation of warning signs, imposition of regulations to restrict use to certain locations, and enforcement of those regulations. If the gorge is 20 miles from the nearest road over a very primitive trail, the requirements of *due care* are obviously lessened.

This brings us to a final concept called *voluntary assumption of risk* (VAR). You cannot assume that participants engage in VAR just because they enter an area of their own free will. Instead, visitors must understand the perils, the danger that they face, and then voluntarily assume responsibility. This places greater emphasis on proper design of access systems and any associated facilities along with warning signs and other verbal communication.

IDENTIFICATION OF HAZARDS

Types of Hazards

Managers should be able to recognize various types of natural hazards since recognition is the first step in minimizing danger. The following is a general list:

---

* For a more formal discussion, see A. N. Frakt and J. S.Rankin, 1982.

1. NATURAL—LAND

a. Lightning

One of the deadliest threats to recreationists is lightning, particularly on high, exposed sites. Lightning-strike patterns are predictable, so known lightning zones can be avoided.

b. Cliffs

Cliffs and other places of abrupt relief like chasms and pits should be identified and avoided through proper mad and trail location. Jeopardy can also be reduced through adequate site preparation, including such items as safety barriers.

c. Landslides and Falling Rocks

Local areas of medium to high relief that have unstable soil or rock outcroppings should be avoided. You can usually identify these by early signs of erosion or sloughing. A knowledge of soil types, along with an understanding of geology, helps you to predict loose rock breakup and massive soil movement.

d. Snow and Ice Avalanches

Areas of avalanche activity are generally known and identified easily by old avalanche paths. The environmental conditions under which avalanches occur are temporal and must be monitored to predict an event. If possible, avoid planning sites in avalanche areas. In places where diverse winter sports are offered, managers should monitor for avalanche conditions; ideally they can then curtail any activity in these areas during critical times. Unfortunately avalanches can occur in the most unlikely places, so consult a specialist.

e. Ice Fields, Snowfields, and Crevasses

Ice fields pose many hazards for recreationists. First are weather conditions. Whiteouts due to fog and snow are not unusual, and without guiding landmarks travel is extremely hazardous because of sheer drop-offs and crevasses. Heavy snowfalls over short periods and low temperatures also add to this risk. Even mountain rescues are often difficult both because of the weather and not being able to locate the injured party.

f. Vegetation

Overstory vegetation can be a hazard in developed sites due to environmental conditions such as heavy wind, shallow soils, and high soil moisture or due to rot or dieback caused by mechanical injury.

g. Wildlife

Wild animals such as bears, moose, buffalo, and rabid coyotes present real danger to recreationists. Often user areas are deliberately located on the edge of prime wildlife habitats so that people can observe these animals.

h. Others

Other land hazards such as volcanic action [20] and dust storms may prove harmful to recreationists.

2. NATURAL—WATER

Any body of water is a potential hazard to people depending on how well they are both physically and mentally prepared. Water hazards are probably more obvious but should be enumerated anyway:

Figure 18-2.   Plague warning related to squirrels near Glacier Point, Yosemite National Park. (Photo by B. W. Twight)

a. Tidal Changes

Abrupt tidal changes can prevent use. They may cause people to make irrational decisions that they would not think of under ordinary circumstances.

b. Ocean and Lake Currents

Water currents may not appear on the surface but can still be very hazardous to users. A knowledge of local conditions is essential for understanding and locating water currents.

c. Water Obstacles

Obstacles to normal movement over water, such as boulders, log jams, rapids, and waterfalls, create danger. Some people are qualified to handle these difficult situations; others are not. Certain obstacles are acceptable as part of one recreational opportunity, but not for another.

d. Flooding

Flooding creates hazards for users as well as nonusers; each may suffer if they happen to be in the flood zone. Although high water is usually predictable, many places support a large amount of recreational use, and managers are pressured to develop and encourage activities within the flood plain.

e. Others

Other water hazards include harmful animal life and water pollution. Exact problems vary with local conditions.

3. MAN-MADE

Man-made hazards are potentially the most difficult to manage because people often do not recognize their precariousness.

a. Buildings

Poorly maintained or abandoned buildings, rotten bridges, and similar man-made objects are often focal points in a landscape and thus attractive nuisances.

b. Road Design

This encourages or discourages speed levels, traffic bottlenecks, blind turns, and other problems. Roads are often overlooked, yet much recreation is auto-oriented.

c. Altered Landscapes

Sometimes man creates natural risks through strip mining, wells, mine shafts, etc.

SURVEY TECHNIQUES

Make local hazard surveys to determine specific hazards and their potential impact. The following are some basic techniques:

Review Accident Records, Tort Claim Records, and Lawsuits

Past occurrences are the best predictors of the types and possible locations of future accidents. All agencies should maintain records of accidents. Other sources include mountaineering groups, law-enforcement offices, and land-management agencies.

Use Aerial Photography

Stereo pairs of large-scale aerial photos help you survey large areas for potential hazards. Thus you accomplish much of your work in the office with minimum cost and delay, provided recent photos are available. Fall photos are generally the best for this type of survey since they maximize detail (because the deciduous leaves have fallen) and depth perception (because of maximum contrast from shadows). You can transfer this information to a base map—preferably a medium-to-large-scale topographic map—and verify it with minimum field sampling. Plotting past accident records may also be helpful.

Inventory work of this nature is usually associated with area planning so that you can take all hazards into account when you allocate land for specific sites. While much of this work can he accomplished in the office, verify results in the field to check the accuracy of photo information. Also, data on water depth, velocity, obstacles, and seasonal changes are better obtained through field studies.

Conduct Intensive Field Studies

Intensive field studies on prospective sites can determine existing hazards and how management can cope with these in the future. For most auto-oriented sites, these are necessary. Many travelling visitors may not understand the potential perils in a casual stop at a developed site. Therefore, managers should try to reduce these hazards during the site planning phase before visitor use begins. On dispersed-use areas, intensive field studies may not be necessary; the information needed to alert visitors to possible dangers can be provided by aerial photos.

For example, suppose a park manager is in charge of a site adjacent to a series of small bluffs overlooking a swift river. Along the base of the bluffs is a tilted ledge. Several drownings have occurred during previous seasons because people walking along this water-splashed mossy ledge have slipped and fallen into the river. Warning signs and complete physical barriers can probably solve the problem. Aerial photos can show the general risk of strolling near the swift river, and intensive development could be directed away from the water. Detailed site studies can indicate specific actions to reduce danger near or within the site.

Monitor Seasonal Use

To ensure the success of any hazard management program, monitor seasonal fluctuations. Certain dangers, such as increased water velocity and flooding, may not show up in measurements taken at only one point in time.

Reconstruct Past History

While conducting surveys of potential man-made hazards, you should attempt to reconstruct the history of man's activities in that particular area. This can help pinpoint potential problems left by previous developments. With a sufficiently detailed history, you can discover the exact locations of old mine shafts, covered wells, and building foundations.

EVALUATION OF HAZARDS

The following criteria should help you evaluate hazards:

Recreation Opportunity

As suggested throughout this chapter, the first and most important criterion is the experience you wish to provide and the alignment of the hazard management program with the overall opportunity. The Smith Gorge roadless area illustrates this point. To move the hazard management program from the existing anchor point, or activity area, towards the modern end of the ROS would certainly reduce the risk to participants. The problem is twofold. First, it escalates costs, which means that we have not sought the most efficient solution. Second, we may dramatically alter an opportunity, or the perception of an opportunity, or even give mixed signals which confuse potential users. Moving sites may also generate public criticism and legal or political opposition.

Transferring a program away from an anchor point towards the primitive end of the ROS does not meet the needs of the intended user population because you signal that risks are fewer than they really are. In the short run, you may save money. In the long run—after a major accident and lawsuit—you may overcompensate by moving too far in the other direction.

Type of Resource

The very nature of the resource may determine the direction that hazard management will take. As mentioned throughout the text, resources, particularly environmental attractors, are the essence of activities and as such should be carefully considered in your program. If a resource is unique and worthy of preservation, hazard reduction should manipulate users rather than environments. On the other hand, maximum modification of the landscape, such as sealing a cave or removing hazardous overstory vegetation, *may* be more appropriate. Also consider manmade developments and their historical significance and condition, like abandoned buildings, pits, and debris, and modify or remove these to reduce danger.

Type of Activity

Consider the activity that you encourage; technical rock climbing may be attractive because of associated risks. Skilled climbers understand and accept these perils; they also minimize them through proper instruction, good equipment, and recognition of individual limitations.

Other concentrated activities—picnicking—should be considered relatively hazard-free and thus planned and managed that way. Make a maximum effort to eliminate, reduce, or modify hazards in developed recreation sites. Intermediate activities, such as hiking and bicycling, may require some decrease in physical risks. You may simply tell participants about others.

Accessibility

Possibly the level of accessibility dictates the type of hazard management program. If an area is somewhat inaccessible, minimal information that stresses potential risks may be most appropriate. On the other hand, when a dangerous area is easily accessible so that people can enjoy its unique scenic beauty,

maximum safety precautions may be necessary. The overlook at the Lower Falls of the Yellowstone River is an example of this kind of situation. We assume a greater responsibility with increasing accessibility.

Levels of Predictability

If the hazard is geographically and chronologically predictable, such as the stability of a bluff zone, then the manager must consider it in program planning. If certain circumstances occur on a predictable basis, use this information and the location in formulating your hazard management plan. Natural disasters like floods, storms, and tornadoes are becoming more predictable. Some are predictable on a cyclical basis; others on an immediate, emergency basis. You can make changes, including possible relocation of facilities, to reduce the effects of predictable hazards. Others require an emergency plan to reduce immediate effects. Unfortunately, if the circumstances are not highly predictable, managers often overlook the need to plan for emergency situations.

Maturity of Participants

Factors considered to this point relate to recreational activity or environmental effects that influence that activity. But you should also consider user reactions. Maturity means both emotional prudence—the capacity for rational decision making in the face of risk—and perceptual acuity—how accurately particular hazards are interpreted. Emotional maturity is usually, but not always, associated with chronological age. Perceptual maturity is usually determined by previous learning experiences or previous exposure to potential hazards. We should also consider who the primary decision maker is in a group of participants since decisions are generally made by group leaders.

People may be emotionally mature and still have had little experience with certain environs or recreational activities; therefore, they may not understand the significance of the hazards they are facing. Many drownings are the result of rational decision making by an individual who incorrectly perceived a dangerous situation as involving minimum risk. When a real hazard is seen as minimal or nonexistent, a much more intensive management program is required.

SYSTEMATIC REDUCTION OF HAZARDS

As defined in the beginning, hazard management is the purposeful action taken by management to reduce the probability of injury, loss of life, or loss of property due to known, suspected, natural, or man-made hazards. Notice that a hazard-free recreational setting is not mentioned in our definition. This kind of setting would most likely be very sterile.

Once you have identified and evaluated hazards using the above criteria, you should classify or prioritize them for management action. Each fits into one of two categories—significant and routine. Each item can also be rated as modification or preservation. Modification means that it is acceptable to change the landscape or the facility to mitigate a dangerous condition. An example of this is adding a rustic handrail along a boardwalk surrounding a hot springs. Preservation means that modification is generally unacceptable; consequently any mitigating measures would involve manipulating visitors or at least warning them of the dangers involved.

Significant hazards receive priority in program development. A modification or preservation rating indicates the direction that the program should follow. Routine programs take less effort; however, it may be possible to immediately implement a program to reduce some routine hazard without a great deal of analysis or cost.

After identifying and rating problems, managers must formulate specific programs. These offer some balance between maintaining a desirable landscape and facility and protecting visitors. An example of poor action is the previous case in which the superintendent failed to seal off an attractive water-splashed rock ledge along a river near a main parking area. Several drownings resulted from people accidentally slipping off the ledge into the water. Instead of tastefully sealing off the ledge and hopefully dropping the number of drownings to zero, he constructed a one-rail, three-foot-high fence. The following year, the number of drownings dropped from six to three.

The exact method of hazard reduction may be dictated by the resource—avalanche zones, unique natural areas, and so forth—or by visitors such as those who demand beachfront activities. But managers must deal with a larger problem—the realization that most hazards cannot and should not be removed; they can only be reduced. The following are common techniques for doing this:

1. *Area Planning.* Through the process of area planning, needs dictate specific site developments which are then given functional locations according to the experience opportunity being provided, the resource, and the existing transportation systems. The same process that determines the location of specific site developments should account for

hazards. If necessary, they can be avoided by redirecting the access or location of facilities along the access.

2. *Site Planning.* Site planning reduces risks to users via carefully designed facilities that encourage particular behavior. For some major hazards, proper site design can minimize the risks and still be appropriate for the immediate landscape. In some cases, the safety factor may override the concern for aesthetics.

In reality, you can use only two methods to reduce the hazards associated with a particular site, assuming that this is the only logical place to locate the site. The first is a

Figure 18-3. Recreation site design that minimizes risk to visitors: An overlook from the south rim, Grand Canyon National Park. (Photo by B. W. Twight)

physical barrier that directs people away from a hazard or restrains them (see Figure 18-3). The second is a psychological barrier that theoretically discourages any visitors except skilled participants. For example, a manager is inviting disaster if he or she builds a road into an area reserved for technical rock climbing. This encourages participation by casual climbers who do not have the skill or the understanding of the risks involved.

3. *Hazard Removal.* Hazard removal is a tool for eliminating the risk to the participants. It is simply eradication—cutting dead trees, removing buildings, dynamiting mine shafts. This does not necessarily mean removal is only a last resort. It is simply another alternative for managers to use in particular situations.

4. *Information and Education.* You can devise programs that raise levels of skill, increase awareness of the risks involved, or warn and allow people to make their own choices. Each approach or combination of approaches may be sufficient. However, even if we reduce the risk, we should still attempt to remind people about potential hazards through an information program. Information programs are often the first step toward hazard management in sites that have already been developed. They may be stopgap measures until more sophisticated programs such as trail relocation, close out of a facility, or establishment of permanent barriers can be worked out. Post information signs in conjunction with permanent measures to make people aware that certain dangers still exist. On dispersed-use areas, informational programs may be the best technique for managing associated hazards.

5. *Regulation.* Reducing potential risks by regulation is effective but expensive. Establishing a regulation means creating a concomitant program for its enforcement. This becomes an expensive procedure. One example of hazard reduction through regulation is the requirement that a raft meets certain design specifications, carries specific safety items like life preservers and extra oars, and fulfills certain on-water safety requirements. To enforce this regulation, qualified technicians must inspect rafts and boat patrols must ensure that users comply with on-water safety regulations and have all specified equipment on board.

To reiterate a previous question: How far do you take this? We could perhaps regulate an activity to such a point that it is no longer satisfying to the using public. This type of regulating is mostly reserved for situations in which there is great potential for loss of life or property. Much depends on the activity, the danger to others, and general societal values. For example, to obtain a hunting license, a hunter safety course is now required in many states. To obtain a permit for technical mountain climbing, a statement of experience and qualification is now necessary in some climbing areas. The number of permit requirements like these are increasing. We should first check to see if we have done a thorough job of planning, hazard removal and education, before creating stringent regulations.

SELECTED READINGS

1. Bailey, R. G. 1971. "Landslide Hazard Related to Land Use in Teton National Forest, Northwest Wyoming." Ogden, UT: U.S. Forest Service, Intermountain Region.

2. Bryant, E. A. 1991. *Natural Hazards.* New York, NY: Cambridge University Press.

3. Burton, I., and Hewitt, K. 1971. *The Hazardousness of a Place: A Regional Ecology of Damaging Events.* Toronto, Ontario, Canada: University of Toronto Press.

4. Burton, I., Kates, R. W., and White, G. F. 1978. The Environment as Hazard. New York, NY: Oxford University Press.

5. Cuskelly, G., and Sessoms, H. D. 1989. "An Investigation of Selected Park Management Practices Among Local Government Park and Recreation Departments in North Carolina," *Journal of Park & Recreation Administration,* 7(1): 26-40.

6. Frakt, A. N., and Rankin, J. S. 1982. *The Law of Parks and Recreation.* Medford, NJ: Brighton Publishing Company.

7. Gist, R. and Lubin, B. (eds.). 1989. *Psychosocial Aspects of Disaster.* Somerset, NJ: John Wiley & Sons.

8. Jubenville, A. 1983. "Analysis of the Hazard Management Program at Otter Creek Park, Project Report." Park and Recreation Consultants, Alaska.

9. Kaiser, R. A. 1985. *Liability and Law in Recreation, Parks, and Sports,* Englewood Cliffs, NJ: Prentice-Hall.

10. Kozlowski, J. C. (ed.). 1985. Parks and Recreation Law Reports (annual). Alexandria, VA: National Recreation and Park Association.

11. Kozlowski, J. C., and Wright, B. A. 1989. "State Recreational Use Statutes and their Applicability to Public Agencies: A Silver Lining or More Dark Clouds," *Journal of Park & Recreation Administration,* 7(2): 26-34.

12. Lavalla, P., et al. 1989. *Managing Field Operations: An Introduction to Incident Management.* Olympia, WA: Emergency Response Institute.

13. McAvoy, L. H., and Dustin, D. L. 1985. "Regulating Risks in the Nation's Parks," *Trends, 77*(3):27-30.

14. McAvoy, L., Dustin, D., Rankin, J., and Frakt, A. 1985. "Wilderness and Legal Liability: Guidelines for Resource Managers and Program Leaders." *Journal of Park and Recreation Administration, 3*(1): 41-49.

15. Manfredo, M. J., and Bright, A. D. 1991. "A Model for Assessing the Effects of Communications on Recreationists," *Journal of Leisure Research, 23*(1): 1-20.

16. National Recreation and Park Association. 1992. *NRPA-Pacific Risk Management Handbook.* Sacramento, CA: NRPA Pacific Region.

17. Paine, L. A. 1966. "Accident Caused by Hazardous Trees in California Recreation Sites," U.S. Forest Service Research Note PSW-133.

18. Patek, W. J., and Atkisson, A. A. 1982. *Natural Hazard Risk Assessment and Public Policy.* New York, NY: Springer-Verlag.

19. Petersen, J. A. 1987. *Risk Management for Parks, Recreation and Leisure Services.* Champaign, IL: Sagamore Publishing, Inc.

20. Saarinen, T. F., and Sell, J. L. 1985. *Warning and Response, to the Mount St. Helens Eruption.* Albany, NY: State University of New York Press. (especially chapter on U.S. Forest Service).

21. Utah Division of Comprehensive Emergency Management (UDCEM). 1991. *Utah Natural Hazards Handbook: Process, Impact, and Mitigation.* Lake City, UT: UDCEM.

22. Van Arsdel, E. P. 1969. "Detection of Hazard Trees in Recreation Areas by Remote Sensing," *Remote Sensing Conference for Recreation and Resource Managers, Proceedings.* G. R. Hocker, ed. College Station, TX: Texas A&M University.

23. Wagener, W. W. 1963. "Judging Hazard from Native Trees in California Recreation Areas: A Guide for Professional Foresters." U.S. Forest Service Research Paper, PSW-11.

24. Wenger, K. F. (ed.). 1983. *Forestry Handbook.* 2nd Edition. New York, NY: John Wiley & Sons.

25. White, G. F. (ed.). 1974. *Natural Hazards.* New York, NY: Oxford University Press.

CHAPTER 19

Maintenance Management

Maintenance management is closely related to site management (see Chapter 8). However, managing a site means you design and develop the natural environment, its soils, vegetation, landscape, etc., whereas maintenance management means you exercise continual care to ensure that services provided on the site produce a continuing high-quality, safe visitor experience. This means that access developments like roads, trails, and bridges, facilities like outhouses, visitor centers, tables, utilities like solid-waste disposal, sewage disposal, and water supply, are continuously provided at a quality standard which meets visitor expectations, agency policy, and safety requirements for the site's location on the ROS.

For example, at a wilderness campsite maintenance management may only insure that no litter or garbage is present, that human waste is sanitarily covered, that potential drinking water is regularly tested for contamination and warning signs posted, and that trails and bridges meet both safety and aesthetic standards. On the other hand, at a highly developed automobile campground,

Figure 19-1. Poor maintenance of picnic sites creates a bad impression of your agency. Roosevelt-Arapaho National Forest, CO. (Photo by B. W. Twight)

maintenance management may include the following: daily litter pickup throughout the grounds, garbage-can emptying after the dinner hour each evening (reducing the attraction for bears), restroom cleaning three times a day, a full-time tertiary treatment sewage disposal plant, continuous pumping, filtration and chlorination of water for a 200,000-gallon reservoir, the operation of diesel generators supplying electric power to the visitor center, restrooms and ranger stations, scheduled annual painting of restrooms and triennial painting of other buildings, patching and sealing of asphalt roads and nature trails, and weekly shoveling of ashes from campsite fireplaces.

Regardless of the type of activity carried out, maintaining high-quality services is costly, and adequate funding has always been difficult to obtain. Constant care doesn't create capital-intensive developments that elected representatives can point to with pride at election time, either. Thus it has always been easier to obtain funds for constructing a big new visitor center than to obtain them for care over time.

However, by failing to demand a high *standard* of continuous care for grounds and facilities, which creates quality experiences for visitors, a public agency may detract from user enjoyment of a scenic resource. Indeed, an outing can literally go down the drain for the family that has to use a mucky, stench-filled restroom or a garbage-strewn, filthy campsite. Furthermore, an encounter with a lack of neatness and upkeep can often negate any previous public support your agency might have enjoyed from a current visitor, lending credence to the old saying that "if you can't keep it up, don't put it in."

Maintenance management is therefore one of the more important programs in outdoor recreation. Because of this fact, fully half of the annual operating budget in some National Park Service areas goes to maintenance. Visitor management, interpretation, and resource management share the remaining funds.

TWO FACTORS OF IMPORTANCE

Two factors are of primary importance in providing maintenance operations—standards, and cost estimates.

Standards are statements that identify the elements of each maintenance activity. They express in measurable terms results or conditions that exist when activities are managed satisfactorily—that is at a standard level. Standards should be prepared so they express a single level of acceptability. For example such a standard might include: "Buildings must be maintained in a manner that makes it possible to identify the man-hours, materials and funds needed to attain the stated standard." This identification might be prepared then using a time and cost study of the complete job carried out to standard. Such a study might be compiled using work order records from previous maintenance of the building in question compiled on a form such as that in Figure 19-2, p. 292. Activity standards should apply uniformly to all offices and areas in the recreation management agency. That way each member of the organization either knows or readily understands the approved quality level for the activity in question.

An example of maintenance standards for "Buildings, Utilities and Other Facilities," under the subcategory "Buildings, Floors," applies uniformly throughout the National Park Service as follows:

Buildings

Floors

a. All are structurally sound with no signs of displacement or deflection.
b. Coverings such as tile are free of objectionable deterioration, evidence of vandalism, excessive wear, etc.
c. Coverings are clean and protected with acceptable materials.
d. Floors are free of litter, dirt, markings, etc.

Standards such as these are outlined in your agency's administrative manual, by the agency maintenance division's central office, or your local written standard operating procedure. If not, they should be developed and written into a local operating procedure for the guidance of all employees. For measurability, create standards using known and established engineering criteria such as from the Uniform National Building Code, the National Electrical Code, the National Fire Code, and various American Standard Safety Codes published by the American Society of Mechanical Engineers, the U.S. Public Health Service, the American Public Health Association, etc. Useful additional information in regard to the achievement of quality standards and production of quality maintenance work can be gleaned from the works by or about the methods of W. Edward Deming cited in the Selected Readings below.

Standards should also incorporate visitor feedback obtained from complaints and surveys. For example, ask random samples of visitors how satisfied they are with the level of restroom or other facility cleanliness. Also respond promptly to any complaint by increasing the quality level of maintenance to prevent future complaints. Just a few unhappy articulate visitors can soon give your facility and agency a bad reputation, particularly if they write letters to congressmen, newspapers, travel magazines, or organized constituency groups.

Detailed manpower and fund estimates help provide the documentation necessary to obtain funding for maintenance at the quality standard set for your agency's services. As we suggest above, the basic tool for estimating these manpower needs and the dollar costs for each maintenance job is the work order or job order request (see Figure 19-2). As we discussed, work-order forms provide a way of planning proposed maintenance jobs in terms of schedules, standards, and various costs, as well as documenting future budget requests.

The maintenance operating program form in Figure 19-3 (p. 293) provides a way of aggregating and identifying all work orders prepared. The maintenance activity, priority, description, man-days, costs, and scheduled start and finish dates are all summarized on this form. These forms, which can be produced with computer graphics programs, form the basic documentation for routine maintenance programming. Other useful methods of carrying out maintenance programming can be found in the selected readings at the end of the chapter.

Use the basic maintenance operating plan—the work order—to estimate actual job costs, detailed descriptions and standards for a proposed task. You can break down the work into number and type of personnel needed to do the job, number of estimated man-days, and approximate salary cost per man-day. Equipment needed for the job and materials and supplies necessary to complete it are also estimated here in terms of time and cost.

Once the job is completed, enter *actual* costs on the form. This gives you a measure of your ability to accurately estimate. File copies of these completed work orders (or

Form 10-577
(March 1970)

UNITED STATES DEPARTMENT OF THE INTERIOR
NATIONAL PARK SERVICE
JOB ORDER REQUEST
(See Instructions on Reverse)

SAMPLE
H-3-2-5

JOB ORDER NO.

FY _____

JOB DESCRIPTION	LOCATION	DISTRICT
Seal Coat	Route 3	Blue Sky

PROPOSED START DATE	TARGET COMP. DATE	NO. OF UNITS	UNIT OF MEASURE	EST. COST PER UNIT	ACT. COST PER UNIT
7/1	9/1	5.5	mile	$2,170	

STANDARD AND LEVEL PROPOSED

R & T General 1,2,4; Flexible Pavement 1, 2, 3, 4

STATEMENT OF WORK PROPOSED

Seal and chip 5.5 miles Route 3 between Rocky Campground and Valley Overlook.

	POSITION, TITLE, GRADE AND SURNAME	EST M/DAYS	DAILY RATE	EST. COSTS	ACT. M/DAYS:	ACTUAL COSTS
PERSONAL SERVICES	Engineering Equipment Operator	12	46.40	557		
	Moter Vehicle Operator	31	42.00	1,302		
	Laborer	13	32.80	426		
	Road Foreman	2	52.40	105		

	TYPE OF EQUIPMENT	EST HRS./MIS	RATE	EST. COSTS	ACT. HRS/MIS	ACTUAL COSTS
EQUIPMENT RENTAL	Truck, 3-ton	80/hr	4.00	320		
	Roller, 12-ton	20/hr	6.00	120		
	Oil Distributor	10/hr	12.00	120		
	Spreader	20/hr	16.00	320		
	Loader	15/hr	8.00	120		

	ITEM	EST. COSTS	ACTUAL COSTS
MATERIALS AND OTHER COSTS	Chips, 645 tons	6,450	
	Asphalt, RC-800, 52 tons	2,080	

COST ACCOUNT	PERSONAL SERVICES	EQUIPMENT RENTAL	SUPPLIES AND MATERIALS.	OTHER	TOTAL
230	$2,390	$1,000	$8,530		$11,920

REQUESTED BY *(Title & Signature)*	CONCURRED BY *(Title & Signature)*	APPROVED BY *(Title & Signature)*

COMPLETED BY	DATE COMP.	INSPECTED BY	DATE INSPECTED

Figure 19-2. An example of a work order for action on a maintenance job.

Form 10-576
(March 1970)

UNITED STATES DEPARTMENT OF THE INTERIOR
NATIONAL PARK SERVICE

H2-6

OPERATING PROGRAM FY __7X__

(See Instructions on Reverse)

AREA OR OFFICE Great National Park								ACTIVITY Buildings and Utilities	
PRIOR. NO.	ACCT. NO.	STD. LEVEL	JOB DESCRIPTION	MAN-DAYS	EST. COSTS	SCHEDULE START	COMP.	REMARKS	
			Refuse contract	—	15000	7/1	6/30		
			Maintain signs — B & U	20	874	7/1	6/30		
			Paint comfort stations (3)	30	1240	3/5	4/27		
			Clean and operate maint. shops						
			Mountain park boundary						
			General maintenance on buildings	50	2459	7/1	6/30		
			Rehabilitate campsites						
			Paint maintenance shops (2)	50	1873	5/28	6/29		
			Paint VC-Admin. — Int.	30	1149	5/7	5/25		
			Paint VC-Admin. — Ext.	20	885	9/15	9/28		
			Operate & clean VC — Admin. Bldg. & mow lawn						
			Operate campground						
			Litter collection B & U	50	1525	7/1	6/30		
			General supervision	468	22410	7/1	6/30		
			SUB-TOTAL.....					XXXXXXXX	

PREPARING OFFICIAL *(Title and Signature)*   APPROVED BY SUPERINTENDENT *(Signature)*

Figure 19-3. An example of a maintenance operating program form that summarizes a series of work orders involving a general maintenance activity area.

computerized records) are valuable development tools and supporting documentation for future operating plans and budget requests.

Use a maintenance operating program form that summarizes all work orders by type of activity to plan actual yearly work schedules. Then you can schedule work which can be done in the winter to provide year-round employment for key maintenance personnel. The total cost of all work orders is aggregated with this program plan, then compared with the actual budget available. When the budget is less than the summated cost for all maintenance work, use the priority number and standard level you have entered on this form to eliminate less-important jobs or to reduce their standard level. Those are two ways you can bring the cost of programmed work into balance with the funds available.

The number of man-days estimated for each job and scheduled dates for work tell managers how many people are required to get the job done and when they need to be hired. These latter estimates also help determine when you should contract work out because of insufficient agency personnel. Operating program estimates, when multiplied by an inflation factor, also give you a basis for making both preliminary and final budget request estimates for the three-year federal budget cycle or any alternative cycle at other governmental levels. Additionally, operating program forms provide recreation managers with documentation that justifies each year's budget request up the agency chain of command. Summaries of major types of costs from compilations of these documents can be used by the agency senior staff to justify and support agency requests to congressional appropriations committees.

A further requirement for manpower and funding estimates, as well as the final budget, is to have extra dollars available somewhere to handle any maintenance emergencies. You can often obtain these at the regional or main-office level if the director or regional director has an appropriated contingency fund. At the field level, handle emergencies by canceling or postponing the completion of one or more lower-priority *funded* work orders until nearly the end of the fiscal year. Should an emergency occur prior to that time, such as culvert washout or the wrecking of a critically needed vehicle, sufficient funds may then be reprogrammed locally and the lower-priority jobs canceled are then postponed until the next fiscal year. It is therefore important to have *some* noncritical budgeted work orders so that such funds are available for an emergency.

MANAGING A MAINTENANCE OPERATION

You can best carry out these tasks by planning, budgeting, and programming. Plans must identify *what* services and facilities are to be maintained, each service or facility's useful life (how long it is to be maintained before replacement), and what schedule of maintenance is necessary to ensure a high standard of operation until that useful life is finished. For example, the interiors of heavily used public restrooms may require repainting once every year for high-quality surfaces that resist moisture, stains, cleansers, disinfectants, and vandalism. Other facilities such as water chlorinators may require chlorine replacement and filter cleaning every two weeks during the operating season. Trail grading and light bulb replacement may be necessary only once a season. Each task, however, requires a plan for manpower, equipment, and supplies. Perform periodic inspections and keep a written record of these on file to insure that you schedule planned maintenance often enough to keep each facility up to your standards.

It is obvious that planning such activities requires a thorough knowledge of equipment and facilities, of the work to be done, of the tools needed, and of necessary materials and supplies.

You can generally learn how to plan and estimate maintenance work through extensive experience with the particular jobs to be done. If recreation managers do not have that type of experience, they can acquire the information by hiring a maintenance supervisor who does or by using written records and manuals that document the learning of others. This is where files or computerized records, spreadsheets, etc., of prior work orders, and maintenance operating programs showing the actual costs of jobs in previous years, become invaluable sources of information. You can better estimate the cost of operating a particular facility by multiplying the costs incurred in earlier years by the yearly changes in the consumer price index or other inflation factors.

As suggested above, work order records are even more useful if you enter the data from them into a computer file. Then you can make various comparisons and develop spread sheets of summary statistics easily. Some agencies also provide in-service courses for maintenance management problems like these. For example, the National Park Service conducts maintenance management courses at its Mather Training Center, Harpers Ferry, West Virginia. Sometimes these courses are open to personnel from other agencies. Contact the Training Center director or the Chief of Maintenance in the National Park Service's Washington, DC office (U.S. Department of the Interior).

Budget requests with inflation-corrected estimates for the next and following fiscal years can also be developed from prior years' work orders and summarized operating programs. You can project minimum amounts of the necessary "person" power, along with supplies and equipment, from such data. Then you can use it as a basis for planning, purchasing, and maintaining necessary inventories of such items as toilet paper and spare parts, for hiring seasonal personnel, and in leasing pickup trucks for the summer ahead. All of these actions, however, depend on your records of operating costs from the existing operation or similar operations.

Programming maintenance operations is necessary to carry out maintenance plans and get high-priority work done efficiently and in time to ensure a high-quality recreation experience for most visitors. Several components are necessary for effective and efficient operation of a maintenance program. According to John A. Rutter, for many years a demanding well-organized manager of various U.S. National Parks, you should first create a basic schedule of routine operating and maintenance requirements.[8] *This is a schedule of what must be done.* Second, you should have a complete inventory of maintenance, rehabilitation, and operating deficiencies. *This is a statement and schedule of what additionally needs to be done.* Third, you should do a cost analysis of the routine maintenance operating requirements. *This is the cost of what must be done.* Fourth, you need a stack of work orders compiled for other-than-routine job requirements. Finally, you should make a spreadsheet showing the distribution of operating funds for the current fiscal year according to the broad categories of potential expenditures, personal services, equipment rental, supplies and materials, etc.

Former Superintendent Rutter's programming guidelines are worth repeating here, particularly for less-experienced managers. They go as follows:

1. Programming must be realistic in cost and scope.
2. No work should be performed outside the scheduled written programs except in the case of unforeseen emergencies. (Spur-of-the-moment decisions and expenditures for nonemergencies cannot be tolerated or costs cannot be contained).
3. Costs must be determined for routine operations in order to plan for special operational projects.
4. Program planning *must* reflect input from all levels of operation and supervision.
5. Program planning *must* reflect input from the appropriate unit manager.
6. Program planning should be initiated at the lowest possible effective supervisory level. Job supervisors and foremen must participate in planning their activities and determining job costs, as much as possible. (Cost-consciousness and job planning are supervisory musts.)
7. Programming should be done as far ahead as *practical* in the most usable increments—quarterly, seasonally, yearly.
8. All work must be covered by a work order, and no work, except in emergencies, should be performed without a work order.
9. After an emergency, a work order must be made out to cover the time and cost involved (and kept on file for future planning and programming).

After the work orders and costs have been summarized, the next step in programming is placing all jobs in sequence. Maintenance managers should determine the sequence for each job by surveying needs or priorities and determining if the job is required or not. After needs and priorities are identified, you must plan the work as follows:

1. Survey the extent of job. Be sure you end up with a completed, usable unit.
2. Prepare a site plan if appropriate (see Chapters 8 and 17).
3. Prepare a sketch of the work to be done with sufficient detail to fully portray the finished product, if that's appropriate.
4. Secure plan approval as necessary from your:
   a. landscape architect,
   b. agency engineer,
   c. forest or park superintendent or district manager.
5. Prepare a detailed work order for the job.
6. Enter the work order in the work program in the order of its appropriate priority.
7. Review work orders for the following:
   a. approval by the appropriate foreman,
   b. a checklist of materials needed.
8. Order and secure materials needed far enough ahead of time so they are available when work is scheduled. A critical path analysis helps for larger jobs (see Civil Engineering Handbook).
9. Make sure *all* purchase orders are signed or countersigned by the division head responsible for the funds involved.
10. Check the availability of the equipment required.

11. Check manpower requirements and availability.

Now the maintenance program is ready for the year's work, so you are ready to execute it. The responsibility for getting the job done rests with the job foreman. The foreman has, or has been provided with, the skills, material, equipment, standards, and work orders necessary to do the job. In carrying out maintenance work, remember the following important factors:

1. The responsibility for execution *must* be placed at the job level.
2. Standards set by the agency or the area superintendent are acceptable minimums only. You should gladly accept a better job at the same or less cost.
3. Each employee responsible for performing a job or series of jobs should be encouraged to use maximum initiative and ingenuity to accomplish his or her work for better production at less cost.
4. If sacrifices must be made, it is best to accept less work of better quality. Each dollar invested in a project must be well-invested, as you cannot afford to redo a job or waste effort.
5. A planning process *must* be completed before starting any regular maintenance job.
6. All material should be on hand, all equipment arrangements made, and all manpower requirements met. Figure out what you are going to do, get what you need to do the job, and then do it. Do the job on your terms— not the terms of expediency.
7. Supervision and inspection must come from established sources and through established channels.
8. Changes or modifications should be accepted only if they come through proper administrative channels. The right hand *must* know what the left hand is doing.
9. *Don't over-man a job.* If anything, underman it. We all work better and accomplish more under a little pressure. The job foreman should be held directly responsible for efficient use of equipment and full use of manpower to complete a thoroughly satisfactory job.[8]

MAINTENANCE OF EQUIPMENT AND PHYSICAL FACILITIES

Earlier in the chapter, we discussed the work order and the work program as ways of planning, budgeting, and managing maintenance work. Three important items on the work order form shown in Figure 19-2 (p. 292) are estimated costs for wages, equipment operation, and materials and supplies. As fees for personnel, supervision, and materials and supplies are generally paid from funds appropriated for maintaining particular categories of park or recreation facilities, it should be obvious that such labor and materials costs are proportionally distributed or prorated over each job by type of expense. It is not as obvious how equipment costs are handled.

It should be noted here that equipment costs are also prorated for each job under "equipment rental" on the work order form. This means that hourly or mileage costs for each job are charged on the basis of operating rates set for equipment. Since equipment is often very costly, such items as dump trucks, backhoes, and power saws are considered to be "rented" for each maintenance job. The rate is set according to the established useful life of the particular piece of equipment and is generally paid into a local "revolving fund" or account. At the end of the useful life of the truck, tractor or other piece, this account (if properly costed and collected) contains sufficient money to purchase a new piece of equipment.

Useful life generally ends at the number of miles or operating hours when the annual cost of repair begins to exceed the prorated annual cost of a new purchase. Public agencies that use proration methods of "renting" their equipment to each maintenance or other job, and accumulate proceeds into a "revolving" equipment replacement fund, generally have new or relatively modern equipment to work with. Those that don't use such methods are easily identified by their archaic, run-down, inefficient gear, excessive repair costs, slow rate of job completion, and low morale among maintenance employees. Similar revolving funds or "clearing accounts" are sometimes used to accumulate limited funds, and to prorate maintenance costs for other types of facilities—like employee housing where the agency is authorized to retain employee rental payments for housing maintenance.

Maintenance for facilities other than equipment generally involves care and upkeep *to-standard* of buildings, utilities, communications and electrical systems, garbage and trash disposal systems, grounds, camp and picnic sites, and sewer and water systems.

Other facilities that must be maintained are signs, roads, trails, and their appurtenances. Roads and trails include pavement, right-of-way grounds, bridges, culverts and snow fences, grading and drainage, and snow and ice control. Except for housing and large

equipment, as mentioned above, maintenance for each of these facilities is generally funded by annual appropriations according to priority. Priorities are generally set highest for "must be done" items —those critical to public safety and the overall existence of the recreation operation.

Also of highest priority are the facilities which the public sees and uses most often. These attract and maintain public support for the agency. The only time that public-use facilities don't receive top priority is when a top-level agency decision dictates that the public become aware of an agency's need for additional funds. At such times you may find severely run-down and perhaps closed facilities, along with employees who explain to unhappy visitors that the facility is run down and/or closed because of lack of funds. However, it is politically risky for agency heads to try to obtain public support in this manner. Elected officials may feel that such actions do not indicate that agency officials loyally support the administration's cost-cutting or retrenchment policies.

Finally, a word about signs. It is particularly important to keep them in good condition because they communicate directly to the public. Signs can be regulatory, interpretive, and informational, as you have seen earlier in the text. Agencies post them in all the various segments of the recreational activity provided. Therefore they not only have to be functional and visible, but aesthetically pleasing and *cared for* to effectively communicate. This generally means that signs not only be uniform and eye-catching, but also well-painted or otherwise finished, damage resistant or easily replaced, mounted solidly, and checked regularly for damage or necessary replacement. Signs which command respect are those that are well-cared for—not "jack-legged" or homemade. Extra signs of the type most often damaged or stolen should generally be kept on hand for quick replacement during the busy season.

The importance of maintenance is probably best illustrated by the fact that many agency personnel often seem preoccupied with second-guessing the maintenance operation. Everyone has his or her own maintenance program. Everyone knows how to improve the maintenance operation. The management problem is how to make this interest helpful and productive.

While maintenance is often a separate function, performed by special maintenance division employees, it *is* in everybody's interest to fully cooperate with these efforts. Maintenance standards for facilities seen and used by the visiting public must be the highest practicable, so please remember these principles:

1. Clean, neat, well-organized facilities receive good respectful use.
2. Junky, poorly maintained facilities are abused and poorly used.
3. Once inside a park or recreation area, visitors probably have more contact with maintenance employees than with any other group. Hence these employees should be neat, polite and informed with answers to common questions.
4. Visitors are very responsive to maintenance activities since they usually involve personal convenience or personal participation.
5. An otherwise completely satisfying park experience can be destroyed by poor maintenance or a poorly indoctrinated maintenance employee.
6. There should be no "jack-leg" or "homemade" solutions, particularly signs. *Appearances do count.*

7. Be careful to follow your agency's established standards for design, materials, techniques, and procedures.[8]

You should have very definite ideas as to what end product you want from your maintenance program.

Remember that its aim is to produce a quality experience for visitors active in the particular segment of the recreation opportunity spectrum that you are providing at that site. You want your maintenance and other programs to leave them 1) satisfied, 2) knowing what agency provided their quality experience, and 3) feeling like providing future support for your agency's efforts on their behalf.

SELECTED READINGS

1.   Anonymous. 1990. "A Methodical Approach to Park Maintenance," *Park Maintenance and Grounds Management*, 43(12)Dec: 4.

2.   Deming, W. E. 1986. *Out of the Crisis.* Massachusetts Institute of Technology, Center for Advanced Engineering Studies.

3.   Gabor, A. 1990. *The Man who Discovered Quality.* New York, NY: Times Books.

4.   Merritt, F. S. (ed.). 1983. *Standard Handbook for Civil Engineers.* 3rd ed. New York, NY: McGraw-Hill.

5.   National Recreation and Park Association. 1986. *Park Maintenance Standards.* Alexandria, VA: NRPA.

6.   Parmley, R. O. 1981. *Field Engineers Manual.* New York, NY: McGraw-Hill.

7.   Rudman, J. 1989. Park Maintenance Supervisor's Examination. Syossett, NY: National Learning Corporation.

8. Rutter, J. A. 1966. "The Superintendent's Viewpoints." Mount Rainier National Park Operating Procedure, mimeographed. Longmire, WA: National Park Service.

9. Sharpe, G. W., Odegaard, C. H., and Sharpe, W. F. 1983. *Park Management.* New York, NY: John Wiley & Sons.

10. Sternloff, R. E., and Warren, R. 1984. *Park and Recreation Maintenance Management.* 2nd Ed., New York, NY: John Wiley & Sons.

11. Stephens, W. B. 1985. *Civil Engineering Technicians Ready-Reference Manual.* New York, NY: McGraw-Hill.

12. USDI - National Park Service. 1976. Management System and Maintenance Programming Course. National Capital Region. (Materials for the mid-level managers course on the relationships between basic resources, park mission, and planning, programming, and standards for all maintenance activities are offered each year by the NCP Maintenance Division.)

13. Walton, M. 1990. *Deming Management at Work.* New York, NY: Putnam.

14. Walton, M. 1988. *The Deming Method.* New York, NY: Perigee Press.

15. Weisbord, M. R. 1988. *Productive Workplaces.* San Francisco, CA: Jossey-Bass.

16. White, M. J., Clayton, R., Myrtle, R., Siegel, G., and Rose, A. 1980. *Managing Public Systems: Analytic Techniques for Public Administration.* North Scituate, MA: Duxbury Press.

CHAPTER 20

Concession Management

Concession management refers to planning, developing, and supervising visitor services that enhance the quality of the experience. Managers must first decide what services are needed and where they should be located. This is critical—to decide what is needed and where.

Too often we assume that any service the public may wish to have should he provided. However, we need to evaluate each amenity by a set of criteria so that we, as park and recreation area managers, can determine whether or not we should provide it. To evaluate a service, the guiding terms here are *necessary* and *desirable.* Each service should be necessary to the enjoyment of the particular outdoor recreational opportunity we wish to promote. Necessary, in this case, refers to something that is absolutely required for a particular activity—overnight accommodations, food service, a winter sports site, etc. Next, any service must meet the test of desirability. Should you locate it within park boundaries or outside of them?

Figure 20-1. A major park concession area is often necessary to provide visitor services, Old Faithful Inn, Yellowstone National Park. (Photo by B. W. Twight)

The *necessary* and *desirable* criteria should reflect the type of recreational opportunity being provided, and the needs of the expected visitors. Some environmental settings may be so fragile or important to the visual and ecological integrity of the park or other reserved area that they are obviously off limits to concession development. Yet other recreation areas can easily accommodate such development, possibly even visually absorb it into the landscape, with minimal impact on the environment and maximum positive impact on the experiences people receive.

An example is a small state park that is attractive for camping, fishing, and hiking. Because of a new interstate route the park is being pressured to expand camping opportunities. It is unable to accommodate such an expansion without reducing fishing and hiking quality—the primary recreation opportunities within the park. Two nearby landowners have been successfully encouraged by state officials to develop campgrounds and the state park is being changed to foster primarily day use. A happy ending—with this unique partnership, the park has thus been able to provide *more*, rather than less, of its primary opportunities for users.

In another example, a major national park found it necessary to offer overnight accommodations and food service so visitors might enjoy their stay. These services were deemed necessary because the normal travel distance to the park and the length of stay are fairly long. However, with the large numbers of visitors, any major development could detract from the total opportunity because of resource impact, visual intrusions, or significant changes in the intended recreational opportunity. Therefore, although some services are necessary, they may not be desirable in a particular management unit within the particular park. In this case, the solution may be to encourage them in some management units and not in others. Possibly a mass transit system could move more visitors between units. After all, as shown in Chapter 3, the environmental setting represents the essence of the recreational opportunity.

PROVISIONING FOR CONCESSIONS

In the United States, development, although controlled, is often diffused throughout parks. Some countries have used the enclave concept to develop visitor service. They do this by establishing enclaves in places where intensive development can handle the visitor needs. Then other portions of the parks can be maintained with fewer disruptions. Banff National Park in western Canada is a good example of how concessions are encouraged within the town site. Three primary considerations in provisioning for concessions are area planning, type of ownership or operation, and specific leases.

Area Planning

Ideally we should try to cluster visitor services where they are most needed, but in an area that is environmentally sound. By clustering, we can often provide more services in a more economical way, with a minimum effect on space and the total environment. Clustering has been used in some national and state parks; it will probably be used increasingly as the rise in recreational participation places more demands on the limited parkscape.

The first step in this process, of course, is to determine normal travel patterns and activity participation for a particular park and then locate and develop those facilities that are *necessary* and *desirable* to facilitate or enhance travel and activities.

The second step is to make the facility easily accessible and visually harmonious with the landscape. Some areas may be properly located but difficult to reach from the main road—consequently, they are not efficiently used. In most park units, managers understand that the development must blend with the landscape. Yet there may also be considerable pressure from concessionaires, particularly larger, more powerful companies, to deviate from this requirement. Remember that it is important to maintain the integrity of the visual environment for visitor enjoyment and possibly the protection of the resource base.

The third step is cooperation with the private sector in the area planning process. This is essential if we are to offer a wide spectrum of services, or even all services, to satisfy the interests of all visitors. Sometimes we ignore certain legitimate needs. We cannot continue in this manner. If we are to do a reasonable job of providing amenities and meeting the criteria of *necessary* and *desirable,* we must recognize the role of the private sector outside the park and cooperate with it through the area planning process. The latter approach can also help to build support for the park among nearby communities, particularly those whose business activities may be hurt by its establishment.

Type of Ownership/Operation

After we have determined what is needed and where it is needed within the park, we must determine who develops and operates the concession.

Government Ownership and Operation. This means that the administering governmental agency develops and operates the concession service. Generally, this is undesirable because managers may have difficulty in establishing and enforcing regulations themselves. Then the pressure for tourist development may become so great that we forget the basic planning criteria of *necessary* and *desirable.*

For instance, in a county park system the local park district developed and operated a short-order restaurant adjacent to a beach. In the first year, the restaurant netted nearly eight thousand dollars, which was used for park operations. Because of this success and the scarcity of appropriations for park operations, the park district decided to add other short-order restaurants near the remaining beaches. As a result, maintenance of the beaches themselves suffered. This decision illustrates what can happen in concession development when you ignore the original goals for an area and do not evaluate specific service needs and alternatives to meet those needs.

Government Ownership and Private Operation. This is a reasonable alternative in which there is a large investment in development with a marginal return. In other words, an agency develops the facility and then leases it for operation to a private concessionaire—sometimes the only way to get the needed services if you do not choose to have an agency provide them. In this case, the agency should thoroughly evaluate the need for a concession since a large investment is required to develop a facility that may serve only a small number of visitors. There must be some criteria for determining the limit beyond which no facilities are provided.

Private Ownership and Private Operations. This has generally been the most desirable way to develop a service since it involves no government investment and less government control. First, agency managers go through the area planning process to determine what is needed within their own boundaries. Then they develop and distribute the concession prospectus to all potentially interested private investors. This prospectus should show what is needed, and where it is needed, and what constraints there are on operation.

Next, managers must allow the private sector to respond with specific proposals on facility development and services to be offered. These proposals are evaluated according to whether they meet the service needs of visitors as well as protect the environment. The individual selected is then offered a concession lease based on the original proposal or a modified version of it. It is the responsibility of managers to create the provisions of the lease.

Quasi-Public Corporation. Sometimes certain services are needed, but the private sector is not interested in providing them. In this case, if agency operation is not desirable, establishing a quasi-public corporation to handle the operation is the only solution. That way, the agency does have to regulate itself but can still provide necessary concession services.

You should make sure an actual demand exists for these amenities. The real question is how these corporations are going to be subsidized. With public monies? Special tax exemptions?

The Concession Lease

The concession lease or special use permit is a legal document that defines the basic relationship between a concessionaire and an agency. It is an explicit statement about the services to be offered, the administration of the operation, any special considerations such as pricing and advertising, and the monitoring of the operation.

Everything that you expect of concessionaires and the way you evaluate their services must be a part of the lease contract or permit stipulations. This protects both parties and leaves little doubt as to roles and performance standards. For a small operation in a single park or forest district, the contract or permit may be very short with a minimum of requirements; on the other hand, for a large, diverse operation you need a very detailed and complex contract. No matter what the operation, you must recognize the lease contract or special use permit as the vehicle that establishes the quantity and quality of amenities in any park or forest recreation area (see Figure 20-2).

Unfortunately many concessions have been allowed to grow within park and forest recreation areas without management direction. Perhaps while they are small they are of little concern; however, they later reach a point where they create problems and seem "unmanageable." A detailed concession lease or permit minimizes uncontrolled growth and theoretically maintains only *necessary* and *desirable* services at specified levels. *The lease or permit stipulations are the management control mechanisms.*

Figure 20-2. Concessionaires now provide scenic tours where visitors were once allowed to drive their own vehicles. Yosemite Valley, Yosemite National Park. (Photo by B. W. Twight)

CONCESSION VARIABLES

The following are variables that you should consider when dealing with concessions.

Competition

It is important to examine competition. Should we encourage it as a means of regulating prices and service quality? In America, where capitalism is encouraged, the answer for park and forest concessions is not clear. In general, managers should adhere to the "necessary and desirable" principle, supporting only specific services that are deemed appropriate and controlling costs through *regulated* monopolies.

Our primary concern is providing necessary services at a reasonable price so that park visitors can enjoy an uncluttered landscape. For pure competition to exist, there must be sufficient business for two or more companies "to operate at something approximating lowest possible cost."[24] If there is insufficient supply, costs are high. This drives prices up, or one or more operations goes out of business, perhaps leaving a building to weather and become a blight on the landscape. Since the amount of available open space is already limited, it seems prudent to minimize the space needed for services and try to maximize the actual activity space for recreational use. Thus regulated monopolies are usually encouraged to meet identified service needs, minimize spatial requirements and utilities, protect important park features, and keep prices down and the quality of service up.

Many regulated monopolies already exist; they are not unique concepts to park and recreation areas. Concessions, unlike other monopolies, are often faced with real competition from areas immediately adjacent to parks. This may cause real problems since the concessionaire is not allowed to adjust his business quickly enough to match the competition.

Sometimes we even regulate a concessionaire out of business. While you could argue that he or she should not have been there in the first place, we attract and encourage such development. Typically we adjust the lease to keep the concessionaire going. Perhaps we should ask why we should try to develop a service inside our park if there is a great deal of competition from the outside.

There are no simple answers, and obviously conditions change. For example, during the early development of our national parks, maximum overnight accommodations were in demand because of the time involved in traveling to the parks. Large hotel complexes were built to accommodate urban visitors, particularly from the eastern states where political support was important to the development of the original National Park system.

With the increased mobility of the modern traveler and more general support for parks, these services no longer have to be provided within parks. In addition, developments have sprung up on the outskirts that meet changing behavioral patterns and demands. It is not surprising to see more long-range plans for moving concessions outside parks where they can compete within the private sector. This requires, as suggested earlier, maximum coordination between the public and private sectors. However, removing historic hotels from parks like Yellowstone, Glacier, Yosemite, and Grand Canyon may never be politically feasible or desirable.

Economy of Scale

Scale of operation is important to efficient management and the economic soundness of concession operation. Consider scale of economy in initial planning so that you can attract potential concessionaires, particularly those you prefer to have operating within the park.

The small-family operation may be the most desirable, but because of the seasonal nature of the business and other factors, this type of venture may be doomed to economic failure. How do you balance economy with both visitor needs and protection of park and forest scenic values? The answer is simple: "within policy constraints you just do it." You have to make certain value judgments based on present conditions, then adjust things later as the conditions change. Possibly systems analysis or simulation modeling can help determine where services should be located and what effect they will have on concession and park management. This can give you more objective input into decision making. Ideally you should attempt to foresee effects on visitor use patterns and associated developments. Otherwise, concessions must be as flexible as possible—to expand or contract as conditions dictate. Indeed, in certain situations, outside business consulting firms, such as Arthur D. Little Co., have been contracted by the government agency to determine potential profit margins and cash flow, length of season requirements, etc. This was done to determine the feasibility of different types of concession prospectuses and the length of leases required or offered, as part of the process of motivating bids from private firms to provide services.

Managers should also consider clustering concession services so as to increase efficiency and make a concession attractive to private developers. Campgrounds are good examples. Most campgrounds on public lands are small and scattered over large areas; this often makes them uneconomical in terms of concession management. If they are clustered at desirable locations, they may be operated economically and become more attractive to entrepreneurs.

The problem that we must solve is one of the trade-offs. Are campgrounds properly located to provide necessary overnight accommodations? What have we done to convert small, scattered camps into a single large, centrally located one? What are the acceptable trade-offs? Remember that changing campground size or development level character can alter the opportunity and create social succession—the displacement of one type of clientele in favor of another.

Conditions of the Lease

Consider the following factors when you develop a concession lease:

Roles and Responsibility. The roles and responsibilities of each party entering into the lease, as indicated previously, must be explicitly stated in the lease agreement. Nothing should be implied. Any loopholes or misunderstandings over the wording of the contract can lead to strained relationships and ultimately a decline in the very service the agency wishes to offer the public. It is only fair to both parties to clearly outline roles and responsibilities—both morally in terms of service management and legally to protect all involved.

Location and Level of Development. The location and level of development should be completely agreed upon by both parties. The agency makes the basic decision, possibly negotiating between the parties in considering changes. That way the location and level of development (with negotiated changes) both become parts of the lease.

Included in this process is a phasing-in schedule to make everyone aware of the actual timing of each stage of the development. Some provision should also be made for extending deadlines, if necessary, and each party should have some flexibility in future commitments. Therefore you must allow for future expansion. You can provide for this in the lease with nothing more than a statement of management philosophy—clustering developments or adding to existing ones—if future conditions may demand it.

Utilities and Energy Conservation. Energy conservation is extremely important from both an economic and a philosophical standpoint. If we are to promote conservation as well as protect many unique natural features, every phase of this operation should foster these ideals. The type of utility needed and its long-term effects must be considered in regard to scarcity of energy resources. Possibly we should consider an alternative power source, like solar collectors, and use parks and open spaces as demonstrations that man and nature can live in harmony. We suspect that in times of critical energy shortage, many park and recreational facilities will be denied energy resources needed to operate.

Maintenance, Sewage Treatment, and Refuse. Caring for the concession area and buildings is essential to protect both the capital investment and the overall aesthetic appearance of the park. We also need to concern ourselves with utilities such as sewage treatment and solid waste disposal to preserve the environmental setting and the well-being of visitors. Ideally we utilize regional sewer and water systems to minimize maintenance of on-site treatment facilities and reduce treatment costs. In solid waste disposal, a properly developed sanitary landfill is essential. This usually means cooperating with the local government to use existing facilities. Whatever the course, specify the requirements and roles of each party in the lease.

Quality of Service. Quality of service is a must if the visitors' needs are to be satisfied, but quality *per se* is a nebulous term. Since the concession lease initiates service, state the standard of quality you expect in that service in realistic, measurable terms. Included should be agency policy criteria as well as any other federal, state, and local requirements established by law. Sometimes a provision is even included in the statement of quality that makes low-cost services available to low-income visitors.

Franchise or Lease Fee. The annual fee paid to the government for the right to operate a concession may be a flat rate or a percentage of gross receipts. The choice of fixed versus fluctuating is a matter of management preference (see U.S. Senate 1990[30]). For some managers, these charges are basically designed to cover lease supervision. Others feel they are a means of obtaining additional monies for other programs. Still others use them as a way of evaluating demand for a service.

The fixed rate is usually used for small operations in which a full accounting of receipts would not be necessary. For larger concessions, the percentage-of-gross-receipts method requires a complete accounting and shows changes in participation from year to year adjusted for yearly increases in cost of service. However, a more modern method is the "division of profits."[24] This simply means that you determine a "break even" point for the business and assess a percentage for gross revenues above that point. That way you provide service first, then assess excess profits. The concessionaire also covers expenses and gets a reasonable return on his or her investment, making up for unprofitable years and getting rewarded for efficient management.

Division of profits ensures a reasonable profit, in the long run, to better stabilize business. In the past, concessionaires did not receive a break during lean years and were possibly charged an excess profit fee during good years. They could not win either way.

Length of Lease, Guaranteed Renewal, and Exclusive Rights. The length of the lease should be commensurate with the investment by the concessionaire; this makes the investment more financially attractive. The ordinary length equals the expected life of the facilities—i.e., the number of years over which they will depreciate. Typically, this is a maximum of 30 years, but it can be as few as one to five with little investment needed.

The agency should set contract length at the minimum necessary to attract a desirable lease, yet maintain flexibility to allow for future changes. Concession contracts with guaranteed renewal clauses are controversial. Many people feel that the agency should handle all contract options. On the other hand, people are reluctant to invest their money and effort in a concession when there is no guarantee that they will continue to operate after the lease expires. This does not mean that the old contract is automatically renewed if you have a guaranteed renewal. First the concessionaire has to meet the terms of the original lease; then, under the guaranteed renewal clause, he or she has first option on the new lease. Provisions for facilities, maintenance, services, and so forth may change in the negotiated contract because of changes in service needs, legal requirements, and management philosophy. Yet this guaranteed renewal clause may be the best way to attract and keep good concessionaires.

Under ordinary circumstances, use patterns, management philosophy, or service needs do not change sufficiently to alter the new lease; consequently, a renewal clause is a logical way to continue the concession. You should not use lease renewal simply as an administrative prerogative to get rid of "bad" concessionaires. If the lease contract is well-written and the provisions properly monitored, administrators should be able to release undesirable concessionaires because they did not fulfill their contract obligations. They should not have to wait until lease-renewal time. Furthermore, experience has shown that many long-term concessionaires have great respect for their park or recreation area and for management's philosophy. Consequently, they support and protect many of the public values associated with that particular landscape.[15]

Exclusive right guarantees current concessionaires that they will receive the first option on future concession additions and expansions. This is usually done in the interest of reducing competition and increasing economy of operation, like incorporating a new service into existing facilities. The new concession service is simply an "add-on" to the original concession contract without the need for a formal contract bidding process. Also, managers do not have to worry about whether or not the new service will be large enough to attract a new investor.

Season of Operation. The length of seasonal operation or the annual negotiated dates of operation should be stated in the lease so that the agency has reasonable control over the period of service availability. In this way, early- or late-season visitors can at least expect minimal services; otherwise, they may only be offered during peak season to maximize profits. A change in local conditions, such as year-round public schools, may also dictate a different operating season for concessions in a local or regional park. Changing winter recreational use patterns have caused changes in season length for many concessions.

Architectural Styles and Building Materials. Controls on architectural styles and building materials ensure reasonable harmony between the natural landscape and the existing development. A pleasant man-made environment provides visitors with a more desirable opportunity by emphasizing the prime park values, including open space, while subordinating man-induced changes. This can be done effectively even in relatively developed parkscapes.

The types of materials used also may affect the visual harmony of the development. Native timber and stone are very attractive yet expensive in construction and long-term maintenance. If you want to use those materials, perhaps you can adjust lease provisions to compensate the concessionaire for increased costs in development and maintenance.

Possessory Interest. Possessory interest means the right of ownership to buildings and related real property if they are located on public lands. Possessory interest in developed or acquired facilities must be stated in the lease in the event that the lease is legally terminated or not renewed. Even if a facility is located on public land, the concessionaire usually is given possessory rights if his or her money went into developing or acquiring it.

This usually means that he or she is justly compensated for such a facility at the termination of the lease. Just compensation can mean "book value" (original cost less depreciation) or "present market value" based on an appraisal. The method to be used should be so stated.

Insurance and Bonding. The concessionaire should be required to carry a reasonable amount of insurance for fire, public liability, employee liability, and other business risks. Bonding should also be required to guarantee construction of proposed facilities and the "faithful performance of other obligations under the contract."[31]

Politics

Concession operations within our parks and recreation areas have come under a great deal of political scrutiny. Some politicians feel we are being too lenient with concessionaires; others feel we are too harshly controlling them. Often there is only a fine line between the two.

A concessionaire should not be continually looking over his or her shoulder, waiting for the "axe to fall." The park manager should take a positive approach to concession operations by planning, developing, and supervising as needed. Requirements should be explicitly stated in the lease, for example, to reduce the impact on normal park operations from external and internal politics. While pressure groups and individual politicians obviously influence the operation of an agency, such influence can be regulated within the constraints of the lease.

MANAGEMENT CONSIDERATIONS

The following is a summary of those considerations through which managers can exercise rightful control over concessions:

Planning

A basic service philosophy must be adopted before you can conceivably develop a concession management program. This should be the overall guiding doctrine in determining service needs and consolidating those needs into specific concession operations. We are all affected by our beliefs and attitudes when we develop management programs; this is especially true in controversial areas like concession management. Consequently it is important to outline a basic service philosophy, then compare it to agency management guidelines and the normal behavior of visitors. If tradeoffs are to be made in providing concession services, what are you, as the manager, willing to sacrifice?

Area and Site Planning. As indicated in the beginning of this chapter, area planning that incorporates the basic service philosophy can determine specific visitor needs (including concessions), allocate space, and select proper locations for needed facilities. This is the most important step; if these facilities are improperly located or not developed to meet the needs of visitors, they will not be used adequately. Then, no matter what subsequent decisions are made, many visitor needs may go unmet or park values may be sacrificed. Without planning, certain services can increase or decrease without regard to overall needs.

Good site planning blends development that both fits the landscape and makes it functional. We remember a well-located camp store that was not well-utilized, primarily because of difficult access from the main road and a poorly designed parking lot that often created safety hazards to pedestrians and motorists alike.

Prospectus. In this document we make service needs known, describe how they are to be handled, and encourage the private sector to provide these services on public lands. The prospectus responds to the concession questions of what, where, when, and how, and should include:

a. Needed service facilities, their locations, and details of their operations,

b. All provisions discussed under Conditions of Lease, at least in summary form,

c. Statutes and regulations under which the concessions will operate,

d. A description of the area, including location, transportation systems, climate, existing use patterns, projected demand, and other data pertinent to the particular project,

e. Submission of offer (all submission requirements, including time schedule should be stated), and

f. The criteria by which the applicants will be judged.

Special criteria are usually used in selecting the successful concession applicant—i.e., how appropriate is the proposed development, how well can the service be provided, and how financially stable will the operation be? Competitive bidding for the lease fee that concessionaires are willing to pay is important but generally not a prime criterion. Thus it is a good practice to require a background resume and a complete financial statement from each applicant.

Partnerships. Agencies must face smaller budgets, yet greater demand for certain services, even some unique services. To balance this, there is said by some to be a greater need for reliance on *partnerships.*[7] Partnerships can be alliances with other agencies or nonprofit groups who can sometimes provide particular services at a lower nominal cost, or paid for by the participants. They can be the classical concessionaire who provides specific services to visitors such as overnight accommodations on a pay-as-you-go basis. Even the simple contract with a local business to clean and maintain a campground, or the use of a campground "host" (for better or for worse) may be thought of not just as a concession but as a partnership. In an effort to make dollars go farther while still providing some level of public service, the U.S. Forest Service has established many such "partnerships" in the past ten to fifteen years.

However, remember that these private companies, or contracted for stand-ins—in lieu of career agency employees—are often employees of a relative monopoly, operating in an isolated location, without much fear of ever having a competitor, even for renewal of their monopolistic contract. Their primary motivation is to make a profit from performance of their contract; service to an individual visitor comes second. And making a profit unfortunately often requires "cutting corners" on what is provided, whether it means rigid adherence to minimum standards of cleanliness or slightly less, or cost-saving measures like hiring poor-quality personnel, buying poor-quality foods, and laying off required personnel early in the season while pleading unavailability of replacements. Some concessionaires in the past have fed garbage to the bears to avoid disposal costs and at the same time attract a sideshow for their visitors, and some have failed to change the bedsheets regularly, etc., all detailed specifications which may not have been written precisely into the contract and may require many hours of inspection, negotiation and enforcement to gain contract compliance.

An important side effect of noncompliance, of course, is that generally it is your agency—not the concessionaire—which gets the bad name and loses public support because of poor performance or service by a private contractor. Furthermore, using an intermediary contracted concessionaire removes an opportunity for the agency to earn public goodwill for its programs and mission. No contractor is going to sell your agency; they are going to sell themselves, if anyone. Any time people conduct business on public land under a legal agreement, permit or contract, these individuals generally do much more than that. They meet and greet the public and provide the minimum specified necessary (hopefully more, but not enforceable) service to complete the desired recreational opportunity.

Another disadvantage which recently made front page news in the national press, is the tendency of some private contractors to squander federal funds when they are not supervised quite closely. Unauthorized and at times illegal expenses have been billed to the government, including tickets to sporting events, lavish cruises and excessive salaries for executives.[27]

Thus, there are trade-offs between these cheaper private services (or perhaps no services) and providing the service at government cost and with career government personnel. On the one hand, it can be argued that

without such partnerships, there would be fewer recreational opportunities and much higher costs for the ones offered. It is also argued that standards and service levels can be strictly specified and rigorously inspected for compliance. On the other hand, it can be argued that *thorough* contract supervision also costs money and requires extra government employees to adequately supervise contract compliance and assure performance at specified standards. Also, maintenance work and lodging facilities supplied by career government personnel in civil service positions sometimes provide a higher quality service, longer voluntary work hours, and longer open seasons than a private operator can afford or be motivated to supply. The West Virginia State Park System provides a good example of the latter type of public employees.

As suggested above, it is also often true that government civil service personnel are better "ambassadors" for their agencies. Being career employees who generally love their work as well as the countryside they work in, they often have a stronger motivation to provide high quality "meeting and greeting" of the public (for career positions, generally better educated and trained personnel can be hired). It follows then, that carefully selected and well-trained government employees are likely to be inspired to perform a higher quality job because of their career motivations and morale, and they generally understand the need to build strong clientele relationships and public support for *their* agency.

Furthermore, carefully selected, indoctrinated, and trained career government employees can have a high level of organizational commitment to service—not found in the temporary contractual relationships more characteristic of private companies formed for short-term purposes. Private companies, quickly organized for such a particular purpose, more often have a *compliance* rather than a norm or professionally motivated culture. Indeed, it takes many years to develop the traditions and organizational culture, sometimes termed "esprit de corps" or élan, that only old private corporate cultures such as IBM and Xerox can legitimately claim to have. Self-interested contract-tied private employees of a regulated monopoly can seldom create that type of culture, except perhaps if they adopt the Japanese management style recently being touted for large U.S. companies (e.g., the GM Saturn Division), and then it will occur only over a long period of time (see the works by and about "Deming Management" in Chapter 19).

Privately employed persons are more under pressure to cut costs and increase profits for their contractually employed company. Thus they may not produce either the quality of work or class of communication which meets the tastes of often cultivated longtime outdoor recreation clientele, as well as the visitors whom the agency might like to retain as clientele (see discussion of clientele building in Chapter 15, Interpretive Services). This may explain why the blue-collar retirees and seasonal nonprofessional "campground hosts" of the U.S. Forest Service (and more recently the Park Service) do not make the high class, learned and enthusiastic impression on recreation clientele that traditionally better educated and better trained U.S. Park Service personnel (both career employees and summer employed school teachers) have made for many years.

Finally, as was pointed out in the recent administrative debate over contracting out maintenance and other services in Glacier National Park, government employees are more likely to be available for emergencies, and are more likely to be loyal to agency needs for contributions of overtime, etc.[16] Even though well-trained career employees may cost more per individual to employ, they often produce more work at a higher quality level than do persons from the subculture of private personnel which follows the "hotel trade" around the country. Thus the debate over "partnerships" may really center around the differences among employees who *see their work either as a career or as a short-term profit-making operation,* a utilitarian view rather than a perspective motivated by the "family" membership and morale factors more often inspiring the employees of career professional organizations and agencies.

Consequently, the decision to provide a particular type of service with government employees and facilities or with private contractors must be carefully considered from all angles.[16]

Assessing Environmental Impacts

After you select a proposal that best meets your criteria, you should assess the total project in terms of its environmental effects. Develop mitigating measures to alleviate these problems, or modify or relocate the project to reduce environmental impact. A plausible approach to this is presented in Chapter 6.

Supervising

Once any concession contract or project has been given final approval, concession management for privately owned or operated services is a matter of supervision. This starts with the groundbreaking and includes:

1. Monitoring construction to ensure that facilities meet the specifications set forth in the plan,

2. Monitoring services to ensure that they meet specified minimum requirements,
3. Monitoring potential environmental effects to adjust programs if problems arise,
4. Monitoring site maintenance to ensure the adequate protection and appearance of facilities, and
5. Monitoring concession users and other agency clientele to ensure that they feel the concession provides quality services which enhance the visitors' experiences.

SELECTED READINGS

1. Absher, J. D. McAvoy, L. H., Burdge, R. J., and Gramann, J. H. 1988. "Public and Commercial Managers Predicting Recre-ationist Opinions," *Journal of Park and Recreation Administration,* 6 (3):66-77.

2. Barber, E. H. 1989. "Customer Service: the Competitive Edge," *Journal of Park and Recreation Administration,* 7(4): 10-20.

3. Buchinger, M. 1968. "Concessions and Service Arrangements in Various Parts of the World," *Canadian National Parks: Today and Tomorrow.* J. G. Nelson, and C. C. Sace (eds.). The National and Provincial Parks Association of Canada and the University of Calgary.

4. Busser, J. A. 1990. *Programming for Employee Services and Recreation.* Champaign, IL: Sagamore Publishing, Inc.

5. Cahn, R. 1969. "Will Success Spoil the National Parks?" special reprint from articles published in *The Christian Science Monitor.*

6. Chamberlain, C. J. 1970. "A Profitable Concession." *Parks and Recreation,* 5(3): 29.

7. Dulac, D. 1987. "Partnerships for National Forest Recreation," Washington, DC: USDA Forest Service Commission on Partnerships.

8. Ellis, T., and Norton, R. 1988. *Commercial Recreation.* St. Louis, MO: Mosby College Publishing.

9. Epperson, A. (ed.). 1986. *Private and Commercial Recreation.* State College, PA: Venture Publishing.

10. Everhart, W. C. 1983. *The National Park Service.* Boulder, CO: Westview Press.

11. Frome, M. 1992. *Regreening the National Parks.* Tuscon, AZ: University of Arizona Press.

12. Hileman, R. 1957. "Concessions vs. Direct Operation." *Parks and Recreation,* 4: 151.

13. Holman, K. 1991. "Essay on Concessions in our National Treasures," McNeil-Lehrer News Hour, PBS Television Videos, November 11, 1991.

14. Hummel, D. 1987. *Stealing the National Parks: The Destruction of Concessions and Park Access.* Bellevue, WA: Free Enterprise Press.

15. Ise, J. 1963. *Our National Park Policy: A Critical History.* Baltimore, MD: Johns Hopkins Press.

16. Janofsky, M. 1992. "Parks Workers with Fewer Rules Test Stereotype About Public Jobs," *New York Times,* November 16, 1992, Page A-1.

17. Kuss, F. R., Graefe, A. R., and Vaske, J. J. 1990. *Visitor Impact Management,* Vol.1, *A Review of Research.* Washington, DC: National Parks and Conservation Association.

18. McKim, W. 1968. "Townsite Administration and Management in Canadian National Parks," *Canadian National Parks: Today and Tomorrow.* The National and Provincial Parks Association and the University of Calgary.

19. McMillan, B. 1984. *The Old Lodges and Hotels in Our National Parks.* South Bend, IN: B.& L. Publishing.

20. Memmel, B. G. 1963. "A Manual on Concession Contracts for Park and Recreation Executives." Wheeling, WV: American Institute of Park Executives.

21. National Parks and Conservation Association. 1988. *Investing in Park Futures—the National Park System Plan: A Blueprint for Tomorrow.* Vol. III, Parks and People: A Natural Relationship. Washington, DC: National Parks & Conservation Assn.

22. Oehlmann, H. 1965. "A Concessionaire Talks Back." *American Forests,* 6(7): 13.

23. Rubini, F. F. 1969. "Fees and Charges, Leases and Contracts, other than Food." *Proceedings, 19th Annual Great Lakes Park Training Institute,* Angola, IN, p. 83.

24. Rubini, F. F. 1970. "Specifications and Contracts with the Concessionaire," *Proceedings, 20th Annual Great Lakes Park Training Conference.* Angola, IN, p. 136.

25. Runte, A. 1987. *National Parks: The American Experience.* 2nd ed., rev. Lincoln, NE: The University of Nebraska Press.

26. Sax, J. L. 1980. *Mountains Without Handrails.* Ann Arbor, MI: The University of Michigan Press.

27. Schneider, K. 1992. "U.S. Admits Waste in its Contracts," *New York Times,* December 2, 1992, page A-1.

28. Shankland, R. 1970. *Steve Mather of the National Parks,* 3rd. edition, New York, NY: Alfred H. Knopf. (Basic NPS concession attitudes are stated in here.)

29. Stanford Research Institute. 1976. *The Concession System in National Parks: Background, Services Performed, Public Attitude Toward, and Future Consideration.* Palo Alto, CA: Stanford University Research Report.

30. U.S. Senate. 1990. *Oversight Hearings on National Park Concession Policy.* Committee on Energy and Natural Resources, Sub-Committee on Public Lands, National Parks and Forests. Washington, DC: U.S. Government Printing Office.

31. U.S. General Accounting Office. 1992. *Report on the Federal Lands: Oversight of Long Term Concessions,* GAO/RCED-92-128BR, May 1992.

BOOKS FROM VENTURE PUBLISHING

The Activity Gourmet
    by Peggy Powers

Adventure Education
    edited by John C. Miles and Simon Priest

Behavior Modification in Therapeutic Recreation: An Introductory Learning Manual
    by John Dattilo and William D. Murphy

Benefits of Leisure
    edited by B. L. Driver, Perry J. Brown and George L. Peterson

Beyond Bingo: Innovative Programs for the New Senior
    by Sal Arrigo, Jr., Ann Lewis and Hank Mattimore

The Community Tourism Industry Imperative—The Necessity, The Opportunities, Its Potential
    by Uel Blank

Dimensions of Choice: A Qualitative Approach to Recreation, Parks, and Leisure Research
    by Karla A. Henderson

Doing More With Less in the Delivery of Recreation and Park Services: A Book of Case Studies
    by John Crompton

Evaluation of Therapeutic Recreation Through Quality Assurance
    edited by Bob Riley

The Evolution of Leisure: Historical and Philosophical Perspectives
    by Thomas Goodale and Geoffrey Godbey

The Game Finder—A Leader's Guide to Great Activities
    by Annette C. Moore

Great Special Events and Activities
    by Annie Morton, Angie Prosser and Sue Spangler

Internships in Recreation and Leisure Services: A Practical Guide for Students
    by Edward E. Seagle, Jr., Ralph W. Smith and Lola M. Dalton

Leadership and Administration of Outdoor Pursuits, Second Edition
    by Phyllis Ford and James Blanchard

Leisure And Family Fun
    by Mary Atteberry-Rogers

The Leisure Diagnostic Battery: Users Manual and Sample Forms
    by Peter A. Witt and Gary Ellis

Leisure Diagnostic Battery Computer Software
    by Gary Ellis and Peter A. Witt

Leisure Education: A Manual of Activities and Resources
    by Norma J. Stumbo and Steven R. Thompson

Leisure Education II: More Activities and Resources
    by Norma J. Stumbo

Leisure Education: Program Materials for Persons with Developmental Disabilities
    by Kenneth F. Joswiak

Leisure Education Program Planning: A Systematic Approach
    by John Dattilo and William D. Murphy

Leisure in Your Life: An Exploration, Third Edition
    by Geoffrey Godbey

A Leisure of One's Own: A Feminist Perspective on Women's Leisure
    by Karla Henderson, M. Deborah Bialeschki, Susan M. Shaw and Valeria J. Freysinger

Marketing for Parks, Recreation, and Leisure
    by Ellen L. O'Sullivan

Outdoor Recreation Management: Theory and Application, Third Edition
    by Alan Jubenville and Ben Twight

Planning Parks for People
    by John Hultsman, Richard L. Cottrell and Wendy Zales Hultsman

Private and Commercial Recreation
    edited by Arlin Epperson

The Process of Recreation Programming Theory and Technique, Third Edition
    by Patricia Farrell and Herberta M. Lundegren

Quality Management: Applications for Therapeutic Recreation
    edited by Bob Riley

Recreation and Leisure: Issues in an Era of Change, Third Edition
    edited by Thomas Goodale and Peter A. Witt

Recreation Economic Decisions: Comparing Benefits and Costs
    by Richard G. Walsh

Recreation Programming And Activities For Older Adults
    by Jerold E. Elliott and Judith A. Sorg-Elliott

Research in Therapeutic Recreation: Concepts and Methods
    edited by Marjorie J. Malkin and Christine Z. Howe

Risk Management in Therapeutic Recreation: A Component of Quality Assurance
    by Judith Voelkl

A Social History of Leisure Since 1600
    by Gary Cross

The Sociology of Leisure
    by John R. Kelly and Geoffrey Godbey

A Study Guide for National Certification in Therapeutic Recreation
    by Gerald O'Morrow and Ron Reynolds

Therapeutic Recreation: Cases and Exercises
    by Barbara C. Wilhite and M. Jean Keller

Therapeutic Recreation Protocol for Treatment of Substance Addictions
    by Rozanne W. Faulkner

Understanding Leisure and Recreation: Mapping the Past, Charting the Future
    edited by Edgar L. Jackson and Thomas L. Burton

Venture Publishing, Inc
1999 Cato Avenue
State College, PA 16801
814-234-4561